A'ūdhu billāhi minash-shaitānir-rajīm.
I seek refuge in God from the accursed satan.

Bismillāhir-Rahmānir-Rahīm.
In the name of God, the Most Compassionate,
the Most Merciful.

PRAYER

PRAYER

M. R. BAWA MUHAIYADDEEN ﷺ

FELLOWSHIP PRESS
Philadelphia, PA

The source of the calligraphic drawing on page 280 is unknown.

Library of Congress Control Number: 2017934801

Muhaiyaddeen, M. R. Bawa.
    Prayer / M. R. Bawa Muhaiyaddeen ☺
    Philadelphia, PA: Fellowship Press, 2017
    p. cm.
    Includes index.

    Trade paperback: 978-1-943388-32-5
    Hardcover: 978-1-943388-33-2

    1. Allāh. 2. Prayer. 3. Islām. 4. Qur'ān. 5. Prophet Muhammad ☺.
6. Sufism. 7. Religions. 8. True man. 9. Good qualities. 10. Truth. 11. Wisdom.
12. Shaikh and disciple. 13. *Dhikr.* 14. Five-times prayer. 15. Ways of worship.
16. Waking up at four a.m. 17. Ablution. I. Title.

Printed in the United States of America
by FELLOWSHIP PRESS
Bawa Muhaiyaddeen Fellowship
First Printing

Muhammad Raheem Bawa Muhaiyaddeen ☺

CONTENTS

A'ūdhu billāhi minash-shaitānir-rajīm.
I seek refuge in God from the accursed satan.
Bismillāhir-Rahmānir-Rahīm.
In the name of God, the Most Compassionate,
the Most Merciful.

FOREWORD

Bismillāhir-Rahmānir-Rahīm

O' reader,

You are holding a treasure in your hands.

The words of Muhammad Raheem Bawa Muhaiyaddeen ۞ are clear gifts of wisdom.

It is the resonance of the Mysterious Secret that is being unfurled before you.

Every word is filled with meanings and experiences that await your discovery.

This book is the experience of wisdom speaking directly to you.

Prayer by M. R. Bawa Muhaiyaddeen ۞ is a map to success.

However, true prayer is not easy, it is a journey of self-discovery.

Prayer reveals us to ourselves.

We make choices to follow our mind and desires or to ascend to another level of discovery where we ignore our mind and allow wisdom to reveal an experience.

This is our life, how we spend the time of our life is critical.

The choices we make have consequences.

Choose wisely dear friend, and follow the wisdom presented here for you.

This is an opportunity to begin the journey to "Merge with the divine presence of your Creator." (*Prayer,* p. 81)

It is an opportunity to "Put an end to the torpor and darkness. Dispel the darkness that is crushing you. Endeavor to drive away satan. Reach God, the All-Powerful One." *(Prayer,* p. 82)

To pray we must be awake, alert, and sincere.

Prayer requires focus, concentration, and love, and then prayer becomes an experience.

Pray as though your life depended on it.

If we pray with the belief and the intensity of focus that this could be our last moment, our last day, then we can understand what real prayer is.

Please, dear reader, go deeply within each word of this book and explore each experience with wisdom.

Do not give up.

The words of wisdom in this book will melt your heart and draw you deeper into the endless, immeasurable love God has provided for us all within prayer.

Prayer is the remembrance of God, that remembrance is the love of God.

Search for it.

Muhammad Abdul Lateef (Kelly) Hayden
Publisher
Fellowship Press

A'ūdhu billāhi minash-shaitānir-rajīm.
I seek refuge in God from the accursed satan.

Bismillāhir-Rahmānir-Rahīm.
In the name of God, the Most Compassionate,
the Most Merciful.

INTRODUCTION

أَعُوذُ بِاللهِ مِنَ الشَّيْطَانِ الرَّجِـيمِ

بِـــسْمِ اللهِ الرَّحْمٰنِ الرَّحِـيمِ

اَلْحَمْدُ للهِ رَبِّ الْعَالَمِينَ وَالْعَاقِبَةُ لِلْمُتَّقِينَ وَالصَّلَاةُ وَالسَّلَامُ عَلَى رَسُولِهِ سَيِّدِنَا مُحَمَّدٍ

وَعَلَى آلِهِ وَصَحْبِهِ أَجْمَعِينَ وَعَلَىٰ مُحْيِ الدِّينِ أَبِي مُحَمَّدٍ عَبْدِ الْقَادِرِ الْجِيلَانِي وَشَيْخِي

مُحَمَّدٍ رَحِيمٍ بَاوَا مُحْيَّ الدِّينِ رَضِيَ اللهُ عَنْهُمَا! آمِين، آمِين، آمِين، يَا رَبَّ الْعَالَمِينَ!

The praise is Allah's, Lord of the Universes, and the Destination for
those who guard their morality. And blessings and peace be upon
our liege, Muhammad, and upon all his people and companions, and
upon Muhyid-din Abu Muhammad Abdul-Qadir al-Jilani, and my
Shaikh, Muhammad Raheem Bawa Muhaiyaddeen, may Allah be
pleased with them both! *Āmīn, Āmīn, Āmīn*, O Lord of the Universes!

May *Allāhu ta'ālā* grant His love and peace to all those who
seek His guidance to the knowledge, wisdom, justice, and behavior
which will enable them to experience His closeness and acceptance.

It is my great pleasure to introduce to you an excellent repre-
sentation of the entire range of instruction of Muhammad Raheem
Bawa Muhaiyaddeen, may Allah be pleased with him, regarding the
myriad aspects of the progressive steps of prayer and righteous behavior necessary for the purification of the seeker's heart, and opening

out the wisdom and knowledge that is its inherent enlightenment.

If one wishes to fashion a building to ascend to the heavens, and beyond to the proximity of God, it must have a strong foundation. One day, as I sat in the presence of *Shaikh* Bawa Muhaiyaddeen ☺, he said to a seeker, "You are trying to construct the upper story of *ma'rifah,* divine knowledge, in your building without having first established the strong foundation needed to support it. Eventually the building will fall down." He was referring to the level of *sharī'ah,* and the practices in it necessary to establish stability of faith.

One of the enormous benefits of a true *Shaikh* is that he will inform you when you are dreaming that you are awake, dreaming that you are enlightened while you are still veiled in darkness.

In his book, *The Fast of Ramadan,* p.10, he said: "However, your *īmān* is not strong. Your foundation is not strong. You still declare, 'I,' 'I.' If your taproot is not strong, you will fall. When your taproot is not strong, what then is your foundation? Your foundation is the secondary roots, the support roots. The taproot of *īmān,* certitude, determination, and Allah is not present."

Later, on p. 11, he ☺ drove home the point: "For ten years now I have been shouting here so that the taproot can take hold. I have been trying to embed this taproot. But if you gain personal fame and begin to discriminate, saying, 'I' and 'you,' you will be hurled around. As soon as the 'I' arises, it will knock you over. When you think, 'I am a guru,' or, 'I am a sheikh,' you will be hurled around. When you think, 'I am learned,' you will be tumbled down. Money, learning, titles, lust, desire, and praise will all toss you down. All these things will knock you down. Then you have no balance, no root. You will fall down on the ground. You will not be able to stand upright, so you will fall on the earth. You need balance. You should check on this and develop that root. Each child should do this.

"Religions will knock you down, caste will knock you down, and color will knock you down. Thoughts of 'my family,' 'my wealth,' 'my freedom,' 'my wife,' and 'my child' will hurl you around and separate you from others. You should think about this. Contemplate what I am telling you. Faith must develop; the supreme root must grow. Only then will our desires be controlled. Thank you. Reflect on this and act accordingly. Do you understand?"

In his book, *The Resonance of Allah*, the 30ᵗʰ chapter is devoted to one of the necessary acts needed to establish the taproot of *īmān*, the unwavering establishment of *salāh*, the five obligatory prayers during the day and night. The *Shaikh* ☺ quotes two traditions of the *Rasūl*, Muhammad ☺:

"'*Qālan-nabi, sallallāhu 'alaihi wa sallam: Likulli shay'in 'alamuw-wa 'alamul-īmānis-salāh.'* Our noble Prophet ☺ has said, 'Everything has its own distinguishing mark or sign, and the distinctive hallmark of *īmān* is *salāh*.'

"The Prophet ☺ said further, '*As-salātu 'imādud-dīn; faman aqāmahā faqad aqāmad-dīn; wa man tarakahā faqad hadamad-dīn.*'

"This means: The *salāh* is the pillar that provides the foundation, strength, and stability for the fortress called *Dīnul-Islām*, which protects and saves us from unceasing sorrows, difficulties, afflictions, and many, many other hostile elements that torment us. Therefore, whosoever stabilizes himself with certitude in the *salāh* strengthens this fortress of *Dīnul-Islām* and protects himself from suffering and torment. Whoever disregards the *salāh* has certainly demolished this fortress. As a result, he will get trapped in the nets of those hostile elements and will experience endless sorrow, difficulties, and torment, from which he cannot be redeemed.

"When the Prophet's ☺ time on earth was ending, his perfectly pure soul, as it was departing from the immeasurably vast–open space of his inner being, said, '*Ūsīkum bis-salāti, 'ūsīkum bis-salāti, ūsīkum bis-salāh.* My final parting instruction to you is that you must establish yourself firmly in the *salāh*, foster it, and cherish it.'

"Anas ibn Malik ☺ reported that the above saying was repeated three times. Therefore, my brethren, please reflect deeply upon this and all the other beautiful things that the Prophet ☺ has said."

In the translation of that book, *as-salāh* is simply translated as "prayer" which unfortunately gave an amorphous idea of one of the necessary practices needed to establish the foundation of spiritual acts leading us to Allah and avoiding the crumbling of efforts. However, in addition to the five obligatory prayers, practices of *dhikr, fikr,* many other aspects of *'ibādah,* strict adherence to accepting what is good and permitted by God, and resolute avoidance of things that are bad and prohibited by God are necessary to build a firm foundation and all floors of the building of our approach to God, from the lowest to the highest.

We thank *Allāhu ta'ālā* that now a beautiful and comprehensive sampling of the advice of *Shaikh* Muhammad Raheem Bawa Muhaiyaddeen ⓢ about practices, obligations, both the apparently mundane (but not actually so), and the sublime, are finally brought together in this beautiful volume, simply entitled *Prayer.* May endless blessings be upon our Prophet, Muhammad, his people, companions, and community, and Muhyid-din Abdul-Qadir al-Jilani, and my beloved *Shaikh,* Muhammad Raheem Bawa Muhaiyaddeen, all of whom worked so hard by the command and permission of Allah to open out the entire path of enlightenment leading to the *wajhullāh* (the Countenance of Allah). It is only the Countenance of Allah that will endure. As Allah has said in Suratul-Qasas, a.88,

$$\text{وَلَا تَدْعُ مَعَ اللهِ إِلَهًا آخَرَ ۖ لَا إِلَهَ إِلَّا هُوَ ۚ كُلُّ شَيْءٍ هَالِكٌ إِلَّا وَجْهَهُ ۚ}$$

$$\text{لَهُ الْحُكْمُ وَإِلَيْهِ تُرْجَعُونَ}$$

"And do not supplicate another god along with Allah! None is God but He! Everything is doomed to perish except His Countenance! To Him you are returning and final judgment is His!"

May *Allāhu ta'ālā,* out of His plenitude of grace and unfathomable love, forgive our faults, eradicate our ignorance, motivate us toward good deeds, morality, and actions, enlighten our hearts and our faces with divine knowledge and wisdom, lead us from step to step, and not withhold from us the splendor of His Countenance! *Āmīn, Āmīn, Āmīn,* O Lord of the Universes!

Imam Muhammad 'Abdur-Razzaq Miller

PRAYER

PRAYER

ROOMS IN A HOUSE

August 25, 1978, Friday, 5:08 a.m.

B*ismillāhir-Rahmānir-Rahīm. Anbu,* love. *Vanakkam,* greetings. Children, I give you my compassionate and loving greetings. My precious children, you who are the life within my life, the love within my love, the light within my eyes, and the love within my *qalb,* my innermost heart—my dearest children, I give you my love. May Allāh guide you on the straight path.

Precious jeweled lights of my eye, every day and every second you must search for God and love God. You must search for God with very much love. You should always intend Allāh, and search for Him with love. Whether it is in the sun or in the rain, in the night or in the day, it would be good if that awareness develops within you. And may Allāh search for you, may He intend you and look at you. May He grant you His grace.

Precious jeweled lights of my eye, we need to worship Allāh. There are many ways that we pray. There are many methods of prayer and there are many steps for prayer. Dearest children, we need to understand that our prayer is like lighting a house. Just as we put light in a house, just as we decorate a house, and just as we clear and beautify it, we must do this to our own house, the cage of our body; we must clean our house like this. We must decorate it, make it pure, beautify it, and place light within it. Precious jeweled lights of my eye, to do this in our cage is called prayer.

1

The way we worship is similar to what we do to a house: we clean that house that has been built with earth, fire, water, and air; we pour the cement there, beautify it with paint and marble, and decorate the interior with different objects. This is what we do to our house that is built with earth, fire, water, air, and ether. We build that house and find whatever is necessary to make it clean. We clear it, level it, and make it beautiful. We apply the necessary paint and plaster and marble. We clear it, clean it, and add the rooms that are needed: a bathroom, a shower, a kitchen, a room for prayer, a bedroom, and a hall or parlor to receive visitors. We also add a dining room in which to serve food; we place a table there, and whatever else is necessary. We have a *secret room*[1] to conduct affairs that are secret and a *public room* to conduct our public affairs. Like this, for prayer and for our life, there are ways in which we conduct ourselves in public and ways in which we worship by ourselves. There are ways in which we conduct the world and family matters and there are ways in which we conduct ourselves in secret.

In our homes, there are different rooms for this. In a single house there will be a prayer room, a living room, a bathroom, a kitchen, and a public room. This is how we live in one place. The secret of our life is like this. Prayer is a secret room, prayer is a pure room. Our life is also a secret room.

Although a bathroom is common to all, when you enter the bathroom you should enter it alone, with modesty, shyness, reserve, and fear of wrongdoing. Like this, just as we differentiate between the use of the various rooms in our life, we must fashion different, beautiful rooms for devotion to God, for prayer, for duty, for service, for the spiritual teachings, and for secrets. This is how we can live an exalted life. Just as we build a house on the outside, we must also build a place to worship God on the inside. It is in this way that we can live a life of excellence.

In each particular room you must do the duty that is appropriate

---

1   Bawa Muhaiyaddeen ☺ often used English words in unusual ways. For the sake of clarity, these words have been italicized.

to it. When you go to the kitchen you must do kitchen work, that duty. Sometimes you will cook alone and sometimes you will join with others. But even if the family is united, even if you are in union with the family, even if you are one family, even if the family is your own blood tie, nevertheless, when you are conducting your life in the room of sex, that is a place where others should not go. Others should not see that. That aspect of your life should not be shared by others, it must be done in secret. It is not the business of others to see that.

There are many different places that must be fashioned in that secret house of our life. This is a subtle house with subtle wisdom, and each kind of work must be done in its own room according to its own nature. Each kind of work must be done in its proper place. Some work can be done outwardly, while some work must be done inwardly. This is the exaltedness of life.

Therefore, there is life, there is the world, there is unanimity, there is unity, there are blood ties, there is God, there is prayer, there is purity, and there is the merging with God where we speak with God. Like this, whatever it is you are doing and no matter who you are doing it for, it must be done in the correct way and in the proper place. Whether it is the world, God, the truth, or darkness, we must know how to separate each thing and keep it in its appropriate place. If a person is able to discover each place, if he is able to fashion these places, and if he is able to clear these places, then he will be able to direct each thing to its rightful section. If he can send these things to their proper places, then he will be able to pray alone in that pure room, that clean room, that room for prayer—that room that is his alone. If he can clear that room and place light there, then he can pray to the One who is worthy of worship, all the time.

Jeweled lights of my eye, this is the excellence of life, this is the subtlety of life, this is the exaltedness of life, and this is the way we must understand life. It is in this way that we must understand the states and subtleties of prayer.

Beloved children, gems of my eye, there is a subtlety to prayer. That subtlety exists. We have not seen God and we have not seen the Truth. Because we have not seen that Treasure of Truth, we are unable to see the Treasure that is God. Truth has no shape. God has no form and God has no color. His grace has no end. Wisdom has no state or end. Our life has no limit. The exaltedness of our worship has no beginning or end, it is complete. That completeness is called *vanakkam,*[2] that completeness is called *toluhai,*[3] that completeness is the only state that we can call prayer. It is called pure Light.

Therefore, precious jeweled lights of my eye, if we want to find out what *toluhai* is, if we want to know how to search for *toluhai* and *vanakkam,* it depends upon how each one fashions his vessel, how he adorns and lights his house. Whether one goes high or low in his worship depends on each one's *qalb,* his soul, and his wisdom.

What is prayer? It is desire without desire. You must develop a desire that has no desire, a hunger that has no hunger, a thirst that has no thirst, a wisdom that has no wisdom, and an attachment that has no attachment. If you develop this, if you develop this state and make it firm, then that is the state of prayer.

When a person is hungry, he immediately starts searching for food. There is an awareness that exists within him. In the same way that he searches for food when he is hungry, he should develop another awareness within him, he should develop an awareness within his body, the hunger to search for God. That awareness must form within him. When a person is thirsty, he cries out, "Water! Water! Water! Water!" is that not so? In the same way that he searches for water when he is thirsty, he must develop that love, that thirst for God. Just as he has a thirst for water, the thirst for God should always be forming within his *qalb.* This should always be forming. Just as he needs his physical vision so that he can see, just as he says, "I need my eyes, I need my eyes," and just as he protects those eyes, he must develop the eye that can see God, he must develop the certitude of the eye of *īmān.* He must establish that faith.

The state that can give him either happiness or sorrow is always with him. He will search for what he wants, saying, "I want to be

2 *vanakkam* (T) Prayer, worship.
3 *toluhai* (T) Prayer, worship; most often refers to the formal five-times prayer in Islām.

happy, I want to be happy." This is the way that he must melt with love for God. That search for Allāh, "I need Allāh, I need Allāh," must be established, that striving must be fashioned. Just as he searches for what he needs, "I need wealth, I need wealth, I need wealth," he must search for Allāh's undiminishing wealth of the *ākhirah,* the kingdom of God. "I need the wealth of grace, I need the wealth of grace." This awareness must be fashioned in his *qalb.* The search for this must be established.

Like that, for whatever he intends from Allāh, "I need Allāh's qualities, I need those qualities, I need those qualities!" he must search for those qualities. God's actions should develop within him, "I must have those actions, I must do that duty, I must have Allāh's qualities, I must perform Allāh's actions, I must perform those actions, I must perform those actions!" He must establish that *'ibādah,* that service to God, within him. He must discard whatever else he trusts and trust only in Allāhu, "I must establish that trust within me." He must bring that feeling and awareness into being within him.

In this way, with every intention, at every second, that awareness should be established within him. That feeling and the awareness that he should pray to Allāh should develop within him. That thirst, that search, that love, that devotion, that trust, and that wisdom should develop within him. Once that search develops, once that clarity develops, then certitude, faith, and determination will become firm. If that faith and certitude flow into him, if that grows in his *qalb,* if that determination which is *īmān* becomes strong, then that prayer will form within him. That *īmān* will be the strength of his prayer, and it will be a support for his search. It will be an aid to that awareness. When that state of awareness and *īmān* is established, it will join with his life and with his *āvi,* his spirit. When that merging occurs, when the *rūh,* the soul, operates without his being aware of it, then that prayer will form in his breath. It will flow in the same way that a current works, automatically. That prayer will work by itself, automatically.

Until this state develops in a man, until this longing develops within his body, until this love develops within him, until this awareness develops within him, until this certitude develops within him, his prayer will not be permanent, his connection will not be permanent, and his determination will not be permanent. Until that state develops, then it is these five times a day prayers, these three times a day *pujās,* these mantras, these other prayers, these magics, this yoga, this charity, this worship, and this meditation that he will call prayer. He will consider all of these to be permanent.

All of the things that are connected to his intentions—whatever the *nafs* seeks, whatever desire seeks, whatever the mind seeks, whatever his thoughts seek, and whatever his arrogance, karma, and maya seek—are like going to a friend's house for a visit. It is like visiting each house, and drinking a cup of tea there. When you do your prayers in this way, you should not think that you are entering the house of God. You are entering the house of the elements and the intentions of the mind. With the thoughts of your mind, you are visiting the elements, the *nafs,* desires, illusions, the four hundred trillion ten thousand spirituals, the ghosts, animals, satans, dogs, and foxes. If you visit these forms, if they receive you, if you drink with them, and after that if you come to pray, then these forms will become your prayer. If we go and visit with the forms that we make with the elements, with the desires that make us happy, with the things that the mind and desire seek, with the things that earth seeks, the things that fire seeks, the things that air seeks, and the things that ether seeks, and if we go to pray taking these things with us, then it will be as if we are going on a holiday. It will be as if we are going every day to see a friend, and to show our love for him. All of these prayers are like this. These are the prayers of the mind, they are like making a social call.

There are certain celebrations that we observe. One day we have one kind of celebration, another day we have a different celebration. There are celebrations for high days and for low days. There are celebrations for New Years, there are celebrations for birthdays. There are birthdays for that person, birthdays for another person, birthdays for the prophets, celebrations for that day and this day. There is a birthday for us and a birthday for you. We have celebrations like this, they are set for certain days and times. There are prayers for the stars, the moon, the sun, and the fire. All of these celebrations are the prayers of the elements, the intentions of the elements, our thoughts, the earth, the fire, the water, the air, and like this, the four hundred trillion ten thousand kinds of energies and cells. We meet and speak with these forms and are happy. We praise these celebrations.

The prayers that we are now doing are being done in this way. All of the elements that we nurture are accompanying us to our prayers. We take with us the demons that we have, the shaitāns, the seven shaktis of mind, desire, earth, fire, water, air, and ether, the four hundred trillion ten thousand miracles and mantras, the demonic forces, and the *sittis,* the occult powers. We take these with us when we pray. It is the same as going to visit a friend. When true awareness, wisdom, and yearning look at this, they see this state.

There *is* a way to worship Allāh. It is like the example of the house that we spoke of earlier. You have to be alone, hungry, and awake. You must be alone, hungry, and awake, and join with God. You must be One. Your prayer should have no duality.

You must be alone, hungry, and awake, and you must merge with God. Then you will be worshipping God as God. This is the meaning. In this state it is necessary that you stay alone in that room, and worship there, by yourself.

There is such a huge world within us! We contain so many tens of millions of animals, dogs, foxes, people, donkeys, horses, vultures, eagles, and birds. We contain the sun, the moon, the stars, the clouds, lightning, thunder, angels, jinns, fairies, satan, torpor, darkness, arrogance, karma, maya, and like this, the intentions of the elements and the running of the elements, the intentions of the mind and the running of the mind, the earth and the desires and hypnotic fascinations of the earth, the flowing of the fluids and the flowing of attachments, the blood and the blood ties, and the relatives and relationships. Like this, we have taken on so many attachments, and it is with these intentions that we bow and prostrate in prayer. This is how we are now doing our prayers. We must remove these. We must find the way to worship God.

First, the yearning for God must develop within man's body. Just as he searches for water when he is thirsty, the yearning, the thirst for God, must develop in his body. Awareness must join with his body. Once awareness has joined with his body, faith must join. When faith has joined, certitude must join. When certitude has joined, the plenitude called *īmān* must join.

It is said that when hunger comes, the Ten (Commandments) will fly away. When hunger comes and we are searching for food, we will have the state where the Ten fly away. Like this, we must have the kind of hunger that searches for God. If a person, in his search for God, is to have the kind of hunger where the Ten do not fly away, then yearning, wisdom, feeling, awareness, clarity, and that faith must flow into his body. He must know that *vanakkam*. Just as a man is able to see when his eyes are open, he will be able to see God when his eye of wisdom is open. He will speak with God, he will merge with Him, and he will commune with Him. That eye will search for That.

This must be established within our body. This wisdom must be fashioned. Having fashioned this, then faith and determination, that *īmān* must be established, it must become plenitude. So, if we can develop this state, then we will be able to understand the ways of prayer. First, this state must be established in our body. This search must form within us. Only if this is established will man have the intention to search for God, both in the night and in the day.

Precious jeweled lights of my eye, we must establish this state within our bodies. Following this, there will be so many hundreds of thousands upon thousands of things that we will need to understand—secret rooms, secret times. This can be done while we are living in the world, while we are living with God, and while we are living in the truth. We must stay in a specific place for each of the duties that we do in the world, we must be in that place. We must do each particular duty at its particular time and in its particular place. There is a time and place for that duty, for that work.

In this way, when one speaks with God, he must speak in the place where God is. When an *'abd,* a slave, speaks with God, then

God will speak with that *'abd*. When God's duty is done, then that is Duty. When God's justice is done, then that is Justice. When prayer is prayed with God, then that is Prayer. When the service of God is done, then that is Service. This is the way that we should do our duty. Although we live with this body, we can perform so much duty.

It is like this. The *kalimah*[4] is composed of twenty-four Arabic letters. The twenty-fourth then becomes the twenty-fifth. The twenty-four letters of the *kalimah* form our body. The twenty-fifth letter is the soul. The twenty-four can be seen, but the one letter which is the soul cannot be seen. The twenty-sixth letter is wisdom, and the twenty-seventh letter is the Nūr, Light—resplendence. That is the day we meet the Light.

The night of the twenty-sixth letter, when wisdom comes, will be the Night of Power, *Qadr*.[5] After the twenty-sixth night, when the twenty-seventh day is dawning, when *pērarivu*, divine luminous wisdom, appears, when that Qutbiyyah[6] appears, when that Light comes down to us, when the Light of the Qutbiyyah descends, then that is called the *Lailatul-Qadr;* it is called *Qadr*. When that becomes the twenty-seventh, that resplendence is called the Nūr. Allāh and the Qutbiyyah merge together, that Light joins with the body. When both the Qutbiyyah and Allāh join together, when that Qutbiyyah, the Light that is wisdom, Allāh, and the Nūr, the *Nūrus-samāwāti,* join together, then that is when the twenty-sixth letter becomes the twenty-seventh. They become One. The twenty-eighth letter is *amāvāsi,* darkness, torpor.

---

4 *kalimah* (A) *Kalimah* is used by M. R. Bawa Muhaiyaddeen ☺ to refer to several different phrases. In most contexts it either is the statement, *lā ilāha illAllāh, Muhammadur-Rasūlullāh,* or the *dhikr, lā ilāha illAllāh.* If twenty-four letters are mentioned it is the former. However, it may also refer to the *dhikr* used by specific prophets, or the series of statements he referred to as the Five *Kalimahs,* which include the *shahādah.* Literally, a word, phrase, or short sentence.

5 *Qadr, Lailatul-Qadr* (A) The Night of Power or Destiny. *Lailatul-Qadr* is the night the entire Qur'ān was revealed to Prophet Muhammad ☺.

6 Qutbiyyah (A) The state of *pahut arivu,* divine analytic wisdom, the sixth level of wisdom that explains the truth of God to the wisdom of the human soul.

If man can merge with God, if wisdom and the Qutbiyyah become one with God, then that will be plenitude. The body will have been destroyed. The body that has been destroyed is darkness, it is creation. After that, the world appears dark to man. When man has merged with God, the world remains dark. That is *amāvāsi,* the twenty-eighth letter, Adam ☺. If Adam ☺ becomes light, the earth remains as earth. The earth is darkness, and Adam ☺ becomes light, plenitude.

We are that. When, through our prayers, what is plenitude joins with Allāh, then the earth of Adam ☺ will stay as the earth and the world will continue to function, creation will continue on. The one who has reached that station (of plenitude)[7] stays with God and the world stays where it is, creation continues. What has appeared continues to exist, while the one who has reached that station stays as plenitude.

Like this, there are twenty-eight letters that make up this house of the body. This cage is comprised of twenty-eight letters. One letter represents birth. That is *amāvāsi,* darkness, torpor. That is creation: it is arrogance, karma, and maya. This maya, arrogance, and karma are connected to the body. That is earth. Earth, fire, water, air, ether, mind, and desire, that is what takes rebirths. The other is plenitude. One who sees the twenty-seventh, which is plenitude, will have discarded birth. If he has not seen the twenty-seventh, he will be born again. He will again become Adam ☺, and he will take another birth. Then the world and torpor will come. In this way he will become prey to tens of millions upon millions of births. We must understand this.

Precious jeweled lights of my eye, we need to realize this. We must know the methods of prayer. We must know what *vanakkam* is and we must know what *toluhai* is. We must climb up, step by step. Generally speaking, it is easy to climb. It is not difficult. There is not

---

7   The editors put words or phrases in parentheses when they are inferred, but not literally said by Bawa Muhaiyaddeen ☺; these words have been added for clarification purposes.

much distance between God and man. The distance is the world that is the mind. If we can cross this world that is the mind, then we can see the grace that is the kingdom of God, and God. This world of the mind is the distance that exists between God and man. This must be crossed. If we can transcend this, then we will see that God and we live in the same place.

This is the mind. If we cross this mind, then the *qalb* becomes a flower, a *qalb-pu,* it becomes a flower garden. God is the fragrance in that flower garden. He is the fragrance in the flowers. When we enter that garden, that fragrance will immediately develop within us. That kingdom is His kingdom, and all of the flowers there have that fragrance. Wherever you look, the flowers have that fragrance. Your *qalb* will take in that perfume; that flower of the *qalb-pu,* will accept that perfume. So, you will be joined with Him, enjoying the fragrance. That fragrance, that perfume will forever be intermingled with you.

Like that, when the *qalb-pu* accepts that fragrance, then that fragrance and that beauty will join with man, they will join with his *qalb.* That is God's kingdom. When the flower and the scent intermingle, then the flower becomes fragrant. This is how the *qalb* and God merge. God is the fragrance of that flower, the perfume of that *qalb.* The *qalb* and God are intermingled, the flower and the fragrance are intermingled. They are never separate.

Therefore, to cross the mind, there are four hundred trillion ten thousand spiritual veils that we must cross. These shaktis are present. To cross the mind, we must first transcend these shaktis. Then we can cross the mind. These shaktis are the mind-people, the armies, the attachments, the forces, *sittis,* cells, viruses, energies, *baktis,* and miracles. There are many shaktis like this—mantras, tantras, and prayers. We must transcend all of these and go beyond. Once we have crossed the mind, it will become very easy.

We must reflect upon this with wisdom. Think about this, my precious children, jeweled lights of my eye. We must discover the way to pray. We must develop the thirst that wants to find the way to worship God. Then wherever we are, we will be able to pray.

We will never get tired, we will never forget. It will not be like going to meet a friend in a certain place and then returning home; we will not meet with God in the same way that we meet with someone else.

God said to Moses ☺, "One who sees Me will not commit any faults in the world." One who sees God once will not commit any faults in the world. This is what God told Moses ☺. The one who has seen God will not commit any faults in the world. The one who has seen God will remain as God and will not commit any faults, he will do God's duty. God told this to Moses ☺.

Like this, if we can speak to God once, then hell and the world will leave us, they will die. That is *vanakkam*. If we are able to see God even once, then hell, desire, the mind, and the world will die. This is how Moses ☺ died on *turshshanam* mountain, on *shī-nai* mountain.[8] When you say "Moses ☺ died," it means that his mind and desire died. After that, Gabriel ☺ had to revive him. When Moses ☺ was revived, God said, "You are wearing slippers made from the skin of a dead donkey. Did you not put on the donkey's skin upon which satan rides? Remove those slippers and become pure!"

The skin of the donkey upon which satan rides is now covering us. When Moses' ☺ mind and desire died, God spoke to him and gave him the Ten Commandments. This body which is the skin of the donkey must die. It was the body of the mind and desire of Moses ☺ that died. After that the elements were revived, and God gave Moses ☺ the Ten Commandments. God said, "Rise up, Moses!"

Therefore, we must remove these slippers of mind, desire, and satan's qualities that we are wearing, and climb the *turshshanam* mountain of the mind. What is this *turshshanam* mountain? Man's

---

8 *turshshanam* mountain *(malai)* (T) The mountain of the evil qualities of the mind. Evil, wickedness, lewdness. Bawa Muhaiyaddeen ☺ is punning on the Arabic word for Mount Sinai, Tūrus-sīnā', where Moses ☺ received the Ten Commandments from Allāh.

Shī-nai mountain (Sanskrit & Tamil) is also a pun on Mount Sinai. *Shī* is an interjection of contempt and disgust. *Nai* means dog. "Get away, dog!"

evil and differences. *Shī-nai* is the dog of desire that must be discarded. It is not the mountain that is in (the Sinai Peninsula). There is a *shī-nai* mountain within you, a mountain of the dog that is desire, the *turshshanam* mountain. It causes divisions, commits vicious acts, murders others, shows differences, and creates fanaticism. This is *turshshanam* — evil. It is the *turshshanam* mountain that shows differences. It is the *shī-nai* mountain, the mountain of the dog of desire. You must go above this mind. You must go beyond this dog, this *shī-nai* mountain of the mind. The mind is the *shī-nai* mountain, the mind is the *turshshanam* mountain. You must cross this mind and go beyond, God said to Moses ☻, "Climb up, climb up, come up. Cross over this mountain and come." Once he travelled above that mind, Moses ☻ met God.

Muhammad ☻ crossed the seventy thousand veils, he crossed the mind. He crossed the seventy thousand veils and the eighteen thousand worlds. Having transcended all of these worlds, he arrived at the *dhāt,* the essence of Allāh that is the Nūr, and spoke to Allāh. He crossed all of these and spoke to Him. That was the *mi'rāj,* where Muhammad ☻ met Allāh and spoke to Him directly.

Like that, we must understand what needs to be crossed so that we too can meet God. This mind must die so that we can meet and speak with that Treasure that never dies. We must be reborn. This body, this mind, and this desire must change, and with God's qualities, the Light must be born. These must die and that must be born. Once this mind and desire, these thoughts, earth, fire, water, air, ether, arrogance, karma, and maya die, then God's qualities, God's actions, God's Light, and God's plenitude must be born. That form must be born. Once that is born, the *wahy,* the revelations, will come.

God said, "Moses, rise up!" and then gave him the Ten Commandments. At a later time, God addressed Muhammad ☻, "Muhammad, come here! Cross over everything and come! Cross these veils and come!" He said, "Cross the mind and come." There, God gave instructions to Muhammad ☻. He gave him the explanations about *toluhai,* He gave the explanations about *vanakkam,* He gave the explanations about his *ummah,* his followers, He gave the explanations about hell, and He gave the explanations about heaven. He told Muhammad ⊕ everything.

Therefore, each one of us must come to that place and hear God's words. We must hear the *wahy.* To be reborn does not mean that you die, it means that this body of Light is born. One is Light and one is birth. You must take the form that is Light. You must discard the form that is the mind and take the form that is Light. If you take that, you will see.

This is the way we need to pray. Then we will be able hear the *wahy,* we will be able to hear the sound of God, and we will be able to hear the word of God. This is the state in which we can do this.

Therefore, precious jeweled lights of my eye, we must think about this. Please strive in this way to pray God's prayer. Please try. *Āmīn.*

Allāh is the One who is sufficient for all. May He give us His plenitude. May He give us all of His explanations. *Āmīn, āmīn, āmīn. As-salāmu 'alaikum wa rahmatullāhi wa barakātahu,* may the peace, the beneficence, and the blessings of God be upon you!

A'ūdhu billāhi minash-shaitānir-rajīm.
I seek refuge in God from the accursed satan.

Bismillāhir-Rahmānir-Rahīm.
In the name of God, the Most Compassionate,
the Most Merciful.

HOW ARE WE TO PRAY TO GOD WHEN HE HAS NO FORM?

July 13, 1982, Tuesday, 6:10 a.m.

My sons and daughters, my brothers and sisters, my grandsons and granddaughters, how can we prove God's words? This is something we have to think about. From *al-awwal* to *'ālamul-arwāh,* from the time of creation to the world of the souls, God has revealed His teachings, His actions, and His words to us through the prophets. The Qur'ān speaks of twenty-five prophets. The Bible and the Torah also speak about these twenty-five prophets. All three speak about these prophets and the explanations they brought.

So, a thought came to my wisdom about this. A thought came to my wisdom, to my *qalb,* my innermost heart, that there are similar words in the Tamil (Purānas) where God is described as the One who has no likeness, no self-image, and no form. He is called the Paraparam Vastu, the Supreme Being, the Param Porul, the All-Pervasive Treasure.

My love you.[1] In the Qur'ān, in the Bible, and in the Torah, God is described in this way, as One who has no form. The Qur'ān says that God has no likeness, self-image, or form. God says, "I am not like the sun or the moon. I am not a light like the sun, or a light like the moon, or a light like the stars. I am not like any of those lights. I am not One who is like those."

---

1 *My love you:* Bawa Muhaiyaddeen ☉ often said this phrase in English in his discourses. He taught that love should have no "I," no separation.

My brothers and sisters, with our wisdom, in our *qalbs* we must understand that there is a meaning to the words that God spoke. We must think about this. He has no form or shape, nor is He like the many kinds of lights—He is nothing like that. As this is so, we must think. The children who have wisdom must reflect deeply upon this. We must consider: What should we know and understand from His words? What is God?

God has created the three worlds of *'ālamul-arwāh,* the world of the souls, the *dunyā,* which is the world of man, and the *ākhirah,* the kingdom of God. He has created all these worlds, as well as the eighteen thousand universes. Allāh says that He has created all of these, and that there is a heaven and a hell. The prophets tell us this. If we research into the story (of those creations), we can know and understand this. Since this is so, we need to reflect on what God is like. He tells us to perform *vanakkam,* worship, *toluhai,* the five-times prayer, *'ibādah,* service to God, and *tiyānam,* meditation. Like this, Allāh has told us to do many things.

My love you, my sons and my daughters. For everything that He has created, there is an origin, a form, a word, and a basis, to show a meaning. It is through these creations that He shows a meaning. The earth, the sky, the world, the netherworld, the sun, and the moon... He created the sun and shows light. He created the darkness and shows the light of the moon and the stars. He created the trees and shows the fruit. He created the earth and shows the grass and the gems. He created the form of the fire and shows heat. He created the water and with that He quenches thirst and shows coolness. He created the section called air to give us health and make it possible for us to breathe. He created the sky and shows the clouds, the lightning, and the thunder, so that through them, we can understand a meaning. It is through all of these that He makes us understand both good and evil, and He makes us understand hell. Everything that we look at has been created with a form, and it is through the understanding of that form that we can know wrong and right.

He created the eyes and shows us the light within them. He created the body and shows us what is within the body. He created the nose and shows and makes us understand the smells and fragrances within it. He created the ears and placed *arivu* and *putti*, wisdom and intellect, within us to discriminate the sounds of wrong and right. He created the tongue and shows us the speech and the different tastes within it. He created the mouth and shows us how to speak in many ways. He created the hands and shows us that we can receive and give both good and evil with them, and He gives us the wisdom to discriminate. He created the legs and shows us how to go on the good path, and He shows us how to use our intellect to discriminate. In this way, He explains what is within each thing. He created the *qalb* and shows the mind and desire, good and evil, heaven and hell, and the four hundred trillion ten thousand spiritual thoughts and actions that are within it.

All of these are created as examples. They have a form, and are examples. All God's creations have been created in this way; they have a story into which we can research. It is through this that we can understand, learn, and know.

God has created an atom, and shows the nature that is within it. Whatever we research into has a form. *Āvis,* spirits, also have a form. Earth, fire, water, and air have a form. Ether, which is maya and torpor, has a form. We must understand what maya and torpor are. In this way, He has placed each of these forms as an example, and through that example shows a meaning.

My love you, my son, my children. We need to reflect on this. God is the only One who has no form, no shape, and no cause and effect through which He can be understood. He is the only One who does not have a form and who cannot be seen through an example. We need to think about this. Everything else has a point that we can see. My love you, my children, this is something we need to reflect on. We need to realize this, think about it, and understand it. It is essential to consider: What is the wisdom and the teaching that will give us understanding? For everything, with the exception of God, something can be shown. Nothing can be shown through which we can know or see God.

God has created the *nabīs*, prophets, the *rasūls*, messengers, and man so that we can understand Him. But instead, human beings worship satan, through satan himself, or through a darkness, or through a torpor. They worship a point. They see a tree and pray to the tree, they see a cow and pray to the cow, they make these into forms. Man looks at all of the four hundred trillion ten thousand points, and prays to those points. Man prays to what he sees. The sun, the moon, and the stars, forms, shapes, demons, and ghosts, all of these are points, they are examples. They are things that have a form.

My love You, my God! My love You! When we pray to something that is dear to our *qalbs,* when we pray to God, how should we pray? What is the point for That? That has no point, It has no example that can be seen. It has no form, no example. So, what is the point for That? No basic foundation can be shown for It. What is that Thing? To what can we direct our prayer? That has no form. Earth, fire, and water all have a form; there is some sign, some point we can pray to. But for God there is no point that can be seen. Is there a point for Him? All of you are praying to God. Does He have an origin? Does He have a history? Is He like the sun, like the fire, like the water, or like the air? What is He like? We have to think about this. What is God?

All creations have an origin, a history, a point, a form, a shape, and a way in which they have been created. Everything created has a point, a form, a shape, something to identify them. They have a story or a word by which you can describe what they are. They have been created with a form, and that form can be seen. But for God, Allāh, you cannot see a point, a form, or a shape and say, "This is God!" You cannot say that.

God is not *like* a light, He is not *like* a resplendence. So, if He is not like a light or a resplendence, how can He be described? If you say that He is a light, then that becomes a comparison. The Qur'ān says that Allāhu is the Sustainer, the One who has no comparison or helper. It says that you should pray to that Allāhu who has no comparison and that you should not keep anything as equal to Him. If you do keep an equal, then that means you are those who are keeping a comparison to Him.

We cannot keep a form or a shape and pray to Him. He has no form or shape on which we can focus our prayer. So, what point is there? What is the point that we can pray to? We cannot see a point. There is nothing we can see that we can focus on.

Some say to pray facing the west. The west is a point. A particular direction is a point. Some say to pray facing the east, while others say to face towards the north or the south. So, each of those directions becomes a point, a form that we are keeping in the mind. How can we pray to Him through that form? If we say that God is in "this direction" or "that direction," then we are keeping a comparison to Him.

Please think about this with wisdom. Through what form, what shape, what story, and what point can we pray to Allāhu who is that Param Porul, that All-Pervasive Treasure? What is that point? Some describe it as being "like this," while others describe it in another way. In a book there will be a different description of what that point is, and some will make what is described in that book into a form.

But God is One who has no form or shape. How are we to pray to Him? What kind of Being is He? What is He like? What is the point we should be praying to? What is prayer?

God is One without equal. He does not have the six evils. He has no wife or children, no birth, no end, and no destruction. He transcends beginning and end. He exists eternally, and dwells in everything. If not for Him, not even an atom would move. They say all of these things about God. So, what is this Being? What form does It have? If there is a Being like that, how can we pray to It? What point should we pray to? If you pray facing a certain direction, then that direction becomes a form. You have kept a form for That, you have created a form. Once you say, "He is like this," then that is creating a form, a comparison to Him. You are keeping a parallel, an opposite.

Therefore, what is prayer? He tells us to pray to Him. What is the point for That? He has no form or shape. What is He like? Are we to pray to a light, or are we to pray to the fire? Are we to pray to the light of the sun, or to the coolness and light of the moon, or to the stars? We have to think of this with wisdom. What is the point? Please think about this.

What is *vanakkam*, what is *toluhai*, what is *'ibādah?* How are we to pray to Allāhu? In what way is it done? What is the point? If there is no point, then what is that? But if there is a point, then what is that? It is a comparison. If there is a point, it is a comparison.

So, how can we pray to Him? How can this be done? Doctor Tambi, please speak, tell us what you think.

ANSWER

It is part of the question I asked yesterday.

BAWA MUHAIYADDEEN

What do you have to say about this, Radio Tambi?

ANSWER

You cannot compare. He is greater than anything you can think.

BAWA MUHAIYADDEEN

Ah, that is enough! You cannot compare Him to anything. If you do, then that is not prayer. If you have kept a point, then how can you pray? So, in the world, no one is really praying to Allāhu. Everything is a comparison. People could be praying to earth, woman, gold, or possessions.

We need to understand what we are really praying to. Is it to religion, race, philosophy, or scriptures? These are points. Religion? That is a point. Race? That is a point. It has a form. Can we do this prayer through a form? Is He contained within this? Is He the form of religion, or is He the form of race? No.

As this is so, we need to think a little. What is that Treasure, and how can we worship It? What is it that is called prayer? We need to reflect on this. If we do not think about this, if we do not understand this, if we do not know this...

Every creation has a form, and it is through that form that the meaning can be understood. But God does not have a form, nor does He have a shape. He is One without estimate. So how can we pray to Him? How can we know Him? We need to understand this.

Only when we realize this will we be able to pray. We must understand this.

My love you, children, jeweled lights of my eye. Every other prayer that we do is prayer to the elements, to evil, to shaitān, to the *nafs,* the demons, the *āvis,* the books, the writings, the stories, or the words. This is what we are worshipping, a point. Whatever side we turn to is a point that we have kept. But Allāh dwells in all lives, everywhere. He is not in just one particular direction. Without Him, not even an atom would move. He is everywhere, within everything. Not an atom would move without Him. He is present everywhere. He is the One who gives nourishment and food to all of His created beings, the One who watches over them, the One who is the Rabb, the One who creates, protects, and sustains, the Rahmān, the Rahīm. Like that, He is the Creator, the Protector, and the Sustainer.

My love you, children, jeweled lights of my eye. How can we know Allāhu and pray to Him? What kind of a Being is He? What kind of a Treasure is He? How can we do this prayer? In what place is He? What is His form? What is His color, what is His hue? We need to think about this. What is meditation, and what point are you meditating on? What is prayer, and to whom are you directing your prayer? If a point has come, then you are creating a parallel to Him. Whatever you are praying to will become something that is a comparison to Him.

This is a *palakkam,* a training exercise. What we are now doing is a learning. This is not *vanakkam,* this is *palakkam,* a habit. Just as the sun and the moon move in their orbits, what we are now doing is being done automatically, out of habit. An explanation needs to come, an understanding needs to come, through the doing of this. My love you, we should gain understanding through the doing of this. Only when we have reached that understanding will it be *vanakkam.*

In this time itself you must finish knowing each and every form. When you have understood that, then that is prayer. Please understand this. Everything you see is an example, and within each thing there is a cause and effect. There is the example and the form, and within that is the story and the words. Yet, you think that all of these shaktis and *sittis* are miracles. All of these miracles are useless.

My love you, we need to think about what this Being called God is. It is possible that He, too, may have something through which He can be shown.

My love you, jeweled lights of my eye. Man himself is the point, the example through which God can be known. Man is the proof for God. Man needs to know God. Man could be that point.

God is a Power. That has no light, heat, anything. That is a Power that controls everything, That is a Power that exists everywhere, in all of everything. Man is the point, man is God's example. God exists within this form of man. Once man knows himself, once he understands himself, then he will be God. He will have that Light, that *beauty-form,* that *zīnah,* that wisdom, that quality, God's actions that are the ninety-nine *wilāyāt,* that compassion, that conduct, that speech, that behavior, and that resplendence. When man knows himself, then he becomes That. When he knows himself and performs God's actions, then his qualities will be God's, that grace will be God's, that speech will be God's, that word will be God's, that gaze will be God's, that sound will be God's, that fragrance will be God's, that taste will be God's, that heart will be God's, and that *qalb* will be God's. That alone is what will be evident within man.

Man is a point. When he knows himself, when he understands himself, when he has cut away earth and maya, when God's qualities fill him and when all other qualities die away, when the desire for earth, the desire for woman, the desire for gold, the desire for possessions, and the world are cut away — when everything dies away from him, then when he looks at himself, he will be without any form, and that Power will resplend within him. After everything within him has died, God's reflection will come within him. Only then will youthfulness, light, wisdom, and God's qualities, speech, actions, and sound come within him. That speech will come within him, that word will come within him, that beauty will come within him, that gaze will come within him, that remembrance will come within him, that compassion will come within him, that truth will come within him, and that wisdom will come within him. All of those qualities will come within him. He will be one who has understood that section. That is *vanakkam,* prayer, where one understands himself, where one knows himself. Man will know and understand himself.

So, man is a point. Man is the point for God. He exists as a form with *pahut arivu,* divine analytic wisdom. It is through man that God can be known. We can know the section of hell through all the other created beings, but through man we can understand that Power, that reflection. The reflected image of God is man. When man's own reflection is destroyed, then the section of God comes. Man now becomes Light. That is a cooling Light. Compassionate love: that is that Light. Patience: that is that Light. Tranquility: that is that Light. Wisdom: that is that Light. Peacefulness: that is that Light. Mercy: that is that Light. Tolerance: that is that Light. Love: that is that Light. Kindness: that is that Light. To embrace with affection: that is that Light. Truth: that is that Light. Justice: that is that Light. Equality: that is that Light. Serenity: that is that Light, that Power. The awareness that the hunger of others is like one's own hunger: that is that Light. The clarity of wisdom: that is that Light. To know the vast *qalb* that is a vast world, the vast *qalb* that contains the eighteen thousand universes, is *'ilm,* divine knowledge, and that is that Light. His qualities are that Light, His actions are that Light, and His Power is that Light.

You need to understand this. If you understand yourself, and if through this understanding, you make all of these other things die, if you make these *nafs,* the *dunyā,* desires, attachments, divisions, and differences die in you, if the connections to these seventy thousand veils and blemishes of birth die away from you, if they are annihilated and you regain your youth, then you will understand that point, that Power that is within you. That is God, the reflection. Once the whole *dunyā* within you is destroyed, that Treasure will resplend as a reflected image within you, and It will speak from that place. That is God. This is wisdom. This is the explanation.

This is what the Rasūlullāh ☺ saw on *mi'rāj,* his night journey through the heavens. This is the point he saw when he saw Allāh. He saw a youth of sixteen years, he saw himself reflected in Allāh's

Mirror. He saw Allāh's Power within himself. Allāh said, "This is your own *zīnah*, light, plenitude, and beauty that you see. This is Me. I created the *dunyā,* hell, and everything else as something for you to understand. It is through you that I can be understood. You cannot search for Me within a form. Search within your *qalb* and find Me. Search through wisdom, through '*ilm,* and through My qualities. Search within yourself and find Me."

My love you, please think about this. Remove the seventy thousand veils and blemishes that are within your *qalb.* Cut the connection to earth, woman, and gold. When you cut these away, you will see God within you. When you see that Completeness, then that is *vanakkam,* prayer. You will understand this with each breath. Understand? This is the meaning.

You need to reflect on this. Whatever you focus on other than Him is a comparison. When you discard something from yourself, that is prayer. When something evil is cut away, that is prayer. When you knock away any comparison to Allāh, that is prayer. But whatever you pray to as equal to Him, is a comparison.

Prayer is to discard everything other than Allāh. Anything else you see as a support is a parallel to Allāh. To beat away what is within all of these sections, is prayer. After you have discarded all of this, after you have finished with everything, that Light will come within you, that Power will come within you, that Beauty will come. Then you will understand.

My love you, please think about this. Understand? This is that point. You are a point, your *qalb.* You are the point for God. What reveals you is God and what reveals God is you. Your *qalb* reveals Him. He explains you and you explain Him. You are the meaning. This is the history. He is within you and you are within Him.

Thank you. *Āmīn.* Please think about this. From within our prayers we need to understand each and every thing. We need to know and understand this.

Thank you. Is there anything else? Ah! Finished.

As-salāmu 'alaikum wa rahmatullāhi wa barakātuhu. We need to think about this.

THE BENEFITS OF PRAYER

May 30, 1984, Wednesday, 9:28 p.m.

Man thinks about, works for, intends, and searches for many different things. Man does all these things for his own sake. What he does in his life is not for others, but for himself. So, no matter what things he searches for, it is for himself. He does not give to others, what he does is for his own self. He spends his entire life searching in this way.

Although most people are searching for their own sake, there are a few who search for the sake of God, there are a few who accept the meaning. When they perform their *vanakkam,* fasting, and *toluhai,* when they tie their hands at *takbir* and make their intention for prayer, they say, "This is for the sake of Allāh." They say they are doing this for Allāh. But if we look at the meaning, we see that it does not matter to Allāh whether we pray to Him or do not pray to Him, whether we perform *toluhai* or do not perform *toluhai*. That is nothing to Him. However, the treasure that we give for the sake of Allāh, the treasure of the open *qalb*—love, truth and purity—what we have fashioned through His qualities and hand over to Him, He accepts *that* with joy.

As a Helpmate, God stands behind anyone who acts with His qualities and His actions. Whoever acts according to His intention, God will stand behind that intention and be the One who is his Helper. If one acts according to God's qualities, God will be the

25

Ruler, the Friend, and the Helper to those qualities. If this state exists, then when a man who has compassionate qualities and a perfectly pure heart says, "I am doing this for Āndavan," He will accept that. If the prayer he does is for the sake of God, if the *toluhai* he does is for the sake of God, if the good actions he performs are for the sake of God, and if his earnings are dedicated to God, then God will return those earnings to him.

If a man plants a crop in the earth, for whom is the benefit? If he plows, fertilizes, and tends the earth carefully, the earth returns the benefit, it gives the profit to him. It does not retain it for itself. If a man plants a tree carefully, tends and nurtures it, then when it bears ripe fruit, to whom does it give the fruit? It gives it to the one who nurtured it. If a man raises a cow and brings it up to maturity, then the cow gives its milk and its benefits in return. Whatever is cultivated will give back a share, whether it is the earth or whether it is a life.

Therefore, the results of the good actions a man performs and the benefit of the worship he does in the name of God will be given back to him. That good benefit is returned. The profits and the fruits are given back only to us. God does not keep any of them. The result of every action that we perform is returned to us, whether it is good or bad. We receive the results of our actions. God does not keep it for Himself. We give the responsibility to Him, and He gives us our share. That is our share. The earnings of whatever we give into His responsibility are returned to us, the good or the bad. It might be the bad that is given or it might be the good that is given, but He gives back our share.

Therefore, for everything that we do or give in the name of God, the earnings come only to us, it is not for Him. If we reflect on this with judgment, with truth, and with wisdom, we will realize that whether it is good or bad, the results come back to us.

The benefit of the prayer that we do is the good that is returned to us. It is through that prayer, through that goodness that we are given the crown of *gnānam,* divine wisdom. We are crowned with the crown of *gnānam* and given heaven because of that goodness.

Whether it is through our *toluhai,* through our good actions, through the good benefits that we bestow, through the duty that we do, through the help that we give to others, through the equality, peace, and tranquility that we exhibit, through the unity that we bring about, or through the good conduct and behavior that we have, we are the ones who receive the reward of great blessings. In return for what we do, we are given the crown of *gnānam,* and attain the kingdom of the Father of *gnānam* and the station, the beauty, and the Light of that kingdom. Having given us that, God sends His *malaks, malā'ikah,* and houris to escort us to that kingdom of heaven. The heavenly beings and angels adorn us and take us there.

In this state, no matter what we may set out to do, the earnings belong only to us. Āndavan gives, He does not receive the benefit for Himself. The earnings of what we have searched for are returned to us. If we perform a prayer saying that we are praying for the sake of Allāh, we will be the ones who receive the benefit. He accepts that prayer and returns the good to us. He accepts every word and gives the good to us. If we do something bad, He gives that to us. If we do something good, He gives that to us. He gives the earnings of every thought to us. He gives the earnings of every intention to us. Therefore, we alone are the recipients of what He gives as the result of our intention. It is not that it brings Him happiness to receive what we give.

If we take a drop of water from the ocean, it does not mean that the level of the ocean decreases because of that. So, the prayer we do does not increase or decrease the level of Āndavan's ocean. It is like taking a drop of water from the ocean. A great *daulah,* wealth, does not come to God through the prayers we do. It neither increases nor decreases that ocean. He is the One who is worshipped by all lives, beginning from the crawling ant to the eighty-four thousand different kinds of lives, the mountains, the sun, the earth, and the sky. The prayers of these lives create a great resonance. So, what is *our* breath going to do? Hmm?

We all praise ourselves, saying, "We are great, this is great, that is great," but that is not how it really is. We receive the benefit. We alone receive the benefit for what we have done. There is nothing for Him. We say, "We are doing this for Allāh. We are doing this for Allāh's sake. We do everything for the sake of Allāh." But if you turn around and look, you will see that you are really doing it for the sake of your wife and your children, your relatives, and your community. You turn another way and say that you are doing it for Allāh, but later you say, "*Aiyō,* I did this for the sake of my child, *aiyō,* I did this for the sake of my wife, *aiyō,* I did this for the sake of my grandchildren!" When you look in another direction you say, "I am doing this for the sake of Allāh." This is how we think, but this is not how it really is.

We need to reflect upon this. Regardless of the subject of our speech, we must speak the truth. We need to open the straight path to God. We should not create mountains between us and God. We should not create veils or differences between us and true human beings. We must open our hearts, we must have an open heart. Open heart! Then it will be easy to commune with another. If we do it in this manner, we can see so much beauty.

We should think about this, children. It will be very good if those who love God, those who truly love the qualities of God, act with those qualities. To want God without having God's qualities is not enough. To want God without having God's actions will not give much benefit.

First, we must acquire the section of God's beauty. We must acquire that from God. The blessing we receive through that will be the greatest blessing.

When we observe the work that a cow does or the work that a tree does...a cow or the earth or the soil or a forest will return a benefit for whatever we do for them. They will give us a benefit in return for what we do. So, will not God who is so great also do that? Will He not give back that benefit? If we do something for the sake of God, He will give something back to us. Even if we think with a small amount of wisdom, we will realize that He will give us everything. Will not Āndavan give the benefit? Hmm? Even when our thoughts are the smallest in wisdom, He understands and gives us that benefit. He does not keep the earnings for Himself, the earnings are for us. Therefore, we need to reflect on this.

God is One who has ears and eyes, He has everything. He cannot be without seeing, He cannot be without hearing. Whether we are praying for His sake or for ourselves, God will know. He smiles. He says, "The crop that you harvest from your land is for you, is it not? Although you are dedicating it to Me, you alone are the one who receives the benefit." This is what God gives.

Therefore, in our life our true hearts must open. It is common practice to say we are praying for the sake of Allāh, but in truth, the heart must open. We must acknowledge, "O God, although I am doing each duty in Your name, I am the one who is receiving the benefits." We have to plead, "O God, please forgive my faults. Whatever I ask from You, I am asking for my own sake. Please forgive me, O Allāh."

My precious children, this is the way we must attain clarity. We must acquire wisdom and we must attain clarity. We must make our hearts pure and resplendent. We need that unity and harmony. Peace is found within ourselves, not within the world. If we cannot find it within ourselves, we will not find it in the world. The world will not give us peace. Peace is right within us, *shānti* and tranquility are right within us. When unity comes, peace will follow.

Yet, one man kills another man without mercy. This man has blood and that man also has blood. That blood should make a person dizzy. At the sight of blood a man should say, *"Atch!"* As soon as he sees it, he should tremble, *"Sha!"* The sight of blood should do that, his head should spin. His heart should tremble and his head should swirl at the sight of blood. But instead, these men are like tigers and lions, they are like beasts. They even drink blood. They butcher other human beings and spill their blood in the same way that they butcher goats and cows. They are called the human race, but they are really the animal species, they are tigers, lions — vicious beasts.

Can we ever imagine that God would give something good in return for such evil intentions? They commit evil without the slightest fear, without the slightest pity. They abuse and kill others without any compassion. How can any benefit come from that?

O God, You are watching. There is no help other than You. You see everything. Man keeps on destroying man.

Bismillāhir-Rahmānir-Rahīm. Ah *shari,* very well. *As-salāmu 'alai-kum wa rahmatullāhi wa barakātuhu.*

A'ūdhu billāhi minash-shaitānir-rajīm.
I seek refuge in God from the accursed satan.

Bismillāhir-Rahmānir-Rahīm.
In the name of God, the Most Compassionate,
the Most Merciful.

FOCUS THE CAMERA OF THE *QALB*

May 24, 1983, Tuesday, 9:14 a.m.

Bismillāhir-Rahmānir-Rahīm. Doctor Tambi, *pillai,*[1] you asked about prayer, *vanakkam.* The most important thing you need to know about *vanakkam* is subtlety. To know the meaning and subtlety of prayer and then to pray, is prayer. In life we need to fashion this state in the proper way. To focus on the state where we can join with God is an essential state for prayer. We need to establish this. As long as that state has not been established, the signs of the connection between God, prayer, and us will not be there. The connection will be to other things.

There are eighteen thousand universes, four hundred trillion glitters, and countless thoughts that dwell within us. Along with this, there is earth, woman, and gold. In addition, there is arrogance, karma, and maya. And there is *tārahan, singan,* and *sūran,* the qualities of birth. There is lust, anger, miserliness, lasciviousness, fanaticism, envy, rancor, impatience, hastiness, pride, jealousy, backbiting, telling lies, treachery, vengeance, selfishness, and doubt. All of these dwell within our body and our mind.

Many countless numbers of thoughts and sections dwell within us. They do not allow us to fulfill this state of prayer. They do not

---

1 Bawa Muhaiyaddeen ☺ often referred to his children as *pillai,* child, and *tambi,* little brother.

allow us to establish the connection between God and us. We need to fashion a state where we can cut these other connections. Having fashioned that state we must stand steadfast, with faith, trust, and *īmān*. With that strength, we must join *īmān* in Allāh with wisdom, join wisdom with Muhammad ⊕, join Muhammad ⊕ with the resplendence of the Nūr which is the completeness of wisdom, and then take that completeness and join it with Allāh.

Prayer is the state where we are joined with Allāh. To establish that state is prayer. If we do not have that state, these other sections will not allow us to establish our prayer, they will change us. They will change the connection between God and us, the gaze that looks at Him and us, the speech that speaks to Him and us, and the love that has love for Him and us. They will change our focus from Him to other places, to other pictures. We must know this subtlety in our *vanakkam*.

Children, this is indeed a great subtlety—a subtlety of prayer, a subtlety of *toluhai, 'ibādah, vanakkam,* and *dhikr.*[2] We must think about this state.

When you are taking a picture of this world, or of the eighteen thousand universes, or of life, or of beautiful things, or of things that are not beautiful, you have to hold the camera in your hands and focus correctly on the point you want to photograph. From where you are standing, you need to focus very carefully on the point you want to take a picture of. Before you click the shutter, you must first check to make sure that everything appears in the picture. It is only a small point, and once you click the shutter, *"tak,"* that is the picture you will get. After that, if you want to enlarge the picture you can enlarge it, or if you want to reduce it you can reduce it. But, if the focus is not right, then the picture will not be right, it will not be composed correctly. Instead of focusing, you looked here and there, you turned slightly, or you looked around.

---

2 *dhikr* (A) The remembrance of God. Of the many *dhikrs,* the most exalted *dhikr* is *"Lā ilāha illAllāhu:* Nothing exists except Allāh. Only You are Allāh." All *dhikrs* relate to His *wilāyāt* or His actions, but this *dhikr* points to Him and Him alone.

Like this, in our prayers, when we fail to correctly establish the state of focus between God and ourselves, we will not be able to connect with the section of subtlety that was described earlier. So, that will not be prayer. We will have made a different connection. We will have turned towards something else, we will have looked elsewhere. If we look at things other than Allāh, then the direct connection between Him and us will not be evident. We must realize this state and understand how to establish it.

Just as a camera has to be focused correctly on an object, the *qalb,* the innermost heart, must be focused. That *qalb,* which is the camera of *īmān,* must establish the focus of wisdom. To catch hold of the connection between God and us, to focus on Him and to take that picture, is prayer. We need to have this state.

Allāh is not an atom, He is beyond the atom. He is extremely tiny, He is so very small. Yet, He is so vast. That is something that cannot be seen with the eyes. It is a Mystery. If we want to catch hold of that Mystery, we have to do so in a very subtle way. We have to capture It with that focus. We have to focus the camera of the *qalb* with that intention. That focus will establish the connection between Him and us. We must fashion that state. In this way, we must establish that state, that point, that focus, that thought, that intention, and that prayer.

When this has been fashioned, what will that state be like? If a person has had a mental shock, he is unaware of anything else. He becomes a *dumb man.* He is not aware of anything. He does not know how to speak, he does not know what someone next to him is saying, he does not know if he is being hit, he does not know if he is being pulled; he is immersed in only one thought, in one point. This is how he will be, is that not so?

The state of prayer is also like this. When we prepare for prayer, we should be like a person in shock. There should be only the point of prayer between Him and us. We should have the state where we are not aware of anything else. No matter what happens, we should not be aware of it. The *qalb* should be like this. The sections of the body should not come and disturb us; the body should be in shock, and the *qalb* should not be aware of anything other than the focus on that one point.

If we can establish this state, if we can be as if we are in a state of shock, then our prayer, our intention, focus, *toluhai, 'ibādah, dhikr,* and whatever else we intend, will gaze on only one thing, that connection between Him and us. If we have that focus, we will not turn to look at anything else.

For a person in that state, the *nafs,* the base desires, will come and shout. All of the four hundred trillion things that were mentioned earlier will come and shout and cry. They will yell at him, and hit him! But he will not be aware of any of these things, is that not so? Like that, no matter how much noise they make, he will not be aware of it. He will only be aware of that one point. He will remain with that focus, that one gaze.

We must correctly establish this state. We must fashion and do our prayers in this way. Only when we establish and do our *toluhai, 'ibādah, vanakkam,* all our prayers, in this way, will the picture of the direct connection between Allāh and us be formed correctly. Only then will the picture of that connection be printed, with that proof. He will be looking at us and we will be looking at Him, the two looking at each other. He will catch hold of us. His *rahmah,* His grace, will be looking at us. And our *qalb* will catch hold of Him, and take that picture of Him. That state of union is prayer. He will have our picture and we will have His picture.

When God's qualities, His actions, and His section come into us and when our section goes into Him, when these two join together and become one, then that state is prayer. When we realize this state, from that time forth, we will understand what prayer is. We need to understand how to establish this state.

So, you must try to fashion this. Only then will your prayer be fulfilled. Then, you and I will have reached that state of completion. This will be the focus and subtlety between Allāh and us. He knows how to catch hold of us, but we need the care, the focus, and that point to make the connection with Him, to catch hold of Him.

When we reach that state, our prayer will be complete. We will not hear the other sounds, the sounds of the connections to the *nafs*, the blood ties, the world, earth, woman, gold, and possessions. We will have completed the process of joining His sound and speech with our sound and speech, His connection with our connection. We will have completed that prayer, we will have finished that *waqt*.

To try to establish that state is the way of prayer, its state and its benefit. That *rahmah* is the most exalted blessing we can attain.

You, I, and every child must think about this. We must try to establish this state. Only then can we receive the *rahmah* of prayer— His treasure that is the *mubārakāt,* the wealth of the three worlds. This is certain.

Āmīn. May Allāh give us this, and grant us His grace.

A'ūdhu billāhi minash-shaitānir-rajīm.
I seek refuge in God from the accursed satan.

Bismillāhir-Rahmānir-Rahīm.
In the name of God, the Most Compassionate,
the Most Merciful.

DHIKR DISCOURSE —
AUGUST 9, 1976

August 9, 1976, Monday, 7:50 a.m.

(This is the first of three from a series of nineteen early morning discourses given in Philadelphia between August 9, 1976 and
August 28, 1976, in which Bawa Muhaiyaddeen ☺ teaches and
demonstrates the silent *dhikr.*)

E arly in the morning, about four-thirty or five a.m., everyone
must wake up. After you get up, you should wash your face,
hands, and feet and then drink some water, or something else. By
four forty-five or five a.m., you should pray to God. All of you
should go and sit in the seats downstairs, or sit somewhere else
downstairs. Everyone, both male and female, must go. You should
go every day.

You must make your *niyyah,* your intention, and then recite the
SubhānAllāhi Kalimah, the Third *Kalimah,* three times. Blow that
into your hearts. After that, make your requests to God:

"O my God, the One of limitless grace, the One of incomparable
love, the One who gives the undiminishing wealth of grace, please
remove all of the faults that are in our *qalbs.* Please cast away all
of the evils that arise in our thoughts. Please cut away all of the
attachments, all of the illnesses, and all of the distresses that come
through our mind and desire. We cannot bear our bodily ailments,
the diseases of blood, the diseases of air, the diseases of earth, the

diseases of birth, and the respiratory ailments. Like that, we cannot do anything with these illnesses. Please remove them. May You take all of our evil qualities. Whether You burn them, whether You keep them, or whatever You do with them is Your wish. Please remove all of these from us.

"*Yā* Āndavanai! *Yā* Allāh! Please give us Your qualities. May You give Your beauty to our bodies. May You give Your qualities to our bodies. May You give Your love to this body, may You give Your grace to this body, and may You give Your justice to this body.

"May You give us Your truthful word, Your compassion, Your peace, and Your tranquility. May You give us Your *wilāyāt* and Your grace. May You grant us Your limitless qualities, grace, and plenitude. May You protect us from the evils of satan.

"Every moment, every second, may You give us the love, the wisdom, and the *īmān,* faith, certitude, and determination, by which we will never forget You. May You give us Your perfected *wilāyāt,* and grace us. May You give us Your Light.

"Āndavanai, may You accept us at this very second. May You accept responsibility for our *qalbs* and may You accept responsibility for our bodies. *Āmīn. Yā* Allāh. *Al-hamdu lillāh.* All praise and praising belong to You."

You must say this!

A 'ūdhu billāhi minash-shaitānir-rajīm. Bismillāhir-Rahmānir-Rahīm. All praise and praising are Yours.

Lā ilāha, there is nothing other than You, O Allāh. If you are sitting with your feet on the floor, look at your feet. As you breathe, the breath of *lā ilāha* should flow from the left foot, the left big toe, or from the left hand, or with a slight movement of the left eye or the left eyebrow. *Lā ilāha* must flow with the breath.

IllAllāhu, You are Allāh. Your right thumb should rise, your right big toe, or your right eye should move slightly. From that, you will know where the breath is.

(Bawa Muhaiyaddeen ☉ demonstrates.)

Lā ilāha.

DOCTOR MARKAR explains

The breath should go out from the left nostril. And when you say *illAllāhu,* the breath should come in through the right nostril. You should blink from the right side slightly, so that the Light can be drawn in and focused in the heart, the chest.

BAWA MUHAIYADDEEN

(Bawa Muhaiyaddeen ⊕ demonstrates the *dhikr* further and then continues speaking.)

This is how you should do it. You must distinguish between the breaths, either by a slight movement of the toes, the thumbs, the eyes, or the eyebrows. Until you learn this, you might say it out loud with your tongue, or you might say it silently, or you might say it with a slight sound. After that you should say it with the breath; after that you should say it with the tip of the tongue; after that you should say it without the movement of the tongue; after that you should say it through the *rūh,* your soul; after that you should say it through the light of *īmān.* Then you should say it through remembrance. After that you should take in the breath through *unarchi,* feeling, then take it in through *unarvu,* awareness, and then balance it through *putti,* intellect.

Later, through *arivu,* wisdom, you must distinguish between the breaths, and stop the breath, here and there. Through *madi,* judgment, you must control the breath, you must understand where it is. After that, through *nuparivu,* subtle wisdom, you must know how to raise and lower the breath — where it is going, where it is coming from, and in which passageway and in which nerve it is working. This is done through subtle wisdom. Next, you should discriminate with *pahut arivu,* divine analytic wisdom. You will be able to find out what is wrong and what is right, and where the evils are. You will be able to know where the good is and where the evil is. You will be able to see this in the breath itself. The Light will come by which you can see this in the breath, and you will be able to discard the evil and accept the good.

After that, when you take in that breath with *pērarivu,* divine luminous wisdom, you will be able to see all of the universes that are within you. You will be able to understand the worlds that are inside you and the worlds that are outside, the evils that are inside your heart and the evils that are outside, and the angels that are inside you and the angels that are outside. You will be able to understand the light that is inside you and the lights that are outside. You will understand all of this. You will understand the ocean of maya that is inside you and the ocean of maya that is outside. You will understand the hell that is inside you and the heaven that is on your right. You will understand all of this as if you were seeing it in a mirror.

When you do the *dhikr* correctly and establish that state, then it will automatically flow with your breath, both night and day. The *rūh* and the wisdom of the Qutbiyyah will be doing the *dhikr*. This will flow with the breath. Then that remembrance, that thought, that focus, that light, that soul, and that wisdom will automatically operate with the breath. In a little while it will operate automatically. Then, only the light of Allāh, the sounds of Allāh, the grace of Allāh, the speech of Allāh, the resonance of Allāh, the wisdom of Allāh, and the qualities of Allāh will be within you. It is then that you will understand what tranquility is and what peace is.

You must establish this state. You have been doing this *dhikr* incorrectly for five years now. You have not been doing it the right way. We have been wrong and you have been wrong. We did not demonstrate it to you correctly and you did not do it correctly. Therefore, from now on you must do this every day. I have to leave in nineteen days, so for those nineteen days, I need to show you how to do this correctly. You must learn it.

Doctor Markar Tambi, must go and sit there and demonstrate this. I might also come at that time. Whether it is the evening or the early morning, or before you go to whatever job you are working at, or when you return from work, or after finishing your duties, you should have this remembrance and do the *dhikr*. In between these times, you should not waste time. Whenever you have time to spare, you should sit down and do the *dhikr*. If you have work to do, you should do that work. The rest of the time you must do the *dhikr.* When the female children have their monthly cycle, for those five or so days they should wash their hands and feet, stay where they are, and recite the *dhikr.* They should do the *dhikr,* but separate from others. The rest of the time, they should join the others and sit downstairs and do it.

Like this, you must do this as your duty. Each of the Fellowships should do this. If you do not do it, then that is useless.

Secondly, when there is a meeting being conducted here, some of you go and sit outside. That is wrong! Even if you have already learned everything, you must still go and sit in the meeting room and do your *dhikr.* You must do your *dhikr* while you are listening to what is being said in the meeting. Your *tiyānam,* meditation, should be ongoing, your *dhikr* should be ongoing. No matter who is speaking, no matter where you go, whether you are working, standing, or sitting, you must do that *tiyānam, dhikr, fikr,* and *vanakkam* to God.

What is the use of your wasting time? There is no use in coming here if you waste every single second you have. There is no point in my coming here and there is no point in your staying here.

Each one of you must do this *dhikr* as your primary duty. Only then can you earn your wages for the kingdom of God. You can receive His grace. You can receive a place in His house. You must give your illnesses to God and receive His bliss. Every day you must ask for this, and give all the responsibility to Him.

As soon as you wake up, you must give the responsibility to God, and then go to work. You must search for His grace. Then you can go to work. In the mornings you must get up, give all the responsibility to Him, and receive from Him all that He has. You must give Him the responsibility for the illnesses that have come to you, receive His qualities from Him, and then go to work. This is how you should do it.

Before you go to work, do this *dhikr.* Every second, every moment, you must give the responsibility to God. Then He will take a share of all the difficulties, illnesses, and accidents you may encounter. He will break apart all of the difficulties that come like a huge mountain to crush you. Without reciting these satan mantras, demon mantras, idol mantras, *sitti* mantras, and toy mantras, you must remember God, speak to God, and receive His help.

You must do this, you must do this every day, in the evening and in the afternoon. Do you understand? Do it this way. For these nineteen days, before I leave, you (Doctor Markar) should teach this.

Type everything I have said now, and give everyone a copy. This will tell them how to set their *niyyah,* their intention, and how to do the *dhikr.*

Everyone has illnesses, everyone has demons, and everyone wastes time. Throw off all of these, give the responsibility to God every day, and then go to work. Before you go to sleep, you must wash your hands and feet, give all responsibility to God, and recite this *dhikr.* Before you lay your head down, give all responsibility to God. When you return from work, after you eat and wash, you must give the responsibility to Him, and then do your other work. You must do it like this in the morning and at all other times. It must always be within your hearts.

You must do this. There is no point in just sitting here and sitting there, sitting here and sitting there! Eating, sleeping, sitting somewhere, and going rounding is *no good.* Do you understand? Does everybody understand this? Do it this way.

Shari, all right, the children who are going to work, go to work. The children who are going to eat, go to eat. *Shari.*

QUESTION

What was the line you say before you start the *dhikr?*

DOCTOR MARKAR

A ʿūdhu billāhi minash-shaitānir-rajīm.

BAWA MUHAIYADDEEN

A ʿūdhu billāhi minash-shaitānir-rajīm. A ʿūdhu billāhi minash-shaitānir-rajīm.

A ʿūdhu billāhi. Yā Allāh, please protect us from satan who was cast out from Your heavenly kingdom, that satan who is an enemy to man, an enemy to Adam ⊙. *A ʿūdhu billāhi.* Protect us from satan who has been an enemy to man from the time Adam ☺ was created. Protect us from satan who was cast out of heaven, who was thrown out of heaven.

A 'ūdhu billāhi minash-shaitānir-rajīm. Minash-shaitān. May You protect me from that satan. Please protect me. *Minash-shaitānir-rajīm.* Like *minnal,* like lightning, may You burn satan away from me with Your grace. With Your Light, may You cast him away. Like lightning, may You cut away his connection to me.

Bismillāhir-Rahmānir-Rahīm. God is the One who is the Creator, the Sustainer, and the Protector. O God, please protect me. *Āmīn.*

Shari, do this. Only if you can do this can He give you His *rahmah.* But if you sleep in corners, this *tambi* in one corner, you in another corner, that child in another corner, and the next in another corner, who will accept you? You must get up early in the morning, do *tasbīh* to Allāh, and give all responsibility to Him. If you do not do that, who will accept you? You must give the things you cannot bear into His hands. You must take from Him what He has and give to Him what you cannot bear. That should be your intention.

You are just wasting your time. Get up my child, and do it like this. Tell everyone to listen to this. You must pray.

A'ūdhu billāhi minash-shaitānir-rajīm.
I seek refuge in God from the accursed satan.

Bismillāhir-Rahmānir-Rahīm.
In the name of God, the Most Compassionate,
the Most Merciful.

DHIKR DISCOURSE—
AUGUST 11, 1976

August 11, 1976, Wednesday, 5:00 a.m.

My loving children, jewels of my eye, when we commence to pray we should say: *A'ūdhu billāhi minash-shaitānir-rajīm.* Everyone must say this.

Precious jeweled lights of my eye, who are children within my heart, in our lives we must go on the path of our Father, on the path of the resonance of Allāhu. In this state, as we go along, we must search for His earnings.

Here, there are two ways of searching. One is the search for Allāh's *rahmah.* which is the heavenly kingdom called *swarnapati.* The other is the search for the accursed hell, *lahannam.* Some people search for hell which is the *dunyā,* the world. They prefer *lahannam.* Others prefer Allāh's *rahmah.* So, there are these two. Some people search for the *dunyā,* while others search for the *ākhirah.* Both are His kingdoms.

The wages of the *ākhirah* are not found on the outside. It is the wages of the *dunyā,* the wages of hell, that are found on the outside. All of the things that we search for outside are the hellboards of *lahannam.* Therefore children, jeweled lights of my eye, we must perform *tasbīh,* glorification to Allāh, within our *qalbs,* and try to attain Allāh's wealth. As *qalb* within *qalb,* as *īmān* within *īmān,* as wisdom within wisdom, as *dīn* within *dīn,* as Light within Light, as Nūr within Nūr, as *insān* within *insān,* and as Allāh within Allāh...

45

Allāh is the One who is plenitude within plenitude. We must focus our intention from the inside, from within the *qalb,* the innermost heart. We must search for this wealth. This is the treasure, the *rahmah* that we must seek. One is the earnings that we search for within, while the other is the earnings we search for outside, in the world. These are the two kinds of wages. We must understand this.

Precious children, there are two kinds of wages that exist in this world. We must differentiate on the outside and the inside, between the wages of the *ākhirah* and the wages of the *dunyā.* What we do for the sake of respect, for the sake of religions, and for the sake of scriptures, the many things like this that we display on the outside without having inner clarity, are done for outer wages. But when the inside is clear, then that is God's wage, our earnings.

Therefore children, jeweled lights of my eye, you must first focus your intention. You must turn your *qalbs* directly towards Him. Of the two kinds of wages, the perfect wage is Allāh's wage. That is the place of prayer. You must establish that place of prayer within your *qalbs.* First, you must seek Allāh within your *qalbs.* You must establish that search through remembrance. That remembrance should become your *niyyah,* your intention. That *niyyah* should flow into your *unarvu* and *unarchi,* your feeling and awareness. Feeling must change to awareness. Then, when feeling has changed to awareness, you must understand that *dhikr,* that *vanakkam.*

That awareness should flow through you in the same way that blood flows through your body. As it flows, the *dhikr* should also flow. Inside that flowing that is like the flowing of blood, the sharp point of *putti,* intellect, must work. Within that sharp point of intellect, *īmān,* faith, must work. Within the resplendence of *īmān* is *madi,* judgment. *Toluhai,* the five-times prayer, must flow within the resplendence of *īmān,* as *'ibādah.*

The city inside the body will be the three realms of *al-awwal, ad-dunyā,* and *al-ākhirah.* The *'ālam, 'ālamul-arwāh,* and all of everything exist within *insān.* The *dhikr* must flow through your nerves, skin, bones, and marrow, and through your yearning, focus, and *niyyah.* That *dhikr* must flow through your veins, nerves, and blood;

that *vanakkam* must flow. When that flowing takes place, then that is *toluhai,* that is *'ibādah.* You must establish that remembrance.

In the same way that the pulse of the blood works within you, the *dhikr* should work. *Dhikr* is like that pulse: *lā ilāha,* breathing out, and *illAllāhu,* breathing in. It is like playing a mandolin. That intention, *illAllāhu,* must resonate. Your wisdom must strum the strings of the *rūh,* the soul. That is the resonance of Allāh. Like that, your life-pulse must flow in that state. You must make your intention *this* intention. You must make this intention before you pray. This is how you must do the *dhikr.*

Having made the *dhikr* flow, you must stand with only one focus, looking directly at Allāh. Your *qalb* must be as Ahamad ☉, and your eyes, your gaze, and your face must be as Muhammad ☉. Look only at Allāh. These two (Ahamad ☉ and Muhammad ☉) must be there, in front of you. With these two in front of you, you must do *tasbīh* to God, you must do *'ibādah* to Him. Remaining in that state, you must give all responsibility to Him.

"*Yā* Allāh, may You take away our illnesses..."

Please recite this after me.

"*Yā* Allāh, may You take away our illnesses. May You grace us with Your life that has no illness. *Yā* Allāh, may You change our qualities and accept them. May You give us Your qualities and grace us. *Yā* Allāh, may You take away our stomach ailments, and grant us Your "illness" of having no hunger. *Yā* Allāh, may You take away the illnesses of our nerves, and give us the happiness of a life of health, without the illnesses of the nerves. *Yā* Allāh, may You take away the illnesses of the bones from this body, and give us instead the health of Your body of purity.

"*Yā* Allāh, may You take away the illnesses that are travelling along our nerves, and give us a life without any illness. *Yā* Allāh, may You take away the illnesses that arise from the tissues of the body, and give us the peace where we have no illnesses of the tissues. *Yā* Allāh, may You take away from us the diseases of the blood, the diseases of the eyes, the diseases of the ears, the diseases of the nose, the diseases of the mouth, and the diseases of the teeth, and give us

Your beautiful eyes, Your beautiful ears, Your beautiful nose, Your beautiful tongue, and Your beautiful speech.

"*Yā* Allāh, may You take away our *qalbs,* and give us Your *qalb. Yā* Allāh, may You remove the illnesses of our anus, the illnesses of our kidneys, our rheumatic illnesses, the illnesses of our nerves, the illnesses of the fluids of our bodies, the ninety-six bilious diseases, and the gaseous diseases. May You remove all of these, and grant us the plenitude of the Light of Your Nūr. May You grant us Your beauty, a long life without illness, a complete life, and the complete prayer, the perfected prayer and worship of You.

"*Yā* Allāh, may You cure and take away, with Your grace, all of the diseases that are within us, such as tuberculosis, vomiting, coughing, asthma, and cancer. May You remove all of our karmic diseases. May You give Your Light to our bodies, in completeness. *Yā* Allāh, may You grant us Your qualities, Your actions, Your behavior, Your good conduct, Your compassion, Your selfless life, Your duties, Your patience, Your mercy, and Your three thousand gracious qualities.

"May You take away all of our qualities. *Yā* Allāh, please dispel our jealousy, vengeance, differences, separations, evil qualities, lust, anger, miserliness, fanaticism, religion, race, sects, and divisions, arrogance, karma, maya, and all the other evil and satanic qualities like these. May You give us Your beautiful treasures of *sabūr,* patience, *shukūr,* contentment, and *tawakkul,* trust in God. *Yā* Allāh, may You give us a long life, undiminishing love, perfected worship, and a life of plenitude.

"*Yā* Allāh, during our sleep and in our happiness and sorrow, may You grant us Your watchfulness. In our lifetime, while we are walking or sitting, happy or sad, may You take away all of the illnesses, diseases, and accidents that come to us. At all times, may we have Your *tānam, nidānam, avadānam,* and *gnānam:* surrender, perfect balance, absolute focus, and divine wisdom. May You give us these four explanations.

"*Yā* Allāh, may You accept our *qalbs,* may You accept our lives. May You accept our prayers, may You accept our sight, may You accept the sounds of our ears, and may You accept our noses. May You accept our speech; may You stand in front of us and behind us as our speech, and speak for us.

"*Yā* Allāh, may You forgive us. Every day, at every *waqt*, may You turn us to the straight path. At every *waqt*, in every word, may You be with us, face to face, and guide us. *Yā* Allāh, may You grant us Your grace so that we never worship any god other than You. May You protect us from the evils and the evil magics of satan.

"*Yā* Allāh, please protect us and prevent us from being led astray by the miracles of satan. *Yā* Allāh, please give us Your grace so that satan does not deceive us through magic, miracles, *sittis,* and his many evil qualities. Please guide us along the straight path. May You grant us the grace of Your straight path. May You give us Your beautiful qualities and Your beautiful perfection. May You give us a life without illness, and grant us Your undiminishing wealth and Your *rahmah*. May You make our *qalbs* pure. *Āmīn*.

"*Yā* Allāh, may You accept our responsibilities, and give us Your wealth. May You completely cut off all of the envy and jealousy in our *qalbs*. May You accept our lives as Your life. From today on, please accept us as Your babies, Your children. May we live as faultless children at every *waqt*. May You give us Your qualities. At every moment, may You give us Your grace so that we may be Your children with Your Light. May You cut away by the roots all of the evils that are within us. May You remove them. *Āmīn*. *Āmīn*."

First you must recite the *Sūratul-Hamd*. Then recite the *Subhāna Kalimah,* the Third *Kalimah,* three times, and blow it into your *qalbs*. Establish your *niyyah,* and then, focusing on Allāh, do the *dhikr*.

(Bawa Muhaiyaddeen ☺ demonstrates.)

Lā ilāha…lā ilāha…lā ilāha…lā ilāha…illAllāh. Lā ilāha, lā ilāha, lā ilāha, lā ilāha, lā, lā ilāha, lā, lā ilāha, lā, lā ilāha, lā, lā ilāha, lā, lā ilāha.
Breathe.

(The *dhikr* continues in silence. Then Bawa Muhaiyaddeen ⊕ recites the Third *Kalimah* three times, and blows it into his chest. Everyone then repeats what he says.)

> *"SubhānAllāhi wal-hamdu lillāhi wa lā ilāha illAllāhu wallāhu akbar wa lā haula wa lā quwwata illā billāhi wa huwal-'alīyul-'azīm.*
>
> *"SubhānAllāhi wal-hamdu lillāhi wa lā ilāha illAllāhu wallāhu akbar wa lā haula wa lā quwwata illā billāhi wa huwal-'alīyul-'azīm.*
>
> *"SubhānAllāhi wal-hamdu lillāhi wa lā ilāha illAllāhu wallāhu akbar wa lā haula wa lā quwwata illā billāhi wa huwal-'alīyul-'azīm.*[1]

"*Bismillāhir-Rahmānir-Rahīm. A'ūdhu billāhi minash-shaitānir-rajīm. Bismillāhir-Rahmānir-Rahīm. Yā* Allāh, You are our Creator, the One who has created everything, the One who provides food, the One who gives the *rizq*, the sustenance, the One who has made clear the Day of Judgment and the Day of *Qiyāmah.* You are the One who has created Judgment Day, the Day of *Qiyāmah*, the *nabīs*, the *olis*, the angels, the earth, and the heavens. You are the One who has made everything rise up, who gives *hayāh*, life, and causes *maut*, death. *Yā* Allāh, may You grant the grace so that everything dwells within Your state of plenitude. *Āmīn.*

"*Yā* Allāh, every day, every moment, may You keep us awake, may You keep us in purity as Your Light, as Your *'abd*, Your slave. *Āmīn.* May You face us directly at every second. May You remove our qualities and grant us Your qualities. *Yā* Allāh, may You end all the poverty that occurs in this world and all the illnesses that affect man. May You remove all of the gales, winds, and rains that are brought by the jinns to the creations. May You protect and sustain us with Your wealth in the *ākhirah* and Your wealth in the *dunyā. Āmīn.*

---

1 Translation of the Third *Kalimah:* All glory is to Allāh and all praise is to Allāh, and none is God except Allāh, and Allāh is greater, and there is no majesty and power except with Allāh, and He is exalted, supreme in glory!

"May You grant goodness to all lives, and grace them. May You give us the qualities and the compassion by which we can live, recognizing other lives as our own life. May You give us good intentions and good qualities towards other lives. *Yā* Allāh, just as You grant us a life without illness, may You grant other lives a life without illness. *Yā* Allāh, may You grant Your good grace to our homes, to the homes to which we go, and to the homes from which we have come.

"*Yā* Allāh, in the countries where we live, may You protect the rulers and those kingdoms from any evil. May You grant Your *rahmah* to all, from the king to the beggar. May You dispel all the distresses that may exist in those countries: the rains, storms, and volcanoes, and may You dispel the difficulties and divisions caused by satan. May You protect and sustain us with Your *rahmatul-ʿālamīn,* Your grace. May You protect the kings, the people, the birds, the reptiles—everything—with the benevolence of the *rahmatul-ʿālamīn.* May You end all of our suffering, guide us on the path of bliss, and grant us Your grace.

"*Yā* Allāh, may You be our Helper in this world and in the next. May You be the Ruler of Grace in our sight, in our thoughts, and in our intentions. May You be the Light in our *nafs,* in our thoughts, and in our wisdom, and guide us on the straight path. *Yā* Allāh, may You make our *īmān* strong, so that it will never waver, and may You grant us certitude so that we may focus on You, and pray to You alone.

"*Yā* Allāh, please protect us so that sadness does not come to us. May You grant us the wealth of the grace of Your straight path, the wealth of wisdom, the wealth of the soul, the wealth of patience, the wealth of *sabūr,* the wealth of peace, the wealth of Your justice, the wealth of *shukūr,* the wealth of *tawakkul,* and the wealth of Your selfless duty. May You give these qualities to all lives. May You give us the perfect certitude and determination on the straight path that no other God exists but You. May You give us the strength of *īmān.*

"*Yā* Allāh, there is no God equal to You, no God other than You. May You establish this certitude in each life, may You establish this certitude in each child. From the king to the beggar, may You establish this certitude in their hearts. May You make all Your creations accept that You are Allāh, the one God. May You open their hearts and make their hearts into *swarnapati,* may You make their hearts into heaven. May You make their hearts the resplendent Light of the Nūr. May You make their *qalbs* into *firdaus,* paradise. May You make their *qalbs* Your throne. May You make their *qalbs* Your home. May You make their *qalbs* Your seat of justice. May You make their *qalbs* into a mosque. May You make their *qalbs* the station of judgment on *Qiyāmah.* May You grant their *qalbs* the plenitude of the Light of the Nūr.

"*Āmīn, yā Rabbal-'ālamīn.* O One of grace, *yā* Allāh, may You protect us with Your *amānah,* Your trust. May You take all of our qualities and grant us all of Your qualities and actions. Every second, may You accept us and carry us as Your babies. Every second, may You remove our sins and embrace us with the completeness of absolute purity. May You forgive all of our faults. *Al-hamdu lillāh.*"

(Bawa Muhaiyaddeen ☺ recites the *Sūratul-Fātihah* and the *Sūratul-Ikhlās.*)

Bismillāhir-Rahmānir-Rahīm.
In the name of Allāh, the Most Compassionate,
the Most Merciful.

Al-hamdu lillāhi Rabbil-'ālamīn;
Praise be to Allāh
The Cherisher and Sustainer of the Worlds;

Ar-Rahmānir-Rahīm;
The Most Compassionate, the Most Merciful;

Māliki yaumid-dīn.
Master of the Day of Judgment.

Iyyāka na'budu wa iyyāka nasta'īn.
Thee alone do we worship,
And only Thine aid do we seek.

Ihdinas-sirātal-mustaqīm,
Show us the Straight Way,

Sirātal-ladhīna an'amta 'alaihim,
Ghairil-maghdūbi 'alaihim wa lad-dāllīn.
The way of those on whom
Thou has bestowed Thy Grace,
Those whose (portion)
Is not wrath,
And who go not astray.
Āmīn. Āmīn.

Bismillāhir-Rahmānir-Rahīm.

Qul: Huwallāhu ahad;
Say: He is Allāh,
The One and Only;

Allāhus-samad;
Allāh, the Eternal, Absolute;

Lam yalid, wa lam yūlad;
He begetteth not,
Nor is He begotten;

Wa lam yakul-lahu kufuwan ahad.
And there is none
Like unto Him.

Āmīn. Āmīn. Yā Rabbal-'ālamīn. Your *amānah,* Your trust...
Āmīn.

Today, we did the *dhikr* for a very short time. You must gradually increase your prayers. You should do this before you go to
work. You must have *himmah,* resolve. You should not do your
dhikr in just a casual way. Your breath must be focused on the
dhikr. With every breath, you must have that focus, that intention,
that subtlety, that search, and that gaze. You must look deeply
and do this with the subtlety that is within subtlety. Do not waste
your time! You must truly change yourself to this path. You must
change, with that *dhikr.* If you have this focus, then there will not
be any other focus.

Children, jeweled lights of my eye, please do it like this. May God guide you and take you on the straight path. *Āmīn, āmīn, āmīn. Shari,* very well, go and do your duties.

As-salāmu 'alaikum. May the peace of God be upon you.

A'ūdhu billāhi minash-shaitānir-rajīm.
I seek refuge in God from the accursed satan.

Bismillāhir-Rahmānir-Rahīm.
In the name of God, the Most Compassionate,
the Most Merciful.

DHIKR DISCOURSE— AUGUST 14, 1976

August 14, 1976, Saturday, 5:30 a.m.

A*'ūdhu billāhi minash-shaitānir-rajīm.* Yā Allāh, please protect us from satan, who became proud when Adam ⊕ was created— that satan who developed the thoughts, the *nafs,* and the desires to cause harm to Adam ⊕.

Adam ⊕ was sent down from the heavenly world to this earth-world, and here satan causes suffering to Adam ⊕ and his children. Satan separates them from Allāh and turns them towards the world of hell. Yā Allāh, may You protect us from that satan, and take us back into You again. Please join us within You.

Yā Allāh, may You protect us so that none of satan's qualities, his wickedness, or his intentions ever touch us again. *A'ūdhu billāhi minash-shaitānir-rajīm.* Like lightning, through Your grace and Your Light, may You cut him away from us so that he will never be able to creep into our hearts. May You remove our evil qualities, our *nafs ammārah,* desires, hunger, lies, backbiting, treachery, scheming, cunning, arrogance, karma, maya, and other qualities such as these. May You remove the darkness of those qualities, and open our hearts of purity. May You join us within Your heavenly kingdom. May You grant us Your grace.

May You make our bodies faultless and blameless. May You make our forms faultless and blameless. May You make our *sūrahs* resplend without blemish or fault. May You make our hearts resplendent.

May You make our beauty into Your perfectly pure beauty. May You make our *qalbs* flower, and may those *qalbs* have only Your fragrance and scent. Please show us the way to fulfill Your commands, and give us Your beauty and excellence.

Āmīn. Yā Rabbal-'ālamīn. May You protect and nourish us. *Āmīn, āmīn. Bismillāhir-Rahmānir-Rahīm. Yā* Allāh.

My children, jeweled lights of my eye, we must establish a *niyyah,* an intention. Before we pray to God, we should establish an intention within us. With determination, we must focus that *niyyah.* It is through this determination that we must pray. This intention must be directed towards God. Our *qalbs* must be focused so that we intend God with every breath. At every moment our intention should be directed towards Him. This is how our *niyyah* should be.

Children, precious jeweled lights of my eye, when you make the intention to do *tasbīh* and pray to Allāh, you must have certitude of *īmān.* With certitude, you must place that *īmān* in your *qalbs* and focus intently on Him. When you do *tasbīh* to Him, that certitude should be focused within your *qalbs.* That intention, that concentration, that *niyyah,* that determination, and that *īmān* must be there at each *waqt* of prayer. This must spread throughout the entire body and *qalb.* This point must be fixed before starting the *dhikr.* The *qalb* should be brought to one point, we must strive to bring it to this one point. Once we have done so, we can begin doing *tasbīh* to God.

In this way, once this has been done, this point must be established in the many *waqts* of prayer. That intention should be established within *unarchi,* feeling. It should be perceived by *unarvu,* awareness. When we do that *dhikr* and when we pray to God, awareness must further be understood by *putti,* intellect. The sharpness of that intellect must carefully understand this in every part of the body. With the sharpness of that intellect we must, with certitude, focus our *īmān* directly on God.

Then, with *īmān,* we must differentiate between the two breaths, sending out the left breath of *lā ilāha,* and drawing in the right breath from Him. We must start the *dhikr* from the left big toe, with the left breath of *lā ilāha.* With faith, certitude, determination, and intellect, the left eyebrow should move slightly towards the left side. Your sight should be directed to the left big toe and the breath should be drawn upward, through feeling and awareness. The breath should rise up. Bring that breath to the *qalb*, and from the *qalb* to the *'arsh*, the throne of God. With *unarvu, unarchi, putti,* and *īmān,* the left breath must make sure that this happens. Say *lā ilāha,* and breathe out from the left side.

This can be said without making a sound with your tongue. The tongue should move in the same way that it moves when playing a flute. In the same way that the strings of a mandolin or a veena vibrate when they are strummed, the tongue should vibrate. The sound of that feeling, the sound of that awareness, the sound of that faith, and the sound of that *īmān* should come like the sound that comes from a flute. That sound should come through the movement of the tip of the tongue. Then the explanation of that sound should come within feeling, awareness, intellect, *īmān,* and determination. The explanation should come within the nerves. Just as you are able to feel an ant crawling on your skin, when you are reciting the *dhikr,* when you have that intention, and when intellect understands this, you will experience that meaning, that *vanakkam,* and that clarity. You must be aware of that *niyyah,* that *īmān,* that focus, and that *vanakkam* as it flows through your body.

On the right side, with *īmān,* with determination, and with that *niyyah,* you must draw in God's Resplendence. God is everywhere within your body, but you have to focus on Him at one point within your *qalb.* With a slight tremor of your right eyebrow and a blinking of the right eyelid, you should draw that Resplendence into your *qalb.* This can be done simultaneously with your breath. With your outgoing breath, the left thumb and left big toe lift slightly. And with the incoming breath the right thumb and right big toe lift slightly, the right eyebrow lifts slightly, and the right eyelid blinks slightly.

There are many ways of doing this, but your intention, focus, and *īmān* must be concentrated on that point. Feeling must be focused there. Awareness must be focused there. Intellect must be focused there. *Imān,* absolute faith, must be focused there. Certitude must be focused there. This is the way you can make all of the *waqts* of prayer into one. You must focus that *dhikr* on the *qalb.* From that *qalb* the *dhikr* must spread through the 4,448 nerves, as if through a wire. It must flow within awareness, and spread within *īmān.*

Once the right side has finished, the left side should start. Then, from the right side, you must once again draw in that *dhikr* of *illAllāhu,* and fall into God.

It is through the *niyyah,* that intention, that this becomes the seven prayers before prayer itself. You must develop that one-point-edness, that *niyyah,* and that concentration within your *qalb,* so that you can perform this prayer correctly. Your focus and your *niyyah* should be in the state where the prayer of *sharī'ah,* these seven times of prayer,[1] can be performed within this *dhikr.* The concentration, focus, and *niyyah* of this *dhikr* should embrace these seven times of prayer. This *niyyah* should be established before you do the seven *waqts* of the *sharī'ah* prayer.

This is the primary intention that we must place within ourselves before we begin our *toluhai* and *'ibādah.* Only after that should we do our prayer. That prayer is the prayer where we surrender to Allāh, it is the prayer of the *'abd,* the slave. To become a slave to God is *dhikr.* That is where we give all responsibility to Him. That *vanakkam* has no *waqt,* no time, while *toluhai,* the five-times prayer, is subject to time. All of our thoughts are subject to time. The sun and the moon have certain times. Just by looking at them, we can tell the time, we can determine the hour of the day.

In the creation of God, the sun and the moon (appear to be) rotating around the world. But, in fact, it is this world that is rotating around the sun. Therefore, as that rotation occurs, the moon and the sun are seen in their place. Similarly, the correct point for prayer is to stay in the place where you are. As the world rotates, it

---

1   seven *waqts* of *sharī'ah* prayer: These may refer to the five obligatory prayers of *subh, zuhr, 'asr, maghrib,* and *'ishā',* and the two additional prayers of *tahajjud* and *witr.* Bawa Muhaiyaddeen ⊕ does not specify what seven prayers he is referring to.

creates time. But *vanakkam* has no time. God, who has no time, is a Resplendence that stays in one place. The world rotates around the sun. Similarly, a point is rotating around God. Creation, time, and what has appeared are rotating around Truth. Everything in the world: creation, beings, time, seasons, the sun, and the moon are rotating around God. They are revolving around Him.

Therefore, everything else — time, *waqts*, seasons — keeps on changing. There is not just one time. Time does not have just one point. There is one time that is calculated for the east, one for the west, one for the south, and another one for the north. In one place it will be nighttime, while in another place it will be daytime.

So, there are these differences in time because of the rotation of the earth. Because of this rotation, there is what is called *sharī'ah*, which is subject to time. Time changes. Time is created because of man's intentions and thoughts. That is *sharī'ah*. Your prayers must be completed at a certain time. This is obligatory, you must focus on God at specific times.

But, if you are truly praying and doing *'ibādah*, you should be rotating around God. All of everything should rotate around God. God is the true point. He is the complete point of Resplendence. In your concentration, focus, *īmān*, *niyyah*, intellect, certitude, and determination, you must be pointed towards that Resplendence. Your state must be that of a slave pointing towards That. That has no *waqt*. This state is called *vanakkam*, *'ibādah*, *dhikr*, and *fikr*. This state transcends *sharī'ah* and becomes *tarīqah*. It transcends *tarīqah* and becomes *haqīqah*. It transcends *haqīqah* and becomes *ma'rifah*. And it transcends *ma'rifah* and becomes *sūfiyyah*. There you become an *'abd*, a slave of God.

This is how our *'ibādah* must be transformed. We must change. Instead of revolving around the world, instead of wisdom revolving around the *dunyā*, we must point that wisdom and *īmān* towards God. That is the state that is called *'ibādah* and *vanakkam*.

Therefore, jeweled lights of my eye, when you wake up, and before you go to pray, you must establish your intention. Before every *waqt* you must establish this focus, this *niyyah*, this one-point-edness. You must do this before you pray, after waking up, when you go to sleep, at every moment, at all times. That should be the point where the world and all of everything is rotating around God. Otherwise, there will be differences of time, differences of qualities, differences of intellect, and differences in the creations. You must think about this. You must point your *dhikr* towards God. You must point it towards the right side. At every *waqt*, at every time, at every moment, while seated or walking, while sleeping or awake, in happiness or in sorrow, you must focus that *niyyah* on this point, and draw everything from Him.

You must try to do all of your *vanakkam*, *'ibādah*, and *dhikr* in this way. That will be the perfect prayer of the one group, where *'ibādah* is truly directed towards God.

Precious children, jeweled lights of my eye, you must firmly establish this *niyyah* daily. The seven *waqts* of prayer should be done with this determination. Make your intention, focus, and thoughts firm, bring that into feeling, join that within awareness, bring that into *īmān*, and bring that into determination. Then focus that *īmān* on Him. Have the certitude that there is nothing other than Him. Then make yourself an *'abd* to God. Your point must be that of becoming a slave to Him.

These are the seven *waqts* of *toluhai*. Beyond these, we will perform *dhikr*, which is the prayer of *firdaus*, paradise. Then, wherever we are, we will be God doing *tasbīh* to God from within God. We will be doing *tasbīh* to God from within the Light of God. That is the eighth sphere. We will be doing *tasbīh* to Him from the heaven called *firdaus*. This *niyyah* must be established as our (primary) intention. Having established it in this way, we must then perform *tasbīh* to Him with our every breath. That is heaven.

In this state we must give all our responsibilities, our sounds, and our speech to God, and take on His qualities and His sound. We must give our body to Him, and pray to Him through His Light. We must give Him our body, our *niyyah*, and all of our responsibilities, and pray to Him through His Light, His resplendence, His qualities, and His sound. That is that *vanakkam*.

Now, jeweled lights of my eye, please recite. Please do *tasbīh* to Allāh.

Lā ilāha...lā ilāha illAllāh, lā ilāha illAllāh...

(Bawa Muhaiyaddeen ☺ demonstrates the silent *dhikr*. Then he recites the *Sūratul-Fātihah* and the *Sūratul-Ikhlās*.)

As-salāmu ʿalaikum.

A ʿūdhu billāhi minash-shaitānir-rajīm.

   Bismillāhir-Rahmānir-Rahīm.

   Al-hamdu lillāhi Rabbil-ʿālamīn;

   Ar-Rahmānir-Rahīm;

   Māliki yaumid-dīn.

   Iyyāka naʿbudu wa iyyāka nastaʿīn.

   Ihdinas-sirātal-mustaqīm,

   Sirātal-ladhīna anʿamta ʿalaihim,
   Ghairil-maghdūbi ʿalaihim wa lad-dāllīn.
   Āmīn.

   Bismillāhir-Rahmānir-Rahīm.

   Qul: Huwallāhu ahad;

   Allāhus-samad;

   Lam yalid, wa lam yūlad;

   Wa lam yakul-lahu kufuwan ahad.
   Āmīn.

Qul: Huwallāhu ahad: For all of everything, He is the *ahad*. He is the secret, He is the mystery. He is the One who is the secret and the mystery. He is the One who is hidden within all creations. He is hidden within all the fruits, He is hidden within all the flowers, He is hidden within all the trees, the shrubs, the flowers, the unripe fruits, and the ripe fruits. His mystery is within all beings. His beauty, form, taste, flavor, sweetness, fragrance, and qualities can be seen within everything. He is within the *ʿālam*, this world, *'ālamul-arwāh,* the world of souls, and all of everything. He exists as the light of the sun, as the glow of the moon, and as the glitter of the stars. Like this, He is within everything. He is within the earth, within the form, within the sky, and within the creations. *Qul: Huwallāhu ahad.* He is the One who is *ahad,* the One who is the mystery. *Qul: Huwallāhu ahad.*

Allāhus-samad: He is the One who exists equally for all lives. He is the *Allāhus-samad* for all lives. For everyone, for those who are good and for those who are evil, He is the One who has equality. He is the One who protects without separation. He is the Almighty One who exists equally for all of His creations: for the creations of the ocean, the creations of the hills, the creations of the earth, the jinn creations, the fairy creations, the creations of darkness, the creations of light, the creations of water, the creations of air, the creations of ether, the creations of fire, the creations of land, and the human creations. He treats all of these creations equally, and provides them with food. He understands the needs of all, and gives whatever they ask for. He is the One who treats everyone equally whether they blame Him, scold Him, deny Him, praise Him, or exalt Him. He exists equally for everyone. *Allāhus-samad.* He is the *samad* for everyone.

He is the One who has transcended all differences of race and religion and gives equally to all. He has transcended colors and hues and gives equally to all. He has transcended hatred, sadness, difficulties, and everything else and gives equally to all. He is the One who is complete, the One who is perfected, the One who has equality. He is *Allāhus-samad.* He is the One who gives equally to everyone. He gives peace to everyone. He is the One who can embrace everyone, and comfort them. *Allāhus-samad.* He is the One who can give solace to every heart, who can give *shānti* to every sadness. He can give peace to every person. He can give peace and tranquility to every state, regardless of the storms that may come. *Allāhus-samad.*

Lam yalid: He is there in every breath, in every being. He is the One who is *lam yalid* on our left side and on our right side. When any creation takes a drink, He is the sustenance on the right side. When you realize the taste, He is the taste on the right side. When you recognize His taste through your wisdom, He is the taste that resides on the right side. He is your nourishment when you eat and when you drink.

Wa lam yūlad: He is there on your right and on your left. When you eat your food, He is there as the food. When you recognize the taste, He is the taste. *Wa lam yūlad.* He is always there within the taste. He is the One who is there at all times, within the taste, on the right. *Wa lam yūlad.* Through that food He makes you grow, and through that taste He makes you realize Him. He is the only One who can do that. *Wa lam yūlad.*

Wa lam yakul-lahu: He is there as the Light of Truth, hidden within all of everything. He is the Truth hidden within your intention, He is the Truth hidden within your focus, He is the Truth hidden within your prayer. *Wa lam yakul-lahu.* He always exists as the Truth within all of everything. He is there as your true intentions, He is there as your true focus, He is there as your true prayer. *Wa lam yakul-lahu.* He is the One who exists within all of everything on the right and on the left. He exists in the world of heaven and He exists in the world of hell. *Wa lam yakul-lahu.* He is within the ant and He is within man. He gives food to the ant and He gives food to man. *Wa lam yakul-lahu.* For all of everything He is the Sustainer. There is a certain kind of food for the earth, the sun, the moon, the stars, and for each thing that He has created. The sun needs food, the moon needs food, the stars need food, each creation needs food. For everything, *wa lam yakul-lahu,* for each of His creations there is an essential food, and that food is known only to Him. *Wa lam yakul-lahu.* He is the taste and He is the food.

When you understand the taste He will be on the right, when you understand the food He will be on the left, and when you eat that food He will make your body grow. *Wa lam yakul-lahu.*

Kufuwan ahad: He is the *ahad* for all of everything. He is the secret within your heart. He is the mystery within your heart. He is the light within your body. *Wa lam yakul-lahu kufuwan ahad. Kufuwan ahad.* He is the *ahad.* He is the mystery, He is the secret, He is grace, He is light, He is the soul, He is resplendence, He is wisdom, He is clarity, He is resonance, He is the explanation, He is the One who knows, He is the One who creates, He is the One who is clear, He is the One who gives food, He is the One who corrects, He is the One who has peace, He is the One who has tranquility, He is the Judge, He is the seat of justice, He is the One who gives the verdict, He is the One who inquires, He is the Eternal, True One, He is the One who is without beginning and end. *Wa lam yakul-lahu kufuwan ahad.* He is the secret for all of everything. He is the mystery.

We must meditate on God, and do *tasbīh* to Him. That is our responsibility.

This is His *Qul: Huwallāhu ahad sūrah.* First there is the *Sūratul-Hamd,* and this is the second *sūrah,* the *Qul: Huwallāhu sūrah.* All of the 6,666 *āyāt,* verses, of the Qur'ān reveal who He is. These are His words. These words reveal His story. These words reveal the story of creation and God's story. Therefore, gems of my eye, we must consider this and reflect deeply on it.

Āmīn, āmīn, yā Rabbal-ʿālamīn.

Yā Allāh, may You protect and nourish us. May You remove all of our illnesses and give us all of Your happiness. *Yā* Allāh, may You cure all the diseases of the nerves, the diseases of the skin, the diseases of the eyes, the diseases of the nose, the diseases of the ears, the diseases of the teeth, the diseases of the tongue, the diseases of the back, the diseases of the taste, the diseases of the neck, the diseases of the membranes, the diseases of the hands, the diseases of the *qalb,* the diseases of the desires, the diseases of the mind, the diseases of the body, of the veins, flesh, muscles, bones, marrow, blood, water, fire, air, and ether, the diseases of the anus, the diseases of the brain, the diseases of the arteries, the diseases of the kidneys, the diseases such as asthma, tuberculosis, and coughing, the diseases of the bile, the diseases of craziness, the diseases of the gases, the diseases of the stomach, the diseases of the intestines, and the diseases of the saliva. *Yā* Allāh, may You give us Your life that has no illness, an undiminishing life of grace, and a long life. *Āmīn.*

Yā Allāh, may You unite us within You. May You give us Your beauty, Your qualities, Your *qalb,* Your nature, Your actions, Your conduct, Your love, Your faith, Your three thousand gracious qualities, Your tolerance, tranquility, justice, honesty, duties, patience, forbearance, *sabūr, shukūr, tawakkul,* and peace. *Yā* Allāh, just as You give all of these qualities to us, may You give them to all of the creations who are with us, in the places where we live in the world and in the countries where we reside.

May You give peace to all creations and to all mankind. May You give peace to every human being, to every heart. May You give a life of peace to all, in the kingdoms where they reside, and may You protect us from gales, storms, volcanoes, and fires. May You protect us in the kingdoms where we live, so that none of these evils and evil diseases affect our kingdom. May You protect and sustain us in the countries where we live, in the cities where we live, in the places where we dwell, in the places we trust, in the places where we worship, and in the places we can see. May You remove our illnesses and protect the kings, those who rule these countries, and all of the people and other creations who live in those countries. May You protect and sustain all of everything, and grant Your grace. *Āmīn, āmīn.*

May you dispel our jealousy and arrogance. May You dispel our evil qualities and evil thoughts, and rule over us. Please give the people unity, exalted qualities, peacefulness, and tranquility. May You give us Your grace. *Āmīn, āmīn, yā Rabbal-ʿālamīn.*

O Gracious One, may You protect us. May You understand the states of our minds and give us peace. May You remove all of our diseases. *Āmīn, āmīn, yā Rabbal-ʿālamīn.*

There is no God other than You. May You give us that *īmān* and certitude. *Āmīn, āmīn. Al-hamdu lillāh. As-salāmu ʿalaikum wa rahmatullāhi wa barakātahu kulluhu.*

Bismillāhir-Rahmānir-Rahīm.

Al-hamdu lillāhi Rabbil-'ālamīn;

Ar-Rahmānir-Rahīm;

Māliki yaumid-dīn.

Iyyāka na'budu wa iyyāka nasta'īn.

Ihdinas-sirātal-mustaqīm,

Sirātal-ladhīna an'amta 'alaihim,

Ghairil-maghdūbi 'alaihim wa lad-dāllīn.

Āmīn.

Bismillāhir-Rahmānir-Rahīm.

Qul: Huwallāhu ahad;

Allāhus-samad;

Lam yalid, wa lam yūlad;

Wa lam yakul-lahu kufuwan ahad.

Āmīn.

Āmīn, āmīn, āmīn, yā Rabbal-'ālamīn.

Children, each of the female children should now make your intention to give *salāms* to one another. When you do this, you should cut away any separations that you have in your minds. You should give your *salāms* with the intention that you and the other person will be united in the next world, just as you are united in this world. Both of you should give these *salāms* in unity, looking at the other person's face. You should give the *salāms* with the intention that all of your faults should be completely removed and that both of you should live in unity, tranquility, and peace in the heavenly world and in this world. Like this, all of the male children should also make this intention and give *salāms* to the male children.

If you do it in this way every day, if you join together as one and make this intention, then your faults will leave you and your unity will grow. All the differences in your minds will be cut away with the giving of these *salāms*. The doubts within your minds will be removed. The wealth of grace and the wealth of beauty will develop in you.

If you do it like this every day, all of your doubts, anger, and sins will leave on their own, and you will feel happy. You will develop love and trust in God. Therefore, when you join in this way it will bring joy, and each person's faith will increase. Your faith and the faith of the other person will increase. It will strengthen your faith when you look at each other. This will be a way for each of you to grow with clarity.

This is the reason we are now giving you these explanations. Earlier, for the past five years, we were teaching you wisdom and the ways of conducting yourself in the world. We were giving you explanations about God and explanations about the world and the four religions. We were teaching you about the four steps, and giving you explanations about the family of man and the qualities of the animals.

Now we are teaching you, for a short time, a beginning lesson on prayer. You must take a firm hold of this. From now on, you must grow by doing this. As you grow, you can ask for whatever you need. One time you may want to see heaven. As you recite the *dhikr* you can ask, "What is heaven like? O God, how can I attain heaven? What is hell like and what is heaven like?" You can ask this in your intention. After that, close your eyes and perform the *dhikr.* When you ask your Shaikh directly in this way, he will show you. You must intend this within wisdom. "O my *Pidā,* O my Father, please come. Please show me whether this is heaven or the stench of hell, whether it is good or evil." You must ask your questions within feeling, awareness, knowledge, and wisdom. Ask, and then that explanation will be given by your Father within your *qalb.*

When you look within your heart with the certitude of *īmān,* you will see the form of your Father, the form of your Guru. That form will be seen in front of you. He will show you each thing. If you ask, "What is heaven?" he will show you, "This is heaven!" At that time you will forget yourself. Only then will that explanation come to you. The explanation will be revealed to you within and without, through the eye in the center of the forehead. You will be able to understand about heaven and hell. You will understand all of the wonders that you see.

If you continue to ask for an explanation about something, he will give a reply. He will give it within your *qalb* and he will also give it on the outside. An explanation will be given for whatever you ask. If you ask, "What is heaven?" he will not only show it to you, but he will also show you what you need from there. He will not only grant you heaven, he will show it to you. He will show you what is in the *'ālam* and *'ālamul-arwāh*. Whatever you want to see, you will be able to see. If you want to see your birth, you will be able to see that birth.

So, without wasting your time, if you can have the intention to realize the grace and explanation of the connection between yourself and God, then that would be good. If you can place that Perfect Guru within your *qalb,* then to whatever questions you ask through *īmān,* you will be given a reply. Within a second you will be able to see all of everything in this world and the world of the souls. It will be just an atom, a tiny particle. Therefore, your vision must be sharply focused. That is a very tiny, subtle, and sharp point. That is that camera, that is that television. You must develop that subtle wisdom and subtle vision. That subtle faith, that subtle eye, that subtle wisdom, and that subtle *īmān* must be focused, and when you question through these, you will get the reply.

You will be able to see so many gems and so many colors in the world and the world of the souls, in the earth and in the sky. You will be able to open out and see what is in the sun, what is in the sky, what is in the earth, what is in the body, and what is in the nerves. You can open out and see your diseases. You can open out and see what is within your *qalb*. You can open out and see your blood. You can penetrate into and see everything within your body. You will be able to delve into and see each section. You can see it directly. This will be the clarity of your prayer, and through it you will understand the connection between yourself and God.

This is the state you must have in order to worship and do *'ibādah*, service to God. It is then that you will be able to ask these questions. You have to be in this state when you ask. Otherwise, you will not understand.

You must keep your Shaikh within you, and ask through him. For that, you need subtle wisdom. You need subtle *īmān*, certitude, and determination. When you close your eyes and then ask your questions from your heart, when you ask through wisdom, you will see him in your heart. When you see him like that, you can ask your questions. Then you will understand everything, you will see everything, you will see everything that is going to happen. You will see the destruction of the world and the ruling of the world. So, you will see everything. You can ask everything in this prayer.

Therefore, try to firmly establish your *vanakkam*, certitude, determination, and *'ibādah*, and reach the state of peace. This is the state where you transcend the four religions, and then do *'ibādah*. This is *'ibādah* within *'ibādah*, *vanakkam* within *vanakkam*, *toluhai* within *toluhai*, focus within focus, *niyyah* within *niyyah*, wisdom within wisdom, Light within Light, Nūr within Nūr, and Allāh within Allāh.

There is so much more to learn; this is just the beginning. There are more and more and more and more explanations.

Therefore, the four *vēdas*, scriptures, and the four steps are within us: *sarihay, kiriyay, yōgam,* and *gnānam; sharī'ah, tarīqah, haqīqah,* and *ma'rifah.* When we transcend these four steps that are within us and then transcend the fifth step, we will come to the sixth step where we join with God. *Az-zabūr, al-jabbūrat, al-injīl,* and *al-furqān* are the four steps, the four scriptures. We must go beyond these.

It is not good if you are harboring doubts about the words of your Father. If you fail to follow him, if you take a cross path, then that will not be good for you. You will arrive at the place where satan is. Therefore, you must accept whatever your Father says, and surrender to that. If you fail on even one point, if you have even one doubt within you, then *wa lam yūlad,* your Father will let go of you. In the same way that the mother hen separates herself from her chicks, the Father will separate himself from you. That is the point.

Like this, if you do not accept what the Father says with absolute certitude, then that is what will happen. He does not profit from that. He does not benefit from it. He will just say, "*Shari,* all right, go!" He will not hurt you, he will just say, "No. Go! You are not searching for it, so go!" It is nothing to him.

Therefore, you need to have certitude and determination. Then you can progress on this path. *Āmīn.*

You must understand this. *Āmīn, āmīn.* Please give your *salāms.* May God help you.

A'ūdhu billāhi minash-shaitānir-rajīm.
I seek refuge in God from the accursed satan.

Bismillāhir-Rahmānir-Rahīm.
In the name of God, the Most Compassionate,
the Most Merciful.

SAY *LĀ ILĀHA ILLALLĀH*— DO NOT WASTE YOUR BREATH

June 18, 1975, Wednesday, 7:00 a.m.

Say, *"Lā ilāha illAllāhu."* Do not waste your breath. In every breath, say, *"Lā ilāha illAllāhu."*

Say this always. Do not ever be idle. You need to continue to say these words whether you live here or anywhere else. You need to say these words with your breath. Although you are not saying them out loud, say them with the tongue inside your mouth, *"Lā ilāha:* There is nothing other than You. *IllAllāhu:* You are Allāh."

You need to take "There is nothing other than You" into your awareness, and say it. That movement needs to be there. *"IllAllāhu:* You are Allāh." With awareness that sound has to enter through wisdom, and be seated in the *qalb,* the innermost heart. You need to say this at all times, no matter where you are.

That remembrance, these words need to continue to move with your breath while you are walking, while you are sitting, while you are awake, when you first arise, while you are working, and while you are sleeping. This needs to be understood with *unarvu, unarchi, putti, madi, arivu,* and *pahut arivu:* perception, awareness, intellect, judgment, wisdom, and divine analytic wisdom. After understanding it through divine analytic wisdom, you need to know exactly where it is moving. Awareness must know where it is going and where it is coming from. Its sounds, its explanations, the light, all of it, must be monitored and understood by *pērarivu,* divine luminous wisdom.

Say it like this. Do not waste even one second! The *dhikr* must be seen and understood by your thoughts, perception, awareness, intellect, judgment, wisdom, divine analytic wisdom, and divine luminous wisdom. These need to be joined together as you say it.

Whether you are seated here or somewhere else, you need to say this. It is good to say it no matter what work you are doing. You should not just spend your time laughing with each other. This needs to be ongoing in your memory no matter what work you are doing. It needs to go on continuously. As it goes on, you need to extract the appropriate wisdom and actions from it, take on the qualities of God, bring them into action, and do God's duties. Please do this.

Do not waste your time. Now you go over there, somewhere, and laugh together. Or you go to the park and laugh together. Or you just talk to each other in an idle manner. You should not be like that! You need to do this work no matter where you are. These words must continuously move in your hearts in this way, with wisdom and awareness. Whether you are in the park, the back yard, the front yard, the left side of the house, or the right side of the house, these words need to keep going. This prayer, this unity-work to merge with God, needs to go on continuously.

You *must* do this. All of you, each one of you, must do this. You should not spend your time uselessly. You should continue to recite this even when you come here to listen to wisdom. You should come here at the correct time and listen to the discourse, listen to wisdom. At other times, whether you are here or anywhere else, you need to continue to hear those words. You need to continue to act in this manner.

This is the most important thing you need to do. There is no benefit in being idle. This work must go on at all times. You must do this when you come here to listen at the appropriate time, and the rest of the time you must also do this work. It is only then that the crop will grow, it is only then that the light will resplend, it is only then that the unity will become oneness, and it is only then that we can do our duties merged in unity with God. This will be the indication that you are working in unity with God.

You cannot do this by being idle. Do not waste your time! Children, please do this. Tell this to every child and do it yourselves. Each child must encourage the other children to do this, and must do this himself. Get two or three people together and say this. Invite the people who are wasting their time to join you. Tell them about this, and do it.

Each of you, all of you, please do this exactly as you would give milk and nourishment to an infant. Children who know this need to feed the other children. Children who know this need to feed God's milk to the other children. Give it to them to drink. You need to do this. Do not think that you already know it (and thus do not have to do it). You need to do this and you also need to encourage others to do it. Do it like that.

Do not waste your time! There is very little time left. In that time we need to do this duty and this work. My sons and my daughters, please pay careful attention to this. Many of you listen only when I am speaking, but you waste the rest of your time. That is not correct, that is not the way.

Do not think that you need to be in this room to do this; you can be in another room or in another place. But you need to establish this *dhikr* and do your work. You can come here when it is time to listen to wisdom, at the time wisdom is being taught, when it is time to make the truth understood. However, you must do your work no matter where you are. You need to help the other children grow and you yourself must grow.

This is one statement—one part on the left, one part on the right. Say these words. This is a statement of absolute purity. It is a statement that contains nothing other than God. God Himself is seated within it. If you keep saying it, you will be in unity with the Ever-Existing One; you will become one with Him.

Please do this. It is only if you do this that it will be a *good morning*. Otherwise, it will be merely a morning. Ah? Please say this with certitude. Then it will be a good morning for us. All right. Go and have your breakfast. I am going to do a little rounding.

(When you repeat this *kalimah* silently, when you say,) *"Lā ilāha,"* there will be a *tick* sound. (And when you say,) *"illAllāhu,"* there will be a *tick.* You will feel it as a pulse when your heart beats, *tick, tick, tick, tick, tick.* You need to realize in your awareness how it beats, just as you feel it in your blood vessels. That is how you must discover it. It is like finding the pulse in someone and counting how many times it beats per (minute). When you raise up that *dhikr,* you need to find the section that operates there in that same way — with awareness.

You will know when wisdom and awareness go there. As *lā ilāha* is breathed out through the left, and *illAllāhu* is raised up through the right, and when your awareness understands, you will know it and feel it.

A'ūdhu billāhi minash-shaitānir-rajīm.
I seek refuge in God from the accursed satan.

Bismillāhir-Rahmānir-Rahīm.
In the name of God, the Most Compassionate,
the Most Merciful.

THE WAKE-UP SONG: COME TO PRAYER[1]

August 18, 1976, Wednesday

The sound is resonating, look.
God's sound is resonating, look.
The sound is resonating, look.
God's sound is resonating, look.

The sun is shining, look.
The sun is resonating, look.
The sound is resonating, look.
The sound is shining in the world, look.

Heaven is resonating, look.
Everyone, heaven is resonating, look.
The angels and the heavenly beings are resonating,
listen to the sound.
The angels and the heavenly beings are resonating,
listen to the sound.
O creations born with me, look at this.
Focus your intention
on the Great One who belongs to us.

---

1 Bawa Muhaiyaddeen ☺ asked that the recording of this song be played each morning at four a.m. to wake everyone up for the early morning prayers.

Focus your intention
on the Great One who belongs to us.
It is three o'clock, look.
Everyone, wake up, get up and come here.
Everyone, wake up, get up and come here.

Listen to the prayers of the heavenly beings.
Listen to the prayers of the heavenly beings.
All of the birds and winged creatures
that have been formed there with such beauty
are resonating, look.
The cocks and the cranes are sounding the call.
The cocks and the cranes are sounding the call.
They are calling, awakening there
and coming together, look.
They are calling, awakening there
and coming together, look.

Listen to all the sounds.
Look at the resonant sound of God.
All the lives are gathering together
and worshipping the One, look.
The sun has risen, listen.
Wake up and come together by four o'clock.
The sun has risen, listen.
Wake up and come together by four o'clock.

Cleanse your body, your hands, and your feet.
Make the face of that body beautiful.
Perform the ablution of the hands and feet
and then come here to worship your Creator,
and then come here to worship your Creator.

Everyone, gather together as one.
Come here to worship God.

Come, come, please come.
Everyone gather together as one and come here.
Gather together one by one.
Search for the grace to pray to the One.
Search for the grace to pray to the One.
Look for that grace within the resonance
of the *salawāt,* the blessings of God.
Everyone is worshipping the One who is alone, listen.
The prayer begins at four-thirty.
Cut away all of the "I" and the "you" and pray.
Look there without religion or race.
Everyone, worship the Almighty King.

All who dwell
in the *'arsh,* the *kursī,* and the *qalam,*
the throne of God, the eye of wisdom, and the pen,
have gathered—
all the angels, the archangels,
the lights, the *qutbs,* the prophets,
the sun, the moon, the stars, and the atoms.

The birds, the winged creatures, the reptiles,
the snakes and the scorpions are praying, look.
The frogs and the fish all are awake, awake;
they are leaping and calling there.
They are swimming, swimming,
rising to the surface, look,
searching there for a peaceful life, look.
They are searching for food from God.
They are singing His names of grace.
See how beautifully they do that
on time, at that *waqt.*
See how beautifully they do that.

Oy, children, gather together as one!
Come here and gather together as one.
Pray as love within love.
All of you who are the children of Adam ☺,
gather together as one.
Search for our Father.

Say *"illAllāhu"* there.
Say it without saying it, with just your tongue.
Merge with the Treasure of liberation.
Recite this day and night,
until the sound *"Allāhu"* is resonant.

Then all the universes in the *qalb*, the inner heart,
will be illumined.
Join together in
the *'arsh*, the *kursī*, and the *qalam*
in *'ālamul-arwāh*, the world of souls.

Make the *"illAllāhu"* resonant.
Search for His grace in the heart of your *qalb*.
The Light is an omnipresent resplendence.
The Light shines within the *qalb*, look.
When the face and the heart become one,
the heart, the *aham*, is Ahamad ☺;
the face, the *muham*, is Muhammad ☺; and
the Light is Nūr-Muhammad ☺.
These three exist within you as the Triple Flame.

Place your heart into God.
Turn your face towards God.
Let the Light speak to Him.
Look at Him with that face of Light.

Place all of this into the meaning.
Believe in the Divine Grace of your Creator.
Stand and pray with good conduct.

All who have been born with me, please come.
All of you, please come here.
Search for peace in this life.

This is the goodness that will complete your lives.
Our lives must be good.
All of you, gather together as one.
Wake up and come here.
Search for grace from God.
Gather together with faith in Him.
Come with certitude.
Merge with God of that divine realm,
with God of that divine realm,
in the Triple Flame.
The *'arsh,* the *kursī,* and the *qalam*
are appearing in *al-awwal,* the time of creation, look.
Look deep inside.

Everyone, gather together as one and come here.
Please come to recite here.
Search for the One who is the Almighty One.
Clear your hearts.
Increase the light in your faces.
If you follow the wisdom and look,
Ahamad ☺, Muhammad ☺, and Nūr-Muhammad ☺
will be there in the Triple Flame.
They will resonate inside the beauty of your form.
The subtle meanings will be understood.
The *'arsh* of the universes will shine.
The *rūh,* the souls, that shine in *al-awwal* will be seen.

Salawāt after *salawāt,*
the blessings of the One alone will resonate.
The heaven known as *firdaus*
will become yours with certainty, look.

While you are in the *'arsh,* the throne of God,
open your heart and look inside.
Dispel the darkness there.
Endeavor to make the *"illAllāhu"* resonate
in your heart.

Come, come, everyone.
Come, everyone.
Gather together here,
come, wake up to your birthright.

Everyone gather around the God who is Love.
All the creations are awake.
They have come into the presence of God.
They have the intention to pray to Him.
All the lives are awake.
Come at this time.
Our hearts must be made resonant.

Look at the birds and the winged creatures.
Come here, do not lie in your beds!
There is work that needs to be done at four o'clock.
We must worship our Beloved.
We must know our Father.
We must know our Original Father, our Ādi Pidā.

We must reach the Light.
We must attain a life of liberation.
We must attain a life without illness.

We must live without troubles.
We must regard other lives as our own.
All the lives must pray to God.

Oy! The torpor must be dispelled.
Children, get up and come here.
It is speaking without speaking at this time.
See how it is shining without shining.
The meaning is understood without understanding,
sparkling, sparkling, gathering together and
becoming light.
Going deeper into yourself,
reciting the appropriate *dhikr*,
the remembrance of God,
you must endeavor to become resonant
with the explanation.
Merge with the divine presence of your Creator.

Merge with the divine presence of your Creator.
Oy, come, come, everyone.
Come here and please look,
please look at the world,
at the birds, the tigers, and the bears.
Look at the animals,
the fish and the frogs.
The open blossoms of the lotus flowers,
the wonder of the flowers,
how they open and bow down.

The sun is rising, look.
The sun is rising, look there.
Wake up with wisdom and come here.
Children, all of you, please come.
Endeavor to dispel that wordless darkness.

Come, come, children.
Come to look at God, children.
All lives dwell there,
worshipping the Light of God.
If you look at this state,
increase your worship,
and come to penetrate the torpor,
then all of us on earth can join together as one.

Come, come, everyone.
Come here and gather together, everyone.
Make the intention to pray to the Almighty One.
This will be prayer, look at it.
Do this in the way it has been ordained.

Come, come, children.
Come here and join together as one.
Sing, sing of His grace.
Search, search for His qualities.
Sing, sing His name.
Learn His secrets in both worlds.
Please come at this good time.

Look at everything in the light of the dawn.
Put an end to the torpor and darkness.
Dispel the darkness that is crushing you.
Endeavor to drive away satan.
Reach God, the All-Powerful One.
Dispel all your sins.
Live a life entirely without sin.
Live with freedom upon freedom.
Live forever as the free ones.
Ask God for lives without illness.
Live without any troubles.

You can obtain the boon of eternal life.
You can reach peace and absolute truth.
You can live lives that do not end.
We can see the God who is our birthright.
We can join together as grace with grace.
We can merge with Him as love with love.
We can understand the *awwal,* the *dunyā,* and the *ākhirah,*
the beginning, this world, and God's kingdom.
We can join with our Father.

We can all gather together as one.
Our hearts can resonate together,
and we can live together in equality.
O my precious children,
do not give up the birthright
God has bestowed upon you.
Come to pray!
Do not give up the birthright
God has given you.
Come to pray!

O humankind,
you are creations of God.
Look with wisdom.
Search for the Treasure that is your birthright.
Place your intention on the One
who belongs to you.
Pray, look deep within your *qalb*
and see what is there.

Jeweled lights of my eye,
jeweled lights of my eye,
who are my birthright.
Pray to God every day,

Search for Him and realize Him
with wisdom and with love.

Make your hearts resplendent.
Dispel the darkness.
Drive out the torpor and the maya.
Reach salvation in this birth itself.
Place your intention on the grace of God.

Please come.
Please come and look at what is here.
Gather together as one.
Join together as one.
Say that One Word.
Endeavor to worship Him,
He who is One.
Everyone, gather together here as one.
Everyone, open your mouth and sing.
Sing only that One Word.
Listen to how it resonates with that One.

Come, come here, everyone.
Come to see, to see this Treasure —
It is our Master, alone with Himself.
It is the Silence that is intermingled with the earth.
It is the Creator who dwells in the *qalb*.
It is the Creator.
It is the One who is the Omnipresence
in the fetus and in the form.

Attain the Light that is your birthright.
Believers, come, everyone.
Please come, look at what is here.
Pray to the Great Treasure.

Ask of the Able One.
Establish the *"illAllāhu,"*
establish the *"illAllāhu,"* in your *qalbs*.
Pray until your hearts become resonant.
Please come, everyone.
Gather together here.
Join together as one.
Place your intention at the feet of God.
Search for His grace.
Endeavor to pray with love.

Āmīn. Āmīn.
This song can be played at four a.m. to wake everyone up.

A'ūdhu billāhi minash-shaitānir-rajīm.
I seek refuge in God from the accursed satan.

Bismillāhir-Rahmānir-Rahīm.
In the name of God, the Most Compassionate,
the Most Merciful.

ON *DHIKR*

Talk to Mr. Johannes Witteveen
Managing Director of the International Monetary Fund

February 1, 1978, Wednesday, 4:30 a.m.

Bismillāhir-Rahmānir-Rahīm. Tambi, my brother, there is a point I would like to speak about. We have now gathered together for the early morning prayer. All religions have prayers of this nature. Islām has five times of prayer a day, some religions pray three times, some two times, and others one time. Yet, no one has seen God, no one has seen God with his eyes.

Man, however, has an awareness within him; he has an inner mystery. That mystery is proof that there is a Treasure within. It is shown in that awareness and in his faith. This awareness and yearning that are within man enable him to act in situations that are beyond his capability. It takes him to places that are beyond his reach. Man can do many things, but there are certain things that he cannot do. It is in these situations that something else does it for him. It does it for him. It demonstrates that something else exists. So, man's wisdom and awareness realize that there is something beyond us. That is called "God." Man becomes aware of this.

God is not a form. God is not like the sun, the moon, or the stars. That cannot be discovered by comparing It with anything that can be seen. Yet, man's faith leads him to say, "God is like this." "He is like that." "He is like that."

Man creates many forms and statues. He makes forms such as animals, *hayawāns,* four-legged animals: dogs, cats, elephants, peacocks, vultures, eagles, foxes, and rats. He asks, "Is God like this?" or "Is He like this?" or "Is He like that?" He makes them into deities, he believes in them, and he begins to worship them.

Each section, regardless of what it accepts, regardless of its wisdom and what it creates, has a belief, a mystery, a secret that understands that there is something beyond man. This is a faith. This faith exists in man, it exists in everyone. It is a mystery that exists within man, it is a mystery that cannot be understood. A secret can be understood, but a mystery cannot be understood. It is something that one knows, yet does not know. Such a Power is called God. The faith in the existence of God develops within man as he realizes that there is something that explains and enables him to do what is beyond his capability.

Human beings worship God in many different ways. They call it prayer. Some deny that God exists, while some say, "There is a power that exists. It has no form, it is a power, a light," and they worship that. Some make idols and worship them. Others make forms of animals and worship them. This is how it is. Man has all these various ways of worship. There are so many different sections.

Truth, however, is a different section. Prayer and truth are an entirely different section. Those who perform this prayer in the world are very rare; to do this is very rare. It is rare in the world to learn to do this prayer. This prayer is different. To do this prayer, the one who is praying and the One who is being prayed to must be one. They must be one. That is *vanakkam*.

So, the many religions, many scriptures, and many people pray in many different ways. In Islām there are five *waqts* of prayer; it is called the five-times prayer. Let us now speak a little about these prayers. In Islām, they pray facing the west, towards the *qiblah,* they turn from the east to the west.[1] This is how they pray. This is their prayer. They say that when they pray in this way they are worshipping Allāh. They say that you must keep Allāh in front of you when you pray.

---

1   This discourse was given in Sri Lanka. The direction of prayer there is towards the west.

However, according to the meaning of the Sufis, God exists in all directions, He exists in all sections. There is no place where He is not, there is no place where He cannot be seen. He dwells in everything. He is a Power. Just as there is water within the earth, just as there is fragrance within a flower, just as there is fire within a rock in the earth, just as there is air throughout the earth, and just as there is a light, a life-force, within everything that grows, God exists within all lives, within all creations, as the Soul, the Light-Soul. He exists within everything. There is no place where He is not. The Sufi realizes this, he realizes that there is no place where God is not.

According to the word of Islām, one should turn from the east towards the west to pray. That is one meaning. The meaning in Islām is to worship God by facing the west, by facing towards the *qiblah*. But the prayer of the Sufi, the true way in which he prays... for a Sufi the world is a prayer mat. Wherever he looks, wherever he turns, he is praying to God.

So then, what is the meaning of the practice in Islām of turning from the east towards the west? One is born in the east, he appears in the east. The west is where he disappears, where he is finished. He appears here and he disappears there. In Islām, this is the point of facing towards the west. This is the meaning of facing in that direction. In his prayers he must disappear. Since he is born here in this world, he must die in prayer, he must disappear. He must die in the west; he must die there. It is for this point, this reason, that they speak of turning from the east to the west. One must disappear in the west.

From the section of the east, the Sufi goes to the west. The west signifies God. That is the place where the Sufi disappears in the end. He dies in his prayer. His body and his every aspect die there. That is his prayer. To disappear in the west is the prayer of the Sufi. All of his thoughts and everything that appeared must die. The mind, the desire, and his form are controlled. All of these are kept under control. By subduing these he dies, he surrenders. This is prayer. If a person prays in this state, if he dies in this way, then for such a one, that is called prayer. The one who is born must die in order to reach God, he must die. Only if he dies can he reach God. Whatever world he holds on to, that world must die. Whatever world he has appeared in, that world must die away from him. Only then can he see the place in which he existed earlier. Where was he before? What place was he in before? Where did he come from? Only if the world that he has come to dies, can he return to the world that he was in before—God. Earlier he was in God. Now he has come to this world, and if this world dies he can return to that earlier place. That is *vanakkam,* that is prayer. Only prayer in this state can be said to be prayer in the station of the Sufi.

The prayer of the Sufi does not require being seated in a particular way. It is not like that. What is this state like? The 43,242 breaths per day are connected with God. Only when each breath is working with God can one be called a Sufi. A Sufi speaks without speaking, smiles without smiling, talks without talking, looks without looking, understands without understanding, walks without walking, sleeps without sleeping, and eats without eating. There are so many meanings like this. This is what is called "Sufi." His prayer consists of 43,242 *sajdahs* to God a day. Each breath surrenders to Him. He performs 43,242 prostrations a day. This is not done just three times or five times a day.

A Sufi does not use ganja, opium, or marijuana. A Sufi does not take opium or marijuana and become intoxicated. A Sufi does not get married, have children, and raise the children "this way" or "that way." Sufism is Sufi-son/sun. A Sufi is a sun to the world and a son to God. He is a son to God and a sun to the world. To the world he is a *sūriyan,* a sun, and to God he is a son, a Sufi-son/sun; he is a light to the world and a *mahan,* a son to God. He is a light to God, a *dhāt,* a grace to Him. He is a treasure that came from God. For the world he is a sun that gives light to everything. That is Sufi-son/sun.

To do this prayer one must control the mind, control the desire, control the physical visions, control the elements, control the semen, and control the scenes of the world. He needs to control all of these aspects. One who has subdued these is a Shaikh. He is a Sufi Shaikh, one who shows the path. If these have not been subdued, then his state is that of a *supi*, a pacifier that a baby sucks. A Sufi-son/sun exists in that other state.

Every created being is born in this world and every created being dies. Everything has been born and everything will die. It appears and it dies. Similarly, whatever has appeared must die within prayer. If one is truly in prayer, then everything will have died. When one worships God, everything must die. That is prayer.

Otherwise, if a man places on the outside the animals that are within his mind, and worships them, then that is not prayer. If the monkey that is within his mind is put on the outside and worshipped, then that is not prayer. If the elephant that is within his mind is put on the outside and worshipped there, then that is not prayer. Prayer is not like that. There will be an elephant inside and an elephant outside, there will be an animal inside and an animal outside, there will be a dog inside and a dog outside, there will be a snake inside and a snake outside, there will be a monkey inside and a monkey outside. This is not prayer. Only when these die is it prayer.

When the animals within us die and when the world that we see dies, then that is prayer. Only when we come to the state where they have died can that prayer be said to be the *vanakkam* of the Sufi-son/sun. This state is Sufism. This is what is called Sufism.

This, my brother, is a little of what we are trying to learn here. These children and I are trying to practice this a little. This is why we wake up at this time.

When there are fields and crops to be irrigated, it is the work of the overseer to open the sluice gates that will release the water from the storage tank, but it is the work of each individual to see that the water is directed to his own field. Each one has to do that work for himself. The one who releases the water will not divert it to the individual fields. Each farmer must divert the water to his own section.

It is the same way in Sufism. Our duty is to open and reveal. We open the sluice-gates, little by little, and reveal to you the manner in which the water flows. But it is the responsibility of each individual to divert the water to his own field and to cultivate it. That is not my responsibility.

This (early morning) time is a time of torpor for man. Torpor also comes immediately following a meal. He feels tired and wants to sleep. At eleven a.m. or at twelve noon, the same feeling of torpor comes. It is like the pangs of hunger that come at certain times.

At three o'clock in the morning we feel sleepy. Satan comes and makes us want to sleep. We must shake ourselves free and wake up at that time. That is our responsibility. Otherwise, satan, the world, and the elements will grab hold of us. This is why the world wakes up at this time, and this is why the prayers have been prescribed at this time.

Man will be unable to pray as long as the world has not died within him. He will be unable to pray as long as he has not controlled the mind. The mind must die and the world must die. Only when whatever he is holding on to dies will he be able to pick up something else. Only when the many things he holds on to die can he take on something else. While he is carrying a load, if he desires something else, he will not be able to hold it. There will be no room. But if man can make the kingdom of hell die, if he can let this go, then the kingdom of God is his. If the elements die, then God is his.

It is like this, *tambi*, to apply this in our life is Sufism. In this prayer of Sufism we say *lā ilāha*. *Lā ilāha,* there is nothing other than You. *IllAllāhu,* You are Allāh. This is *vanakkam*. With each breath, this sound should come from our tongue, without the tongue actually moving, like music, like the playing of a flute. In the same way as the heart works, *lā ilāha illAllāh* should work. It should work like the heart does.

Open: Lā ilāha.

Stop: IllAllāh.

Our breath must move with the beating of the heart. When the heart is open, the breath goes out. When it contracts, the breath comes in. When it contracts: "*IllAllāh,* You are Allāh." When it is open: "*Lā ilāha,* other than You there is nothing else. You alone are that point." Everything else disappears. It is born, appears, and disappears. "You are Allāh. I am not, you (others) are not, there is nothing else. *Lā ilāha,* there is nothing other than You. *IllAllāh,* You alone are Allāh."

Lā ilāha: The breath goes out through the left nostril. *Open: Lā ilāha.* Just as one faces the west, his wisdom and his faith must point towards the Power that is God. They must point towards That, and draw It in. His faith should draw It in. His wisdom should draw It in. Bring It in with *illAllāh,* You are Allāh. On the right side, bring It in with the incoming breath, and stop It there.

Lā ilāha illAllāh. This is what the Sufi says: "Not I. You. There is nothing other than You. You alone are Allāh." To prove this is prayer. That proof is God. There is no self, the self is dead. There is no world, there is nothing else. "There is nothing other than You." That is prayer.

With each of the 43,242 breaths a day, we should do *sajdah* to God, whether we are walking or sitting, sad or happy, asleep or awake, in our speech and in our breath. So how should this keep moving? No matter what work man is doing, his heart keeps on pumping. Similarly, that breath should keep on pumping within him. Prayer is the pump. That faith, that point, that magnet, and that remembrance should keep on pumping, no matter what work he may be doing.

That is a separate thing and this is a separate thing. That is mind-work and this is truth—this is certitude, it is the certitude of faith. This is the right hand and that is the left hand. Both must do their respective work. Just as the heart goes on working, that prayer should go on working. So, there are two kinds of work. There is the work of the world and there is God's work. Our prayer, our work, and our worship should go along with the breath. To understand both and act accordingly is Sufism.

If one has not become a Sufi, if he has not become a Sufi-sun, then he will not be praying. That will not be prayer. Only a sun knows the seasons of the world. When it sheds its light, it understands what is happening in the various places. If one does not become a sun, he will not understand this. Like that, only when his wisdom, his truth, and his prayer reach that state, will he understand about prayer. Then he will understand God and prayer. Otherwise, he cannot.

This is what is called Sufi. Therefore, that is prayer. If these children can learn this...

When someone is learning to drive a car, he grabs hold of the steering wheel. If he holds on to the steering wheel and practices steering, then later he will be able to drive. But there is no use in just learning how to drive. To drive, one should also know the map of the road and the mechanics of the car. If he does not know the mechanism of the car, it is not enough to know how to drive. He must know all the subtleties of the mechanism of the car. If he is driving along, the car may stall; something may get blocked, or a nut may come loose, and the car will stop. If this happens and he does not know the mechanics, he will get stuck somewhere. If, however, he is a mechanic, he will quickly be able to fix the problem and drive on.

Like that, one who practices Sufism must know the mechanics and the map. This is the reason, *tambi,* that we are practicing a little. My children and I are learning. We need to practice.

Lā ilāha.
(Bawa Muhaiyaddeen ☺ breathes out through the left nostril.)

IllAllāh.
(Bawa Muhaiyaddeen ☺ breathes in through the right nostril.)

Lā ilāha illAllāh. The sound should come in the breath. The sound should come in that movement.

When someone plays a flute he does not sing, yet a song emerges, music comes forth from the flute. A guitarist does not sing, but a song comes forth when he strums his guitar. What is within him comes out. Similarly, the 4,448 nerves in our body should be strummed with certitude, determination, and faith. When you are strumming, the sound should come from those 4,448 nerves. There are 248 pieces of bone, 236 plus 12 more, and the sound should come from those bones. This sound should come from the membranes, the muscles, and the blood. It should come from the 105 million skin pores. That sound should come forth.

This sound that comes without actually being made by the mouth should come from within. Like the heart that is continually working, that sound should come. Everything should move silently. Each time one breath goes out and one breath comes in, there are eight hundred million prayers, eight hundred million sounds that come forth. Eight hundred million prayers are coming from that one word. If you take count, a man has eight hundred million mouths. Only one breath goes out, but everything that is within him—all the nerves, the skin, and the bones—is saying that word. To say that word with such power is Sufi. It must be said in that state, with each breath.

Lā ilāha is not a simple matter. Let us now say it.

Lā ilāha illAllāh. Lā ilāha illAllāh. Lā ilāha illAllāh. Lā ilāha illAllāh.
With movement, send the breath out of the left nostril: *lā ilāha.* Then, draw it in through the right nostril: *illAllāh.* Faith should leap into God and draw this in.

Please take this (breath) in with that movement, like this...

(Bawa Muhaiyaddeen ☺ demonstrates the *dhikr*. When the tape resumes, it is dawn and the birds are singing.)

The sun is now dawning. As the sun dawns, it rises from the ocean, from below the horizon. It rolls and comes up. Now it is the color of blood or fire. This is a time of accidents. There is a magnet in the earth. Man also has this magnet, this connection, within him. That red fire is the connection that is mingled with the blood. While the sun is rising, man's mind will go up and down. The magnet in the earth will pull him, that current will attract him. His mind will pull him and his blood ties and attachments will pull him. This is a time of accidents.

Man himself is a world. There is also a world outside. There is a sun and a moon within him and there is a sun and a moon outside. There is an ocean within him and there is an ocean outside. The ocean of illusion is within him and there is an ocean of water outside. When the sun rises, it pulls him; that power, that shakti pulls him. This time is the time of accidents. The sun has a red color, it has a red color when it sets and when it rises. Similarly, when man is born he has blood ties and when he dies he has blood ties. These are the two times.

A Sufi has none of these attachments. For a Sufi these have died, these connections have died. For a true Sufi these are dead. There are no attachments, so he does not get pulled. A magnetic current can pull only if there is iron, but if there is no iron, then the current cannot pull. Like that, for a Sufi there is no world, so the world cannot draw him in.

One who has the world will be pulled by the world. When he is being pulled like this he should not continue doing this prayer. He should stop praying (while the sun is rising). If he is being pulled, it means that he still has the world within him. He should stop praying. He is iron and that is current, so that current will pull him. If there is no iron, the current will not pull. He will be like a log of dead wood. Wood will not attract a current.

If he has that state, if he is like a log of dead wood, then these rules do not apply to him, he can go on praying twenty-four hours of the day. But, if he retains the iron that can be pulled by the magnet, by the current, then his prayers must be performed only at certain times of the day. Prayer during the time of sunrise is suitable only for the Sufis. For everyone else, prayer that is done during this time will result in turmoil, it will not be suitable.

To understand what prayer really is, we must learn to pray in a subtle way. We must understand the ways to pray, the ways to sit, the ways to recite, and the ways to take this in.

Let us look at a mosque. The call to prayer is given loudly five times a day—*Allāh, Allāh*. This sound, *Allāhu akbar,* is sent out like the ringing of a bell. The call is again given when it is time for prayers. Then, when the people are praying, the sound of *Allāhu akbar* is lower—*Allāhu akbar.* When they bend down in *rukū',* *Allāhu akbar* is recited even softer. And when they perform *sajdah,* it sounds even softer.

Like that, the *sharī'ah* has a very loud sound. But the sound gets softer as one continues to pray. As one continues, the sound gets less and less. And as you continue even further, it gets even less.

Similarly, when you first say *lā ilāha,* you will say it with a little sound. Then when you say *illAllāhu,* the sound will be less. As you go on saying this, the sound will be finished. There will be only the motor and the current, *kkhhss, kkhhss, kkhhss, kkhhss.* That is what will be working, *kkhhss, kkhhss, kkhhss, kkhhss.* You will not be aware of the current that is flowing through the wires. You will know it only if you touch it. If you touch it, you will get shocked.

Alternate and direct current are extracted from earth, fire, water, air, and ether. This current is extracted from the water, from the earth, from the air, from the fire, and from the ether. Earlier the current was in unity, joined with the elements, but once it is separated, it can kill someone. If the current comes in contact with water — *srrrr!* It sends out sparks. If it comes in contact with iron — *srrrr!* It sends out sparks. It is not like it was earlier, it is not accident-free like it was earlier. Before that, the elements and the current were friends. Now they are not friends.

Like this, we must extract prayer from the five elements. It must be extracted. The D/C must be separated in the proper way. If we can separate the D/C from the five elements of earth, fire, water, air, and ether...earlier it had a connection to them, it was within them, but now we must extract it. Now it becomes electricity. At first it was the elements of earth, fire, water, air, and ether. Now it is an *electric-city,* now it is a *current-city.* Earlier it was the world, the elements, but now it is a current. When it becomes a current-city, it is light. As soon as it comes into that section of current, and if the earth, fire, water, air, and ether make contact with it, they will be hurled away. Therefore, if one has this connection, he should not go and touch it. Earlier the current was joined with the elements, but now it is not joined. Now it is electricity.

Man needs to extract prayer in the same way. After that, he should not touch it if he has a connection to this earth. He should not touch it with thoughts of this body. He should not touch it if he retains a connection to the earth or to the fire. If he touches it with this connection to earth, fire, water, air, and ether, it will shock him and toss him away. He will meet with an accident. So, he should not have that connection.

This is electricity, it is D/C. It moves without our being aware of it. You can see an electric cord, and it is possible to see the rubber insulation and the copper wires inside the insulation. But you will not be able to see the current that is flowing through the wire. You will not know how it is flowing. You will have to use an instrument to determine its movement. Only then will you know. Even when you look with an instrument, you will not see the current, you will only see a light.

Prayer is like that. You need to insert a light bulb. If you insert a bulb and then turn on the switch, you will see light. Without that bulb, without that switch, you will not know whether there is a current. Prayer is the connection between God, the switch of faith in God, the light that is your prayer, and the body that is this world through which the current flows. Prayer flows along like the current that flows through a wire. The connection between your prayer and God continues to flow, but no one will be aware of it. It is not something that you can discover by trying to touch it.

In this way, first, *lā ilāha*. Next, *illAllāh*. When the sound becomes less and less, when the prayer goes along with the breath and works automatically, it will be like the current that flows through a wire. It will be so slow, so imperceptible. If anyone who has the five elements touches it, he will be hurled away. Only God will know. Only the wire, the current that is flowing within it, the magnet, God, and the light will know. This is how that prayer will keep on going, going, going, going, and going. It is like a current that has been extracted. It keeps on moving by itself. It will not be evident, it cannot be shown. But if one who has the elements touches it, he will be tossed away.

This is the way the prayer of a Sufi is. My children, this is first said out loud. Later, when it becomes easier and easier, when it has been extracted, it will flow like the current in a wire. It will not be seen outwardly. A Guru will know it, he will be able to check and observe it. God will know that bulb, that light. And a true Kamil Shaikh will check it as it keeps on flowing.

Therefore, it is in this way that we should perform the prayer of a Sufi. In this state, in the twenty-four hours of the day, both the negative and the positive can go on working. This can work and that can work. Both must be done. This is a duty and that is a duty. This is negative and that is positive. Both should go on working. This will work on one side and that will work on another side. Both should not run together, or they will ignite. Both should not run together. Let one work by itself and let the other work by itself. Then there will be light. They should not make contact with each other. This is prayer. The two should not run together. *Vanakkam.* If they touch each other, they will ignite.

This is the prayer we should perform, the prayer of the Sufi. Each child should apply this correctly and pray in the proper manner.

Even though I had other work to do and even though the prayers of some of the children may have been disturbed, it was necessary for me to speak about this today.

Please bring fruit and give it to this *tambi.* Also, bring some tea.

Wherever you go, please do this prayer. My work could have gone on longer, but my brother also has work to do, so we should not detain him. I had to speak because my brother had a thought. He was wondering, "What is worship, what is prayer?" You might have been thinking about this, "What is the meaning of prayer?" It is for this reason that I had to speak for so long.

Whom does one worship? What is prayer and to whom does a Sufi pray? God praying to God is *vanakkam. Lā ilāha,* other than You nothing exists. *IllAllāh,* You are Allāh. These are the words of God praying to God.

Once a person records something on a tape, it will no longer be necessary for him to be there. The tape will produce the sound. Similarly, if man has recorded himself onto God, if he has surrendered to Him, then God Himself will go on giving that sound.

MR. WITTEVEEN

I am very grateful for his explanation. It is very, very clarifying. Thank you very much. I hope I didn't disturb too much.

BAWA MUHAIYADDEEN
No, no, work goes on its own. Please serve the fruit and tea.

A'ūdhu billāhi minash-shaitānir-rajīm.
I seek refuge in God from the accursed satan.

Bismillāhir-Rahmānir-Rahīm.
In the name of God, the Most Compassionate,
the Most Merciful.

THE BANK OF THE GURU, PART ONE

March 14, 1977, Monday, 5:30 a.m.

(Every morning in Sri Lanka, the song tape from August 18, 1976 was played at four a.m. to wake everyone up. Then, at 4:30 a.m., a tape from the August 1976 *dhikr* series was played. Everyone would follow along with Bawa Muhaiyaddeen's ☺ words and instructions, and would then perform the silent *dhikr* until sunrise.)

BAWA MUHAIYADDEEN

In Philadelphia, you get up at four o'clock, pray to God, and worship. You do the *dhikr*. But, after coming here, you are sleeping. The men should do the *dhikr* in the boys' room and the women should get up and do it in the girls' room.[1]

CHILD[2]

We do it down in the girls' room where they play the tape.

BAWA MUHAIYADDEEN

You must pray. Did you come here just to sleep? It is true that you sleep only a little here. You do go to bed late. But you do the

---

1   This discourse was given in Jaffna, Sri Lanka. An extension to Bawa Muhaiyaddeen's ☺ ashram was under construction at the time. Daily, Bawa Muhaiyaddeen ☺ would oversee the construction. The dormitory-style rooms that the men and women stayed in were referred to as the "boys' room" and the "girls' room."

2   Bawa Muhaiyaddeen ☺ referred to everyone as his children.

same thing there in Philadelphia. Everyone should get up early. Not only you, everyone here should get up.

CHILD

In Philadelphia, if all the people get up early that means that all the people go to sleep earlier, too. There, by ten o'clock they go to sleep.

BAWA MUHAIYADDEEN

Ah! You say they go to sleep at ten o'clock in Philadelphia? There, the people do not leave until twelve midnight, or sometimes one a.m. It is only after they leave that you can go to sleep. It is like that wherever I am. If I am there, it is like that, and if I am here, it is like that.

You are only paying attention to your sleep. You are not paying attention to the One who feeds you. You are not paying attention to the One who gives you sleep, to the One who gives you food, to the One who gives you health. Here, we are short of space and we lack many things. Nevertheless, even though there is very little room, some people do not waste their time, they wake up early in the morning.

If you want to be healthy, this is the way to be healthy. This is how to be well. Otherwise, you are just going to be sick. This is an herb that gives you health. It is an herb for your heart, it is a medicine. You are going to get sick if you just sleep. It is because the men are doing the *dhikr* that they are able to work night and day. They are able to do so much work. It is because they get up that they are healthy. They do so much work, they start early in the morning and work until about eight, nine, or ten o'clock at night. The masons leave at about ten p.m., and then the men go to bed. They lie down and think about getting up to do *tasbīh* to God. Because they do this, even though they may have a good deal of pain and even though they may have a fever, by the next day or the day after, they are well. You are not like that. This medicine is working in them, this grace is working. They are healthy. That is the reason.

You are not like that, you are just wasting your time. You are wasting your time like this other child is wasting her time. Do not be like that. You must trust in God and have faith in Him. You must seek Him, intend Him, think of Him, and trust Him. You must be looking at Him. The *qalb,* the eyes, and the wisdom must be looking at Him. You must be looking at Him with your intention. That will be the food for your life, for your *rūh,* your soul. That will make you grow. It will remove your sadness, it will remove your pain and illness. Please think about this a little. If you do this, it will be good. Then you could benefit from having come here. It will benefit you in that world and in this world. If you do not understand this, then you are just wasting your time. Please reflect on this.

You must do your duty. When you get up early, how healthy you will feel! If you do that duty to God, see how well your body will feel. You will be healthy and happy. But if you sleep late, then you cannot even get into the bathroom! You will have to stand in the queue until about seven or eight in the morning, and it will be so difficult. The whole day you will be coughing and complaining, *heh, eh, eeih.*

CHILD

There is not very much room here, there is not a really proper place to do *dhikr* at four o'clock in the morning. We need a proper place to do *dhikr.*

BAWA MUHAIYADDEEN

It can be done, it must be done. It is not really easy here. But once the building is finished and everything is cleared away, there will be space where we can all get together and do *dhikr.* Later, when all the work is completed, we can do this. For now, do the *dhikr* wherever you can. When the building is finished, you can all get together and sit in the hall. You will have room to do it there. The hall will be clear, the hall upstairs will be clear and you can do it peacefully. It will be clear and open. There will be no confinement. Now, there is very little space.

You must do it. You must strive. This is an herb that will cure your illnesses. Whether I am there or not, you must not wait for me to carry on with your work.

CHILD

Then should we use the tape? Or does it matter? Is it an individual preference?

ANOTHER QUESTION

Teacher (Mrs. Ramachandran),[3] some people like to do *dhikr* with the tape and some people like to do it by themselves. So, some people want the tape to be really low because they don't want to hear it. We don't know what is the best thing to do.

BAWA MUHAIYADDEEN

How can you do anything without your Guru? The tape is your Guru calling you to wake up and do this.

CHILD

No, not the song, the *dhikr* tape—*aparam pattu,* after the song. Everybody likes that.

BAWA MUHAIYADDEEN

You must play the *dhikr* tape and follow along with it. First, put on the song to wake everyone up, and then put on the *dhikr* tape. In Philadelphia, they told me to sing a song to wake everyone up. You must play that song, and then when you are all awake, you should come and recite the *dhikr*. After that, there is no song. You must get up and come together, put the *dhikr* tape on, and do the *dhikr* in the way that it should be done.

Put on the song in the early morning, and get up. Put it on at four o'clock, and by four-thirty you should be ready and come. You should be ready for *dhikr*.

CHILD

...put on the *dhikr* tape?

BAWA MUHAIYADDEEN

If you can do it alone, then do it. But if you have been sleeping-

---

3 Mrs. Ramachandran was the translator of this discourse. She was a schoolteacher and was addressed by all as Teacher.

in, then the tape is necessary. You are not doing anything. You think you are doing *dhikr,* but you are really only saying, *"om, am."* What you are really doing is reciting, *"om, am, shiva, sootcha, vatcha,"* like some of the other children.

CHILD

Explain, so I can understand.

BAWA MUHAIYADDEEN

All right. It is because this must become impressed in your heart: "*Lā ilāha,* there is nothing other than You. *IllAllāh,* You are Allāh." You should do this in your dreams, in your thoughts, and in your sleep. This should be recited continuously. If you recite this all the time, you will use these words in your dreams, you will use these words in your thoughts, and even when death comes, you will use these words. That light will be formed.

You must do this. That would be good. This is your search. Do not look to me, I will have to leave. This is how you should do it.

CHILD

Teacher, I do not understand. It seems to me there is a big difference. When I listen to Bawa pray, I am not praying, and when I am praying by myself, it seems much more strong than just to listen to Bawa praying. It seems more important to pray myself, rather than to listen to Bawa pray on the tape. I am just sitting back, like watching a movie.

BAWA MUHAIYADDEEN

You must follow along! *I don't know!* You must say it along with the words. You do not seem to have the strength to do it like that. When those words come, you must be strong. You must accept them and follow along with them. It is like the current that comes through a wire, like the light that comes in a bulb.

CHILD

He says one good prayer and I start chewing on that and trying to make that deeper, and already he's like on three more prayers.

BAWA MUHAIYADDEEN

You have to follow along with the Guru's words. Either the Guru must be present in front of you or you must follow along with the (recorded) words of the Guru. The Guru's words have to come into your heart. His words must be present. Or else, you must be sitting in front of him. You need to immediately accept those words and establish that prayer. Otherwise, that (sound) will not come to you; it will be like a bulb without light, a bulb without current. You need that certitude.

Even when you are alone, you need the words of the Guru, he must be in front of you, in your heart. You must listen to the Guru's words, and the Guru must be within you when you recite. Even when you are not listening to the tape, you need to hear the sound, that sound must be heard on the inside. Only then will there be light. Otherwise, that light will never come.

Whether the Guru is there or not, that sound must be heard in the *qalb*. You must have that certitude. You must recite those words from within. If that certitude does not come, then no matter what you do, it will be useless. Whether you hear the sound on the outside or not, you must place it inside you. You must hear that sound on the inside, that resonance must come. You must establish that explanation in your intention, with certitude. Otherwise, it will not give any benefit. You must realize that certitude, faith, and determination in your heart.

Either you must hear the sound on the outside or it must be understood from within the heart. As soon as you intend it, you should hear that sound. The tape has to come inside. If you do not hear the sound on the outside, then you must hear the sound on the inside. It must be recorded. Then it will be beneficial. Do you understand?

CHILD

I am not sure. I strive very hard to pray to "Muhaiyaddeen" inside. That seems to me *the* most important thing. But I still...I find it difficult to do that when the tape is playing outside.

BAWA MUHAIYADDEEN

Who is on the outside? What is outside must come inside and speak within. You have to take it inside. First it must come inside. If the sound on the outside does not go inside, how can the tape be recorded? It must go inside and then come out from within. If the sound does not come from here and go to there, how is that sound ever going to come again?

It is like a tape recorder taking in the sound and recording it. Unless you take in the sound, how can it be recorded? The sound must emanate from within. If you do not take in that sound, how is it ever going to record? How can it come inside?

CHILD

Yesterday in his prayer, the first thing he said was, "O Lord, teach us to understand that everything is Yours. Teach us how to have absolute trust in You." And when he said that I thought, what a good thing, you know, to try and meditate on, to have absolute trust in God. So then, I grabbed on to that. But then, very quickly he was making all kinds of other prayers. And I didn't know whether to go cling on to that one idea of trust in God or to go with the next prayer and the next prayer and the next prayer and the next prayer.

BAWA MUHAIYADDEEN

Athe shari, that is all right. Let Bawa continue to say what he is saying. Do you accept all of it? If you do accept it, your *qalb,* that intention, will say, "O God, I accept this."

When I am praying, when I am saying, "O God," you have to stay behind me. Do not go in front! At that moment, you must not go ahead. What is there for you to think about? You have to hold up your hands and beseech God with the Guru's words. That is a *lift,* an elevator. So how can you go in front of the Guru?

When the Guru says, "O God," then God has to speak. The Guru has to be in front to speak with God, and you have to stay behind him. The Guru goes ahead and you have to stand behind, you have to surrender and stay behind him. What is there for you to think about? He is like a lift that will carry you, and you have to surrender and stay behind him. Why should you think that you should go in front of the Guru?

CHILD

When he prays, he is on an airplane and I'm just walking.

BAWA MUHAIYADDEEN

Someone who is walking cannot follow a plane, the Guru cannot lift him into the plane. One who is walking will just be walking around over there, in the bathroom. That is useless. So, you have not surrendered to the Guru. You must hold on to him and then proceed.

There are many people like this. There are many ignorant people in Philadelphia with those kinds of qualities. They say, "Don't pray. Why should we do that? Why should we wake up early?" There are two or three people there who are thinking like that.

You went high very fast, and you fell down just as fast. You have gone down very deep. You think you are very high, but you really have gone down very deep. You think that you are very high, but you have gone down very low. Some people are like that in Philadelphia.

Even so, there are many children who have surrendered. They are coming along quickly. When you look at them, you will see that point. You will see that, from their faces. What is in their hearts will be seen on their faces. I will know who is working there. It will be clearly seen. That picture can be clearly seen. I know that form. I know what is inside them. I can look at their faces and look at their hearts and know who is working there.

CHILD

We have been hearing the tapes for four months now. Is there ever going to be a time when we can turn them off and pray by ourselves? We have heard the tapes for so long now. We have heard the tapes for so long. Can we ever do the prayers by ourselves?

BAWA MUHAIYADDEEN

You have to put on the tape until it is recorded within. Until that sound comes within, you have to do that. After it comes within, you can stop the tape. Once that is recorded within, you can stop the tape.

CHILD

That never ends!

BAWA MUHAIYADDEEN

Until then, you must do this. Until that certitude comes, until you hear the sound on the inside, you have to do this. After you have recorded the tape within, you can stop the outer tape. Look at yourself. See whether you can hear the sound of that record within. With certitude, with that subtlety, with that penetrating wisdom, with that ear of *īmān,* make your *qalb* determined in the Guru, and look. Say, "My Shaikh, my Guru must reside within me. I must hear that sound."

Look deeply. See if that beauty is there. You have to think. See if each sound arises within you as a vibration. See if you can see that form, see if that record, that sound is understood there, within you. See if you can hear it with the ears of *īmān.* Look with the eye of wisdom. Look and see if you can see that form. Then, it will be a mirror, and when you look, you will see what is within. You will see that form. That sound, that record will have come there, and you will hear it in your ears. Your body will hear it.

That sound will be heard within one body. If you hear it and if you pay attention to it, then it is correct. As soon as you have taken in the *dhikr,* that sound will come. It will come within you. The two sounds will become one. You and the Guru will be one *picture,* the two sounds will become one. As soon as you think of it, the sound will come; when you think of it, the sound will come and you will pray. Then there will be unity. One! One body, one sound, one gaze, one ear, one voice, one worship, one prayer. You will be merged with the Guru. The two will be merged as one, and then you will no longer need the tape.

Until then, you will not have certitude. Until then, your *īmān* will not be clear. Until then, your prayer will not be clear. So, until that sound comes within, you must do this. Only after that will you be clear.

If you have to respond to someone, if you have to speak to him and give a reply, and if you cannot provide the answer, then you should immediately say, "O my Guru." Look in your heart a little. Then ask, "O my Shaikh, my Father, please answer this. I cannot speak. You must speak. What is it that I can say?" As soon as you think like this, the answer will immediately come. The vibration will come and you can reply. "I cannot speak. You have to speak, you have to give the answer."

It is like putting water in a bottle, carbonating it, and putting the cap on. When you open it, that answer will come out, *tak!*—it will immediately come out. That is truth. Then, whatever question there is in your intentions will be answered. Until then, until the record, that picture, and that Light come to be within you, until you accept that only the Guru must speak and that you must give up your own speech—only when you accept that, will you be the microphone and he be the speech. You have to be the microphone and the speech has to come from there.

The Guru must speak and you must be a microphone that brings forth that speech. You must come to that state. Then it will be correct. No matter what happens, that must be the state. No matter what you say, you have to speak in that state.

Whatever you do not understand…If you want to see heaven, then ask the Guru: "O my *Pidā,* O my Father, what is heaven like? Please show that to me, I want to understand it. What is hell like? I want to understand it." You must remember the words that the Guru said about this earlier. Remember what he said about hell. Remember that. If he spoke about heaven, remember that. Then say, "Please show me."

Look at your Guru and say, "Please show this to me." Ask this in your *qalb.* Say, "Please show me," and if you look in this way, you will see. You will see it here and you will see it there. Look here, look here, look here, look at hell. You must look with *īmān* and with wisdom. Close your eyes and look! Open your eyes and look!

Close your eyes and look! You can do whatever you like. When you look, as soon as you remember what he said earlier, you will see what is happening there. No matter what you think of within, whether you want to know what the angels are like, what the 'adhāb, the punishment is like, what hell is like, what the fire of hell is like, what kind of work is going on there, who the sinners are, what snakes are found in hell, what is going on there, if you ask and ask, you will immediately see what is happening there. You will see what everyone is doing. You will see everyone who is being tortured, and you will hear the questions that everyone is being asked.

Whatever you ask about, you will see it. Both of you will see it. The Guru will show you. He will say, "This is this angel, this is the 'adhāb that is going on, this is the sin that that person has committed." He will tell you which hell it is. You can ask and ask, and you will see it with your own eyes, you will see it with your own form. You will be able to see it and you will be able to hear it. You will be able to do all this. That is the state you will come to. You can ask about the seven hells, you can ask and ask. If you keep the Guru within, you can ask and ask. He will show you. If you remember everything that the Guru has said about heaven, and then if you look, he will show you. You must ask within. If you listen and look, then as soon as you look, you will see, you will see everything about heaven. You will see it, you will see it wherever you are. Whether you look here or there or up or down, when you say, "Please show me," immediately he will reveal it. If you look up you will see it and if you look down you will see it. People say heaven is like a flower garden. What is it like? They say it is a resplendence, they say it is the *takht,* the throne of God. Everything that the Guru has told you will be like a picture, like a television. You will see everything. You can just sit there and he will take you along. You will be surrendered, and you will see the picture. You and he will travel together and see everything. But you must stay within that surrender. Only then can he take you with him.

You may be seated there, but he will take you along and show you everything. That is that form, that Light-form. You can just sit there. Your eyes will be closed and the speech will be going on. There is the kind of form that exists on the outside. That will be present. But this is the kind of form that exists on the inside, the Guru who can go and see everything everywhere. Each thing will be shown, one by one. He will reveal what this is, what that is, everything. He will show you where each thing is and he will show you where you are. The Light-form will be on the inside, the Guru will be on the inside, and both of you will be speaking and speaking with each other. Every sign will be revealed. You can ask and ask, and he will show you. He will say, "This is Judgment Day. This is where the punishment is given. This is heaven. This is the eighth heaven." He will reveal all that to you. You might say, "I want to go around the world and see what the world is like." He will reply, "The world is an atom." Immediately, he will show it to you. "This is the world. Look!" He will show you each thing, one by one.

Now, all that you are doing is sleeping over there. You must go round with the Guru, you must understand with the Guru, and you must speak with the Guru! You have to see the entire world with the Guru! You cannot see God, the Qutb ☺, or the Nūr-Muhammad ☺ as a form. They are Light, they are a Power. They are formless, they have no pictures. Everything else can be shown, but if you ask what they are like, they will be seen only as Light, as a very great Power.

Everything else, all that is good and evil, will be understood. Then, this picture will be understood. You will understand this picture, you will see it directly with your eyes. You will act directly, you will fly directly. Sometimes you will have to fly. The Guru will hold on to your hand and embrace you. He will carry you, and fly with you. (Bawa Muhaiyaddeen ☺ claps.) "Go there!" he will say. Then he will say, "Come here!" He will call you and embrace you. Some places you will have to go alone, while sometimes he will embrace you and take you within himself, as one. He will say, (clap) "Let us go there! Can you hear what is there? Now look! In this place we cannot go as two. One! Only one can travel on this path, two sections cannot go. Therefore, you and I have to become one. Now, do you hear this? Do you see this? Did you see everything as I brought you along? Did you understand? Now you have seen all of this. The One is the Light."

So, you will see everything but you cannot speak. He will take you along and he will ask you, "Have you seen this? Have you seen this?" He will explain each thing to you, he will show it to you. Ah, whenever you ask a question, he will answer.

This is what the Guru's journey is like and this is the journey of the children who have surrendered to the Guru. But until this time, until you see that place, everything you do is baby-ignorance.

I have spoken about this in *The (Ten) Wonders, The Guru's Explanations — The Pattu Pudinam.*[4] Out of two hundred thousand wonders, only ten wonders have been written down. They tell you how to travel on the path. Only when you come to that state will you be in the state in which the Guru can lift you up and reveal everything. There are ten wonders out of two hundred thousand that have been written down. If you come to the state that is revealed in these *Ten Wonders,* then wherever you go, the Guru can show you everything.

Until then, everything you do is ignorance. You will be one who has no certitude.

CHILD

Teacher, when I'm saying my prayers to God, you know, I am like confused on the physical things. It seems like we get what we pray for you know, but I'm confused whether I should just ask for God to clear the path to Him on the inside or whether He should also clear the obstacles in the world. I am confused what to ask.

BAWA MUHAIYADDEEN

You will not be able to ask God. There is a great distance between God and you. First you have to ask the Guru. There is a huge mountain between God and you — the mind. You cannot ask. You need a lift, an elevator, for that. The Guru is the lift. You have to ask the Guru. If you surrender to the Guru, then, after you surrender, that

---

4 *The Ten Wonders,* also known as *The Ten Mystical Experiences,* was related by Bawa Muhaiyaddeen ☮ in the 1950's.

lift will carry you there. That mountain will be broken down, and you can speak face to face with God. Do you understand?

CHILD

Kunjam, a little.

ANOTHER CHILD

Teacher, Bawa speaks about doing prayer, about *niyyah,* or focus...

BAWA MUHAIYADDEEN

You have been studying for so long. You have studied from so many gurus in the world. You have recited mantras. But you cannot study those things here. That is not how it is. All those things you have studied with those gurus will not apply here. Man-God, God-man, man within God and God within man—this is the learning you have to study here. It is an incomparable learning, a learning without any equal. Mantras, tantras, magic, and miracles cannot be studied here.

You have to go directly to God. God has to be within you. Here, you have to study the ways in which you can break down the dark, black mountain known as the mind, the mountain of maya that stands between you and God. You need that Light, that tiller, that bulldozer to break it down. You have to fashion that engine, you need that bulldozer. That is wisdom, faith, and truth. With that, we must break down that mountain. Then we can go directly to God in our life. God will be within us and we will be within God.

You need to understand and know that unity. To achieve that unity, you need to surrender to the Guru. That is the bulldozer. That is the lift and the bulldozer. With that you can break down that mountain.

(Bawa Muhaiyaddeen ☺ addresses a man who comes into the room.)

Are you sad? Are you worrying? Ahh, that is okay!

(Bawa Muhaiyaddeen ☺ continues speaking to everyone.)

When someone sees that another person is having difficulty, he must help him. Some people only care about themselves and do not care about others. They only pay attention to their own suffering and their own health. They do not pay attention to the difficulty, poverty, or suffering of others. Is that God's fault or is that our fault? That is man's ignorance, his selfishness. That is his lack of knowledge. We need the patience and tolerance that can chase away the darkness and ignorance. Then those things will not torture us and darkness and ignorance will be dispelled. We need patience to do that.

So, that person is a little sad, he is a little worried. Until we have the wisdom and the awareness that the sorrows of others are our own sorrows, until we realize the difficulties of others, until we get that patience, we need to study wisdom. When that comes, it will be good. That is what I think. *Papum,* we will see.

CHILD

How can we surrender to the Guru so that we can hear his voice inside?

BAWA MUHAIYADDEEN

To surrender to the Guru is to have the certitude and *īmān* that says: "There is nothing for me other than that. That is the Father who can lift me. That is the Dēva who can lift me. That is the ship that can carry me and show me the way. That is my life, my existence. That is my wisdom, the ship on which I can journey. That is like a lift that will raise me up out of hell and protect me. That is my wisdom, that is my Light. I cannot reach the shore without this lift. I cannot function in this birth without it. In this birth I must cross over the five elements of earth, fire, water, air, and ether, and cross over mind and desire, arrogance, karma, and maya—these nine hells. The only one who can lift me out of these nine hells is the one *Pidā,* the one Guru, the one Nūr, the one Light. Therefore, I must accept that treasure."

When, with certitude and determination, you surrender to that Guru, you will have to give all responsibility to him. It is like taking everything that is in your hands—all that you earn, your jobs, your wages, everything—and putting it into a bank. In the same way that a bank gives you checks, you will receive a check. That check needs to be in your hands.

So, just as you deposit all your money and wealth in a bank, you must deposit all your earnings, thoughts, intentions, and savings into the bank of the Guru. He will then place the check called *īmān* into your hands. That check must be in your hands. Everything you have must be deposited in that bank. That is surrender. Then, whenever you need something, you can write the check for it. All responsibility will have been given to the Guru. *That* is surrender.

(Roosters crowing, birds singing.)

Shari, all right, morning!

There is God's justice, the king's justice, man's justice, and the conscience. These four kinds of justice are four laws. God's justice has to become the king's justice, the king's justice has to become the man's justice, man's justice has to become the conscience, and that must become law. These four laws have to be understood in the world. If these four kinds of justice are not understood, that country will be destroyed. Accidents will occur, famine will come to that country, and disease will come to that country. It will be subject to accidents by fire, water, air, storms, viruses, and the oceans. Illnesses, diseases, clouds, *cells,* and fires will cause that country to become poor, and then be destroyed.

Like this, these four kinds of justice must exist in each world that is within you. The world exists within you and you are the ruler for that country. Because you are the ruler for your country, you must dispense God's justice. You are the king for this world. Because you are the king for this kingdom called the *qalb,* your heart, God's justice must become the king's justice. It must reign there. You are the king for this country. God has given you that crown. You are the king for the eighteen thousand universes. You have to deliver the judgment for that. You have to deliver the justice for that. You have to inquire into the guilt and innocence there, and according to the results of that inquiry, you must rule over that country.

God's justice has to become the justice of the king, and with that justice you have to rule that kingdom. Within that kingdom you have six kinds of souls, six kinds of inhabitants. Also, there are animals there, there are demons, there are ghosts, there are snakes, there are scorpions, there are demonic qualities, there are elements, there are jinns, and there are fairies. Animals and human beings exist there. Like this, there are four hundred trillion ten thousand things that exist in the eighteen thousand universes. There are so many atoms, cells, lives, elements, and crazinesses. So many kingdoms, the sun, the moon, the stars, and the soul exist there. There are six kinds of souls.

According to the explanation of the soul, you have to be the ruler of that kingdom, you have to govern there. You have to resplend as man, as Adam ☺. That is the Light that comes from the Nūr. That Light of the Nūr is called Muhammad-Ahamad ☺; the two, the *aham* and the *muham* are joined as one. The resplendence of the heart, the *aham,* and the beauty of the face, the *muham,* are made into one and exist as one Light. That Light is the Nūr, the plenitude. The name for that Light is Ahamad-Muhammad ☺. That is man. That is what is known as man. Man must dispense the king's justice and God's justice.

Thus, you have to be the king for this land. You have to be the king for the eighteen thousand universes. You have to bring God's justice to the king's justice, and you have to bring that Light of the king's justice to man's justice. You have to give the judgment to the animals that live there, to the forms that live there, to the maya that lives there, to all the eighteen thousand universes, to the atomic lives, to all the creations: to the animals, reptiles, birds, winged creatures, monkeys, dogs, foxes, cows, horses, and donkeys, and to hell and heaven. God's justice has to become the justice of the king, and as the king you have to dispense that justice. You have to be a human being and deliver man's justice, you have to be a man and act with man's justice.

After that, living as a human being, you must have compassion for all lives, you must have trust for all lives. All lives must be like your own life, all hunger must be like your own hunger, and all sorrow must be like your own sorrow. That is the justice that you must bring into your kingdom.

Then, you must have conscience. Judgment Day. Judgment is the '*arsh*, the conscience. Judgment is the throne, the court. You have to come to that court. That is conscience. You have to come to the judgment called conscience, to that lift. When man comes to that state, when man's justice is brought to that conscience, then you, as the leader of that pure kingdom, must give the judgment.

You must carry out these four kinds of justice. If you do not dispense those four kinds of justice, that country will be destroyed. In the way that we explained earlier, you will destroy that country, you will destroy that kingdom. You will destroy that country through disease, illness, demons, ghosts, arrogance, karma, maya, demonic qualities, evil qualities, and poisonous qualities.

Because you are a king, you have to have God's justice. As the king in your kingdom, if you do not dispense the king's justice, and as the king, if you do not dispense man's justice properly, if you do not become human and dispense man's justice, if you do not carry out man's justice and affix the seal, and if you do not carry out the judgment of the conscience properly, then this country and this family will be destroyed by satan. It will be destroyed by karma, it will be destroyed by maya, it will be destroyed by birth, it will be destroyed by your thoughts, it will be destroyed by the elements, animals, demons, and ghosts. It will be destroyed by sadness, illness, disease, poverty, difficulties, storms, fire, water, air, ether, and viruses. This country will be destroyed by all of these things.

So, in this way, whose fault will that be? This came about because you did not carry out justice in your country, you did not dispense justice to what is seen on the outside, to other lands, or to your world that is seen on the inside. This is your world. Therefore, whose fault is that?

You must not deviate from justice. God has given all the responsibility for the kingdom of God to you. He has also given you the kingdom of hell. He has given you the kingdom of heaven, the kingdom of hell, the eighteen thousand universes, '*ālamul-arwāh*, everything. He has given you Himself and His Power. He has given you the king's justice. If you do not dispense it, if you do not affix the seal, if you do not bring it into man's justice, and if you do not pass judgment with your conscience, then you will be destroying that country. Because you have let go of your justice, your law, your conscience, your human justice, your king's justice, and God's justice, you are destroying the country. This is not God's fault.

Therefore, if you understand this, it will be very good. You should not say, "It is God's fault! It is God's fault!" Think about this and turn to the straight path. If you rule your kingdom in the right way, it will be very good.

Shari, very well. People inquire about us. They say, "What is this country like? What is this Guru like? What is this Guru Bawa like? What is he like?"

You ask one person, you ask another person, and you ask another. You ask the wall, you ask the earth, you ask the fire, you ask satan, you ask pharaoh, you ask Abū Jahl! If you go on inquiring and investigating like this, then your own section will be finished. It would be much better if you inquire into yourself. Some are saying, "Who is this Guru Bawa? He builds this and he builds that. He is not teaching anything. He just goes on building. He did this, he's building this, he built in Mankumbān, he constructed this building, he built a God's House. What is he going to do next? What is he doing this for?" If you research into these things, then that is the research of satan. Then you are *poitch,* finished!

If you inquire into all these things, if you investigate and write this down in your books, if you write this down in your *time-books,* in your diaries, then that is useless. What you are seeing is false, what you are looking at is false, and what you are hearing is false. Your judgment is false, your birth is false, your existence is false, your life is false, and your death is false. I do not know what you are looking into. It is a useless investigation. You need to investigate yourself. That is the work you should be doing. You should not be investigating others.

From the time you started, you should have handed over everything to the bank. You have accepted the responsibility of the bank, but you have no way of gaining access to it. You have accepted the responsibility of the bank, but you do not have a key to open it. *Key-nothing.* You have accepted the responsibility of the bank, but you have no way of opening it. Key-nothing. If you give all of your property to the bank, then you need to be able to open it. You have accepted the responsibility of the bank and have come here, but key-nothing.

Therefore, this is the kind of responsibility that you have. That is not good. It will not be of any use to you at all. You will not receive any money. You will not have any money for a bus, you will not have any money for a train, you will not have any money for a journey—you will have nothing, because you do not have a key. You are saying, "I am the banker." But, key-nothing.

Shari. Do your own business without investigating others. You have taken on the responsibility for a bank, but you have no key and you are inquiring: "What is he like, what is his conduct like, what is he doing? What is this work that he is giving us from morning to night! We should be studying *gnānam!*" You have accepted responsibility for the bank, but you have no key. You say, "He makes us break rocks in the morning and then we have to carry sand and rocks all over the place. I have sores all over me, I have blisters, my chest hurts, my hands itch, my body has gotten thin, my strength is all gone, everything is gone, my baggage is gone, my journey is gone. *Aiyō!* Why are we doing this? This is suffering! Is this what we have come here for?"

You do not have the key. You should give your responsibilities to the bank, and then everything will be easy. Then the ticket will come for everything.

Thank you. Go and have breakfast.

CHILD

Can I ask him a question?

BAWA MUHAIYADDEEN

All questions are finished. You have slept all this time, and you have come only now. Now go and eat. Get up at four and pray. Then come and ask questions.

CHILD

I got up at four o'clock but nothing much happened. But I did get up. (laughter)

BAWA MUHAIYADDEEN

You were sleeping and then got up? *Shari*. The crows get up at three or four in the morning. They caw, but they do not search.

CHILD

And me, likewise.

BAWA MUHAIYADDEEN

First do that. Do that first. Search for what you need to search for, and after that you can come and ask your questions. Now we have finished talking. We have been speaking since five in the morning.

(Bawa Muhaiyaddeen ☺ responds to another questioner.)

You say that "Jesus ☺ said" and you say that "Muhammad ☺ said." They would have said this long ago, but now we are giving explanations (directly).

You have not seen Jesus ☺, you have not seen Moses ☺, and you have not seen Muhammad ☺. Even though explanations are given to you directly, you read these other books and discard the explanations that you can see. You discard the speech that comes to you directly. Although you did not know Moses ☺ at that time, you speak about him. Although you did not know Jesus ☺ at that time, you speak about him from books you have read. Although you did not know the people at that time, you speak about them from books you have read. But when it comes directly to you, when it comes directly to you from someone who *does* know Jesus ☺, who *does* know Moses ☺, who *does* know Abraham ☺, and who *does* know Muhammad ☺, when that speech comes directly from someone who knows them, you go and hide, and you disregard it. You do not accept that speech. You disregard the speech that is coming to you directly, and you go and hide and read your books. That is what you accept. It is a big, black mountain that has caught hold of you.

If you would accept this speech that you hear now, if you would accept what you see directly, it would be very good. If you would accept what is being said now, it would be very good. This is the explanation. The difference between the words spoken then and the words that are being spoken now is that these words that are coming to you directly have life!

It has been two hundred million years since this world was created, and in every country what was land has become ocean and what was ocean has become land. Each history, the history of everything that happened earlier, the entire history of birth, is contained in one bank, one book. All of those histories are in one bank. That *system,* that record, is found in that bank. Everything is there. That bank is a huge steamer, a steamship. That steamer contains all of the histories, the research — what is happening now, what happened earlier, and what will happen later. All of this is on that record.

After many ages, a power of God comes. It comes to the world at a particular time and reads that record. It comes to make people remember. That full history, that record, is read and revealed. That power comes once in many, many ages, at the time of destruction. It comes at a time when everything has been forgotten and explains that record, that history of two hundred million years.

That tape reveals everything. All of the histories that have occurred in two hundred million years are on that record. It is revealed as a proof to the people, to make their certitude firm.

So, that is an injunction of God. This is the way God's judgment is. All of the histories will come on that record. All of the points that are recorded there are now coming directly. What was not seen previously can now be seen. That history is coming in its entirety.

This cannot be found in books. That story is not with you! That steamer is not with you! That bank is not with you! You just record and accept things that you have not seen!

That history comes at the time of destruction. His record comes at the time of destruction as a proof (of His existence) — to witness it, and to make it understood. There is a time like that.

If you do not understand what is on that steamer, it is not God's fault. It is the fault of your karma, the fault of the hell in which you reside. That is not God's decree. You should understand and realize this. That point, that time exists as a proof, and when it is read in that place, you must accept it. When the work of the steamer is finished, it will leave. And then, so many more tens of millions of years will go by before that kind of steamer comes again, before His power is revealed once again. That steamer will come at that time and reveal this, and it will also leave. Even then, you must accept it. If not, it is only your ignorance, nothing else. It is not God's fault.

All of the histories that are contained within this have only one point. There is only one history. You must understand this. There is no more room for me to tell you anything beyond this. If anything else needs to be said, that means you do not have wisdom.

Right. All the women go and do your work. The male children have their work, their duty. Go and eat.

This is a day that comes only once in a hundred years. It is a good day, it is a good year. It is a good day. You have received a blessing today. This is a preface, today's speech is a preface. Therefore, please take what was said today and check it, type it, and present it in a clear way. *Shari.*

A'ūdhu billāhi minash-shaitānir-rajīm.
I seek refuge in God from the accursed satan.

Bismillāhir-Rahmānir-Rahīm.
In the name of God, the Most Compassionate,
the Most Merciful.

THE BANK OF THE GURU, PART TWO

March 14, 1977, Monday, 6:30 p.m.

You have to place all of your thoughts, intentions, sadness, sorrows, anxiety, and suffering, everything that you have, into the bank of the Guru. Not what you earn or what you acquire. Do not give that! You should deposit your thoughts, intentions, sorrows, sadness, and anything that you are searching for into that bank.

Then, from the Guru you must get the receipt, the check, that is your birthright. You must get that check of *īmān,* faith, certitude, determination, patience, compassion, tolerance, peacefulness, and the *tawakkul* that gives all responsibility to God. The Guru will give you that check, and you must keep it in your hands. Everything else you must give into his hands. You must give your mind into his hands and receive the receipt of grace from him.

So, like that, you will receive that receipt for what you give to him. The value of that check will be such that you can tear it off and use it for anything you need. The Guru will give you that check. This is the wealth you will receive, he will give you that check.

That is surrender. If that state comes, then just as you deposit your wealth and money in a bank and then receive a check for it, if you deposit the thoughts of your mind, your birth, death, sorrows, troubles, difficulties, all this, into the bank of the Guru, you can use that check that is given to you to withdraw what you need. If you keep that in your hands, then that is surrender. If you give all responsibility to the bank, then you can withdraw whatever you need at the time it is needed.

That is surrender. When you reach that state, that is surrender.

Therefore, whether it is your body or your material things, if you put your thoughts, intentions, worship, prayer, devotion, wisdom, ability, and so forth into the bank, if you give all the responsibility to the Guru, and if you get a receipt from him, then that is surrender. Then it becomes his responsibility, and he must protect everything. As soon as you need something, that point will come to you and you will have peace. Neither satan, nor thieves, nor robbers, nor burglars will be able to come near you, because you have the receipt. No one can come to rob you, so you can be peaceful. If someone wants something, he will have to break into the bank. And the one who protects the bank will stop anyone who comes to steal. Whoever comes there to steal will die; that thief will die.

That is surrender. When you reach that state, then that is surrender to the Guru.

SONG: THE GOOD DAY

August 4, 1977, Thursday, 8:50 a.m.

When will the good day come,
the day that will be a good day for us?
When will the good day
of the resonance of the Grace of Allāhu come?
That day will be a good day for us.
When will the Grace that is Allāhu resonate?
That day will be a good day for everyone,
a good day for us.

When the *qalb,* the innermost heart,
is filled with justice
and truth dawns there,
when the *qalb* is filled with justice,
when the path that is truth appears,
the state of human justice will arise, and
a human being will live as a human being.
That will be a good day.
When that day comes to us,
it will be a good day for us.

Day and night the blessing of Ādi Rahmān
who rules us,
day and night the blessings of Ādi Rahmān
who rules us,
will leap from heart to heart,
melt there and beat
between one human being and another.
When will that day come to us?
That day will be a good day for us.

When we live with justice,
the state of conscience,
melting compassion, patience, tolerance,
good conduct on the path of truth, and
when we live filled with goodness,
that day will be a good day for us.
That day will be a good day for us.
When will that day come?
When will that day come?

That day will be a good day
for mankind and for us.
It will be a day of exaltedness in our lives.
That day will occur on the day
we realize truth in a state of silence.
That will be an exalted day in our lives.
We will be aware of truth,
and we will walk on the good path.
That day will be a good day for us.

The hearts of all mankind will resonate.
The bliss of grace will shine from their *qalbs*.
Justice and exaltedness will overflow from them.
They will live eternal lives of absolute integrity.

That day will be a good day for us.
That day will be a good day for us.
When will that day come to the world?
To everyone?
To all lives?
To those who have been born as human beings?

That will be an exalted day,
a good day.
That will be a good day for us.
That will be a good day in our lives.
Race, religion, and separation will be destroyed.
The peaceful qualities of truth and justice
will live among us.
Compassion for other lives will be most exalted.
Truth, justice, integrity, patience, compassion, love, and
al-hamdu lillāh, giving all praise to God,
will be most loved.

The day that mankind achieves that state
will be a good day for us.
That day will be the day the entire world will praise.
That day will be the day the state
of He who is One will be established.
That day will be the day He will stay with us.
That day will be the day He will rule.
That day will be the day of the praise known as *al-hamd.*

When will that day come?
That day will be a good day for us.
That day will be a good day for us.
On that day the state of
the just Rahmān will overflow from us,
compassion will arise from us, and

the divine Grace of our Creator
will descend into the *dunyā,* the world.

The heart will love this.
The *qalb* will love this.
That day that this occurs
in the life of man will be an exalted day.
That day will be a good day.
That will be a good day for us.
When will that day come?
That day will be an exalted, good day for us.

That will be the target and the arrow.
That will be the grace and the treasure.
That will be God and man.
The day they live as one
will be a good day.
The day they live as one
will be a good day.
When will that day come?

That day will be a good day for us
and for all lives.
That day will be a good day for all lives.
That will be the place
in which the sound will resonate.
That will be the grace
that will dispel our sins.
That will be the place
in which the sound will resonate.
That will be the grace
that will dispel our sins.
That will be the wisdom that destroys
the hypnotic delusion of the intellect.

The day that mankind
searches for this blessing and reaches it
will be a good day for mankind.
That day will be a good day for mankind.

When will that day come?
That day will be a good day for all lives.
It will be a day of service to God.
It will be a day the heart will be resonant
and attain grace.
It will be the day all lives attain peace.
That day will be the day all lives attain peace —
the day of service to God,
the day of service to the people,
the dawning of the day
of the crown of God in the kingdom of God.

When will that day come?
When will that day come?
That day will be a good day for us.
That will be an exalted day
when man lives amidst all lives,
the day of service to God,
the day of service to the people,
the day of dispensing justice
in a state of silence.
When will that day come?
When will that day come?
That day will be an exalted day for all lives.
What day will that come into being?
In death and in birth,
that day will be the exalted day
that belongs to Him.

A'ūdhu billāhi minash-shaitānir-rajīm.
I seek refuge in God from the accursed satan.

Bismillāhir-Rahmānir-Rahīm.
In the name of God, the Most Compassionate,
the Most Merciful.

THE OUT LOUD *DHIKR*

September 8, 1981, Tuesday

(Bawa Muhaiyaddeen ☺ points to one of his disciples.)

He is a Hindu. He belongs to a famous Hindu family, and he knows a great deal of Hindu philosophy. The Hindu religion is vast; it is a very large book. He has studied all of the Hindu mantras. There are so many gods in that religion. His family manages a temple where they worship many gods: Pillaiyār, Murugan, Shiva, Shakti, Pārvati, Paramasivan. So, he knows Hinduism very well— Shakti and Shiva. In this religion mantras are studied.

First (my children), is the religion of creation. Below the stomach is the mantra of creation, maya. Second (Bawa Muhaiyaddeen ☺ points to the stomach) is the Hanal religion, the religion of fire. This fire also exists within Hinduism where there are fire gods, water gods, air gods, earth gods, sun gods, and moon gods. There are so many gods and mantras in Hinduism. Those in the Hanal religion worship the fire, the sun, the moon, and the stars. This is the hellboard of the trench of fire. The third religion is Christianity, the heart. There, they worship the pure spirits and impure spirits, the *nafs ammārah,* the desires, the *rūh,* the *rūhānīs,* and the *nafsāniyyat.* Catholicism and Hinduism are very similar. They both worship statues. Hanal is the worship of fire, of forms. Christianity is comprised of both Catholics and Protestants, two divisions; that is Christianity. Some people

133

worship spirits, some worship statues, some worship the angels, some worship miracles, and some worship the saints. They pray to these.

Hinduism, Hanal, Christianity, and *al-furqān,* Islām, which is the head, are one book. The one form has four steps. Hinduism contains the creation mantras, the Hanal religion contains the meditation mantras, and Christianity contains the spirit mantras. But God is One who has no form. Judaism and *al-furqān* do not have any forms. There should not be a form; you should pray to the Mystery that has no form. In the prayer of *al-furqān* (Islām) and Judaism, the two sections of Qāsim and Banū Isrā'īl, there are no parallels to God.

So, there is one form and four religions. And there are four hundred trillion ten thousand spiritual prayers. The prayer of maya has four hundred trillion ten thousand spiritual prayers. These four religions, these four prayers are one form, one book, and one story. The four religions are the one body. There are four sections: one quarter, one quarter, one quarter, and one quarter. One storybook contains the story of the world, the story of the soul, the story of prayer, and the story of God, Light. There are four books, four sections—one body, four chapters, one man, one God, and one prayer. You must understand *this* (Hinduism), you must understand *this* (Hanal), you must understand *this* (Christianity), and you must understand *this* (Islām). You must understand these four steps.

So, do you know everything about creation? Have you completed that learning? Have you observed what man creates? Man makes the *arts-creations.* But God's arts are the trees, the shrubs, the flowers, the plants, the animals, and the birds. God's arts move, all of it moves. But all of man's arts are statues. That is creation, the Hindu religion, the arts that do not move, the prayer of creation. There are sixty-four *līlais,* sexual games, and sixty-four *kalais,* arts and sciences. That is Hinduism; that is the prayer of the arts—the sixty-four *līlais* and sixty-four *kalais.* In the nighttime, it is the *līlai vinotham,* and in the daytime, it is shown as an act on the outside. So that is the *creation part,* the section of creation. That is Hinduism.

So, the forms that God creates are like this and the forms that man creates are like that. Everything that God creates moves. You must learn all of this, you must study everything.

Does fragrance come from what you have created? Do fruits grow from what you have created? Does taste come from what you have created? Does what you have created contain a soul? Nothing comes from this artwork that you create. Do the gods you have created have souls? Sometimes people place many statues under certain trees. They also place lights, fire, and incense there. Do these statues speak, do they eat? These are things that man has to carry, things that the monkey mind has to carry. They do not speak.

This is how the Hindus worship. These are the sixty-four *kalais* and sixty-four *līlais,* the arts, and the maya shaktis. All of these mantras, studies, ragas, music, songs, and dances are part of this learning. This is a form. This is what they do, this is their prayer. There are dog gods, cat gods, elephant gods, snake gods, rat gods, eagle gods, vulture gods, vampire gods, tiger gods, lion gods, fish gods, crow gods, and peacock gods. There are countless gods like this.

What are these gods? Have you finished with this karma? Have you given up maya, desire, attachments, the monkey mind, differences, religions, castes, separations, colors, hues, and the "you" and the "I"? Have you cut away all of these? No, you have not cut them away. Have you attained peace, tranquility, and equanimity? Man-God, God-man. Have you become God? No. You have not become That.

Only if you cut away all of these things can you become God. Then the hunger of others will be your hunger, the suffering of others will be your suffering, the life of others will be your life, and the well-being of others will be your well-being. Have you reached that state? You have not reached it. You have not given up all these forms. Since you have not given them up, you must study. You must understand these. Only when understanding comes will you be able to give these up. If you do not understand, you cannot learn or attain that high state. If you do not give up these forms, you cannot achieve that high state. So what are you going to do? It is as if you have fallen into a very deep, deep, deep place and you cannot climb out of it. If a man falls into such a deep place, will he be able to climb out of it? He cannot get out.

Likewise, God is very deep. God's Power is very deep. It is a place that has no limit, no end, no state, it is a place that cannot be understood. *Lā ilāha,* there is nothing other than You. *IllAllāh,* You are Allāh. One point. I am nothing, You alone are God. Have you come to that state? Has anyone reached that? No one has reached that. You have not come to that understanding. So, what *is* your state?

I have been teaching in America for the last eleven years, but your color differences have not left, your desire has not left, your creation (section) has not left, your doubt has not left, your anger has not left, your hastiness has not left, your jealousy has not left, the "I" has not left, your hunger has not left, differences have not left, lust has not left, torpor has not left, impatience has not left, arrogance has not left, karma has not left, and maya has not left. So how can you learn? How can you understand? How can you go to that place? Instead, you are like worms that have fallen into fire. It is as if you have fallen into that place. When I look, it seems as if you have gone into that place.

I have given one million discourses, but not one discourse has gone into you! Not even one point has entered you! You are like a baby, like a parrot. You learn like a parrot. Not even one point has entered your ears or your hearts. You have not understood; you are just dancing, playing, and jumping. Eleven years have gone by, but you have not understood. There is nothing coming out of you. You must start! You must start, and then I can bring you along, step by step — this explanation, this explanation, this explanation, this explanation, this explanation, this explanation. You have to start from the beginning.

There should be a few of you who have understood, a few of you who should have risen higher. But you have not. You have not read the book, you do not know the meaning. Now you are just making noise with your mind. You do not understand. But we continue to speak, we just go on speaking.

This child has been here for eight months. Does she understand about prayer? Prayer in Islām is one way, but this prayer (the out loud *dhikr*) is different. This point is different. So, what is this section? *Start!* What is this learning? One God! Each word refers to the one God, each word asks forgiveness for our faults, each word drives satan out.

(Bawa Muhaiyaddeen ☺ now gives explanations of some of the words that are recited in the out loud *dhikr*.)[1]

A 'ūdhu billāhi minash-shaitānir-rajīm. "O God, in the same way that You dispelled satan from heaven and from Yourself, please dispel him from us. Just as You banished him from that place, please banish him from us."

The second word is *Allāhu akbar.* "You are the Great One. You are the perfectly pure Great One. You are the Great One. I praise You, You are the Great One. *Allāhu akbar!* You are the Great One who controls and rules over all of the kingdoms. You are the Great One. We praise You."

The third word is *astaghfirullāhal-'aliyyal-'azīm.* "O God, please forgive the faults we have committed. Please forgive the faults we have committed earlier and the faults we are committing now. Please pardon all of the faults we have committed through our thoughts, the faults arising from our vision, and the faults we have committed in our lives because of karma." This is what we say, we ask forgiveness. There is one God, one point.

One by one, step by step…Step by step we must understand. So third, we must ask God to forgive our faults. Āndavanai: He is not the earth, not the fire, not the water, not the air. He is not a form or a shape. You are not asking these (to forgive you). He is not these. He is God. You are not asking the prophets or the *olis.* You are not asking the saints. You say: "O God, *astaghfirullāhal-'aliyyal-'azīm,* please forgive us." With each breath we ask God to forgive the sins

---

1 The out loud *dhikr* that is recited in the Mosque in Philadelphia, PA, is published in the booklet called *Morning* Dhikr *at the Mosque of Shaikh M. R. Bawa Muhaiyaddeen* ☺.

we have committed. We ask to be forgiven and to be made pure. Whom are we asking? We are asking God, Āndavan who has no form, or shape, or figure, the One who has nothing. We are asking the One who has no color, hue, race, religion, or scripture.

Next, the fourth, is the *SubhānAllāh Kalimah*. "O God, *subhān-Allāhi wal-hamdu lillāhi*. You are worthy of all praise and blessings. *SubhānAllāhi wal-hamdu lillāhi wa lā ilāha illAllāh*. You are One. For all of everything, You are the only One. Please cut away all of the darkness in our *qalbs*. Please cut away our torpor, anger, miserliness, envy, jealousy, and treachery, and grant us wisdom, grace, and Your *rahmah*. Please give us wisdom, grace, *rahmah,* and Your Light. Please perform *qurbān* on our *qalbs*. Please perform *qurbān* and cut away all of our thoughts."

Having sacrificed the *qalb* by performing *qurbān,* we surrender to Him. In order to establish a connection between God and us, all of the things within us that separate us from Him must be cut away. "Please perform this *qurbān* and make us pure." This is the fourth prayer that we recite.

Fifth, *subhānAllāh*. "From the time of creation, from the beginning, there is nothing equal to You. Without You nothing would exist. *SubhānAllāh*. You are the only One who can free us from all of the faults we have committed. *SubhānAllāh! SubhānAllāh! SubhānAllāh!* We praise You and beg You to cut away all of the four hundred trillion ten thousand spiritual prayers and spiritual gods. You exist within everything that has been created. Please cut away all of the evils within us and reestablish the original connection between You and us. *SubhānAllāh*." This is what we ask Him.

Sixth, *al-hamdu lillāh*. "We praise Your abundance and You. We praise Your grace and You."

There are countless meanings to these words, but I am telling you a very small point about the praise of Him. There are many meanings, but this is just a small point.

Seventh, *yā* Latīf. "You are the One who understands in a subtle way. You are the One who understands us in such a very subtle way. You have very sharp wisdom. You understand everything in such a

very sharp way, and dispel our faults. You are the One who understands our *qalbs*. You are the One who understands the many subtleties in our *qalbs,* who frees us, and who joins us with Your Light.
Yā Latīf, this is what You do."

Eighth, *yā* Kabīr. "You are eternally holding Your flag. Al-Kabīr.
Your resonance, Your sound, Your flag, and Your Power are in
Your hand. With that Power You rule over all lives. Your Power
protects each life and each body. *Coming, giving, gone, come, give.*
You give, give. You are the One who gives. You are the One who
tells us to go and You are the One who calls us back. You are the
One who gives. *Yā* Kabīr. You tell us to go and later call us back.
You give us Your grace, You give us Your qualities and grace. God.
Is this a mantra? This is His glory, His kingdom, and His Power,
God. This is not like the mantras of *ayum, kiliyum, savum, ahm, eem,
oom, eee.*"

Ninth, *yā* Karīm. "You are the One who appears without
appearance, the One who understands without understanding. *Yā*
Karīm, You understand. You realize the taste in every soul. Within
every soul, You appear without appearance. You realize and understand every taste, You understand every breath, You know every
conversation, You know the *qalb* of everyone. Will You not protect
me, O God? *Yā* Karīm, will You not embrace me? Will You not
pardon my faults? O God, take me back into Your kingdom, Your
pure kingdom, into Your paradise! I came from You; the soul, the
Light came from You, You alone! Please accept that Light back into
You again. I separated from You, I divided away from You. Please
accept me back into You again. O Protector, please accept me. This
is what we ask, *Yā* Karīm."

Tenth, *yā* Rahīm, the Creator, the Protector, the Sustainer.
"Everything came from You. You are the One who gives food, who
created me, who gives me nourishment, and who protects and cares
for me. May You protect me completely. You gave me hunger, disease, aging, and the world, all of these. You gave the body. I seek
nourishment for my soul from You. I seek life from You. I seek to
give the responsibility of my true *qalb* to You. I seek to surrender to

You and to do duty to You. O Rahīm, please accept me." You must ask this. You must beg for this.

Eleventh, yā Rahmān. "There is no place where You are not. No life exists without You, nothing exists without You. Everything that You create moves. You give rizq, food, to every moving thing. Whether it is in the seas, in the hills, in the earth, in the sky, in the sun, in the moon, in the stars, or whether it is in the stones, the gems, the trees, the bushes, or the flowers, You give movement and food to all of them. You apportion this and give nourishment to them. You make them move. You give water and food to the trees. You are the Rahmān for every moving creation. No matter what they do, You do Your duty. O Rahmān, You are the Protector. You are the Rahmān who makes them move. You are known as ar-Rahmān. You treat all lives as Your own life. You treat the hunger of others as Your own hunger. You treat all of the sorrows of others as Your own sorrow. You treat all lives as Your own life. You treat all of the happiness of others as Your own happiness. O Rahmān, You give water and food to even the frog that lies under the stone. You give food to the white ants that are hidden in the earth. You protect and provide for the eggs and embryos that are hidden in the coral in the ocean. You provide for the stars and the lights that are hidden in the sky. You provide for them. You give nourishment that is essential for the sun and the moon. You provide for the snakes that live in holes.

"O Rahmān, You encompass the eight directions and the sixteen corners. You give food to the lives that are hidden and to the lives that are not hidden. You give food to those who remember You and to those who do not. What is the quality of Your protection? What is that protection? May You grant us that protection! O Rahmān, please give us that beauty, that quality, and that wisdom. We ask You to give us this state."

Is this a mantra?

QUESTION

What I do not understand is that if I just say these names without understanding it, then that will just be what I did before.

BAWA MUHAIYADDEEN

You must ask that from a Father, and learn. If you ask him and learn, you will not have doubt, suspicion, and anger, these will not come. All of these are explanations. If you do not understand them, you cannot reach the end. The end will be dead.

If you start from the beginning, it will be easy. But without understanding, if you speak (with doubt, suspicion, and anger), quarrels will arise. *Up, down.* If you understand and then discard these doubts, and if you start from the beginning, it will be easy. If you do not understand and if you think that you can reach the end, it will not happen. I have tried for the last eleven years to bring you all to a state of understanding, but you have not reached that state; only a few have reached that state. Only a few are beginning to understand.

You must first understand. If you reach that state, it will be good. Otherwise, this will not happen. You will be like those in the seventy-two groups, *jahannām's* group, the group that belongs to hell. If you do not understand, you will not surrender to the One. If you understand, you will surrender to the one point, but if you do not understand, you will surrender to one hundred and five million births. How can those one hundred and five million births not come?

God is One who has no appearance, no form, no color, no hue, no race, no religion, no *vēdas,* scriptures, and no *vēdāntas,* philosophies. He is without differences. He is beyond divisions and separations. He is plenitude. Because He is complete, He has the state where He sees all of His creations in the same way. He is ar-Rahmān. He is that quality. He looks at the snake, the gecko, the fish, the dog, and the fox equally, and He gives them the food they need, and protects them. That is His work. Equality, peace, and tranquility are His work. When that state comes to us, when we reach the state of self-knowledge, we will know that state. Without that understanding, there will be "this person is different, that person is different; my race, your race; my religion, your religion; my scripture, your scripture; I am great, you are great." We can only reach that state if we understand God's state and His duties. Then that state will come, and we will understand it. That is surrender to God. The state that is like that is surrender to God.

Very well. There are one hundred and five million births, reincarnations. What is reincarnation? A human being has only this one birth, the birth where there is the connection between man and God. If you miss this birth and are reincarnated, it is *no good.* You will not be able to make the connection with God. God is a Power and man is a ray of that Power. This is the time when the two points, the ray and that Power, must unite and the switch must be turned on. That ray and that Light—that Power which is the motor and the ray—must be drawn together like a magnet. This is the human life, the Light-form life. This is when there is wisdom. If this human-life is lost, then it is water-life. There are six kinds of lives: there is the human life, which is the soul, and the other five kinds of lives. If we miss this birth, the human life will be lost. It will change. It will not be drawn to the magnet, and the form of a *hayawān,* an animal, will come. The human form will have the wisdom of animals and the energy of animals. It will have the energy of the snakes, the energy of the animals and reptiles, and the energy of the five kinds of lives. Man's soul will be lost, that wisdom and that Light-power will leave.

So, we have to search for this, we must search for the connection that exists between God and us, the one point.

Shari, there are one hundred and five million births, reincarnations. The Buddhists say they want to be reincarnated, the Hindus say they want to be reincarnated, and people in certain other religions also say they want to be reincarnated. But the *gnānis* and *sittars* of the Hindu religion say, "If we miss this birth, we do not know what our next birth will be." One who has realized the truth, a wise man, says this. He says, "If I miss this birth, what birth will I get? My birth will be ruined. Please give me the wisdom to make the connection with God in *this* birth." This is the birth that has wisdom, and if you miss this, you will not get another chance. Reincarnation is *nothing,* it is *no good,* it is the birth of the *hayawāns,* the animals, the snakes, the worms, the insects, the trees, the bushes, the grass, and the weeds. What kind of birth will that be!

God is the One who is not born and who does not die, the One who is unchanging and who does not forget us. That is how that Power is. God has so many meanings. He is always natural. He is the One who exists forever. He is God, a Power. He controls everything. He controls all of the shaktis, the energies, the souls, and the spirits. That is God, a Power. That is what is known as God, a Power. He is a natural Power that exists eternally. That is God. Allāh, God, Kadavul, ar-Rahmān, ar-Rahīm, al-Karīm—He is a Power.

That Power always exists. If you surrender to That, if you are in unity with That and are surrendered to It, if you are pulled to that magnet, then you will become That. It has no death or birth and you will have no death or birth. You will have no birth. That exists forever and you will be joined eternally with It. There is nothing opposite to That. It exists forever. It has no birth or death. Therefore, since you have surrendered to That, you will become That, and you will exist forever. That has no birth and you have no birth. That is complete and you are complete. That is plenitude and you are plenitude. That is peace and you are peace. You will have attained that state.

Very well, let us say that you have *not* surrendered to That. A snake has a form. If you take the qualities and form of a snake, what will it be like? The snake has poisonous qualities, those are the qualities that come out from a snake. If you say to the snake, "My god, I accept you and surrender to you," then what will it give you? It will give you its poison. What else will it give? It will give you its form. If someone beats it with a stick, it will die. So, now you are a snake. You are reincarnated.

If you surrender to a dog, if you surrender to the dog of desire and if you pray to and embrace that dog, what will it give you? It licks and licks the *dunyā—lalalalalala*. It licks feces. It gives that form. So, you are born as a dog. If you surrender to a cow, what will happen? It will give you its qualities of pulling a cart. If you surrender to a horse, if you surrender to a tiger, if you surrender to a peacock, if you surrender to an eagle, if you surrender to a vulture, each one will give you its form, the qualities that it possesses. If you surrender to a pig, it will give you its quality. If you surrender to a lion, it will give you what it possesses. If you surrender to an elephant, it will give you that form, that quality. If you surrender to a fish, it will give you the quality it possesses. If you surrender to a crow, it will give you that blackness, that quality.

Whatever form you surrender to, that is the form and the quality you will be given. If you surrender to maya, it will give you that. If you surrender to a demon, it will give you that. If you surrender to satan, it will give you that quality and that form. If you surrender to the earth, it will give you the quality of the earth. If you surrender to a vampire, it will give you the quality and form of the vampire, you will drink blood. If you surrender to the monkey mind, it will give you the form and the qualities of a monkey, that is what it will give.

Like this, if you surrender to every form and every quality you have fashioned, that will be the form and the quality you will be given. That is rebirth. Does God give you this? No, God does not give you this. He does not give you this birth. You yourself take this birth. This birth becomes the form that you take. You surrender to that form and those qualities. You take the quality and form of what you surrender to. Whatever quality and essence exists within the outer form that you surrender to becomes your form. That is reincarnation, it is the one hundred and five million births.

Who is the one who fashions this form? Who is the one who surrenders? Who is the one who takes this birth? Man himself. So, according to this form, God says, "*Shari, po!*—all right, go! Go and experience that." You yourself fashion that quality and form. You take on that form and surrender to it. These forms that are made into statues and kept in the temples are the forms that you surrender to and take on. You take that birth. You recite mantras and surrender to the snake, the rat, the cat, the dog, the fox, and the wolf. That is not God's fault. You yourself have taken that birth, and you surrender to that birth. These are the one hundred and five million births. This is karma. You surrender to the karma of their qualities and their forms. This is karma, it is arrogance, karma, and maya. These are the forms, the births that we take.

But God is not like that. God is One who has no death and no birth. He exists forever. If you surrender to Him and if you take on His qualities, you will take His form, that Light-form, the Light-form of plenitude. Once you surrender to Him and take *that* form, you will be free. You will have no further births. *Reincarnation nothing!* If you take on His qualities, there will be no reincarnation. *Shari,* all right.

Twelfth, *yā* Rabb. "You are the One who creates. You know me. You are the One who created me. *Yā* Rabb, You are the One who created me and You know what You have kept within me. Earth, water, fire, air, ether, mind, and desire are within me. The monkey of the mind and the dog of desire, arrogance, karma, and maya are there, connected to the earth. Everything is within me. *Yā* Rabb, do You not understand me? You have created me like this. Please remove all of this so that only You remain. *Yā* Rabb, You alone must live within me. *Yā* Rabb, *yā* Rabb, *yā* Rabb, please remove all of this and give me that connection where You and I live together. That is my food, that is my life, that is my intention, that is my prayer. *Yā* Rabb, please do this."

Thirteenth, *yā* Sabūr. "No matter how many faults we commit, may You forgive them. Every creation commits faults. All of Your creations make mistakes. I have forgotten You and say, 'I, I, mine, mine, my race, my religion, I, I, I am a king, I am a minister, I am a learned man, I have studied, I am the one who knows, I am a saint, I am a *nabī,* I rule over this world, the heavenly world, and all of the worlds.' Satan speaks like this. Yet, no matter what he says, You, O God, are the One who has *sabūr. Yā* Sabūr, *yā* Sabūr. You have so much *sabūr* that You even give food to satan. You even protect the one who is evil and do duty to him. You do not ridicule him or discard him, You do not show differences to him and You do not hurt him. You even give food to all the created poisonous trees, You give food to a poisonous thing and You protect it with *sabūr.* Therefore, *yā* Sabūr, please give me that quality. Please give me Your *sabūr.*

"*Yā* Sabūr, *yā* Sabūr, *yā* Sabūr, I humbly ask You to give me that. (Bawa Muhaiyaddeen ☻ sings) *Yā* Sabūr, *yā* Sabūr. (Bawa Muhaiyaddeen ☻ speaks) I am asking You to please forgive me. (singing) *Yā* Sabūr, *yā* Sabūr." (speaking) Please grant me that. May I have peace so that I can give peace to those who commit sins. Please give that to me."

You must beg Him for this. You must weep and ask this. The *qalb,* the innermost heart, must cry. Tears do not need to come from the eyes, but tears must come from the *qalb.* It must melt. This is not a mantra. The *qalb* must melt. (singing) "*Yā* Sabūr, *yā* Sabūr, *yā* Sabūr, *yā* Sabūr."

You must beg for forgiveness. "Please give me this quality of *sabūr.*"

Fourteenth, *yā* Quddūs. "Before we even think of it, You can burn everything to ashes. Even before we intend it, You can lift us up. You can give us wisdom, ability, *gnānam,* and light even before we intend it. You can do this even before we think of it. Whatever needs to be done is in Your hands. (singing) *Yā* Quddūs, *yā* Quddūs, *yā* Quddūs, *yā* Quddūs. (speaking) You give grace to those whom You intend. You give grace, You give wisdom, and You give *gnānam.* You are the One who understands everything. As this is so, do You not know my sorrow? Please give me that wisdom, that light, that plenitude, and that *'ilm,* and help me. Please correct our faults and help us."

This is what we ask when we praise Him. We are reciting these words to the one God. All these are His prayer. At every stage, step by step, we are asking Him to grant us this.

Fifteenth. (singing) "*Yā* Haqq, *yā* Haqq. (speaking) Truth. There is nothing else. You are the One and only One. *Yā* Haqq. You are the Truth, You are the Truth, You are the Truth, You, indeed, are the Truth. You are the Truth, al-Haqq — Truth. You are my treasure. That Truth is my treasure. You are the Truth. That Truth is my *haqq.* You are my wealth. That Truth is my wealth! That Truth is my wealth! That Truth is my wealth! That Truth is my wealth! Make my *qalb* into that wealth, the wealth of *'ilm.*"

This is how each of these words are. Point by point, they have been explained. This is not a mantra. When we understand all of this, when we acquire these qualities and finally disappear, then — *nothing!* "I am not. You are God, *illAllāh.*" In the end, we reach this section, having cut away everything else.

We must go before God in the same way that we go before a mirror. We must sit in front of Him and correct our faults. We must cut away and destroy our bad qualities. When we go in front of a mirror, we will see our form and we will be able to cut away and remove our flaws. You must cut away and remove everything in your form. If you go in front of a mirror, you will see yourself. If you see yourself, then you will be able to cut away your faults. You will see yourself in the mirror. In this state of prayer, by going before God, you can cut away each of your faults. You can cut away every quality. You can cut and cut every action, correct yourself, and surrender to Him. This is what you must do.

This is not the only thing. There is so much more. There are so many more explanations. If you cut away these things — *shari,* good. If you do not cut them away, then — *poitch,* finished! Then of what use are you? If you cut these away one by one as I am telling you to, then you will become the mirror. The mirror will be within you. You will see everything, and all those who look at you will also be able to see themselves and correct themselves. If the mirror is present, you can correct yourself and clear yourself. In this way, you can know yourself.

You must not make decisions hastily. You must understand; you must understand each thing. If you go to a university to study, and if you go *up* and *down,* how can you learn? You will have difficulty and loss. You must think hard, reflect, analyze, and investigate all of the subtle things that are there.

If you take on the brain of a flea, everything will go wrong. You must take on the qualities of God and His wisdom, and then look. Then it will be correct. This is enough for now. Come here and ask for what you need. If you do not understand something, come and ask me. When I am speaking here and you have a question, you must come and ask me. You must try to understand and learn. Sometimes you are sleeping, other times…

Now, you have come to Ceylon. You came here three weeks ago. You came at that time to see your Father, to look for wisdom. So, when you look, whatever it is that you look at: in your wisdom you must see the heart, in your love you must see the heart, and in your faith you must see the heart. With love, faith, and wisdom, you must see the Father's unity. If you look in this way, you will have peace, abundant peace. With that love, you will have peace.

But, if you come here and look only at this house and at Sri Lanka, there will be difficulties. That is not tranquility, that is difficulty. That is not peace. When you come here, your work is this *toluhai;* that is your heart-work. If you do not join that prayer, you will not understand. If you look at the house, at the wind, at the waves, and at Sri Lanka...

So, you have come to your Father. You need peace. If you want to attain what is peaceful, you must first have peace. If not, if you think that you can attain peace tomorrow, or in two days, that will not happen.

In order to have the beauty of the heart and the face, you must be like a baby who has affection, wisdom, and love. You must not become like an old man. You must not take on that section; you must not let your skin become shriveled and your face become dark. Your heart and your face must always be beautiful. That will be good. That beauty must remain like that always.

Every child should be like this. You should not become like an old person. Your face should be bright, it should not be dark. You should make your heart into the pure kingdom of God, not into the kingdom of hell. Have faith in God. Have faith in the truth. Have faith in the wisdom of the truth. Become complete in God's qualities. Then you can receive the benefit from that. You will attain that youth, that beauty, that truth, that light, and the plenitude of His qualities, the qualities of grace. Have faith in that. Every child must believe in this. We must attain our freedom. Never believe in the happiness and the sadness of this world, or in the speech and chatter of this world.

There is a certain kind of *tarāsu,* weighing scale, in the supermarket. Whatever you want to buy for the five elements is weighed on that scale, and then you are given that weight. Whether you want a liter or a pound, it must be weighed on that scale. But if you want to buy something for the soul, the scale is here (Bawa Muhaiyaddeen ☺ points to the heart). Faith and truth, it is on this scale that this treasure must be weighed. The food for the truth, the soul, life, wisdom, *gnā-nam*, and the light must be bought from God, and must be weighed on this scale.

So, there are these two scales. One kind of food you must buy from God. The rest you must buy from the supermarkets, from the shops that are here and there. If your heart is clear, you can buy what you need from God and weigh it on this scale of faith. You must establish that. Each child must establish that.

Hastiness is the enemy of wisdom. Impatience eats up wisdom. Anger is the guru of sin. Lust is greater than the ocean, maya is greater than the ocean. Duty is greater than the beauty of God—the beauty of His quality is greater. That beauty, that duty is God's quality, an exalted quality. God will become enamored with that. The karma of one who does not deliberate and reflect carefully on what he sets out to do will lead to the agony of a living death. His life will not leave, he will not be able to die. If we do not think, consider, analyze, reflect deeply, and understand, that will be our suffering. The karma of one who does not investigate and reflect deeply on what he sets out to do will lead to a living death. He will not die. His life will not leave him. It will be pulled between his throat and his chest, *aggh, aggh, aggh.* This is the suffering.

That is not good. You need to think about this. Time is passing. Are you not listening? Did you listen? This morning I was speaking with a German man. He has studied a great deal about everything and he had many questions. But with one word he understood this wisdom. He understood everything. In a short time he was able to understand everything, all the explanations.

You must listen carefully to what comes from a subtle Father. That is the best way. Try to learn and understand what is coming from him. In this way, each one of you must think about this. If you think like this, it will be good.

A'ūdhu billāhi minash-shaitānir-rajīm.
I seek refuge in God from the accursed satan.

Bismillāhir-Rahmānir-Rahīm.
In the name of God, the Most Compassionate,
the Most Merciful.

Song: The Sun Has Dawned

April 27, 1975, Sunday, 5:45 a.m.

O Treasure that I too must become,
 O Treasure of Wisdom, O Treasure of *ādi* and *anādi*
that rises as *Ādavan,* the Sun, throughout the universe,
that rises as the Sun, establishing bliss throughout the universe,
that rises as the Sun, establishing bliss,
establishing bliss throughout the world,
that rises as the Sun throughout the world,
that rises as the Sun throughout the world,
that rises as the Sun throughout the world, establishing bliss.
O Wisdom, O Bliss, you must come to us!
O Wisdom, O Bliss, you must come to us, O Bliss, O Sun!

The Sun has dawned and risen in the darkness.
O ye beloved, O ye faithful, O ye true friends,
please come to praise the Original Great Light.
The Sun has dawned!

O ye beloved, O ye true friends, O ye faithful,
God, *Ādavan,* has risen!
O ye beloved, O ye faithful, O ye true friends,

please come, search for the Grace of God.
Praise Him, O ye faithful, come here.

The Sun has dawned!
The peacocks will dance, the cuckoos will sing,
all the flowers will open with joy, look!
The fish will leap, the frogs will jump,
the fish will leap, the frogs will jump,
the crabs will swim.
The birds will dance, all the winged creatures will sing songs,
the peacocks and the cuckoos will come to play,
the peacocks and the cuckoos will come to play.
They will all come to gather there.
The Grace of God will be there.

Their happiness will be radiant with light,
dawning to resplend in the morning.
There will be well-being and flowing water,
coolness, wakefulness, and happiness,
coolness, wakefulness, and happiness.
There will be well-being and flowing water.
That will grant well-being,
that will bring well-being.
The bliss will be here.

The doe and the elk, the doe and the elk,
the doves and all the birds have come to gather together
to sing at the feet of God,
and to dance the appropriate steps in the appropriate order.
Stand and look at them at this time.

The Sun has risen!
All the living beings will play there.

The Sun has risen, the Sun has risen.
Rise up out of the darkness, come, O ye beloved!
Arise out of this birth, come, O ye beloved!
Search for the Grace of God, O ye faithful!

One, two, three, four—by four the Sun has risen.
O ye beloved, O ye true friends,
the birds and the winged creatures,
all the animals that live in the pond,
the *hayawāns* that live in the jungle,
the fish, the crabs, the frogs, all of them,
the worms and the insects have all gathered together.
The flowers and the insects have all gathered together.
They are dancing, singing, playing, and searching for God.

The Sun has risen!
Arise out of birth, come, O ye true friends.
O ye faithful, O ye beloved, search for the Grace of Ādi.
This is how bliss will become radiant in our lives.
This is how bliss will become radiant in our lives.
Wisdom itself will become the Sun.
That itself will become the Sun.
Wisdom itself will become the Sun.
That itself will become the Sun.
It will become the Grace of God.
It will become Wisdom.

In the life of our birth, in the darkness of the life of our birth,
in the life of the body made of five elements,
the actions, the mind, the desire, and
the *nafs* exist in the darkness that is our life.
This life must dawn.
The shining Wisdom must resplend.

That state will exist as *Ādavan.*
That itself will resonate as the Sun.
That will resplend as the Grace of God itself.
This birth must be changed.
It is for this that the darkness must be destroyed,
Wisdom must be made to dawn, and
the darkness of ignorance must be dispelled.

If you regard this state as a great one,
the Wisdom that shines will resplend as the Sun and
illuminate the microcosm and the macrocosm,
and through that, we will regard our lives with sheer happiness.
Truth will shine everywhere in the world.
In God's creation, all the creations,
the trees, the vines, the bushes, will praise God.
They will search for God while the birds sing songs of bliss.
All the creations will pray to Him.
They will search for Him on the exalted path.
All His creations throughout all the lands
will bow down and worship Him with goodness.

You must understand this state, this state.
You must make the Wisdom known as the Sun resplend as bliss.
You must understand this state.
The Wisdom, the shining Sun known as *Ādavan,*
must resplend for you.
The fish, crabs, frogs, and crocodiles
living in the sea of maya must all be illumined.

The *nafs,* desire, hypnotic delusion,
lechery, malice, greed, lewdness, fanaticism, envy,
intoxicants, lust, theft, murder, and falsehood
will live in that dark sea.

These fourteen will comprise the dark world there.
The three turds that are the arrogance, karma, and maya
in life will become the body of shaitān.
These seventeen comprise this state.

If you are there, you will know, and
when you understand with Wisdom,
you will see this explanation.
Wisdom itself will become *Ādavan,* the Sun.
That Grace, that Light, that Wisdom will become the Sun.
That Light, that Completion will become the Sun.
That Treasure, that Grace will become God.

If we see this Wonder in the world,
if Wisdom shines for us in this world,
we will see God's creation,
the dancing, the singing,
the happiness, the sadness,
the grief, the joy, the sorrow,
the death, the birth.
We will see it all.
With Wisdom, we will see it all.

Understand, be aware, and see.
Search for the way to make the Sun rise in your life.
Make the intention to drive out the darkness.
Search for the Light of Wisdom known as *Ādavan,*
the Sun, that illumines both worlds.
That will become the Sun.
That will become the Completion in our lives.
That will become our rightful Treasure.
That will become the state in which we worship only One.

Know this, O children.
Understand this loving Treasure, O children.
The happiness of the world,
the sadness of life,
happiness and sadness, death and birth will come in life.
You will see it all.
When the Sun shines, all of it will appear.
Understand this, complete this,
understand this Treasure!

You must pray to God.
You need to know, understand, and sing of this.
When Wisdom becomes resplendent,
the darkness will be dispelled
and all of His creations will be known and understood.
That is bliss.
Everything will be clear.

Search for Wisdom in this state!
Sing the Grace of God itself!
See One in the Truth!
Search for the Treasure that is the One who exists as His grace.
Anbu.

A'ūdhu billāhi minash-shaitānir-rajīm.
I seek refuge in God from the accursed satan.

Bismillāhir-Rahmānir-Rahīm.
In the name of God, the Most Compassionate,
the Most Merciful.

EXPLANATION OF THE SONG: THE SUN HAS DAWNED

April 27, 1975, Sunday, a.m., after the song

The *ādavan* has risen. *Ādavan* means sun. It has now dawned. The sun dawns at four o'clock. All of the birds, the winged creatures, the flowers, and the crabs come. All of the flowers open, and all of the birds and the winged creatures come to dance in bliss. They are happy and they sing, *kee, vy, veee*.

This is only a small explanation. You should get the song and translate it. What I am giving you now is only a few words about this. If it is not complete, it will not be right. The section should be fully completed. That is the point. We can give a small explanation now, but later we should translate the entire song.

This is how the sun rises. *Ādavan* means sun. When it rises in the morning all of the birds, the flowers, the winged creatures, the crabs, and the fish arise in happiness. The birds sing happily, the peacocks dance, the cuckoos sing. They are happy. The moment the sun rises at four o'clock in the morning, this starts. The flowers open. The white flowers open and the fragrance comes into them at four o'clock or three o'clock. They are very happy at that time. They sing, all of the flowers sing.

They are singing, all of the birds are singing. The crabs and the fish are singing, *keeee;* they sing their melodies. A sound comes from the water. A sound comes from all of the leaves and from all of the lotus flowers, *sshhh*. When the rays of light from the sun known

157

as *ādavan* touch the trees—the moment they arise, they are joyful. They say, "Ah! The time has come for us," and they feel happy.

(All of the beings) go where they need to go to get their own food. They have to go to work, they have to find their food. They get up and they begin to do this, happily. All of them have to go to various places on their journeys.

Ādavan has risen. *Mādargal,* you too should come out of the darkness. Children, you too should come. The sun has risen.

TRANSLATOR

Mādargal means females.

BAWA MUHAIYADDEEN

No, *mādargal* means everyone. Everyone is female. Only God is male, all the rest of us are female. We are all in love, God-love. We are enamored with Him. Therefore, the birds, the winged creatures pray to God at this time. They are happy, they have come. But you, O people, you have not come. All of creation has come and is experiencing bliss, but you are sleeping!

Come. Your life is still dark. Earth, fire, water, air, ether, your body, and maya are all in darkness. Leave these and come! You can reach God, you can be happy. Make that Sun rise! Make that Sun rise! That is Wisdom. Come, make that Wisdom dawn. We can go to God. That is the Sun, Wisdom is the Sun. All (of the other beings) are happy, only you are in the darkness. Come, Wisdom is dawning. Come quickly. Praise God. Pray. Search for your rightful places.

This is what is said in this song. At dawn, you can see all the worlds, all of God's creation. When the dawn arrives, you can see everything. You will be able to look at everything, you will be able to see everything. You will be able to see all of the joy and sorrow, the destruction and the creation through the Wisdom that dawns as *Ādavan.* Come!

This was a good song this morning. It has a lot of meaning. It is like a song. It has a lot of meaning. For someone's life, for his dark life, *Ādavan* means Light, Wisdom. That must dawn. Only then will his life dawn. Otherwise, it will be dark. Without that, there will only be darkness. He will never experience happiness nor will he see the happiness of God's creation. Yes, this is how it is. It is a good song.

ESCAPING FROM SATAN AT FOUR A.M.

August 15, 1975, Friday, 10:05 a.m.

QUESTION
For the past three nights, the past three mornings, I have been waking up at five o'clock. And then this morning I woke up because I had a dream, I woke up at about four o'clock. When I wake up I feel like I should be getting up, I just feel awake. I wanted to ask you about that and I also want to ask you about the dream.

TRANSLATOR
You want to ask about the fact that you wake up early morning at four o'clock? Is that unusual for you?

QUESTIONER
Yes, it is.

TTRANSLATOR
What time do you normally wake up?

QUESTIONER
Oh, seven-thirty, eight o'clock.

BAWA MUHAIYADDEEN
For so many days satan has had a hold over you, but when you woke up at four o'clock, satan left you.

When you wake up at four a.m., you should pray to God, you should think of Him. You should wash and clear yourself, and then

161

you should pray to God. Then satan will leave you. At four a.m., when everyone is asleep, mūdevi[1] and satan do their work, they enter everyone at that time. So, those who have wisdom, those who have the remembrance of God will wake up and get out of bed right away. They will wake up, and immediately do their duty; they will pray to God.

Now, three-quarters of the people wake up, but a few people in satan's section remain asleep. As soon as someone wakes up, there is no place for satan. Satan runs around. There is no place for mūdevi either. She also runs around. They both run here, there, and every-where, looking around. They keep running and searching for people like you who sleep until seven o'clock. Some of you get up, go to urinate, and then return to bed. You pull your blankets over your-selves and get warm. *"Oooh, oooh, oooh, oooh!"* Then, satan embraces you and says, "Now you belong to me! Everything is finished! Ha, ha! You belong to me!" He holds you down under the blankets. Mūdevi and satan hold you down. If they have caught you, you will not know whether or not it is dawn. You will not have brushed your teeth, you will not have washed your face, you will not even have gone to the bathroom. When you finally wake up and open your eyes, you still cannot get up because satan is embracing you. So, you are unable to get out of bed. Even if you need to go to the bathroom you will put it off until later, because he is holding you down. *"Oooh, oooh, oooh, oooooh!"* When satan and mūdevi catch hold of you it is difficult to get free from them. Some people keep lying in bed, long after daybreak, and when they finally wake up, they ask, "Is it dawn yet?"

After eight o'clock, satan and mūdevi have other people to deal with. They leave these lazy people and go to other places where peo-ple are still sleeping at four or five in the morning. They go there and

---

1   mūdevi (T) The Hindu goddess of misfortune and suffering. She resides in all places that are unclean and represents falsehood, darkness, and what is wrong. For more about mūdevi and her sister, sīdevi, see *Questions of Life — Answers of Wisdom, Volume Two,* pages 6-7.

embrace them. They have work there, so they go. Satan is happy to go and catch hold of those people who are asleep. He has continuous work. He knows that if he goes to a certain place at a certain time he can catch some people, so, when he has finished dealing with one place, he goes somewhere else.

When you get up late, you will have pain here and pain there, because mūdēvi has held you down. You will say, "*Aiyō,* I have pain here, I have pain there!" There will be no light in your face. You will want to go back to sleep, but when you lie down you will be unable to fall asleep. Why? Because even though mūdēvi and satan have left you to go to other people, your monkey (mind) now starts its work with you. The monkey and maya are now working. "*Aiyō,* I can't fall asleep! *Aiyō,* sleep is not coming!" You will toss here, and turn there. That monkey and the desire will roll your body from side to side. Both of them will roll your body about.

Then the next day, at three a.m., satan will return. He will catch you and hold you down, and you will once again stay in bed.

Like this, without letting satan catch hold of you, get up at four a.m. Then satan will not embrace you. It is like this for many people. When you sleep in the daytime, mūdēvi and satan catch you. In the night, the monkey of the mind, desire, and maya catch you and roll you around, and at three a.m., satan comes and catches you.

Therefore, without getting caught by this mūdēvi, get up. Remember God. Wash your hands and feet. Do your duty. Think of God. That will be good.

For many days you did not come here. You went to many other places and satan was with you, holding you down. But since you have been coming here, satan is losing his grip on you, little by little.

To reflect on God at this time is good. To remember God and to pray to Him is good. That will be beneficial.

Do you understand? That will be good.

A'ūdhu billāhi minash-shaitānir-rajīm.
I seek refuge in God from the accursed satan.

Bismillāhir-Rahmānir-Rahīm.
In the name of God, the Most Compassionate,
the Most Merciful.

ALL ABOUT PRAYER

August 15, 1981, Saturday, 5:50 a.m.

A *'ūdhu billāhi minash-shaitānir-rajīm. Bismillāhir-Rahmānir-Rahīm.* Children, I need to speak to you today about a few things. In this time period, in this country, I have been speaking to my children about Allāh, about prayer, and about *gnānam*. I have been giving my children explanations about *toluhai, 'ibādah, vanakkam,* and *gnānam,* five-times prayer, service to God, worship, and divine wisdom. I have been giving them explanations about the section of wisdom.

For many years I have been explaining in many different ways. For eighty or ninety years I have been teaching this in the world. With the exception of the time when I was alone, I have been teaching about prayer and about the connection between man and God.

I have been explaining many different things, in many different ways, so that they can know and understand. I have been teaching, so that they can find peace and serenity, so that their *qalbs* can find tranquility, so that they can understand the connection between God and man, and so that they can understand what belongs to God and what belongs to man. I have been teaching them many different types of prayers so that they can learn this.

In the world, there are many religions, many colors, many races, many languages, many gods, and many prayers. Like this, there are many prayers that are done in many different ways. There are many churches, many temples, many mosques, and many shrines, and according to the different customs, the methods of the prayers will vary.

But, there is only one race, one family, one prayer, one lineage, one God, one truth, and one point. This is the true learning and explanation. This explanation must be understood with wisdom, and it is through this learning that the *qalb* can find peace, foster tranquility, discover the connection with God, and pray to Him.

This one prayer must grow within our hearts. The qualities and actions of this prayer are different from those of other prayers. This is beyond the *vēdas,* the scriptures, and the *vēdāntas,* the philosophies, it is beyond race, religion, and differences, it is beyond *unarvu,* feeling, *unarchi,* awareness, and *putti,* intellect—it is far, far beyond intellect. When we do this prayer, we must cut away the diseases that kill us, the diseases that separate us, the diseases that transform us, and the actions that change the connection between God and us. We have to change all of these. We have to change these diseases that are changing us: race, fanaticism, religions, divisiveness, scriptures, philosophies, magics, miracles, praise, honor, pride, slander, saying one thing on the outside and keeping another within, the differences of "I and you," "mine and yours," "I am great and you are inferior," "my religion and your religion." We must change these diseases and find unity. It is only in this way that we will be able to find unity and tranquility. It is within that tranquility that we can find peace, within that peace that we can find serenity, and within that serenity that we can make the connection to God.

When we make the connection to God, our pure heart, pure wisdom, pure soul, and pure prayer will merge with God who is Purity. This one prayer is the prayer that connects us with God. Earlier, we taught this prayer to many people. I taught them *lā ilāha illAllāh.* It is a short prayer. This is the prayer where you realize the connection between the soul, God, and man.

The (first) meaning is: *Lā ilāha,* there is no God other than You. There is no other God.

The next meaning is: *IllAllāh,* You are Allāh. You! Nothing! I am not! There is no other God, there is nothing else. You are the only One, God. That is the meaning.

Some people might say, "*Lā ilāha*, there is no God." Then they say, "God, You are God. *IllAllāh*, You are God." They think that the meaning is that there is no God. But then they say, "You are God." If there is no God, how can God be there? Some say that this is the meaning, but it is not the meaning.

When you say *lā ilāha*, it does not mean that there is no God. The meaning of that *dhikr*, that word, is that there is nothing other than You (God). That word means that nothing else is like You, not I nor any other creation. There is no equal or comparison to You, there is nothing equal to Your Power. In all creation there is nothing comparable to You. Whether it is in the sun, the moon, the earth, the sky, the gods, the *nabīs*, the *olis,* or in anything else, there is no Power like You. You alone are God. There is none other than You. You have no companion or helper, no birth or death, and no beginning or end. Whether it is in the religions, the *vēdas,* the *vēdāntas,* the 124,000 prophets, the lights, the resplendences, the powers, the researches, the false wisdom, ignorant wisdom, scientific wisdom, true wisdom, or in the seven different wisdoms, there is nothing that is equal to Your Power, Your wisdom, actions, qualities, behavior, patience, peacefulness, tranquility, justice, integrity, conscience, good conduct, or compassion. Nothing can compare to You. No one can dispense judgment like You. In worship and in prayer nothing is equal to You, nothing is comparable to You. There is nothing other than You.

You alone are that Power, the One without birth or death, the One without wife or children, the One without property or possessions, the One without comfort, the One without selfishness or self-business, the One without differences of race or religion, the One without attachments, the One without lust, the One who has no anger, arrogance, karma, and maya, the One without any likeness, and the One without any helper. You stand alone, conducting everything. You are a Power, the Power that controls all power. You are beyond everything that is created. You are God. Nothing is equal to You. That is the meaning.

When that word, that *dhikr*, is recited, you should understand this explanation in your heart. When you have understood that *dhikr,* you will understand this meaning. The breath should say this. When wisdom speaks, it should say, "There is no other God. You alone are God, Allāh." This is what should come forth when you speak and this is what should be written when you write. This is the meaning.

Saying that *lā ilāha* means "There is no God," and that *illAllāh* means "You are God" is not the meaning. You should understand this. We have been explaining this for a long time. We need to give you certain explanations about this, so that you can understand. If you understand this meaning and put it into practice, then each of your 43,242 breaths will do *sajdah* and *rukū',* each breath will prostrate and bow down to Allāh.

In the same way that each breath moves in your body, this prayer should also move. The connection to God, along with the words, should move in and out with the breath. The speech and the words should be merged with you. Then you will understand the eighteen thousand universes, you will understand all of the creations. You will know all of these creations, you will understand the meanings within them, and you will be victorious over them. This is the one prayer, one family, and one God. It is Light.

Children, precious jeweled lights of my eye, here in this country of Serendib, in many other countries, and on the continent of America, I have been speaking about this wealth so that you can understand and be victorious. I have been showing you the short way to wisdom, I have been showing you this short prayer. Some of you have openly accepted this path. Some of you are trying, you are making an effort to accept this and put it into practice. You are making the effort to understand that section of wisdom, that peace, that tranquility, that one family, that one God. Using that wisdom, some of you have set out to find the section of peace.

But some of you are nurturing the section that is separating you from the family of man and from God. You do not have that path, that wisdom, that peace, that tranquility, that unity, and the understanding that there is one family, one God, and one human race.

You have separated from human beings, from peace, and from tranquility. You have divided off, some because of color, some because of religion, some because of race, some because of language, some because of the *nabīs,* and some because of the *olis.* These differences have been growing in some of you. Some of you have separated because of gods, some because of prayer, some because of the different *vēdas,* some because of the four hundred trillion ten thousand kinds of prayers, some because of *sittis,* some because of miracles, some because of mantras, and some because of magics. Some of you are fostering these many different actions.

So, in this way you have separated yourself from God, from unity, from truth, from prayer, from peace, and from tranquility. By nourishing these other things you have separated from prayer, from God, from that peace, from that grace, from that *rahmah,* and from that plenitude. This is the reason, this is one reason.

We must conquer this state. To overcome this, some of you will have to start from the beginning. Some must start from the beginning, while some can start from that final point. Those who have not separated from this station, from mankind, from God, from the soul, and from truth can start with this *dhikr* prayer. They have established the original supreme root, and can take their own water. They have found the spring where the water is. They have established the taproot that goes deep down to the spring, and they can take the water, fertilizer, food, and nourishment from that spring. That supreme root goes deep down and they can take the water of God, serenity, tranquility, and peace—considering the lives of others as their own lives, considering the hunger of others as their own hunger, considering the comfort of others as their own comfort, and considering the bodies of others as their own bodies. They are able to take their original food. They can take that water and food, that prayer, and that peacefulness from the supreme root.

Faith, certitude, *sabūr, shukūr, tawakkul,* and *al-hamdu lillāh,* inner patience, contentment, trust in God, and all praise to God—this root goes deep down, and from that they are able to take their original food. They are able to take it from God. They can take that prayer from Him, that food from Him, that water from Him, the qualities from Him, that *sabūr* from Him, and that peacefulness from Him. They can take these from Him. They will prostrate to Him. Some have established this deep root. If that supreme root goes down to the right place, then they will be able to perform 43,242 *sujūd,* prostrations, per day.

But some people have separated from this connection. We are trying to form this, but they have separated from this. In Ceylon and in many countries, in America, on the continents of Europe and Asia, and in other places like this, some are separating. Some are cutting off this connection, while some are forming this connection.

The point is this: even though we have been teaching and doing this prayer for so long, there are some who are developing and some who are not developing. So, for those who are not developing and not understanding this connection, we have to find a way to make them understand, so that they can overcome the *tattwas,* the forces that are separating them. There are those who are able to take the water and fertilizer from the original root. Others have a connection to arrogance, karma, and maya, to the differences of race and religion, to colors, desires, pride, lust, anger, miserliness, lechery, fanaticism, and envy, to feeling, awareness, and intellect, to scriptures, philosophies, languages, to the many tens of millions of gods, and to mind and desire. Because they have these connections, some people are unable to grow; they are unable to cut these away. They need to see that because of their connection to karma they have separated. For this, we need to give them fertilizer.

The one who has the supreme root is able to take his original food. He has peace. But the many other trees, these flowering trees, fruit trees, and apple trees, have to be given "milk." There are things we have to do to make them grow. We must water the plants for a certain amount of time. We must give them the temporary water, the temporary food, and the temporary fertilizer. We must supply them with this temporary prayer, temporary water, and temporary fertilizer. They cannot take the original food, so for a time we have to supply it.

Like that, this is what we must give for this state. We have to place this prayer, this *toluhai,* this *vanakkam* there. We have to place this *arivu,* wisdom, and this *putti,* intellect, there. This is what needs to be given. When a seed has been planted and is slowly growing, that is the time when it needs fertilizer and water. It needs to be given fertilizer and water at certain times—in the morning, in the evening, at noon, in the daylight, and in the heat. In the early morning we must pour small doses of the proper amount of water on it. We must place the fertilizer there at the correct time. We must do this so that the seedling can develop its original root, so that it can take the water and fertilizer for itself, and grow.

This is why we must now do this five-times prayer. It is necessary for some to do this. For others it is not necessary. Those who have the original root, those who do not have the differences that cause separations, can take what is original. They can take the connection to God, that prayer, that wisdom, those qualities, those actions, that behavior, and that duty. However, there are some people who just take what is on the surface of the earth. They take the water and the germs and viruses that are on the surface. They do not dig deep down to find the original taproot. Consequently, the germs, viruses, cells, and energies come and settle on the tree, and they damage the flowers, the fruits, the seeds, and the unripe fruits. They do not allow the plant to mature. Insects come and try to destroy it, diseases come to destroy it, karma comes to destroy it, demons come to destroy it, and differences come to destroy it. Like this, the four hundred trillion ten thousand kinds of "prayer" qualities come and try to destroy it.

So, we have to win over this. We have to conquer the connection to earth. We have to conquer the connection to water. We have to conquer the connection to air. We have to conquer the connection to fire. And we have to conquer the connection to ether. We have to conquer these connections with the five-times prayer.

Subh, the early morning prayer, is the prayer of the earth. It is the prayer that cuts that connection. This is the prayer that cuts the connection to the section of creation, to blood ties, and to attachments.

We must try to conquer the connection to earth, woman, and gold. This is the first prayer of the day that we must do. We must cut the connection to the earth, the connection to birth.

That is Hinduism. It is called *sharī'ah*. The Hindu religion is the religion of creation. All of creation appears from the connection to the earth. We must try to overcome this section. It contains four hundred trillion ten thousand kinds of shaktis, divisions, and prayers. The fire and the water in these shaktis make up creation. The water becomes blood. We must cut away this shakti. This is the connection of Shakti and Shiva—Adam ☻ and Hawwa' (Eve) ☻—the five elements, mind and desire, the *sittis,* the miracles, colors, hues, races, languages, *vēdas,* and *vēdāntas.* All of these are contained within it. Astrology, the planets, the sun, the moon, and the stars, maya, clouds, maya shaktis, poisonous shaktis, hell, flesh, food, and other attachments like these are contained within this section. We have to overcome them.

This is the section where one kills another, where one separates himself from another, and where one stores everything within himself. There are countless thoughts and countless gods. Countless animals and snakes are made into gods. Animals, snakes, scorpions, birds, fish, elephants, rats, crows, peacocks, horses, donkeys, and lions are made into countless gods and worshipped. All of our qualities are changed into gods, into blood-sucking vampires, shaktis, miracles, and *sittis.* Each demon, each ghost, each quality is changed into a god, and it is through these connections that we kill ourselves. They devour us, drink our blood, and poison us. The evil qualities of the rats destroy our house, the arrogance of the elephant breaks everything, the peacock of the five elements and the five colors separates and destroys us, the black crow blackens our hearts, and the snake poisons us with its evil qualities. In this way, this section contains many colors and hues.

This shakti is Hinduism. This is the first section that must be cut away. Here, water becomes blood, the blood becomes a blood clot, the blood clot becomes a piece of flesh, the piece of flesh becomes flesh, the flesh becomes nerves and bones, and the nerves, bones, membranes, skin, fire, air, heat, water, and illusion become the body. The body becomes the many colors. The colors, beauty, and elements become maya, and that becomes the many holes for the body. These holes become the skin pores. These skin pores become the 105 million openings for the 105 million births. Air, water, fire, and heat move in and out through these 105 million openings. Mind, desire, cells, viruses, falsehood, demons, ghosts, and maya travel back and forth through these openings. Inside and outside, connections are formed through these 105 million openings, they are formed by way of these holes. These connections must be cut away.

This is the first section, the study of creation. We have to study this section of creation, and cut it away. The body was formed from a piece of flesh. We have to cut off its attachments to blood ties, race, religion, *vēdas,* and *vēdāntas.* Once we have cut these away, we must proceed. The first prayer exists to cut these attachments. This is called the prayer of *subh.*

Once these attachments are cut away, we come to the shakti of water, of creation, of lust. The force of this maya shakti pulls us. It brings about the connection where water becomes blood. First is the shakti of Adam ☽ — creation. This next section is the shakti of Michael ☽ — water. The shakti of Michael ☽ has 1,008 different *sittis,* miracles. With these miracles, water is changed into a blood clot. This connection is the connection to the *āvis,* the connection to the demons, the connection to the *nafs,* and the connection to hunger in the world. It has all of these connections: the connections to hunger, disease, old age, and death, to arrogance, karma, and maya, and to intoxicants, lust, theft, murder, and falsehood.

This is the fire of hunger, the hell-fire that is located in the stomach. When hunger comes, the Ten (Commandments) will fly away. Wisdom and ability will fly away. All of our good qualities and good actions will fly away.

This is the Hanal religion. This second section is the section that prays to the fire of hunger. When you pray to that fire of hunger, you will sacrifice everything so that your body, your life, your spirit, and your soul can grow.

So, first you are a slave to Adam ⊕ (creation), and then you are a slave to hunger. In that first section you are a slave to creation, a slave to forms. You are a slave to the forms of Adam ⊕, a slave to the elements, a slave to thoughts, a slave to shaktis, a slave to lust and lechery, and a slave to languages—to these prisons. You must cut away this slavery.

In this second section you are a slave to hunger. You are a slave to old age, hunger, disease, and death, you are a slave to these four. This is the Hanal religion. You become a slave to the fire of hell: the fire of anger, the fire of hunger, the fire of arrogance, the fire of lust, the fire of doubt, the fire of suspicion, the fire of "I," the fire of "you," the fire of color, and the fire of sin. You become a slave to the fire called torpor, and you burn in that fire. You make this fire into a god. This fire of hunger is made into a god, and you pray to it. At night, in the time of darkness, you pray in the glow of the light of this fire.

First, in the time of darkness, you pray to Shakti and Shiva, Adam ⊕ and Hawwa' ⊕—the mother of birth, of maya. Second, you become a slave to the hunger that is arrogance, karma, maya, and the five elements. That is the Hanal religion.

The first prayer is the prayer of creation, the prayer of attachment, the prayer of birth. That is the prayer of *subh*. You must overcome that section and establish *īmān*. Whoever wants to conquer this must extract its essence, and give up everything else.

Second is the fire of hunger that feeds the fire of the elements. You must overcome that. With the sun-god, the moon-god, the star-god, the fire-god, the anger-god, the arrogance-god, the demon-god, the ghost-god, the food-god, the flesh-god, the water-god, and the air-god—with all of these gods, man is praying to the fire of hell. When hunger comes to someone who has this fire, the ten will fly away. His feeling, awareness, and good qualities will all fly away. This fire is the Hanal religion—water and heat.

To conquer this you must perform this second prayer; you must establish *īmān*. When you conquer this connection and establish the connection to the *ānmā,* the soul, then that is known as the prayer of *zuhr*. It is prayed at noontime. This is the time that this prayer should be prayed.

You must extinguish this fire, sever this connection, and cut away that fecal arrogance. This fire is called fecal arrogance. It is arrogance and fanaticism. If you have diarrhea twice, you will lose all your strength. If you have diarrhea twice, your arrogance will leave you. You will not even know what state you are in. So, this will not protect you.

Cut away this connection and try to take your original food of *al-hamdu lillāh*, take the food of *sabūr, shukūr, al-hamdu lillāh*, and *tawakkul-'alAllāh*. At the prayer of *zuhr*, cut away this connection to arrogance.

Your God is not fire, water, or air. The hunger that you have will not allow you to grow. This fire of the sun and the moon cannot nourish you. It is hot and will consume you, it will burn you. As soon as the sun comes up, you will run away from its heat. You will seek shelter under a tree. You wanted the heat, but then you run and run away from it.

You are suffering in the fire of hunger. How much suffering and confusion you have in this fire of arrogance! You are burning in the fire of anger, the fire of the jinns. This is the section of the jinns. God created the jinns out of fire. Those jinns are your fire; they burn as anger, arrogance, lust, and hunger and make you suffer. God discarded this fire, but you are making it grow. You have to cut this away.

This section is the Hanal religion—*īmān, tarīqah*. This *tarīqah* is where you accept God, take the essence, and then proceed. You cut away the diseases that are killing you. Hunger, disease, old age, and death are killing you. Cut these away. This is the Hanal religion, it is the stomach.

Next is *al-injīl*, Christianity, your heart. Having overcome the section of fire and water that is within you, having won over the four sections within that, having won over creation, having conquered the connection of fecal arrogance, having cut away the connection of fanaticism, having overcome the connection to earth, the connection to water and blood, and the connection to hunger—the connections that are killing you—then you come to *al-injīl*, Christianity, the *āvis*, the spirits.

Both the pure spirit and the impure spirits exist here. There is the pure *āvi*, and there are the impure *āvis*. You will understand that the angels, jinns, fairies, spirits, demons, ghosts, and five elements are within you. These *āvis* are joined with you. Air runs within your thoughts and desires, your look, sight, intention, sound, and breath. This air flows in and out, as thoughts and intentions. This is *al-injīl*, the *āvis*. This air, these *āvis* are crucifying you. They have nailed you to the cross of this body of earth. The dog of desire, the five elements, and the monkey of the mind have put you on a cross, they have nailed you there. The five nails are earth, fire, water, air, and ether. You must remove these five nails. Blood attachments are dripping from there. Arrogance and blood ties are destroying you. Arrogance is separating and destroying you. These *āvis* are devouring you.

Your soul is a pure soul, it is God's property. For you, this is *lām*— *alif* and *lām*. The *alif* descends from the *'arsh*, the crown of the head, to the forehead, and extends down the nose. The eyes are the *nūn*. An essence has been placed within that *nūn*. If you look intently at that eye, you will see a *bā'*, and within that you will see a dot. That is what you will see. When you look down, that dot is the world. What do you see within it? Darkness. What is the light that you see there? The fire of hunger and the fire of anger that are within you. When you look at this fire, you will think it is light, but this light can only be seen in darkness. It cannot be seen in the daytime.

This fire can only be seen in the darkness of your mind. You consider this to be *gnānam*, or *arivu*, or resplendence, but wherever you look in the darkness, you see only the lights of the sun, the moon, and the stars. This is what you see in the darkness of your mind. If you did not have darkness, you would not see this, is that not so?

You speak about your prayers, your worship, your color, hue, race, religion, scriptures, and philosophies, but in this darkness you are praying to fire. In this darkness you look at the stars, and think that you are seeing yourself; you think that this is your own life. When you look at the stars you say, "The light that I am seeing is my life." But the moon and stars can only be seen at night, they are impure spirits. These impure spirits have a connection to the lights and fires of the five elements, and can only be seen as light when there is darkness. This is not purity, and it is not prayer. Like this, it is the lights of the sun, or the sky, or the earth that you are seeing in the darkness of your mind.

God is Light; what is called God is Light. But you are nailed to a cross. Blood is dripping from the places where you are nailed, and you are in darkness. Blood is dripping from you while you are in this darkness. The nails of the five elements have you pinned on this cross, and the blood that is your blood attachment is dripping from there. This blood attachment is your darkness. The lights that you see in that darkness are the lights that are within you: anger, arrogance, fanaticism, caste, religion, scriptures, separations, and divisions. These are the many stars, the many lights that you see, the fire, water, and air.

What is seen in darkness is not prayer. You must dispel this darkness of the mind. You must free yourself from that cross. If you remove the five nails, you will be free, you will be free of the "I" and the "you." You will be released from the cross. When you come to the state where these five nails have been removed, you will reach God's place.

The *alif* descends from the *'arsh* to the *kursī*, and extends down the bridge of the nose. If you bend the *alif*, it becomes *lām*, Light. That is the sun. When the *alif* bends slightly, it becomes the *lām*; it is *lām*, Light. That is perfected wisdom. When that *alif* bends a bit more and comes to the nostrils, it becomes a *mīm*. Your eyes are a *mīm* and your nostrils are a *mīm*. When the *alif* bends, it is *lām*. And when it is straight, it is *alif*, Allāh. These three letters can be seen on your face. The *alif*, *lām*, and *mīm* will resplend there, as your *zīnah*, and through this light, your *sūrah* will become the *mīm*, your *sūrah* will become the *lām*, and your *sūrah* will become the *alif*.

Once you have discarded everything, you will become the *alif*.

When you bend in *rukū'*, you will become the *lām*, the Light. When you remove the *nafs*, you will become Muhammad ☉, the *zīnah*, the beauty, the *mīm*. In one state you are the *mīm*, in one state you are the Light, and in another state you are Allāh, the *alif*. You will have no sound. When you are the *alif*, you are one who has no sound. When you are the *lām*, you are one who is pure, one who speaks with wisdom. When you are the *mīm*, you are one who has peace, one who has realized tranquility, equality, peace, and serenity. So, *alif*, *lām*, and *mīm* become your form.

Once you have removed the five nails and once you have seen these three, you will be free of the cross. You will see your pure *āvi*. That pure *āvi* is the sun; when it merges with wisdom it becomes the sun. When the *mīm*-Muhammad ☉ merges with the Nūr, it becomes *lām*, the sun. That is the Light to all creations, the Light to all lives. You will realize that state.

When you free yourself from the cross, when everything is subdued and you can see everything, then you will understand that there is only one Allāh, the *alif*. That has no sound. You are the one who has to give sound to Allāh. *Alif*, *mīm*, and *lām* are Light. That Light of wisdom is what gives the sound of Allāh. It gives Allāh's sound, speaks Allāh's speech, speaks Allāh's words, displays Allāh's qualities, demonstrates Allāh's duty and justice, shows Allāh's ways of integrity, exemplifies Allāh's service and peace, and treats other lives as one's own life.

At *zuhr*, you must cut away hunger. Next there is *haqīqah*, Christianity, *al-injīl*. When you free yourself from the cross, you must proceed, and make the connection to Allāh. That is Christianity. From this state you must proceed further, and make the connection to Allāh, the connection to Ādi, the Primal One.

First, you cut the connection to earth, second you cut the connection to hunger and arrogance, the connection to fanaticism, and the connection to birth. That is *tarīqah*. First there is *sharī'ah*, next there is *tarīqah*, and then there is *haqīqah*. These are the *vēdas* of *az-zabūr*, *al-jabbūrat*, and *al-injīl*. You must conquer the connection to these three shaktis.

Next there is *al-furqān*—the head. This is where the *alif, lām,* and *mīm* are seen as one, as the *zīnah,* the beauty. That is the face.

In the *injīl vēda,* if you have conquered the elements, then that will be Ahamad ☺: God, the heart, the *beauty-form,* God's Light. If you have pulled out the nails, if you have overcome the elements, and if you have vanquished hunger, then that place, the heart, will be a beauty-form. That is Ahamad ☺, the *aham,* the heart. This is the place where the Light of Muhammad ☺, your *zīnah* and resplendence, dwell. If this place is clear, then it becomes Muhammad ☺. This is *haqīqah,* this place is *haqīqah.* This is the prayer of *'asr,* the afternoon prayer.

Maghrib is *al-furqān.* The prayer of *maghrib,* the sunset prayer, is the connection between you and Allāh. This is where you accept nothing other than the commands of Allāh's prophets. His sound has seven causes: the two eyes, two ears, two nostrils, and one mouth. Through these seven openings, sound is given to God. It is not this outer eye, within this eye there is another eye. It is not this ear, within this ear there is another ear. It is not this nose, within this nose there is another nose. It is not this mouth, within this mouth there is another mouth. It is not this tongue, within this tongue there is another tongue. It is not this speech, within this speech there is another speech. It is not this fragrance that you can perceive, there is another fragrance. It is not the light that is within this eye, there is another light through which you can see Him. It is not this ear that you hear with, there is another ear through which you can hear Him. It is not this brain, there is another brain that can speak with Him.

It is not the cross that you wear as a pendant. There is another cross called the Qutbiyyah. This cross is always within you. It starts from the *alif,* it starts from Allāh.

Allāh, Muhammad ☺, and Muhaiyaddeen ☺, these three form that cross which descends from the *'arsh* and meets and crosses at the *kursī.* Allāh and the Nūr, the Light, cross there. This cross is with you, it is not a cross that is worn as a pendant. It is imprinted there.

Alif is Light, resplendence. What resplends from the *kursī* is Light. This cross is not a pendant that is worn for show. Light radiates from

the center of this cross. This is the Qutbiyyah. It is Allāh's Light—
Nūr, the Light. It descends from the 'arsh to the kursī, as Light. This
is the gnāna kan, the eye of wisdom. It is the cross which is located
between the two eyebrows. This cross was imprinted within you in
'ālamul-arwāh. It is the kursī.

Understanding this is al-furqān. The alif, lām, and mīm are your
zīnah, the face, the head. You must give the seven sounds to Him,
and then speak. It is not this outer eye. You must go beyond the
seven causes. When you go beyond these seven causes and look, you
will see God's eye, the eye of wisdom. You must look with that eye.
It is not this eye, you must go beyond the seven. The gnāna kan will
be there; the eye of wisdom will be there. Look at everything with
that eye. Open the eye of wisdom, see with that gnāna kan.

It is not this nose, not these fragrances. You must smell with the
nose of wisdom. Find out which life has what smell, which place has
what fragrance, which qalb has what fragrance. Smell with that nose
of wisdom. Smell with that nose, send out the foul smells, and take
the fragrance of 'ilm, divine knowledge, into your qalb. Join with
that. Draw in the fragrance of rahmah, the grace of God.

It is not these ears. You must listen with wisdom. When you listen with wisdom, when you cross over the seven layers and go to the
eighth layer, then you will hear the resonance of Allāh, His explanations. Ohhh! What you will hear is so very subtle! Listen with that
wisdom, and learn. The heart of īmān and faith will hear the sound of
the pure fragrance—gnānam. This is what will be given there. Join
with that wisdom and listen to the gnānam that is there. Hear with
that ear. Listen to that and speak with Him. See Him, speak with
Him, and smile with Him. Maunam, silence!

It is not this brain. There is Allāh's brain, the Nūr, that brain of
Light. Pray to Him with that brain. This is the prayer that you must
pray, not the other prayer. You must pray without missing even a
second. So many rays are coming forth. Many, many, many rays are
radiating from that brain. At every moment, at every second, that
effulgence is coming forth.

At every second, with every ray, you must perform sajdah, prostration to God. With one word, 43,242 rays must be sent forth. This sound must emanate from the nerves, the muscles, the flesh, the skin pores, the bones, and the hair follicles. These 43,242 rays must be sent forth, and fall at His feet, that sound must be sent out. So much sound must go out, and connect to Him. That is *sajdah*.

That is *maghrib*. That is the *waqt* of *maghrib*. Once you have finished that learning, and have made the connection to God, then that is *maghrib,* the world of *gnānam*. That is *maghrib,* ether. If, in these four *waqts,* you make that connection, then that is *al-furqān*.

The four *vēdas* form one book. This is the book that you are made of. First, you complete your study of the section of creation. Then you complete your study of the fire of hell, Hanal. Then you complete your study of air: the *āvis,* God's creations, the *malaks, malā'ikah, olis,* Gabriel ⊕, Michael ⊕, Raphael ⊕, and Israel ⊕.

First, there is Adam ⊕, you learn about the earth, the body. Second, you learn about Michael ⊕, water. (Third you learn about Israel ⊕, fire.) Fourth, you learn about Raphael ⊕, air. You learn about Israel ⊕, Raphael ⊕, Michael ⊕ and earth — fire, air, water, and the body which is earth. These four creations, these four sections make up one book. You are the book. You are a book with four sections; *az-zabūr, al-jabbūrat, al-injīl,* and *al-furqān* are the four religions. This is your history-book.

If you understand these four sections, if you study these and cut them away, then you come to one point, *'ishā'* — one point, God. That has no night or day. That is *'ishā',* the late night prayer, the fifth *waqt,* where you pray without attachment. That is your history, it has no night and no day.

How will you be praying there? God and all lives will be within you. You will understand that there is one sun, one family, and one God. You will have peace. You will be merged with God, in peace. You will have the tongue that can speak with Him, the nose that can smell Him, the eyes that can see Him, the wisdom that can understand Him, the mouth that can imbibe Him, and the *qalb* that can understand that taste. Whatever is within you will not be different from what is within others. You will realize this truth.

You will see all lives within you, you will see all lights within you, you will see truth within you, you will see compassion within you, you will see duty within you, you will see all hunger within you, you will see the sadness of all lives within you, you will see the suffering of all lives within you, you will see the many difficulties of these lives within you, you will see that service within you, you will see that justice within you, you will see that conscience within you. You will see so many of God's qualities and actions within you.

You will see that all of these lives exist within you, and you will satisfy their needs and give them peace. You will not see any differences. You will see God within you. You will see God's section, His essence, that point within you. You will understand this and do the prayer of *lā ilāha illAllāhu*. When you have come to that place and have found clarity in the four sections, you will do this prayer.

But, today, because you have not understood this, you are separating off. If you can cut away the diseases that separate you, if you can understand this, then that is what is called *sūfiyyah*. You must understand this *vanakkam,* and then study *sūfiyyah*. First you must conquer the four sections, understand *vanakkam,* and then learn about *sūfiyyah*.

It is that wisdom, that point, that I have come to explain. Some of you have grown the supreme root, while others have taken root in the four sections of creation. You have taken root in differences. Some of you have the differences of color and divisions, and these are separating you, they are pulling you down. You are not going up. I have to pour water on you, I have to spread fertilizer on you. I have to give you the temporary water, the temporary fertilizer, the temporary air, and the temporary heat. So, some people need to have the water poured on them. If, however, you can cut away your own history, if you can understand, then you will be able to take your own water. If you can understand this point, you will be able to take your own water. Otherwise, someone else has to pour the water on you. Someone else has to spread the fertilizer on you. He has to pour and pour the water, and slowly cut away your differences, so that the root can grow. Therefore, I see these two sections in this world.

There are four divisions. In each division, people say "I" and "you." They have not read the one book. One who has not read this book will be unable to pray this prayer. He will pray the prayer of the elements. He will pray the prayer of fire, the prayer of air, and the prayer of creation. Only the one who has finished reading this book will be able to pray this prayer. Only then can he do it.

Therefore children, that is the reason. Even though I have been teaching for such a long time, there are some who have separated off, some who have not taken root. Others have taken root; they have reached the state where they are able to take water and fertilizer from the original root. But some, here and there, have not researched or studied this book. To learn these four books is *vanakkam*. Otherwise, water and fertilizer need to be given.

This is *vanakkam*, this is the one prayer. We have to understand this prayer. We need to apply fertilizer, so that the root can grow. Some people are able to do this for themselves, while others need to have this done for them. Some will need to have water poured for them until the root grows; they are unable to take the original water.

Some are growing. Others are not growing. Some understand. Others do not understand. Some understand the final prayer. Others do not understand the final prayer.

This is the work that we must now do. Some people say it is not necessary to do this. Ohhh, *meecham nallam!* Very good! If the 43,242 rays can go out from one breath, very good! If that peace comes to you, good, that is good! If that Light comes to you, good, all lives will recognize that! If that justice comes to you, good! If those qualities come to you, good! That is what you are searching for. If that Light comes, then it is very, very good!

Otherwise, this cutting has to be done, these sections have to be cut away. They have to be cut away, one by one, and fertilizer and water must be added. To cut all these away, and to make the connection with God is called prayer.

There are four hundred trillion ten thousand prayers. You must understand the history. The four sections are one book, four histories. These must be cut away. These four sections are within you. If

you can cut them away, and if you can study this history, then that
will become your own history, the history of prayer and the history
of life. We must understand this.

My love you, my children. It is necessary that I start some of
you at the beginning. Some have to start at the beginning. Others
can start at the end. This is what I am now doing, showing you the
separations that must be cut away. You cannot pray the one prayer
if you have not cut away these sections. The one who has not cut
his connections will be unable to pray the one prayer, while the one
who has finished the cutting will not need to pray the beginning
prayer. If you cut away whatever is separating you, then there is no
more cutting to do. If you cut away what is within you, then there
is no more cutting to do. Once you have cut away each section, if
you have nothing other than God, if you have nothing other than
His Light, then that becomes your prayer. Only if you have finished
this cutting can you do this prayer. You must cut the four sections
and go beyond.

You must study the four books. These are the four steps, the four
religions: *sharī'ah, tarīqah, haqīqah,* and *ma'rifah.* In Tamil these four
steps are known as *sariyai, kiriyai, yōgam,* and *gnānam.* In Arabic the
four steps are known as *az-zabūr, al-jabbūrat, al-injīl,* and *al-furqān.*
In English they are known as Hinduism, Hanal—Fire Worship—
Christianity, and Islām. These are what they are called. This is the
book you have to read.

Please think about this a little. If you do not reflect on this, you
cannot research into it. Some of you, without reflection, are complaining, "He said one thing before and now he is saying this." Your
minds are going round, round, round. When a clock is circling
around, and when you look at the time, you will see that it is travelling from twelve to one and from one to two. This is how some
of your minds are going around. Your mind starts at one and goes
around to twelve and then comes back to one. It keeps going round
and round. Some children are going round, round, round, round.
You rotate around the world in the same way that a clock goes round
and round. You must look beyond this.

This is the world, the mind is showing the world. It is displaying time. You are seeing the same thing, over and over again. The mind is showing the world, it is showing one to twelve. These are the twelve openings. There are ten openings, and two more above these, making twelve openings. It is these twelve openings that this world shows. Only when you go beyond these will God's point, that point of Truth, be shown. You must think about this.

This is the world. The mind is the world, it circles around the world. When you look within, this is how it is. You are seeing the same thing over and over again.

A compass shows the four directions of east, west, north, and south. A compass shows you four directions. You must take that instrument that shows you all four directions and point it in one direction. It points towards both the east and the west. East is the body, west is the soul, God. Make that compass always point west. Then there will be one point.

Until there is that one point, the mind will be like a clock. What time is it now? Ten o'clock. What time is it now? Nine o'clock. What time is it now? Eight o'clock. It goes round, round, round. It circles around, night and day. You are always watching the time. This is the world, the mind. It keeps circling around. You must change to a compass that shows one direction. First, change to the four directions, then change to the four religions, after that change to one direction, then change to one family, one God, one point. That will be prayer, the surrender to God.

So, for that, we must change. We must endeavor to do this. If we keep on circling around the mind, the same things will keep coming back, again and again. The world will keep coming back. It will come back so many times: one, two, three, four, five, six, seven, eight, nine, ten, eleven, twelve. This is how the mind is. Race, religion, scripture, color, and language will keep returning. You must change to a compass. After that, change to one point. Change to the prayer that is between you and God. Prayer must be changed and pointed towards God. Then you will have peace. Then, that will be right.

This is why we now have to do this beginning prayer. In Ceylon, so much time has gone by, and still the original root has not taken hold. Ten or eleven years have passed in America, and still some people have not established that original root. In Ceylon, some people have not taken hold of this and in the West, some people have not taken hold of this. For some, the root is growing but it needs to grow some more. For some we still have to pour water. They need to understand their history, they need to learn, and cut away their connections. It is through this cutting that they can learn.

When you cut one connection you learn, when you cut another connection you learn, when you cut another connection you learn some more, when you cut another connection you learn still more, when you cut the next connection there is prayer, and when you cut the next connection there is peace, God. So, this is what you must do. You have to learn, and cut these connections away. Then you will be God's family—Light. You must give sound to that.

My love you. It is now early morning. We woke up at five o'clock, and we went into the bathroom and washed our face with some water. The children were praying downstairs. We started speaking at five thirty. Today is Saturday morning and this speech came to me. I was told to speak. I asked Doctor Tambi's wife to come here, but she said she had not washed her face yet. I said, "*Shari,* come and translate anyway. I have not finished. There is still more that needs to be said."

So, I had to speak. There was much more to say, there was more that I needed to teach you. I had to tell you this, I had to give you these explanations in order for you to understand your minds. We had to speak a little to the American children and to the Ceylonese children. Whether they are from the West or the North, wherever they are from, we had to speak a little about this section.

If there is no rain, the crops will not grow. If there is no darkness, the moon will not shine, the stars and the moon will not glitter. If there is no sun, the darkness will not leave. So, without darkness, the moon will not shine and the stars will not glitter, without the sun, the clouds will not leave, and if clouds are present, the darkness will not leave.

Like this, to dispel darkness, the sun is needed. For the light of the moon and the stars to be visible and for fire to be seen, darkness is needed. To understand God, wisdom and Light are needed—the sun is needed.

Therefore, we have to show you different things according to each particular section. Certain things have to be dispelled and certain explanations have to be given according to each particular section. So, there were certain things that we needed to speak about today.

My love you. Precious jeweled lights of my eye, please think about this, and do it. It is my duty to tell you. It is God's duty to tell me what to say, and it is my duty to tell it to you. It is my duty to say what I am told to say, and it is your duty to listen and act accordingly. To listen with awareness is your duty, to put this into practice is the duty of faith, certitude, determination, and *īmān,* and to understand this is the duty of wisdom, it is the duty of the clarity of wisdom. If each one of us does his duty, then this will be understood. *Āmīn. As-salāmu 'alaikum.*

Precious jeweled lights of my eye, the reason that this section came this morning…my dearest children, children who are mingled with my life, my body, and my soul, some of you have made complaints. Some children have made certain complaints. There are some who have a grievance in their hearts, and they have been making these complaints. Some children had grievances earlier, some children had grievances after that, and some children have grievances now.

So, the One who has to inquire into these grievances said to me, "Certain complaints have come to Me. What are you going to do about this?" He told me that there were many complaints.

I replied, "I don't know! If there are any complaints that have come, then You must speak. I will then tell them what You say. What You say, I will say."

So, He gave an answer to your complaints, and I spoke that answer into the microphone. I had to speak because these complaints kept on coming. I am just saying what He said. This is not my fault.

Ask the One to whom you are complaining! If you have a grievance in your heart, ask Him.

That Judge said, "These complaints have come to Me. I have heard them. It is your children who are making these complaints."

I replied, "Is that so? I did not know that."

He asked me, "What are you going to tell them?" and I replied, "What am I to tell them? If You have something to tell them, I will certainly convey it to them!"

Then God said, "Tell them this."

So, my children, this is what I told you. The children who are complaining should take in and understand what I have said. Once you understand, you can withdraw your complaints, you can retract them. This is what you should do.

Āmīn. May God give you His benevolent grace. Āmīn. May He give His benevolent grace to my children. Āmīn. Āmīn.

A'ūdhu billāhi minash-shaitānir-rajīm.
I seek refuge in God from the accursed satan.
Bismillāhir-Rahmānir-Rahīm.
In the name of God, the Most Compassionate,
the Most Merciful.

TRUE ABLUTION

February 23, 1983, Wednesday, 9:32 a.m.

QUESTION
I have a question. It's about my prayers. Whenever I start praying, it's very difficult for me to concentrate, and for some reason, whether it's satan or what, I start thinking of worldly things, like people who have hurt me and all, instead. And besides, I have learned it all Arabic-wise, so maybe that's where I am wrong, I should know the definitions...

TRANSLATOR
You don't understand the meaning?

QUESTIONER
Yes, I mean I do because I have been praying all my life, but some of it I don't, it's like, well I can't explain it, it's just that...

BAWA MUHAIYADDEEN
Mmm. It is the same for everyone. That is why no one is praying. There is no one in the world who is really praying. They say they are praying, but when they pray, all of these other things come into their hearts: children, work, husband, property, possessions, sorrow, pain, what happened earlier, and what may happen later. Those reels are running, so there is no one who is really praying to Allāh.

People may seem to be standing in the presence of Allāh, they may have that form, but they are not really there, they are actually

189

wandering all around the *dunyā*. They are wandering here and there in the world. They may be standing there in prayer, but their *qalbs* do not have the state that has given the responsibility to Allāh. Since their state is not right, they are not really praying. To pray correctly is difficult.

Child, these thoughts are called satan. Where is satan? When we see someone who is speaking badly, or who has bad qualities and bad actions, we say, "*Aday*, satan!" Is that person really satan? No. He is not satan, it is those qualities that we are calling satan. When we say "*Aday*, satan!" we mean that his actions and his qualities are doing the work of satan. So, the reason we say this is not because he is satan, but because his qualities and actions are satan. He is a man, his form is that of a man, but we say that he is satan because of his qualities and actions.

If these qualities and actions are within us when we are praying, then that is satan. So, that is satan. Somehow or other these qualities enter a person and will not let him pray. His prayer becomes *bātil*, useless. His thoughts make his prayer *bātil*. Understand? That will not be prayer. His prayer will be useless. It is *khalas*, it is finished. Those qualities will not allow him to complete his prayer. This is what is happening there.

It is because of this that Allāhu ta'ālā Nāyan told our Nabī Peruman Mustāfar-Rasūl, *sallallāhu 'alaihi wa sallam*, to do *wudū'*, ablution. There are sixteen *sharts,* conditions, for doing ablution correctly. That is what *wudū'* is. But we are still not doing it in the proper way. We are not doing even one of the four sections of ablution correctly. If we do not know how to do even one section correctly, how can we pray? We are just doing what someone else is doing. Everyone is praying, so we are praying, everyone is going to the five *waqts* of prayer, so we are also going. We are just going along in this way.

Those of wisdom say, "If a man truly prays even one *waqt* of prayer, hell will be far away from him." If someone prays even one *waqt* correctly, if he meets Allāh-Rasūl ☉, then hell will be far away from him. One *waqt*! In his *hayāh,* if he can truly pray one *waqt*, that will be a great *daulah,* a great wealth. In his lifetime, he must try to at least pray this one *waqt.* That one prayer will be better than seventy thousand years of *toluhai.*

One day the Rasūl, *sallallāhu 'alaihi wa sallam,* was doing his ablution. At his side there was another man who was also doing this. While the Rasūlullāh ⏀ was performing his *wudū',* the other man finished his *wudū'* and got up to go and pray. Then the Rasūlullāh ⏀ turned to him and said, "Please do your ablution again. You did not do it correctly. I saw that it was not done correctly."

So the man did it a second time. Again he got up to leave. The Rasūl ⏀ said, "No, you still have not done your ablution properly, you need to do it correctly."

The man did it for the third time, finished, and again tried to leave. The Rasūlullāh ⏀ said, "No, you still have not done your ablution correctly. Please do it again."

Then the man said, "*Yā* Rasūlullāh, please tell me the way to do it. I do not understand how to do this."

The Rasūlullāh ⏀ replied, "Every man who comes to the prayer brings with him the world, hell, sins, various difficulties, and all of the qualities of satan. That is a great weight. During his ablution he must lay down that load and establish a connection to Allāh. He must unload what he has brought with him from the sight, nose, tongue, ears, and all of the sounds. He must lay down all of these sounds and the other things of the five (senses) that he has brought with him.

"Within the time that we are performing these sixteen kinds of ablution, we must make the connection between Allāh and ourselves. That is when that connection between Allāh and ourselves must be established. We must come to the state where we can see Allāh. We must establish love between Him and ourselves, and prepare our *qalbs* so that our *qalbs* have the state where Allāh sees us and we see Him. Our intention and our prayer should be made complete in this place itself. Here, itself, that *vanakkam* should be made full.

"This state must be established within the time a person performs the ablution. That is when he must bring his *qalb* to this state. He must strengthen his *īmān* and his *qalb,* and form his love for Allāh. This state must be established first. Then, when he goes to pray, he should have Allāh's intention, His *salawāt,* that thought, and that focus. Having established that state here, when he goes to pray there, he should face Allāh alone and follow behind the Rasūl ☻ who is the *imām,* the leader of prayer. That is all he should be aware of.

"Like that, when you go there, you should face Allāh alone and do *sajdah* to Him. You should follow behind the Rasūl ☻ and focus on Allāh, who is in front. That is the only point you should be aware of. You should not be aware of any other point. To start from here, to go there, and then to bow in *rukū',* is *toluhai.*

"But, instead of correctly establishing this state, you are simply washing your hands, washing your mouth, washing your nose, wiping your head, washing your neck, and washing your hands and feet. This is not the way to become pure. The correct way to do ablution is to establish the state that has the connection between Allāh and yourself.

"Allāh has said that if you are in a place where there is no water, you can do your ablution using sand or dust. You cannot put sand into your eyes, or into your mouth, or into your nose. You cannot do any of these things, is that not so? But it is said that where there is no water you can do your ablution using sand. What does that mean? The meaning is that you are establishing that state while you are going through these actions. That is the meaning of ablution. The *wudū'* you do is not just performed on the outside. You must perform *wudū'* correctly on the inside.

"To become clear, is *wudū'.* To establish your *qalb* in the right way, is *wudū'.* To make your *qalb* virtuous, is *wudū'.* To bring it onto the straight path and to make the connection between Allāh and yourself, is *wudū'.* Within this ablution itself, you must properly fashion this state. You must do this," said the Rasūl ☻. He continues, "If you establish that state, then your prayers will not be *bātil.* Once you have established this connection to Allāh, you will see Him and you will do *sajdah* and *rukū'* directly to Him. You will be doing *sajdah* directly to His Light.

"If we do our ablution in this way, our prayers will not be *bātil*. Satan will not come and disturb us, those reels will not be running. Only the reels of the love of Allāh will be running, the connection between Him and us. This is what is known as ablution. If you establish this state, your prayers will be fulfilled. That is prayer. Then you will truly be praying.

"Until we have established this, we are just doing what all the others are doing. Even though a person is standing in *toluhai,* he may be wandering around the whole world. He may tell someone, 'O my friend, wait for me outside. I'll finish my prayers in two minutes and come back.' When he is going to the prayer he uses bad words, and when he sees someone there he uses bad words.

"When you go to prayers, you should go with the *dhikr,* the remembrance of God. As soon as your *wudū'* is finished, you should proceed with the *dhikr.* You must go with that state. If you tell someone to wait outside while you complete your prayers in two minutes, that is not prayer. This is how some people go to pray. But you must go with the state of death, the state where you have died in Allāh. You should not have the thought of returning. Understand? That is prayer.

"I am not saying that you should not pray. Until you understand this, you must do those prayers. But this is the state that you must try to develop. You must try to establish this state in your *qalb.* If you do not do your ablution properly, how can your prayers be fulfilled?"

This is what is known as ablution. Understand? This is what the Rasūl, *sallallāhu 'alaihi wa sallam,* told the man who was by his side doing his ablution. Understand?

Al-hamdu lillāh.

Is there anything else?

QUESTION

I am confused because Bawa has said that everything we do must be done to a limit and we should realize our limits, and even prayer has to be done to a limit. And I understand that it seems like for every person it would be an individual thing. And then I believe I heard Bawa say at a discourse that all these other things have to be done to a limit, but moving towards God, that won't hurt you if you just continue and continue. So I don't know, I don't know how to organize my life because (crying)...

BAWA MUHAIYADDEEN

Boo, boo, booooo, hoo. My love you! When you walk along the road, do you look down? Do you look at your feet as you go along?

QUESTION

Sometimes I'm looking at the ground.

BAWA MUHAIYADDEEN

You are looking down the road! Your eyes are looking ahead as you go along. Suddenly, if a child crosses the road, or a snake crosses the road, your legs immediately stop. Your eyes did not see the snake, but your legs immediately stopped. Or, you might jump to the side. Suppose there is a ditch or a stone on the path. You immediately stop, or avoid it. How does this happen? It is a reflex action of your muscles. The body knows. Your eyes do not necessarily see it, but the body is aware. That section, those muscles are aware of the danger.

Similarly, no matter what duty you may be doing, the remembrance of Allāh, that intention, must always be present. It must be ongoing in your heart, that intention must be constantly within you. Without missing even one minute or one second, that thought should move with your breath. If you have that intention within you, that will be completeness. Focusing on the thought of Allāh, having the remembrance of Him, and having the intention for Him, is the greatest prayer. That is the most exalted prayer.

Even if you do a thousand prayers of *toluhai,* the thoughts, remembrance, and intention of your *qalb* must always give all responsibility to God. This is what God accepts. You give the responsibility to Him, and He accepts it. If that thought is within you, the One who accepts it will take it. There is no limit for that, there is no *waqt* for that. For that intention there is no *waqt,* for that remembrance there is no *waqt*, and for the eye of *īmān* that focuses on that One there is no *waqt*. You must strengthen this. This is your duty. When you do all of your other duties, you should have this in your awareness. This is a duty that you must do!

God is the One who created you, the One who gives you the *rizq,* the One who gives you food, the One who protects you, the One who looks after you, the One who guards you, and the One who gives you a house. He is the One who gives life, the eyes, ears, nose, mouth, hands, feet, and body. He gave you all of these. So, you must remember that One who gave you so much. You must intend Him. You and I should intend Him, should we not?

All of these other things will disappear. You must think of That which exists forever. That thought should be within us, that remembrance should be there, that intention should be there. Our *īmān* should always be focused on That, no matter what we are doing.

Toluhai has a limit, it has a limit, a *waqt.* Everything in life is like this. But there is no *waqt,* no time, for That. This is the *proof.*

Understand?

QUESTION

Sometimes is it better then for us to try to do our duty with that remembrance and with that intention towards God instead of stopping and maybe trying to rush through doing a *salāh?*

BAWA MUHAIYADDEEN

If you do not have this state, then the *salāh,* the five-times prayer, is a duty that you must do. When hunger comes, you eat, do you not? If dust falls into your eyes, you wash your eyes, do you not? It is like this. See, now your nose is running and you are blowing your nose into a handkerchief. It is like this. Are you just letting your nose run? No! It is like this. That is the point.

Anbu. Al-hamdu lillāh.

All right. Will you give me some leave now? I have become tired.

A'ūdhu billāhi minash-shaitānir-rajīm.
I seek refuge in God from the accursed satan.

Bismillāhir-Rahmānir-Rahīm.
In the name of God, the Most Compassionate,
the Most Merciful.

SALĀH IS A BRIDGE

May 25, 1984, Friday, a.m.

(Bawa Muhaiyaddeen ⊕ is speaking about what happens after death.)

The thread of your faith will be fashioned like a strand of hair. Your *vanakkam,* your worship that is fashioned like a strand of hair, will become a bridge, and the point of your *'ibādah,* your service to God, will be spread on top of this bridge. The value from your *'ibādah* and from your *vanakkam* will be spread over this bridge that is the width of a hair, and will broaden it for you.

Your eyes will see the bridge widen according to what you did through your love of Allāh, the *tasbīh* you performed for Him, the *vanakkam* you offered Him, the *salāh* and *'ibādah* you performed to Him with certitude, determination, and *īmān,* and according to how open your *qalb* was. You are the ones whose *'ibādah* must fashion and build that bridge in the correct way. Each person must do this. To cross the chasm of hell you must build your own bridge, with prayer. That is *salāh,* the five-times prayer. That is your *salāh.* This is the path that enables you to cross this *dunyā,* to cross hell and reach heaven.

You must realize this with certitude. It is your *qalb,* your mind that is hell. That could be the fire. Your attachments, your ties, and everything you search for in this *dunyā* are hell, and will become the *'adhāb,* the torment that you will experience in hell. All the sections in

197

the *dunyā* that do not have God's qualities and actions will be spread as the firewood and the sufferings of hell. If you gather these sections, that will be hell. It is not heaven. If your mind and desire gather these things, they will become the burning fires of hell, they will become your place of hell. All of the things that you gather in your life are acquisitions for hell. That is what is known as the fire of hell.

You must make this mind go on the straight path. You must correct and turn your qualities to the path of Allāh, perform all of your actions on Allāh's path, act with good conduct on Allāh's path, acquire love, equality, tranquility, and peace, and show and give others the good benefit, with love. If you do this and gather good benefits, then that will be the profit you receive from your *'ibādah.* That will become the velvet of goodness that will be spread over that bridge, to broaden the path. It will be a flower-like velvet carpet for you to walk on. The Rasūl, *sallAllāhu 'alaihi wa sallam,* will be there, on the other side. The *mīzān tirāsu,* the balance scale, will be there to weigh the good and the bad. Good and evil will be weighed on that scale. In our lifetime, in our *hayāh,* we must see that *mīzān tirāsu.* That is our *qalb.* Sin and merit, hell and heaven, good and evil are weighed with a needle point on the two weighing pans of this scale that is our *qalb.* That justice and conscience…

Of the two weighing pans, one is for the sins that we have committed and one is for the good that we have done. Our *qalb* is a *tirāsu,* a scale. Wisdom must weigh our love and our qualities. The merit we receive from Allāh, our love for Allāh, our intention for Allāh, and our prayers are weighed there. Of that, the section of God that we have completed will be placed on the weighing pan of goodness. It will sit on the pan of goodness. The sections of the *dunyā,* the actions of the *dunyā,* and the attachments of the *dunyā* will be placed on the side of evil. Selfishness, separations, differences, and the qualities of attacking others with your mind, your heart, your actions, and with falsehood and jealousy will all be gathered on the side of evil.

Your *qalb* is the *tirāsu* for you. In your life in the *dunyā,* your *qalb* is the scale. After you die, it becomes the *mīzān tirāsu* where your good and bad are weighed. The *qalb* is the *tirāsu* that you can see for yourself. Each one will be able to see this. Tomorrow, that *tirasu* will be known as the *mīzān tirāsu*.

After death, there are two planks that are planted in the grave, one at the head and one at the foot of the body. Like that, one represents *hayāh*, life, and one represents *maut*, death; one is the *dunyā*, the world, and one is the *ākhirah*, the kingdom of God; one is evil and one is good. These are the two sides that will be weighed. This will be a means for you to understand everything that you have forgotten. The *mīzān tirāsu* will weigh what we did earlier, and then an inquiry will be held on the Day of *Qiyāmah*.

The state of your *'ibādah* and the *salāh* that you perform will be a great help to you for crossing over this trench of fire. Your actions and conduct, the qualities of Allāh and the qualities of the Rasūl, *sallAllāhu 'alaihi wa sallam*—the qualities of patience, tolerance, equanimity, equality, peacefulness, and unity—these qualities will be spread as velvet for you to walk across this bridge. So, when you set out to cross that bridge, it will be broadened for you. That is the bridge called the *sirātul-mustaqīm*, the straight path.

If you do not have these qualities, then your life in this *dunyā* will only amount to the width of a strand of hair that has been split into seven parts. This is how narrow your life will be, it will be the width of one-seventh of a hair. This is how insignificant your life in the *dunyā* will be. If you have fashioned only this small strand, then that is what will be tied across that bridge, and it will seem even smaller to you. You will not be able to walk on it. You will be scorched by the heat of the fire that is burning beneath the bridge. You will fall into that fire. God will make us aware of this. He will make us cross that bridge.

God says, "What *you* seek, not what others seek, will benefit you. The actions of others will not affect you. Your good and your evil are what come with you. I am not one who punishes you, I do not get angry with you. Anger and punishment are in your hands. It is you who becomes angry and you who creates your own punishment. You punish other lives, you get angry with other lives, and you attack others. You cause suffering and pain, and then you laugh and cry. This is within you. You create what is within you. Then you come here and experience your punishment. Your good and your evil belong to you alone."

That case, that lawsuit, will be heard on the Day of *Qiyāmah,* and the judgment will be given on Judgment Day. You must know that this Day awaits you. Before you go there, you must understand that this Day exists. This Day is waiting for you. No matter where you go, in the end you must bring the profit and the loss to your Father. When you come to your Mother and Father's house, you must give this to Them, you must show them the profit and loss. Like this, whatever you have gathered must, in the end, be brought and shown to Them. The profit will be yours, but it must first be brought to the Father. The goodness that you sought is yours, but if you discard the goodness and instead gather the evil, then that is also yours. If you return the treasure of goodness that your Father gave you, then that becomes yours. If you discard what is good and destroy and waste that treasure that the Father gave you, and if you instead gather evil, then that will also be yours. You will receive the punishment according to what you sought and acquired. That *tirāsu,* that judgment, will come forth from within you, and according to that judgment, you will be required to answer.

You have two *malā'ikah,* the two recording angels, that are writing down everything you do. They are witnesses. Each part of your body will be a witness to what it did and will reveal all the sins that it committed. Judgment will be given according to that.

Allāh says, "I do not punish you. What you receive will be in accordance with your own actions, in accordance with the good and the evil you have acquired. I am the Creator, your Father. Until the Day of Judgment I keep giving you food and protection. Whether you do evil or whether you do good, it is nothing to Me. Until your very last breath, I wait for you to ask for forgiveness. Until you are no longer conscious, I am here. I am waiting until your last breath for you to ask for forgiveness. But you have forgotten this. Therefore, the outcome of this belongs to you, not to Me." This is what He says.

Allāh continues, "Therefore, My children, please think about this. Come forward and perform the *salāh*. I have given this message to every *nabī*. Faith, the *kalimah, īmān, salāms, salāh, sadaqah, nōnbu,* and *hajj* are for you to correct your qualities. The *salāh* is for bringing about unity, affection, and one love. When all of you join together in unity and pray as one congregation, there will be no battles, enmity, divisions, wars, or fighting. When you live as one brotherhood, as the children of one Mother, you will create peace. Peace and tranquility are Islām.

"As long as the world exists, you will never find peace in the world. If you search for peace in the world, you will not find it. In the world you have divided into religions. One religion kills another religion and those of that same religion kill each other. One race kills another race and those of that same race kill each other. One scripture kills another scripture and those with that same scripture kill each other. One path kills another path and those on the same path kill one another. Like this, in the world one religion murders another and those in that same religion murder each other. Regardless of which religion you follow, this is what is happening.

"I sent the prophets to unite the children of Adam and to stop this destruction. I sent each prophet with My words, the words of God. Therefore, you must listen to My words. Those prophets are My representatives. It is you who have separated what they brought into religions, you who have separated that into creeds, you who have separated that into different paths, and you who have separated that into different scriptures. The prophets brought the truth, but you have split that truth into different groups. These differences have divided you, and the result is destruction and murder.

"You brought about these divisions. To unite you again, as one, I sent the *sattiya vēdam,* the religion of truth. I sent Muhammad as the Final Prophet, to unite all as one."

Adam, Noah, Abraham, Ishmael, Moses, David, Jesus, and Muhammad, may the peace of God be upon them all, are the eight (chosen) prophets. These eight are the chosen prophets. Muhammad ⊕ was sent to unite everyone. He is the Final Prophet.

Peace and unity are the purpose of *salāh*, of *toluhai*. The purpose of the five-times prayer is to show that state of peace and unity. The *salāh* was given to bring about this unity and to develop *shānti*. There, you embrace one another breast to breast, heart to heart, flesh to flesh, to cut away your enmity and unite as one, to cut away your hatred and unite as one. That is *shānti*. There, that great blessing of *shānti* exists. There, that great blessing of unity exists. There, that peace of the great blessing of the true path of *īmān*-Islām exists. That is the peace of Islām. Tranquility is Islām. Unity is Islām. That group is God's group. This peace can only be attained within one's self. It cannot be attained in the world. It is through *'ibādah*, through *vanakkam*, through *toluhai*, and through *dhikr* that we can receive these great blessings of peace, not from anywhere else.

The religions are paths. Peace comes into our *qalbs* from the *īmān*, faith, determination, and worship that we have. Unity comes from God's qualities and the qualities of the Rasūl, *sallAllāhu 'alaihi wa sallam*—*sabūr*, *shukūr*, *tawakkul*, and *al-hamdu lillāh*. It comes from Allāh's qualities, actions, behavior, conduct, and nature. It comes from His three thousand gracious qualities. When we act with these qualities, when we do our *salāh*, *salāms*, and *toluhai* in the correct way, and when we dutifully perform our acts of worship, we will find peace within ourselves. That is *shānti*.

If we have not found peace, *shānti*, and tranquility within, we will not be able to attain it in this world. Here, everything is murder and sin. One attacks another, one kills another. Each one kills its own kind. A snake swallows and kills another snake, a bird kills and eats another bird, an animal kills and eats another animal. Human beings are also like this. Human beings eat other human beings. Human beings kill other human beings. Human beings deceive other human beings. Human beings cause suffering to other human beings. In the same way, one religion does this to another religion.

The purpose of Islām is not to cause sorrow to other human beings, it is to create unity. This is what is known as Islām. Even though there are so many divisions and so many religions, if this state of unity comes, there will be peace. If the explanation of this state comes within the *qalb* of a human being, if he attains that peace, he will have peace in the *ākhirah* and in the *dunyā*. He will have peace here and he will have peace there in the *ākhirah*. If he attains fulfillment here, then the *ākhirah* will be made complete for him. May we reflect on this.

(Bawa Muhaiyaddeen ☺ recites the *adhān,* the call to prayer.)

Allāhu akbar, Allāhu akbar.
Allāhu akbar, Allāhu akbar.
Ash-hadu al-lā ilāha illAllāh.
Ash-hadu al-lā ilāha illAllāh.
Ash-hadu anna Muhammadar-Rasūlullāh.
Ash-hadu anna Muhammadar-Rasūlullāh.
Hayya 'alas-salāh.
Hayya 'alas-salāh.
Hayya 'alal-falāh.
Hayya 'alal-falāh.
Allāhu akbar.
Allāhu akbar.
Lā ilāha illAllāh.

Allāh is greater, Allāh is greater.
Allāh is greater, Allāh is greater.
I witness that none is God except Allāh.
I witness that none is God except Allāh.
I witness that Muhammad is the Messenger of Allāh.
I witness that Muhammad is the Messenger of Allāh.
Hasten to the prayer.
Hasten to the prayer.
Hasten to real success.
Hasten to real success.
Allāh is greater.
Allāh is greater.
None is God except Allāh.

Recite the *kalimah* and come to *salāh*. Allāh is the Great One. Come close to Him. Perform *salāh* to Him. Open your *qalb*, open the *ākhirah*. The door is open between you and the *ākhirah*. Open your *qalb* and come. Allāh is keeping it open for you. He is keeping the *ākhirah* open for you. Open your *qalb* and come. Do *tasbīh*. Perform *tasbīh*.

His representative, Nabī Muhammad Mustāfar-Rasūl, *sallAllāhu 'alaihi wa sallam*, is acting as the *imām*. Follow him. Follow behind him. He is your Nabī. Follow God's representative. Complete your *salāh*. Come, come quickly. Come quickly.

Hayya 'alal-falāh. Come. *Hayya 'alal-salāh*. Come quickly. Come quickly for *salāh*. Come soon. *Allāhu akbar*. Allāh is the Great One. Come and pray to Allāh. *Allāhu akbar*. Come and pray to Allāh. *Lā ilāha illAllāh*.

Allāh is the Ruler of the *dunyā* and the *ākhirah*. He is the Ruler of the *'arsh* and the *kursī*. He is the Ruler over everyone. *IllAllāh*, He is the One alone. There is no comparison or equal to Him. He is the Great One who has no equal. Come and pray. *IllAllāh*, He is the Solitary One, the One who has no comparison. Come and pray to God.

SallAllāhu 'alā Muhammad...

(Bawa Muhaiyaddeen ☺ recites the *salawāt*.)

SallAllāhu 'alā Muhammad, sallAllāhu 'alaihi wa sallam.

SallAllāhu 'alā Muhammad, sallAllāhu 'alaihi wa sallam.

SallAllāhu 'alā Muhammad, sallAllāhu 'alaihi wa sallam.

SallAllāhu 'alā Muhammad, yā Rabbi salli 'alahi wa sallim.

May Allāh bless Muhammad, may Allāh bless him and grant him eternal peace.

May Allāh bless Muhammad, may Allāh bless him and grant him eternal peace.

May Allāh bless Muhammad, may Allāh bless him and grant him eternal peace.

May Allāh bless Muhammad, O my Lord, bless him and grant him peace.

As-salāmu 'alaikum wa rahmatullāhi wa barakātuhu. May the peace, the beneficence, and the blessings of Allāh be upon you.

A'ūdhu billāhi minash-shaitānir-rajīm.
I seek refuge in God from the accursed satan.

Bismillāhir-Rahmānir-Rahīm.
In the name of God, the Most Compassionate,
the Most Merciful.

THE LANGUAGE OF 'ILM

September 26, 1981, Saturday, 11:50 a.m.

Bismillāhir-Rahmānir-Rahīm. Children, we must live within Allāh's love, Allāh's faith, Allāh's certitude, and Allāh's determination. In that state we must make our *īmān* strong. We must try to plant the crop known as *īmān*-Islām.

Knowledge, wisdom, languages, *vēdas, vēdāntas,* miracles, *sittis, wilāyāt,* praise and blame, titles and positions all exist. However, if we look at the different kinds of wealth, if we look at the languages, if we look at the *vēdas,* if we look at the colors, if we look at the races, we can see that *īmān*-Islām is what is most exalted.

Among the languages there is the Tamil language. It is greater than the ocean, it is like sweet music. Everything is contained within it. It is beautiful. It is beautiful to the eyes, to the ears, and to the tongue. Next is the language of the Hindus, which is called Hindi. Its name is Hindi, but it came from the Hindus. This Hindi language is an even more beautiful language. The Tamil language is expansive. Hindi is not expansive but has a sweetness and a happiness to it.

There is Hindi, Urdu, and Arabic. Like this, there are many languages. What is the benefit, what is the taste, and what is the happiness of these languages? There is no benefit in a language of itself, there is nothing gained by simply studying languages. They show differences. Languages, colors, *vēdas,* and *vēdāntas* all show differences. There are different gods, different prayers, and differences of race

207

and color. Like this, there are so many differences that are shown through prayers, worship, and languages, and these differences create separations and fighting. Everything is separating and dividing. This is war. Divisions are war, fighting. But *īmān*-Islām is one point. If you look at these titles, honors, positions, miracles, and *sittis,* if you look at the *wilāyāt,* if you look at all of these...

The Arabic language has a very beautiful character. Its sounds and its truth come forth from *īmān. Īmān* is Islām. Whoever possesses the wealth known as *īmān* will possess the *mubārakāt,* the exalted wealth of the three worlds of *al-awwal, ad-dunyā,* and *al-ākhirah.* In the world of the *rūh,* in the world of the *dunyā,* and in the world of the *ākhirah,* this exalted wealth is the wealth of *īmān.* Whoever attains this wealth of *īmān* will receive the wealth of *'ilm,* divine knowledge, the original *'ilm.* He will receive Allāh's *'ilm.*

Allāh's *'ilm* will melt rocks. It will make trees cry and flowers bloom, it will cool the grasses and calm the oceans. It will melt the sun, the moon, and the stars. It will melt the hearts of all of everything. It will melt the *qalbs,* the hearts, of the cows, the goats, the animals, and the poisonous beings, and cause tears to flow from their eyes. It will make the most poisonous animals and the most poisonous beings bow down and pay obeisance. Everything that the Rabb has created with His *Qudrah,* His Power, will pay obeisance to that *'ilm* and bow down to that *īmān.* That is what they will do. This state is known as Islām. When a man considers all lives as his own life, then all lives will embrace him. They will bow down to him. They will melt.

This language, this *daulah,* and this *rahmah,* Allāh's *rahmatul-'ālamīn,* are Allāh's *'ilm* and His qualities. This is the wealth of His benevolent grace. It is the wealth of the *rahmah* of His three thousand compassionate qualities, His love, mercy, and kindness. His qualities and actions are the milk of love—white honey. *'Ilm* is like that. When that *'ilm* is joined with *īmān* in a man, then all of everything will bow down to him, all lives will pay homage to him. Snakes, animals, trees, shrubs, water, air, earth, fire, the sun, the moon, the sky, the land, everything will bow down to him, they will pay obeisance to him. This is the way this 'ilm is. Pride, vengeance, black magic, and demons will leave. They will recognize him and leave. Evil will bow down to him and leave. It will pay obeisance to him and go, it will not oppose him. This state is called īmān-Islām. The meaning is that īmān is Islām. This is what is known as Islām.

We think that we are reciting and studying, do we not? We say that we have recited the thirty *juz'ul*-Qur'ān[1] and that we have understood through the Arabic language. But whether it is the Arabic language, or Arabic words, Allāh's words or His *wahys,* revelations, if we understand that language with īmān and if the sweet music of that language, its beauty, sound, resonance, bliss, and tenderness come forth, then that alone will be the music of Arabic that entrances all lives. The prayer that is like that is music. That prayer is music that will make everything melt. Everything will become entranced, all will listen to it. The qalb will melt. That sweet music, that language, that 'ilm will cause the qalb to melt with love.

What we are now reciting is not Arabic, it is just a language. That 'ilm, that Arabic, that *wahy* that came to Allāh's Rasūl ☺ is the *wahy* of grace. It is light, effulgence, that *rahmah,* that white honey. It is the taste for everyone, the joy for everyone. That 'ilm is the Arabic that will give peace and tranquility to all lives, and captivate them. If we recite in this way, if we understand in this way, if we know in this way, if this 'ilm comes to the tongue and if the understanding in the qalb comes forth from the tongue, we will find that there is no other melody as sweet as that, no other taste like that, no other music like that, no other bliss like that, no other tenderness like that, no other perfection like that, no other wealth like that, and no other truth like that. That sound that comes forth is recited in such a beautiful way. It emanates from Allāh as the sound of grace, the sound of Muhammad ☺—the sound of Allāh's "voice." It is the sound of His 'ilm, the sound of His *rahmah,* the sound of His light, the sound of His qualities, the sound of His actions, and the sound of His conduct.

That is the sound that embraces all lives. That music, that sound,

---

1 *juz'ul*-Qur'ān (A) A portion equal to 1/30th of the Qur'ān.

that grace, that resonance, that *rahmah,* that resplendence, that effulgence which shines like a star, that perfection, that sound of Arabic
is the sound that comes from Allāh. That is Arabic.

When you can understand this in the Arabic language, when that
sound resonates from *īmān,* then all lives in the *awwal,* the *dunyā,*
and the *ākhirah* will soften and melt. They will bow their heads and
listen. All of the branches on the trees will entwine and bow their
heads and listen. The grasses will bow their heads and listen. All the
flowers will blossom, bow down in reverence, and listen to that language. Upon hearing that sound—that resonance—the goats, the
cows, and all lives will draw near and bow down to that music. All
the snakes will withhold their poison and stop to worship. All of
the poisonous beings will hold back their poison and stop to pay
obeisance. And all of the birds will fold their wings and stop to listen.
They will be entranced by that sound.

There is no other music as beautiful as that, no happiness as beautiful, no other language as beautiful! It is Allāh's language, a beautiful
language, a beautiful *'ilm,* a beautiful light, a beautiful coolness, a
beautiful *rizq,* a beautiful, perfect food. It will satisfy hunger. It will
satisfy the hunger of the *dunyā,* the hunger of the soul, the hunger
of the *ākhirah,* and the hunger of the body. It will satisfy all hunger.

That is the *'ilm* that will appease hunger. That is that sound, that
is that sweet melody, that is that music, that is that resonance, that
is that prayer, that is that *toluhai,* that is that *vanakkam,* that is that
'ibādah, that is that *dhikr,* that is that *fikr,* and that is that surrender. To
surrender, intoxicated in God, that is that language.

When this sound comes forth from the tongue, when this sound
of *'ilm* comes forth, all lives will bow down. This is the *'ilm* that comes
forth from the Arabic language, Allāh's *'ilm.* This *'ilm* manifests from
īmān, it manifests from faith, certitude, and determination. When it
comes out from Allāh, when it comes out from that Plenitude, you
must take it and make it complete. When it comes forth from the
qalb, when it comes forth from that tongue, and when that sound
resonates, then what will not succumb to that love? There is nothing
that will not be overcome by it.

How beautiful is Allāh's language, His sound! It is His language of grace. It is not like the sounds that we recite. It is not like the sounds that we read. In every *qalb* there is the Light of Allāh, the *rūḥ* of Light. In every letter there is the resonance of Allāh, His sound and His voice. In every word there is the complete wealth which is His *raḥmah*. In every gaze His gaze shines and resplends. It resplends in every *sūrah,* in every word, in every letter, and in every *nuqtah.* If the *qalb* melts and touches that, then we can hear that music, that resonance, that sound.

There is nothing that will not be entranced by that. There is nothing other than that. There are no separations for that. There are no differences for that. There is only One. He alone is. His sound manifests from within that Arabic language. That sound is known as *'ilm.* What is manifested and revealed from that *'ilm* is His qualities and actions. That is Allāh's language. That is buried within that Arabic language.

When we recite with the sound of the treasure that is buried within it, when we extract that section and then read, we will see only One. We cannot see any separations. We will see everything joining with Allāh, and paying obeisance to Him. We will see all lives bowing before Him. We will see the Plenitude that gives the *rizq,* the nourishment, to all lives, and embraces them and protects them.

There is no *raḥmah* other than that *raḥmah.* When we are entranced by that and when *īmān,* certitude, and determination manifest in the *qalb,* the *qalb* will connect with Allāh and will melt. When we extract His *'ilm* from that language and open it out, then that will give gratification and pleasure to the ears, happiness to the eyes, fragrance to the nose, taste to the tongue, bliss and plenitude to the *qalb,* and happiness and satisfaction to the body. All lives will be complete. What will they lack? They will not lack anything. All lives will be without want. This is *īmān-*Islām. It is a beauty that is indescribable and inestimable.

Allāh's grace and *'ilm* are indescribable and unending. Allāh is the unfathomable Ruler of grace, the One of incomparable love. He is beyond description and beyond measure. Nothing is comparable or equal to His love. Such is the speech, the *qalb,* and the *'ilm* of the one who has this love. *'Ilm* is buried within the Qur'ān, within the Arabic language. It is buried within the 6,666 *āyāt,* verses of the Qur'ān.

If we understand what is within this and if we can bring forth this *'ilm* that is buried within the Arabic language, then that will be Allāh's *'ilm.* It is extremely exalted. When this comes forth from the mouth, when these words come forth, all lives will be entranced. Deaf ears will open and hear; blind eyes will see and experience joy and light; muted tongues will speak; noses that cannot smell will open and smell; tongues of fools who have no wisdom will understand and speak; lean bodies will become full; broken *qalbs* will mend; hearts of stone that cannot be broken will break; and hearts that have no faith will bow in obeisance.

In this way, this *'ilm* gives the immeasurable blessing of *rahmah.* There is so much music within this *'ilm.* In the world we can see only an atom's worth of the music that is buried in this *'ilm.* This music emerges from just one atom. Allāh has given one atom of that sound and placed it in copper, gold, iron, silver, stone, trees, metals, bones, joints, the earth, shrubs, water, air, fire, ether, the sun, the moon, the stars, in everything everywhere. He has given it the sound of sweet music. It is only one atom of His sound.

Allāh has split one *nuqtah,* one *sukūn,* into seventy thousand particles, and has given the sound from one of those particles to all places. The sound that comes when you pluck a small wire is the sound that comes from Him, from one particle of that *nuqtah.* The sound that you hear from a tree is the sound that comes from a particle of that *nuqtah.* The sound that comes from air is the sound that comes from that particle. The crackling sound that comes from fire is the sound that comes from that particle. The sound that comes from a stone comes from that particle. The many sounds you hear from metals come from that particle. The sound that comes from the sun is from that particle. The sound that comes from the sky and the earth, from lightning and thunder, all comes from that particle. The sound that comes from the grass, the weeds, and so many other things is from that one particle. One *nuqtah* has been divided into seventy thousand particles and it is from that (one particle) that a sound is produced. This is the music that you study. All of the sounds that come from the bones, the skin, and the membranes are from one particle of one *nuqtah*. How entranced you are by this music! The sound that comes from the tongue, the bones, the joints, the skin, and the membranes is beautiful music that captivates you, is it not? This sound is enticing. Everything is music. You can hear the sounds that come from water and from the ocean. Yet, out of one *nuqtah* that has been divided into seventy thousand particles, this is only one particle of sound. Think what the sound from one full *nuqtah* would be like! All of this exists within the resonance of Allāh, the voice of Allāh, and the sound of Allāh. How much sound is kept within the Qur'ān! God reveals it through the Arabic language in the Qur'ān.

If you take this music and if you read it and bring it forth from your tongue in this way, then what is there that will not be entranced by it? Everything will be captivated by it. The water, air, fire, sun, moon, everything will be overcome. This plenitude is the Arabic language, the sound that comes from Allāh. This sound is buried within the Arabic language, in the Qur'ān. This is the *rahmah,* which is the *mubārakāt.* This is *'ilm,* the *bahrul-'ilm,* His *rahmah.*

Take this sound and make it complete. If you bring this forth from the Qur'ān through the Arabic language, or through any other language—no matter in what language you reveal it, all lives will bow down to what is within that language. This is that *'ilm,* that language, Allāh's language. Everything will pay obeisance to that. One point, one God, one family, one prayer. This does not see any separation. This is completeness. This is *īmān*-Islām. We must understand this. If you do not understand, you will simply be reciting the Arabic language. The Arabic language is just a language, but what is within it is Allāh's sound. The Arabic language is a form, but what is within it is that *rahmah.*

You have Allāh's *rahmah* within your body, do you not? Within a seed there is the *rahmah* that causes it to grow, is there not? Within a flower there is a fragrance, is there not? Within what the Rabb

created and made evident is that *rahmah,* the *'ilm.* It is within. God
has placed a light within a stone, has He not? Like that, He has placed
the light called *rahmah* within the Qur'ān, in the Arabic language. If
you realize this, and if you extract it and read it in that language, it
will be very, very beautiful. That is *'ilm,* that is *īmān-*Islām, *'ilm.* It
melts everything like wax. If you take it and read it, then all of it will
be beautiful music, the music that will enchant all lives. It will break
down everything that will not break, making it melt like wax. Such
is that *'ilm,* the Arabic language.

If you take what is within this Arabic language and open it out,
then the Arabic language will be beautiful in this way. That will be
our *qalb.*

Children, this is very exalted, it is a very exalted *'ilm.* There is no
music other than that. Nothing will give happiness other than that.
There is no wealth other than that. Nothing is complete or gives
long life, *hayāh,* other than that. Therefore, we must try to know this
and make it flourish. *Āmīn.*

May Allāh grant His grace. Every child must try to understand
this. Then, if you can extract this *'ilm,* all lives will surround you.
You will be able to understand all sorrow and joy. You will be able
to dispel sorrow and reveal happiness. You must understand this.

My love you. May God grant His grace. May His love fill us.
May the wealth of *rahmah* that is *īmān* be perfected in us. May our
qalbs melt with His tenderness. May the fragrance of His qualities
come forth from our *qalbs.* May His qualities become complete
within us. Then we will know the completeness of peace, equanimity, and tranquility in this life. *Āmīn.*

May He grant us that grace. *Āmīn. Āmīn. As-salāmu 'alaikum.*

A'ūdhu billāhi minash-shaitānir-rajīm.
I seek refuge in God from the accursed satan.

Bismillāhir-Rahmānir-Rahīm.
In the name of God, the Most Compassionate,
the Most Merciful.

A *HADĪTH* ON PRAYER

July 15, 1981, Wednesday, 7 p.m.

TRANSLATOR

Doctor Markar says that a *rak'ah* is that you have one set of prayers and then one prostration; that is one *rak'ah*. Then, two *rak'ahs* mean two sets of prayers and two prostrations. So he said that in the early morning you are asked to do two *rak'ahs,* that is, two sets of prayers...

BAWA MUHAIYADDEEN

It is because of lazy people that God made the fifty-one *waqts* of prayer into five times of prayer. Because the people could not do this, because they were unable to do this due to laziness and the *nafs ammārah,* the fifty-one *waqts* were reduced by (one-tenth), to five *waqts*. You have been given (one-tenth). That is all you are doing.

There is the prayer at *awwal fajr,* at 3:30 in the morning, the *qunūt*[1] prayer. You are not praying that *qunūt* prayer. Next, when you go to the mosque, there are two *rak'ahs* for the mosque. These are for the sake of the mosque, Allāh's house. You are not doing that prayer. Next, there are two *sunnah* and two *fard*[2] for *subh,* the early morning prayer. I do not see you doing the *sunnah* prayers, although

---

1 *qunūt* (A) *Du'a's* or supplications recited at *witr* and *subh* prayers. See Glossary.

2 *fard* (A) Obligatory prayers; *sunnah* (A) Additional prayers that the Prophet MuhammadÒ usually performed.

you are doing the two *rak'ahs* that are *fard*. So, out of these, you are only doing two.

For *wudū'*, ablution, there are sixteen different *sharts,* sixteen conditions. Out of the sixteen, you are doing only one-fourth. You are not wiping, *mas-hun,* the entire head. Out of the sixteen, this is just one portion. Out of the sixteen, wiping the head is only one portion. So, look at the faults that exist in your worship!

For *zuhr,* the noon prayer, there are twelve *rak'ahs:* four *sunnah* prayers, four *fard,* and then four more (two *sunnah* and two *nafl*).[3] You leave out eight *rak'ahs* and pray only four. You do not understand about the *sunnah.* In this country there are people who do not even understand what *sunnah* is. They do not know about the *sunnah.*

For *'asr,* the late afternoon prayer, there are eight *rak'ahs:* four *sunnah* and four *fard.* The four *sunnah* are done before the *fard* prayer. Of those, you are only praying four *rak'ahs.*

For *maghrib,* the prayer after sunset, there are seven *rak'ahs:* three *fard,* two *sunnah,* and two *nafl.* Of these seven *rak'ahs* you are only praying three.

For *'ishā',* the evening prayer, there are seventeen *rak'ahs.* Because of your laziness you are not even doing one-fourth of what Allāh has ordained.

Fifty-one *waqts* of prayer were made into five *waqts* of prayer, and yet you are not even doing one part of that! You think that this is prayer. You remain asleep and miss the prayer for the mosque, the *qunūt* prayer, and the *awwal fajr* prayer. You rush around, rinse your mouth, do one-fourth of your washing, and do two *rak'ahs* of prayers. Then you think that this is prayer. You were sleeping.

That is not it! You should at least pray the one-fourth correctly. You must understand and pray the *sunnah, nafl, witr,*[4] and *fard* prayers. You have not understood the *sharts,* the conditions of these prayers. Imām ash-Shāfi'īÚ has said that because you have the state where

---

3   *nafl* (A) Optional supererogatory prayers.
4   *witr* (A) According to Abu HanīfahÚ, a necessary *(wājib),* single bow or cycle of prayer, performed after *'ishā'* and before *fajr* immediately following a pair of bows or cycles of prayer known as *ash-shaf'i.*

you do not understand these conditions, you should at least pray the *fard*. This is what the *imāms* say. But what Allāh says is: "You must do the prayers according to My *sharts*."

There were four *imāms:* Imām Abu HanīfahÚ, Imām ash-ShāfiʿīÚ, Imām ibn HanbalÚ, and Imām MālikÚ, and they gave many different explanations for tying the hands at *takbīr*.[5] Some people tie their hands at *takbīr* by covering the eyes. Some tie their hands at *takbīr* by covering the chest. And some tie their hands at *takbīr* by covering the navel. So, some say that you should cover the eyes (with your hands) because the eyes commit sin, some say it is the chest that should be covered, some say to cover the navel: some say to cover above the navel and some say to cover below the navel.

Some people say the navel should be covered, some people say that below the navel should be covered, some people say the breast should be covered, and some say the eyes should be covered. Like this, we must think, which of these is going to protect our honor?

Now, because of these different *imāms* you have become divided. Did Allāh bring about this separation? You must think about how these four *imāms* will cry tomorrow, on the Day of *Qiyāmah*. On the Day of *Qiyāmah*, Allāh will ask these *imāms*, "Did I tell you to create divisions? I said there is one family of Adam, one Allāh, one prayer. Did I tell you to divide them?" He will ask this.

You will say, "This is my *imām*, this is your *imām*." You follow different *imāms* and have different ways of praying. Allāh alone is the Imām, the 'Ālim, the Rahmatullāh. Did He tell us to follow Him, or did he tell us to follow these *imāms?* Whom did He tell us to follow? Allāh might ask about this.

We must pay attention to His words regarding *toluhai, fard, sharts,* and *sunnah*. We must know the *sharts* of *toluhai,* the five-times prayer. We must know the obligations of the *fard*. We must know *sharī'ah*. We must know *haqīqah, maʿrifah,* and *tarīqah. Toluhai* must be made clear.

---

5 *takbīr* (A) To raise the hands and say *"Allāhu akbar,* God is greater," in *salāh* and then to tie the hands, placing the right hand over the left.

When you speak of the *fard*, it is as ordinary as giving milk to a child who does not understand anything. It is like a mother giving milk to a child that cannot feed himself. The first step is like that. This is an explanation of the *fard* that you are doing. It is like that. But, a child who knows how to eat on his own, a child who knows the taste, who knows cleanliness, who knows the flavor, will know how to do all of this. Like this, a child who understands will be able to do this on his own. Earlier the mother has to show the child how to dress and cover his backside. The child does not really understand, so the mother has to show him. Then, one day the child will understand how to do this by himself. That is the state of the child. Like that, when the child has his own awareness, his own wisdom, and his own state, when he has the proper understanding, he can dress himself with a sense of modesty.

Prayer is like that. You must come to a state where you can pray on your own. Then you will understand all of the explanations of good hygiene; you will understand what is clean and you will discard what is unclean. You will understand *sharr* and *khair*, bad and good; you will take the *khair* and act accordingly and understand and discard the *sharr*. You will understand *halāl* and *harām*, what is permissible and what is not permissible, and will take and eat what is *halāl* and avoid what is *harām*. You will understand *dhāt* and *sifāt*, essence and creation, and will take and act according to the *dhāt* and discard the *sifāt*, the attachments. Like this, day by day you will grow and you will realize your state.

It is the same way with prayer. As you continue, you will understand more. That will be *vanakkam*. Then, there is what is called *'ibādah*. What you are now doing is *toluhai*. You have made what is known as *toluhai*, the five-times prayer, into a *tollai*, a difficulty. It is an inconvenience for you.

Vanakkam is to pay obeisance to Allāh. *'Ibādah* is to become an *'abd*, a slave to Allāh, a *murīd*, a disciple. *Vanakkam* is to surrender to Allāh. You accept Him and prostrate to Him. *'Ibādah* is to praise Him alone; you praise only Him. *Sūfiyyah* is to die in Him. You die and study within Him. You understand within Him, you learn within Him, you are aware within Him, you know within Him, and you speak within Him. Like that, to understand these meanings is called *vanakkam* and *'ibādah*.

Toluhai is to learn the first step, it is to learn what is obligatory and to do it. As we understand, we learn more. From there we continue to learn and learn and learn and go on climbing higher. If that state is not present, then it will be like a childless man smelling a dirty diaper. The man does not have a baby, so he carries a diaper with him and smells it so that he can get the smell of the baby. He keeps trying to experience the baby by smelling the diaper. In this way, the childless man keeps on smelling feces. Like that, we are in a state where we are unable to grow. This is what we keep as a smell. We do not understand the meanings we are meant to receive, the explanations we need to know, and the station we need to attain. So, we remain at the place that our limited understanding tells us belongs to us. But, if we look into the real meaning of *toluhai*, if we look into the meaning of *vanakkam*...

There is *toluhai*, *vanakkam*, *'ibādah*, *dhikr*, and *fikr*. The first is *toluhai*, Allāh's qualities, Allāh's actions, Allāh's conduct, Allāh's behavior, Allāh's compassion, Allāh's patience, Allāh's tolerance, Allāh's peacefulness, Allāh's ways of integrity, Allāh's *tawakkul*, trust, and Allāh's duty, His compassionate qualities. These qualities bring peace. To become filled with these qualities and to make these qualities complete within you is *toluhai*.

Once you find that these qualities are complete within you, then Allāh's wealth, His qualities, will grow. You will become an *'abd*, a slave to Him. That is *vanakkam*. *Vanakkam* is where you receive those qualities of Allāh and become His *'abd*. That is *vanakkam*. To surrender to Allāh is *vanakkam*. You receive this wealth and give all responsibility to Him.

'Ibādah is where you distribute whatever treasures you have received from Him. You share it. You spread out and distribute those treasures, Allāh's wealth, those qualities, that *'ilm*, that wisdom, that good conduct, that *'ibādah*, and that *vanakkam*. That is *'ibādah*.

Toluhai is to acquire this state, these qualities of Allāh. You must understand that *shart,* you must understand that patience, you must understand that meaning, you must understand that love, you must understand that *sabūr,* you must understand that *shukūr,* you must understand that *tawakkul. Al-hamdu lillāh. Al-hamdu lillāh.* You must make His wealth complete within you.

We must fill ourselves with Allāh's *'ilm,* Allāh's qualities, Allāh's actions, Allāh's behavior, Allāh's affection, Allāh's love, Allāh's speech, Allāh's resonance, and Allāh's sound. Having filled ourselves with these qualities, then with them we do *tasbīh,* prayers of glorification to Allāh. That is *vanakkam.* To pay obeisance to Allāh is *vanakkam.* To bow down to Him is *vanakkam.* Prostrating to Him is *vanakkam.*

Why do you bow your head? When you see a great man, you lower your head as a sign of respect, do you not? You bend your head in respect. So, to bow down to Allāh is *vanakkam.* You bow your head to His speech and sound, you bow to the words and actions of the Lord. You bow your head in awe, to His explanations. You bow your head to His duty and His gaze. You bow your head to His grace. You bow your head to His *wilāyāt.* You bow your head to His sound. He is known as ar-Rabb, who understands everything. You prostrate to That. You bow your head to His *Qudrah,* His Power. This is the state of obeisance. That is *vanakkam,* that is worship.

To bow down to His justice is *vanakkam,* to bow down to His duty is *vanakkam,* to bow down to His qualities is *vanakkam,* to bow down to His actions is *vanakkam,* to bow down to His love is *vanakkam,* to bow down to His kingdom is *vanakkam,* to bow down to His integrity is *vanakkam,* to bow down to His righteousness is *vanakkam,* to bow down to His good conduct is *vanakkam.* That is *vanakkam. Toluhai* is to fill yourself with all of His qualities. *Vanakkam* is to bow your head in obeisance to Him, to prostrate to Him, and to pray to Him with these qualities. That is *vanakkam.*

'Ibādah is to bow down at His feet, to acquire His wealth, and to make His qualities grow. You take on those qualities, that *'ilm,* that sound, that word, and that action, and make these grow within you.

You give peace to all lives, peace to all hearts, peace to all *qalbs*—peace to the lives, peace to all the beings, peace to all the creations. You make them tranquil and peaceful. You make them prostrate to Allāh, you make them bow down to their Rabb who created them. You make them bow to His justice, bow to His *Qudrah*, bow to His *wilāyāt*, bow to His actions, bow to His love, bow to His compassion, and bow to His judgment. You make them bow down to the One who gives food. You make them prostrate to the One who created the souls and provides their food. This is *vanakkam* and *'ibādah*.

Toluhai is the qualities. Without backbiting and without telling lies, to change your qualities and fill yourself with Allāh's qualities is *toluhai*. That quality is *toluhai*, that action is *toluhai*, that *shart* is *toluhai*, that love is *toluhai*, that peacefulness is *toluhai*. To go on that path of justice, without deviating by even one breath, is *toluhai*. To fill yourself with these qualities and to pray to Him, is *vanakkam*. That is *vanakkam*. Then, when His resonance and sounds are given to others, that is *'ibādah*. *Vanakkam* and *'ibādah*. *'Ibādah*. We bow down to Him, acquire His treasures, and distribute them. We disseminate His explanations and give peace to others. We should think about this.

When we establish this state, then that will be the state in which we die in Him. We merge as one without any duality. There is only one Rabb. We understand that there is nothing other than Allāh, who is One. To merge with Him is *sūfiyyah*. We hear His sound, we speak with His sound, we speak with His tongue, we hear with His ear, and we understand His resonance. Then Allāh is within man and man is within Allāh. Because man's *qalb* is merged with Allāh's *qalb*, man listens to the sound of Allāh's words. They are communing, one with the other. He gives to Allāh and Allāh gives to him. He gives his speech to Allāh and Allāh gives His speech to him. He gives his intentions to Allāh and Allāh gives His intentions to him.

When this state is established, that is known as *sūfiyyah*. That resplends in the *bahrul-'ilm*, the ocean of divine knowledge. This is not found in an (outer) book. This book is called the *qalb*, the innermost heart. The book called the *qalb* and Allāh's Book called *Rahmah*, the Book of Grace, become one. Allāh's resplendence and plenitude and man's *qalb* of plenitude become one. We should think of this. This is the prayer of *sūfiyyah*.

To understand these meanings we have to climb higher, step by step. Doctor Markar Tambi, this is how we have to grow. We must attain wisdom and grow. You have been thinking about how fifty-one *waqts* were made into the five *waqts*. You have been speaking about why there are three *waqts* or two *waqts*, three *waqts* or four *waqts*.

Qunūt. The one who is trying to destroy the *dunyā* is satan, dajjāl. His mother's name is jaddah, his father's name is badda, and his name is dajjāl, jāhil,[6] the one who has gone astray. Every day he licks a rock mountain. Allāhu ta'ālā Nāyan keeps him in a mountain called 'Arafāt and has placed seven mountains on top of that mountain. He has bound him with seventy thousand chains, guarded by seventy thousand *malaks*, angels. These mountains are placed on top of him so that he cannot climb out from under that mountain.

But, he keeps licking from within. He licks and licks and licks that mountain, he licks and licks and licks throughout the night. So, at *subh*, at the *awwal fajr* prayer, it is time for him to free himself and come out. It is then that he sets out to destroy the *dunyā*, the world. That is what is called dajjāl, jāhil.

Like that, within our *qalb*, our innermost heart, there is a rock called darkness, and buried within that rock is this jāhil—the evil qualities. He is the one who has gone astray. He has the qualities of satan. He is buried under this mountain and is bound with seventy thousand iron chains. These iron chains are known as Allāh's *qalam*, pen. In one *alif*, there are seventy thousand *nuqat*, and each of these seventy thousand *nuqat* is a chain. Those chains are the seventy thousand angels, who are the *sukūns*. Allāh has buried jāhil there, in that mountain, and has bound him with these *sukūns*, these *malaks* and *malā'ikah*, to ensure that he does not come out. He licks and licks and licks and licks that *qalb* which is the *'arshul-mu'min*, the throne of the true believer. He is trying to lick his way through and come out with his hell called *jahannam*.

---

6 jāhil (A) Satan, the one who has gone astray. Literally, ignorant, unrestrained.

Some people have a rock of darkness, a *qalb* that is a rock mountain that will not melt. Within that rock mountain is anger and hastiness. This is a *qalb* that cannot be broken. Allāh's word will not be able to melt that place. Allāh's love will not be able to melt that place. Allāh's affection will not be able to melt that place. Allāh's truth will not be able to melt that place. Allāh's patience will not be able to melt that place. His grace, His treasure, and His *rahmah* will not be able to melt that place, that *qalb*. Such is that hard rock! Some people have a *qalb* which is harder than granite stone. This satan keeps on licking within that *qalb*.

God has created the three Lights called *alif*, *lām*, and *mīm*, and with these He protects us from the one with evil qualities, the accursed jāhil, the one who has gone astray—the one who wants to come out to destroy the *dunyā* and destroy you. Allāh protects us from his attempts to destroy our *rūh*, our good thoughts, our *īmān*, and Allāh's *rahmah*.

Therefore, jāhil is trying to arise from within your *qalb*. Through the night you sleep without any awareness, without even knowing whether you are passing gas from your backside. Through the night you do not do *dhikr*, you do not pray. You do not do *dhikr*, you have no thought of God, and you have no fear of God. Those sounds do not resonate there. So, jāhil goes on licking. He is licking from within that rock, from within that mountain.

Earth, fire, water, air, ether, mind, and desire are the seven mountains. The one who has gone astray is buried under these seven mountains. He is bound by seventy thousand angels, seventy thousand iron chains. He is bound with these *nuqat*, these iron links. He is bound with these seventy thousand *sukūns* which exist as angels. That is Allāh's protection.

The *alif*, the Sound that is Allāh, is there as a Light on top of these mountains. It presses jāhil down, not allowing him to rise up. The *lām*, which is the Light of completeness, dispels all of the darkness. And the *mīm* that is MuhammadÒ, Allāh's *wilāyāt*, is resonating there in creation, protecting it. It is because these three go on resonating, shining, and resplending that jāhil is unable to come out. He stays there, licking.

In the nighttime, when your focus (on God), your thoughts, your *niyyah*, that *dhikr*, and those *salawāt* and *salāms* are suspended, jāhil is trying to lick his way out. He is trying to destroy the *dunyā*, the *rahmah* of the *dunyā*, goodness, and the good treasures. That is the quality called jāhil, the quality of differences. So, in that state, if your *qalb* wakes up at *awwal fajr*, and if you pray the *qunūt* prayer, then satan cannot emerge, because Allāh's *Qudrah* will grow over him and he will be pressed down again. He will return again to that place he was in earlier.

Jāhil is licking you every day, trying to come out. Without allowing him to emerge, you must press him down within your *qalb* and bind him with those chains. You must tie up those evil qualities. You must bind up jāhil, the qualities that have gone astray. With Allāh's RasūlÒ, His Nūr, you must press him down. That is why this *qunūt* prayer is done.

The prayer to the mosque is when you place your *qalb* in Allāh; you place the *qalb* called the *'arshul-mu'min* there. This prayer is where you give that *qalb* into Allāh's responsibility. That is Allāh's house, Allāh's *rahmah*. This prayer to the mosque is for the sake of Allāh, where you give all responsibility to Allāh, you give your *qalb* to Allāh.

Awwal fajr is the time when your *hayāh*, your life, emerged. There were two causes that emerged. One is Allāh and one is MuhammadÒ. When the *sirr*, secret, known as MuhammadÒ emerged, it could be seen. That is *sifāt*, creation. That *sifāt*, what is seen, is the *fard*. The *dhāt*, essence, what is not seen, is Allāh. That is the *sunnah*. What is hidden and strong is *sunnah*, while what can be explained on the outside is *fard*, it can be understood.

Therefore, there are two *sunnah* and two *fard*. The form of these two should be understood. What is seen outside is the *fard*, and what goes on resonating and shining within is the *sunnah*. The *sunnah* is heavy. What is on the outside is easy. So, there are two *sunnah* and two *fard*.

Zuhr prayer. There are four meanings that you must understand: *sharī'ah*, *tarīqah*, *haqīqah*, and *ma'rifah*. You must understand the four times four, the sixteen meanings. We must understand these sixteen meanings. Allāh is the Treasure that fills the eight directions and the sixteen corners. There are eight directions and sixteen corners. Allāh fills these. He alone goes on resonating in all of these directions. You must understand this resonance of Allāh in these eight directions. North, south, east, and west are the four directions. There is *az-zabūr, al-jabbūrat, al-injīl,* and *al-furqān.* These are the four religions, the four divisions. There is earth, fire, water, and air. We must understand these four. Earth, fire, water, and air are outside. We must understand this.

These are the four *fard* of *zuhr.* The *sunnah* is inside. The Nūr resplends within *īmān.* That is *rahmah,* that is *sunnah.* The first four are *sunnah,* the last four are *sunnah* and *nafl,* and the four in between are *fard.* That makes twelve. These twelve are your twelve openings. They shine as the twelve *rāsis,* the signs of the zodiac. Four can be seen outside and four can be seen inside. Earth, fire, water, and air can be seen inside and earth, fire, water, and air can be seen outside. *'Ilm* can be seen. Allāh, MuhammadÒ, Nūr, and *'ilm*—the Qutbiyyah, these four can be seen further within. Inside, the *dhāt* will be seen as earth, fire, water, and air. Outside, earth, fire, water, and air will also be seen. What is seen in *'ilm* and what is seen in *'ibādah* are the four causes: Allāh, MuhammadÒ, MuhaiyaddeenÚ—the Light, the *wilāyāt*—and Nūr. These four can be seen within. These are the twelve *rak'ahs.* They have to be seen within, within, within! This must be understood. We must understand this in this *waqt.*

What must be seen in the *waqt* of *'asr* are eight *rak'ahs,* the four *fard* and four *sunnah.* If a man wants to look into this, he will see four *fard* on the outside, in the world, and he should also see the inner *fard,* the four inner steps. He should see the four religions, one within the other. He must discover where they disappear in Allāh. There is nothing other than Allāh. All that was created from AdamÆ was formed from the same earth. *Insān* and Allāh are connected. Allāh is the *dhāt,* He is the Completeness. *Insān* is the *sifāt,* the creation. The *sifāt* can be seen on the outside. The *dhāt* is the grace. Allāh exists as a mystery. We must understand both. This meaning should be understood. This should be understood in your prayer.

Maghrib has seven meanings. There are the three *fard* on the outside. Earth, fire, and water. Earth, woman, and gold. These three are external, they are *fard*. You need earth, you need woman, and you need gold, wealth. These three are needed on the outside; they must be understood on the outside. Inside are the *sunnah* and *nafl*. You have to understand the *nafl*. *Sunnah* is where you realize the state where you merge with Him. Your *maut*, your death, becomes *hayāh*, life that is eternal. You must understand these two that are on the inside. What you see outside is earth, woman, and gold. These are the three *fard* that are outside. We must understand these.

The *waqt* of *'isha'*. There are twenty-one things that you have to consider. There are twenty-one (*rak'ahs*, bows) that you have to understand. When you realize these, when you understand these, you will have cut away your death. If you complete this *waqt* of prayer, that will be *maut*, death, the *fard* of your *maut* and judgment. You will understand that judgment on the outside. You will understand your sorrow and happiness on the outside. Having understood these, you must understand the twenty that are beyond this. If you understand these twenty, you will understand *hayāh*. You will know your death and you will know your life. So, that is *'isha'*. When you understand the *waqt* of *'isha'*, you will understand the blessing that is your *hayāh*, and you will immediately receive the *rahmah*, the grace of that *hayāh*.

Of these five *waqts*, one is the connection to the earth, one is the connection to water, one is the connection to air, one is the connection to fire, and one is the connection to ether, the connection to maya and the *nafs*. If you can cut away these five connections, then that is the five *waqts* of prayer. At each of these five times of prayer, you cut off one of the sections. These are the five *waqts*.

In your life itself there are five *waqts*. When you cut off the earth, you cut off your karma. When you cut off water, you cut off your creation. When you cut off air, you cut off your *nafs*, your attachments. When you cut off fire, you cut off your anger, pride, and arrogance. When you cut off torpor, you cut off your birth. When you cut off the connections to your body, and when you cut away your intentions, you will achieve the state where your intention and His intention are one and the same. *'Ishā'*. There will be no death or birth. You will have life that is eternal. You will always be a sixteen-year-old youth. You will be victorious in this life and in the next. This is *sifāt*.

When we realize the five meanings of the five *waqts*, when we understand this, then Allāh alone is our property, our *hayāh*. He is our property, He is our *hayāh*, He is our life, He is our food, He is our joy, He is our heaven, He is our *'ilm*, He is our very existence. That is heaven. Other than this property, there is no other property that is complete for us. If we can attain *this* completeness, then we are *mu'mins*, true believers. On that Day we will not be asked any questions; we will not be questioned on the Day of *Qiyāmah*.

For those who have no attachments, for those who have no death, there is no Day of *Qiyāmah*. If you keep any property other than Allāh, there will be a judgment for that. If you have only Allāh, there is no judgment for That, but if you have an attachment to something, then it is through that very attachment that good and evil will result. When you have only Allāh, there is no good and evil. There is only Allāh, the Perfection. There is no judgment for That.

You must realize and understand this state. This is the way to pray. If you know this, Tambi, if you pray knowing *vanakkam*, *toluhai*, *'ibādah*, *dhikr*, *salāms*, and *salawāt*, then you will know these meanings. These are the duties that are done by the *mu'mins*. These are the duties that the *nabīs*, the *olis*, and the *qutbs* do. We must also strive hard to do it in this way. When we receive this *daulah*, this *rahmah*, and these treasures of the *mubārakāt*, and when we attain freedom, we will be *mu'mins*. Then everything will intend *you* and come in search of *you*. The *ka'bah* will come in search of you, the *rahmah* will come in search of you, the *nabīs* will come, the *olis* will come, *'ilm* will come, justice will come, and integrity will come. Allāh's qualities will come in search of you, Allāh's wealth of grace, the treasure of His wealth will come in search of you, the wealth of the qualities will come in search of you. Everything will come searching for you! You will be among those who have received the *mubārakāt*.

When these come in search of you, that will be heaven. When you are in a place of *hayāh*, that will be heaven. When you are in the *dunyā*, that will be heaven, and when you are in the *ākhirah*, that will be heaven. When all of these good things come in search of you, that will be heaven. When all the good blessings come in search of you, that will be heaven. It is the *ka'bah* that is coming in search of you. The *ka'bah* is Allāh's *Qudrah* and His *Rahmah*. That will search for you. It is not the Ka'bah in Mecca that comes to you. It is His *Rahmah*, the beauty of that *Rahmah*, His mystery, and His greatness that come searching for you. That is what came to Rābi'atul-'Adawiyyah ☺.[7] That *Rahmah*, that *ka'bah* came to her.

Like that, when the meanings and the light-beings come in search of us, then that is heaven, that is *firdaus*, that is paradise. This is what we must search for. If things that are evil come in search of us, if maya and darkness come, then that is hell. If what is good comes in search of us, then that is heaven, and if what is evil comes in search of us, then that is *jahannam*, hell. We must understand this. If we understand this, we should think about and decide which of these it is best to accept and receive. This is how *vanakkam* and *toluhai* should be done.

Allāh sent down the *rasūls*. He sent down the *nabīs*. He sent down the messengers. He sent down the representatives. He sent down the *qutbs*. He sent down the *auliyā'*. He sent down the *ambiyā'*. And He sent down the *malaks* and the *malā'ikah*. They were all sent down to reveal these meanings to us. They were sent to give us explanations of wisdom and *'ilm*. Through these explanations we will be able to see how to progress and how to reach the house of the *daulah* of Allāh.

---

7 Rābi'atul-'Adawiyyah ☺ (713-801). A Sufi saint who lived in Basrah, Iraq. See *The Golden Words of a Sufi Sheikh, Revised Edition*, pages 453-455.

May Allāh bestow His blessings so that we may reach the house of *'ilm,* the house of *daulah.* Let us try to reach the house of that Blessed One, the house that He has given us, and receive the wealth of His *barakāt,* the wealth of His qualities, the wealth of His grace, the wealth of His treasure, and the wealth of the *ākhirah.* We must strive to find this. Then, the place we live in will be heaven. When goodness comes in search of us, that is heaven. When evil comes in search of us, that is hell. We must understand this. Each child must understand this.

You must reach a good state and strengthen your *īmān.* Make your *qalbs* resplend, make them pure, and try to find victory in your lives. We should try to do more and more prayer, and achieve more and more success and greatness. That will be the complete wealth.

If thoughts such as treachery, falsehood, jealousy, envy, and deceit come in search of you, then that is *jahannam,* that is satan. We must avoid these. *Āmīn.*

May Allāh grant that what is complete be made complete within you. From here on you must try to learn this *'ilm* and this wisdom. You must strive to know prayer. *Āmīn.*

Āmīn. Yā Rabbal-'ālamīn, O Lord of all the universes.

A'ūdhu billāhi minash-shaitānir-rajīm.
I seek refuge in God from the accursed satan.

Bismillāhir-Rahmānir-Rahīm.
In the name of God, the Most Compassionate,
the Most Merciful.

FIVE-TIMES PRAYER

December 23, 1981, Wednesday, 6:30 a.m.

QUESTION
Should the prayers be finished when the sun comes up around six o'clock, or six fifteen? When should they stop?

BAWA MUHAIYADDEEN

The right way is to finish by six o'clock.[1] You might start at five, or five fifteen. Sometimes the prayers might start at four fifty, or four fifty-eight, or five o'clock, or five ten, or five fifteen, or five twenty. *Subh,* the early morning prayer, consists of two *rak'ahs sunnah* and two *rak'ahs fard,* four *rak'ahs* altogether. It does not take much time to do this prayer. As soon as this prayer is finished, you should do the (out loud) *dhikr.*[2] The *dhikr* must be finished by six o'clock, you should finish it before the sun comes up. It would be best to finish

---

1   Time to finish the *subh* prayer: Colombo, Sri Lanka, where this talk occurred, is about seven degrees of latitude north of the equator, so the times for the prayers vary but little through the calendar year. However, at certain northern and southern latitudes the time of first twilight, when the *adhān* for the prayer is given and the time of sunrise, before which the prayer must end, might be much earlier or later. So the times in this instruction are only valid for the community there and people at a similar latitude.

2   Bawa Muhaiyaddeen ☺ is referring to the *dhikr* that is recited aloud every morning at the *subh* prayer. This *dhikr* is published in the booklet, *Morning Dhikr at the Mosque of Shaikh M. R. Bawa Muhaiyaddeen ☺.*

231

the *dhikr* by five forty-five, or five fifty, but it must be finished before six. You might need to reduce some of the *dhikr*.

QUESTION

The call to prayer time has moved forward. It used to be that the call to prayer was at about four thirty-five. Now it is at five o'clock. So, because there is less time, we had to cut short the *dhikr*. And the sun is actually coming up at around six twenty right now, so the *dhikr* is extending a little bit past six o'clock, and in order to say thirty-three (of each recitation)...

BAWA MUHAIYADDEEN

It should finish earlier, it should finish by six o'clock. When the seasons change, the time of sunrise changes. Once you become aware of the light, the sun will have risen, and it is best if you finish a little before that.

The *subh* prayer takes only five minutes to complete. Once the call to prayer is recited, the prayer takes only five or ten minutes. After that you say *at-tahiyyāt*, give *salāms* to the left and to the right, and then recite a *Fātihah*. Once that is over you continue on, and recite the *dhikr*. Some of the recitations of the *dhikr* can be repeated eleven times and some thirty-three times; you can recite the longer ones eleven times and the shorter ones thirty-three times. If you do it in this way, you will be able to finish at the proper time. Once the *dhikr* is over, you should recite a *Fātihah*.

The prayers should be over before six o'clock, while it is still dark. When daylight breaks, a current comes and disturbances arise in the mind. At that time the prayers will not be correct. When the sun is rising, the flow of the blood and the flow of the breath change because of that current. There are four (very forceful) times when the flow changes. These occur at twelve a.m. and six a.m. — at five forty-five or six a.m. — and at twelve p.m. and six p.m. In the same way that the tides of the ocean change, the flow of the blood and the breath changes. In one day there are eight times that the flow changes direction: six a.m., nine a.m., twelve noon, three p.m., six p.m., nine p.m., twelve midnight, and three a.m. It is similar to the changes in the ocean. The flow of the ocean water fluctuates. At certain times of the day the flow will be greater in one direction, and then it will change and become greater in another direction. The flow goes this way, then that way. First it is high tide and then it is low tide, in one place there is no water and later that place fills with water.

There are four times in a day when the waves of the ocean are especially forceful. Like that, in the body there are four forceful times: twelve a.m., six a.m., twelve p.m., and six p.m. Within the twenty-four hours of the day there are these four times: twelve midnight, six in the morning, twelve noon, and six in the evening. At these four forceful times the flow of the blood changes direction. If you have a cut on your body at any of these times, it will bleed profusely. The breath will also speed up. The mind will race without control. It will be agitated and you will have many thoughts.

Therefore, at these times, such as when the sun is rising, it is not good to be praying.

Here in Ceylon the sun rises at a certain time, in the Arab countries it rises at a different time, and in the west it rises at yet another time. The country changes, but in each place the sun will rise at six o'clock, six o'clock, six o'clock, six o'clock. The time for prayer is decided according to when the sun comes up in the different countries.

Tides and airs fluctuate according to the time of day. Just as the water in the ocean changes, the fluids, the breath, the mind, and the thoughts in man change. Therefore, wherever you may be, this state exists. So, if you are in the west, you should follow the time of the west; when you are in the east, in Japan, you should follow the time of the east; and when you are in the north, you should go along with that time of the north.

The mind flows like water. You need to be aware of this. When the mind is disturbed, it causes agitation. And if you pray at these times, then just as the waves rise in the ocean, your mind will be agitated. Your mind will be disturbed and your thoughts will rise and fall, rise and fall, like the waves. One thought will come and

then go, another will come and then go, and the next one will come
and then go. At these times you will not be able to concentrate on
one point, you will not be able to pray correctly. There will be
turbulence. This is why there are the different times for *toluhai,* the
five-times prayer.

One who has become a Sufi is able to control all of this. He can
control these tides, he can control the mind. Once he has controlled
the mind, he is able to pray at any time. His prayer goes along
automatically, like the travelling of the sun. Wherever the sun is, he
follows along with it. There is no darkness for him. Although he is
in the east he journeys to the west. From the west he follows the
light and journeys to the north. From the north he follows the light
and journeys to the south. He follows the light, wherever he goes.
But when *you* go along, it is as though you are in darkness. When a
Sufi travels, he proceeds within the light. He *is* the sun. That is the
difference.

Therefore, you must follow the limits of *shari'ah.* Once you are
able to perform the *dhikr* correctly, you will come to *tariqah.* When
you have completed that in the proper way, when you have established that state and become an *insan,* then you will come to *haqiqah,*
which is the union of God and the heart. Now you are in *shari'ah,*
you are with the world. Some time later, when you change, when
you are able to do the *dhikr,* then that is *tariqah,* where you strengthen
your *iman,* you strengthen your faith — you strengthen that *'iba-
dah,* that faith. Then, when you continue on, you come to *haqiqah.*
You strengthen your heart, you strengthen the connection to God.
Haqiqah is the connection between you and God. It is the prayer of
the heart.

There is the prayer of the world, then the prayer of *iman,* then
the prayer of the union with God, and then *ma'rifah,* the prayer
without limit, where man understands himself. It is a prayer that has
no limit and no night. There is no limit, there is no *waqt,* it is always
light. When man has become a sun, there is no *waqt.* He is Light. So,
there is no limit. He is performing 43,242 *sujud,* prostrations a day.

First is *love,* the world. That is *shari'ah. Tariqah* is to control your *īmān*, to establish *īmān* in Allāh. That is the prayer of *īmān*. *Haqīqah* is the connection between the heart and God. *Maʿrifah* is the connection between the Light of the *rūh* and the Light of Allāh. These are the four kinds of prayer. In *sūfiyyah* there are the 43,242 *sujūd* a day.

The world looks at *sharīʿah*. The *nabīs, olis, malaks,* and *malāʾikah* understand the prayer of *īmān*. *Haqīqah* explains the union between Allāh and you. And *maʿrifah* and *sūfiyyah* are the connection between the Light of the *rūh* and the Light of Allāh. These are the steps.

What we are now doing is the prayer of the world. When you perform *dhikr,* then that is the prayer of *īmān*. You establish faith, certitude, and determination, and unite with God in the heart. Allāh is a *sirr,* a secret. *Haqīqah* is where God and the heart become one. You unite with Him. *Qalb*-Allāh. Both are joined together as one.

Maʿrifah — the *rūh*. It is not this *sūrah,* there is another *sūrah*. When you unite with Him, another form comes. That is a *sūrah* of Light. It is not this (bodily) *sūrah,* but another *sūrah*. There, Allāh and you are in union. He and you are merged. Once the two are united, you become an embryo, a seed within That. Then you have the *sūrah* of Light. When you are merged in Him, in that Light, you take on the *sūrah* of Light. That Light-form of the *rūh* is joined with the Light-form of Allāh. Prayer in that state is *maʿrifah*. There is no darkness. Allāh's form has no darkness, therefore your form has no darkness. That is the Power of God. That is that prayer of *maʿrifah*. This is how it is done.

No one truly understands about prayer. The world looks at prayer from its own place; those who stand in the state of *īmān* look at prayer from their place of *īmān;* those who do *vanakkam* and *ʿibādah* look at it from their place; and those who proceed beyond to *ʿālamul-arwāh,* the world of the souls, look at it from the place of *maʿrifah*. These are the four steps.

Like this, whatever you do, you must do it in the proper way, and then proceed. Do you understand? Step by step, step by step.

First is the world, you control the *nafs*. Second is *īmān,* you strengthen your faith, certitude, determination, and *īmān* in Allāh. Third is union with Allāh. Fourth is Allāh's Power, your soul joins with Allāh's Power. This is the Power. This is *vanakkam*, this is prayer. Within each step you must take the point, and act accordingly.

The currents are flowing in this way. At *subh*, the first prayer of the day which is performed before the sun comes up, the current of the *dunyā* will flow, that water will flow.

Second, when you are doing the prayer of *īmān*, the prayer of *zuhr*, then the *nafs*, hunger, disease, and old age will flow, desire will flow.

At the *waqt* of 'asr, the *nafs ammārah* will flow. The jinns and the fairies will flow. They will come and disturb you.

When you are doing the *maghrib* prayer, then property, possessions, relationships, attachments, and the connections to blood ties will flow. This and that, difficulties and losses will come. These connections will come. The *malaks, malā'ikah,* jinns, fairies, shaktis and *sittis* will come and disturb you.

At the prayer of 'ishā', arrogance, maya, the many thoughts, pride, and jealousy will come and disturb you. The thought, "I am powerful" will come.

Whatever is there will flow. According to the time of day, each of these sections will come and disturb you. In the early morning, the thoughts come: "I have to go to work," or "I have to do this or that," or "I want to eat." The same thing occurs at the prayer of *zuhr*. Desire comes, blood attachments and disturbances of the mind come. The dog of desire and hunger come, you want to eat or go to work. At the prayer of 'asr, the mind and the five elements come and distract you, the mind runs here and there in every direction. At the prayer of *maghrib*, the jinns, fairies, *malaks,* and *malā'ikah* all come and distract you. At the prayer of 'ishā', the *nabīs, olis, qutbs,* and *auliyā'* come; that which is connected to Allāh comes at that time.

In this way, at each time of prayer, each of these sections might come to disturb you. If you inquire, "Who? Who?" and if you identify and understand them, then beyond that you will know the prayer of *ma'rifah*. You will finally understand *ma'rifah*.

These are the five *waqts* of prayer. At the prayer of *subh* you cut the connection to the *dunyā*, the connection to the earth. Second, at the prayer of *zuhr* you cut the connection to the five elements, attachments, mind, and desire. At the *'asr* prayer you learn the nature of the five elements. At the *maghrib* prayer you learn about the jinns and fairies. And at the *'ishā'* prayer the prophets come and you are reminded of their teachings, their lessons, and their books. The prayer of *'ishā'* is Allāh's prayer, the *sūfiyyah* prayer. Once you have understood all of this, the prayer of *sūfiyyah* will be the connection between Allāh and you.

We need to understand this. Step by step, we need to understand. If you go along, step by step, doing what needs to be done at each step, then you will understand each *waqt,* you will understand prayer, *vanakkam.*

At the prayer of *subh* the world is watching what you are doing. At the prayer of *zuhr* the *nafs,* blood ties, mind, and desire are watching. At the prayer of *'asr* the connections of the five elements are watching what you are doing. At the prayer of *maghrib* the blood ties, jinns, fairies, powers, the "I," and speech are watching—the earth, fire, water, air, and ether; the sun, the moon, time, and minutes are watching. At the prayer of *'ishā'* the prophets and their words and teachings are watching.

The prayer of *sūfiyyah,* the prayer of *ma'rifah,* is the *waqt* of Allāh. It has no time, no minutes. The five are finished. Beyond them is the sixth, the connection to Allāh is watching. You do *tasbīh* to Allāh and disappear in Him. You become one with Him. You do *tasbīh* and disappear within Him. Both are joined. You become an *'abd,* a slave to Him. You are one with Allāh in the prayer itself. You merge with that Light. Just as firewood is burned in fire, in that prayer you are completely burned away in Him, in that Light. In the same way that firewood burns and becomes ash, your life is burned in the power of that *'ibādah.* That is *ma'rifah,* that is *vanakkam.* You become one with Him. You are burned away in that prayer, in the same way that the firewood is burned to ash in the fire. You are annihilated. You must reflect on this. This is prayer. These are the ways.

In the world, each one will see this from wherever he stands. This is how it is. When a man is annihilated in God, the two become

one. Once he is *maut,* dead, and is burned to ashes, once his *dunyā* is
burned to ashes and his life is burned to ashes, then what remains is
only man-God, son/sun-God. Only God is there. Man is no longer
there. If man is there, it is like the firewood before it is thrown into
the fire. Anything can catch hold of it. As long as the firewood stays
outside of the fire, ants can get at it, cats can get at it, dogs can get at
it, humans can touch it, *nafs* can catch hold of it. Anything can catch
hold of it. But once it is inside the fire, nothing can go there.

Like that, if a man is annihilated in *'ibādah* to Allāh, if he is annihilated in Allāh, then he is not there. Everything has been burnt
away. His *dunyā* is burnt away. Life, *dunyā,* existence, hunger, disease,
everything is burnt away, everything is gone. Only Allāh remains.
When he has been completely consumed in *'ibādah,* the two become
one. That is son/sun-God. He is God. There is nothing there for
another person to hold on to. The *nafs* cannot touch him, desire cannot touch him, lust cannot touch him, maya cannot touch him. He
is in a place where nothing can touch him. Blood ties, maya, desire,
nafs ammārah, possessions, kith and kin, hunger, disease, old age, and
death cannot touch him. Since these cannot touch him, that is good.
If these cannot catch hold of him, then he is man-God. Since God
cannot be touched, he cannot be touched. That is the state of that
prayer. That is *'ibādah.*

If man does not attain that state, then all of these other things can
come and touch him. Even if he is up in the sky, they can touch him
and pull him down. Fame, name, and honor can catch him and drag
him down, they can touch him. As long as something remains that
can be touched, he will be pulled down. He will be pulled down
by the current of the earth. No matter how high he flies in the sky,
the current of the earth will drag him back to earth. If he has those
connections, the earth will pull him down, and he will be unable to
pray. But if he has been burnt to ash in that *'ibādah* and *vanakkam,*
if he has been annihilated in that Power, then these things cannot
touch him, the worldly things cannot touch him, he is beyond their
limit. Only that Power is there, he is not there.

If you are holding on to anything that can be touched by the differences of the "I" and "you," touched by the planets, touched by *nasīb*, fate, touched by the *nafs*, touched by desire, touched by maya, touched by hunger, touched by old age, touched by arrogance, touched by karma, touched by races, touched by religions, touched by scriptures, touched by philosophies, touched by the "I," touched by the "you," and like this, if you are holding on to the four hundred trillion ten thousand spiritual thoughts, mantras, magics, mesmerisms, fame, status, property, kith and kin, wife, children, livestock, house, and powers, you will be pulled down. If something is there that these can touch, you will be pulled down. You will not be able to merge with Allāh.

But if one has been annihilated within *vanakkam* and *'ibādah*, within that Power, if he has become ash in the same way that firewood is consumed by fire, if he has been annihilated in the Power that is God, then he will be in a place where nothing can touch him. Then, that is *vanakkam*, the prayer of *ma'rifah*, the prayer of the Sufi.

This must be done step by step. One needs to understand this, learn it well, and proceed. That is the point.

You must understand this. *Āmīn*. May Allāh help you.

Please type this.

QUESTION

What is the meaning of the way in which we stand and then bend in *salāh?*

BAWA MUHAIYADDEEN

This is how it is done in the world. You stand, then bend, then stand, then prostrate. This is the way this duty is done in the world. You must do all of this. You stand straight like a tree; when you do this, it is the prayer of the tree. When you bend, it is the prayer of the peacock, the prayer of the animals. When you perform *sujūd*, prostrations, it is the prayer of the fish. When you sit, it is the prayer of the mountain. You sit in the way a mountain sits.

You must stand in the same way a tree stands, without moving. The cow stands like this, no matter how much it rains, is that not so? You must also stand like this. No matter how many floods come, the fish keeps swimming with its head bent down. You must be like that. No matter how many winds and gales come, the mountain does not pay attention to it.

The prayers that we are doing are that of the tree, the good mountain, the animals, and the fish. That is the prayer we are now doing, and from within it we need to extract certitude.

No matter how much suffering comes to the animals, they stand there. We must observe the strength that they have, and understand it. No matter how much the winds shake it, the tree stands there. We must also stand straight like this. We should not fall down under the storms of this world. The cow stands strong no matter how many sorrows and joys of the world strike it, and like that, we must stand strong with faith, certitude, determination, and *imān* in Allāh. Stand strong with that.

A mountain remains firm no matter how many earthquakes, gales, rain, or floods come. Like that, your *vanakkam* must remain firm. No matter how many floods, gales, or high waves may come, the fish swims along in the water with its head down. It lowers its head like that. All others lift their heads, but the fish lays flat and swims along in the water. You must keep your head bent down in *sujūd* to Allāh, in the same way.

We should remain firm on the inside while we do the postures on the outside, like the tree, like the animal, like the rocky mountain, and like the fish that swims along. Although we stand in this way, there is an inner meaning to this. Like the tree, no matter what gales come, you must stand firm and keep your point fixed. In the same way that the cow bears up with patience all of the sorrows that come, you must strengthen your *imān*. Just as the mountain is firm, no matter how many sorrows toss you about in your life, you must keep your *imān* and prayer firm. No matter how much you are tossed about by your blood ties and relatives, you must keep your head lowered in prayer and *tasbīh* to Allāh, just as the fish keeps its head down in the water. No matter how many floods may come, you must keep your head down in *sujūd* to Allāh. This is the inner meaning.

The outer meaning is to be like the mountain, the animal, the tree, and the fish. The inner meaning is to be firm in prayer.

You need to understand the meanings of the five times of prayer, *toluhai*. You must understand this prayer and how it should be done.

Thank you. *As-salāmu 'alaikum,* may the peace of God be upon you.

A'ūdhu billāhi minash-shaitānir-rajīm.
I seek refuge in God from the accursed satan.

Bismillāhir-Rahmānir-Rahīm.
In the name of God, the Most Compassionate,
the Most Merciful.

PROPER CONDUCT IN THE MOSQUE

May 28, 1984, Monday, 6:30 a.m.

Children, female children, I spoke to you yesterday about proper conduct in the mosque. You can play that tape. I spoke about that yesterday morning, and you can listen to that tape.

Your hair should not be visible, it should not be seen externally. Your arms should not be visible, they should be covered to the wrists. If you do not want to wear a *jubbah*,[1] well that is all right. You can wear a long shirt or blouse that extends down to your knees. Beneath that shirt you should wear trousers or a skirt that extends to your ankles. If you wear trousers, they should be loose. Whatever you wear must extend to your ankles, like the women wear in Pakistan, or India, or Yemen. It must cover your legs to the ankles. You can wear a long dress with long sleeves or you can wear a *jubbah*. Wear whatever color you like, but whatever you wear should be modest. It is not necessary to wear a *jubbah*, you can wear something similar to that, or make something from thin cloth or some other material that you like.

No matter what you wear, you must be careful to guard your state of purity, *wudū'*. Good conduct is your responsibility. You have to protect yourselves. In a place of worship, you should be careful not to disturb others. Not everyone comes there to pray. Everyone

---

1 *jubbah* (A) A robe or gown. For women, this is usually called an *abaya*.

has a monkey, a monkey mind. So, they might stare. To protect yourselves, you need *nānam, madam, atcham, payirppu:* modesty, reserve,
shyness, and fear of wrongdoing. You need good qualities.

Females have a beauty. Males have a monkey, they have the
monkey of the mind that tries to act upon what it sees. Since the
males have that potential to act upon what they see, you must cover
yourselves and be modest. You need to have the state where you can
protect yourselves. The females need to have this.

From the time of the Rasūlullāh ☉, this state of modesty has
been established. You must be covered, whether it is in the mosque
or in the house. You should be modest in the house as well as in the
mosque. You should protect your honor, no matter where you are,
because the world will try to catch hold of you. The place of worship is a pure place, and you should have that state of purity. When
you go to pray you must protect your body with your clothes, and
restrain your mind in Allāh's *tawakkul,* trust. That is *vanakkam.* You
should do it in this way.

You can wear any colors you like, but it is good to wear white. If
you do not want to wear white, then you can wear colors, but you
must be covered. There will be different ways of dressing when you
go on *hajj,* different ways of dressing when you go on *'umrah,* and
different ways of dressing at other times. There are these different
ways. Sometimes the females must do what the males do not have
to do.

What is known as *toluhai*[2] is a great treasure. If you wish to fulfill
this prayer, you must become worthy to fulfill it. *Toluhai* is extremely
precious, it is praise to God. God is the One who is accepting that
praise, that great treasure. You are giving that treasure to God. So,
you must be worthy to have God accept it from you. To be worthy,
your *qalb* must be made pure. That is what you must give. Only if
you make yourself worthy to give this praise can you receive the
benefit. This state must exist in both men and women.

---

2 *toluhai* (T) The formal prayers, or *salāh,* performed five times during each
   twenty-four hour day.

What is *toluhai?* It is a very precious treasure. You are giving this precious treasure to God. You are giving this treasure to God, and receiving the benefit from Him. Because you are receiving the benefit from Him, you must be worthy to receive it. Your *īmān,* your *qalb,* your faith, determination, certitude, and purity must be worthy of receiving this. Only then can you receive the benefit. Otherwise you will lose the benefit.

When you go to a place of *toluhai,* prayer, you should not gather *tollai,* trouble. You should go there only for prayer. You should see only God, nothing else. You should not think, "*Aiyō,* I am sweating, *aiyō,* I have no food, this is happening to me, that is happening to me, there is no air in here!" You should not have these concerns there. Your only concern should be surrender to God. If you say, "This is happening here!" or "That is happening!" then that is not prayer, it is not *toluhai.* Your intention should be focused on the one God. You must be finished with those other matters, and be like one who has no memory. You should not remember anything that happened before this, that you saw this, that, or the other.

So, this is the state that you must have to fulfill your prayers. *Toluhai* is very precious, and you must be one who is worthy to give this valuable treasure to God.

It is not good to take small children to the mosque. If the children are old enough to pray or to learn, then it is all right if the mother takes them and keeps them next to her. She should show them how to do their prayers without making any noise. That is how you should do it. Those children should be shown how to do their ablutions, and how to pray correctly. These must be done correctly. You can take the children there who are able to do this, and they can join you in the prayer. They should stay beside the mother, and she should teach them. But if the children are going to play on the carpet, or cry, or sleep, or make noise, you should not take them there. The mothers must see to this. Children who might make noise like this can sleep downstairs, or stay downstairs, or you can keep them in the meeting room.

You must understand this state. You must teach the children

how to behave in the correct way. You must teach them how to do the ablutions, and how to pray correctly. The mother should teach them carefully. She should show the children how to pray and she should also pray. Otherwise, if the children make a sound, *poitch!* it is finished. If a child cries, the prayer will be spoiled, so this is not an appropriate state. If a child goes there and starts crying, or creates a disturbance, *poitch!* the prayers of everyone will be spoiled, it will cause difficulty. You must think of this. My love you, my children, male children and female children, please think of this.

When you go to pray, the *imām* will be in front because he is the leader, and you are required to stand (behind him) in straight, parallel rows, *jib, jib.* You must not just stand here or there, here or there, or anywhere else. If one *imām* is occupied with other work, the *mu'adhdhin,* the *lebbe,* or another *imām* should see that this is carried out correctly, he should see that the lines are straight. The first line should be straight, and the one behind that line should be parallel with it, then the next line should be parallel with that, then the next line should be parallel with that, and then the next line should be parallel with that—like flowers in a row. The first line should be in place, then the next line should be in place, then the next line should be in place. When you look in one direction you should be able to count the straight lines, when you look in another direction you should be able to count the straight lines. When you look here you should see the straight lines, when you look there you should see the straight lines. You must be able to see this from all four directions.

The lines should be like this. Whether it is the males or the females, you must stand in this way. You should not just stand wherever you want. Look to see where the *imām* is. Then each one should stand behind him in straight, parallel lines. This is the way you should stand for *vanakkam* and *toluhai.*

Furthermore, you must do your ablutions. It is best if you do your ablutions at home and come to the mosque without breaking those ablutions. It would be very good if you can do that. You should wear clean socks when you come here, remove your shoes, and then go to pray. There will be people who live here who are doing their ablutions, so if people come in a hurry from their homes, and also need to do their ablutions, that will take up a lot of time because there are only five ablution stations.

If you need to do your ablutions here, you should not wipe your feet with paper towels. Yesterday, many rolls of paper towels were used. The Fellowship has no money, so you should not do that. If you want to dry your hands or feet, you should bring a towel for that purpose. Each one should bring his own towel. If you need to use the bathroom, there is toilet paper there, but you must still be sure to wash yourself with water. Paper towels should be discarded in the wastebasket. Never put paper towels into the toilet, it will get blocked. We must use our brains. In every matter we should use our brains.

We have spoken about how the female children should dress. Now, for the males, when you go to prayers you can either wear a *jubbah* or clean trousers like they do in Pakistan, India, or Ceylon. The *imām* must always wear a *jubbah* to distinguish that he is the *imām,* the leader of the prayers. He must wear a *jubbah* and a *kufi* to show that he is the *imām.*

Clothes differ from country to country. In India, the clothing is different from here. There, the *imāms* and the *'ālims* dress differently. Whatever the place, whether it is Mecca or here or somewhere else, not everyone will wear a *jubbah.* Sometimes they will wear trousers, or some other clothing. Regardless, your clothes must always be clean. Then you can do your ablutions and pray. Your clothing should be clean and loose fitting.

The female children also should not wear tight-fitting clothes. The backside must be covered, a long covering is needed for that. Females should always cover their hair, and all other places except their face. They should cover their front with a loose covering, their arms should be covered to the wrists, their legs should be completely covered to the ankles, and they should wear clean socks. The male children can pray wearing trousers or they can pray wearing a *jubbah* or not wearing a *jubbah.*

What you wear when you pray can vary. In the east, west, north, and south, there are various customs. Here, in Philadelphia, some people wear a *jubbah* as they do in the Arab countries, without understanding the meaning. They wear a robe like they wear in the Arab countries. Both males and females do this, they just wear a robe without knowing what they are doing. There is nothing to that. They are just imitating.

In the Arab countries the sun is hot, so the people will wear a thin, black cloth, or they will wear a thin, white cloth. Whether it is black or white, they do this because the sun is hot. There, it is hot, very hot. We cannot wear that same material here in the west. This is a cold country, and we would die if we did that. So here we need to wear a different kind of cloth, we cannot wear the same clothing that is worn there. We must adjust ourselves to the conditions and nature of the country we are in. Otherwise, if we try to wear the same kind of clothing here, we will perish.

The position of the sun and the moon changes. Time changes. Between the east and here there is a time difference of ten hours; between the Arab countries and here there is a time difference of seven hours; between London and here there is a time difference of five hours; and between California and here there is time difference of three hours. So, there are these time differences. Between the Arab countries and Ceylon there is a difference of two hours, or even three hours, and according to these differences the climate and seasons vary. So, we must conduct ourselves accordingly. We cannot insist that what is done in the east should be done in the west. There, the sun is lower and hotter, and if we do here what is done there, we will perish. The *dīn* is not spread in that way. It is spread according to the conditions surrounding it. If you try to speak only Arabic here, it will not work.

The prayers must be correctly fashioned. Prayer is essential, and it must be done in the correct way. Each one of you must understand the conditions surrounding that prayer.

It is not essential to wear a robe. Here, on the road, I have seen that some people dress their dogs in *jubbahs*. Some people even dress their monkeys in *jubbahs,* or other clothing. So, just wearing a *jubbah* does not mean anything. A prostitute, when she is dancing, will sometimes wear everything and another time wear nothing. There is nothing to that.

Just covering your body like this in the world is not enough. It is useless to say, "That wife wore this, that other wife wore that, so I should wear it too!" What is useful is to dispel the darkness and ignorance that covers your *qalb*. Prayer is to dispel the darkness and blemishes that cover the *qalb*. Prayer must chase away satan and overcome the differences that are covering the *qalb*, taking in Allāh's qualities and actions and securing them there. We must take in the words of the Rasūl, *sallallāhu 'alaihi wa sallam*, and act accordingly. This is what is important, not the clothing that you wear while you are praying.

The clothing that you wear stops at the *qabr*, the grave, where you will be questioned tomorrow. The questions that are asked there are different, those are different questions. You are not questioned about the clothing of the *'anāsir*, the five elements. That clothing belongs to the *'anāsir*. You will not be asked about the clothes with which you adorned yourself. There, the questions are different, they are about good and evil.

Every child must think about this. You have the weapons to protect yourselves. Women must protect themselves. You must protect your honor, you must protect your modesty, reserve, shyness, and fear of wrongdoing. No one else can do this for you. A husband cannot be a guard for his wife, the wife must be a guard for herself. The husband cannot be a watcher over his wife.

Certain places cannot be locked. You cannot put a lock on the mind and you cannot put a lock on desire. The eyes cannot be locked up, the ears cannot be locked up, the mouth cannot be locked up, and the sense of smell cannot be locked up. You may be able to put a lock on your hands and feet, but you cannot lock up these other things. You cannot lock up the backside. It is an open place, and it does its own work. The mind, the eyes, the nose, and the mouth do many, many kinds of work.

So, what is it that can give protection? Each woman must be the protector of herself. A husband cannot do that for her, nor can anyone else. Even if the husband could put an iron padlock on the backside, he would not be able to put a lock on the mind. Even if he could put a lock on the mind, he would not be able to put a lock on desire. Even if he could put a lock on desire, he would not be able to put a lock on the eyes. Even if he could put a lock on the eyes, he would not be able to put a lock on the ears. And even if he could do all this, he would not be able to put a lock on the tongue. He cannot do this. The tongue will do so many things, and he will become crazy. Faith is needed.

A female needs to teach wisdom to these things. She must guard herself with this wisdom. A male must also guard himself. This is not just for women, it is also for men. A man must guard himself, he must guard his mind, he must guard his modesty, reserve, shyness, and fear of wrongdoing.

What is the use of getting angry? If a dog or a fox gets angry, what happens? It gets bitten and its own nose hangs off. It gets bitten and its own ears hang off. One animal bites the other animal, then the ears go, the eyes go. They bite each other, rip each other apart, dog against dog. It is finished. This is what happens when we growl and bite. Our own nose is left hanging and our own ears are left hanging. Our own life is left hanging. This is useless. A wise person will protect himself from this, while the one who does not have wisdom will get bitten, and will lose his nose and eyes and ears.

It cannot be done in that way. A woman must protect herself. No one else can do this for her. She must protect her own mind, her own modesty, her own eyes, her own *qalb,* and her own life. Each female must do this for herself. The husband cannot do it for her. A husband can only guard himself. He must protect himself, his wife cannot protect him or safeguard him. It is the same for the woman as for the man.

So, to live as a man, a man must create his own worth, and to live as a good woman, a woman must create her own worth.

Prayer to God is also like this. You must do it like this. When you go to pray you should not complain, "I am sweating. They are doing this, they are doing that, they are doing this. This clothing is not right, that clothing is not right!" That is like a crazy person. It is like a condemned man who is on his way to the gallows, complaining about the cloth that is covering his head! You are saying, "That is making me sweat, this is making me sweat. This is hurting, it is doing this, it is doing that. Take this cloth off! This cloth is no good, that clothing is no good!" This is the way some of you are surrendering yourselves to God. Some are complaining, "This is making me sweat, that is making me sweat!" To complain like this seems to be your work. Some of the female children are complaining in this way. That is not good. Your *īmān* is not strong. Until your prayers are completed, you should not be aware of anything else. You should be aware of your surroundings only after you have finished praying.

Desire knows no shame. When desire comes to a person, he knows no shame. However, when modesty comes, ignorance will not touch him. When *gnānam* comes, the world will not approach him. When wisdom comes, darkness and torpor will not touch him. When *sabūr* grows, anger will not approach him. And when *īmān* is strong, the evil qualities—what is *kufr*—will not separate him, the qualities that have no belief in God will not come and separate him. Those qualities that have no faith in God are called *kufr*. Those qualities that do not accept God will not separate him. Like this, you must think of each thing.

Prayer is a priceless treasure. You must carry this treasure in your *qalb*, your innermost heart, and give it into the hand of Allāh. He is the One who is worthy of receiving what you are giving and you must be worthy to receive the treasure that He is giving. That is your responsibility. You must be ready to receive the treasure that He is giving.

He is the One who is worthy to receive the treasure that you are bringing, the treasure of your prayer, and when you do your *'ibādah* and *vanakkam* correctly, you will be the one who is worthy to receive what He is giving.

Those who do not pray correctly do not deserve to receive what He gives. Therefore, do not play around when you pray. You must try to do your prayers in the proper way.

Now, some children go to the *subh,* the early morning prayer. And there are some children who sleep through that time. That is wrong. The first seat of the day is *subh.* You must come for the *subh* prayer. If you cannot come, you must pray at home. Those who can should come to the mosque. The second prayer of *zuhr* is at a difficult time, and the third prayer of *'asr* is at a time that is a little more difficult. Although it might be difficult to pray when you are at work, you must try to do your prayers wherever you are. At *maghrib* your work is finished so you can come to the mosque. You will be able to come for *maghrib.* At eight o'clock you can gather here. There are times when you can come and other times when it might be difficult to come. If you were unable to pray at the place where you were, you must come here and make up the *fard,* the obligatory prayers. You must come and do your *salāh.* For *'ishā'* you should come here to pray.

You must cultivate this in the correct way, and reap the harvest you have sown. You are the ones who will receive the benefit. What you receive is for you alone. *Toluhai,* the five-times prayer, is not a game, it is an extremely valuable earning, an earning for the *dunyā* and for the *ākhirah.* It is the highest kind of earning. It is each one's own property. What you earn cannot be given to someone else; you cannot give your wages to someone else. Each one keeps the earnings that he has received.

The person who does not have knowledge may make a mistake, and God will forgive him. But God will not forgive the *imāms* if they make a mistake. The *imāms* are those who have learned. If they make a mistake, God will not forgive them. So, that will be a difficulty for them.

Therefore, we should not play around with God. Prayer is purity, and when we pray we must try to do it with great care, with *īmān* and certitude.

Now, we have built a mosque here, and there is plenty of space in it. How much effort you put into your prayers is up to you. Both males and females should make the effort to pray here. If you bring the children (who do not know how to pray), it could cause difficulties. The children that you bring must be able to do the prayers in the right way. Do not bring the children who cannot do the prayers correctly. Keep them downstairs or somewhere that they can play. That will be good. Female children should not stand beside the males when they are praying. The males pray side by side, therefore a female child cannot stand beside them. The female children should stay with the mother, they should pray beside the mother. Not every child should be taken into the mosque. Only the children who have learned the prayers and who are able to do them should be brought there. Understand? Do you understand?

QUESTION

Can mothers and the children who are almost able to pray, pray downstairs where they can hear the speaker?

BAWA MUHAIYADDEEN

Yes, you can pray downstairs. You can hear the prayers over the speaker, can you not? The mothers can pray here, or they can pray in the mosque classroom downstairs. Whatever place you pray in must be kept clean. Please see to that, and do it.

QUESTION

Should house slippers, slippers that are worn to the toilet, be worn in the downstairs room?

BAWA MUHAIYADDEEN

The slippers should be left outside the room where you pray. The room where the mothers are going to pray must be kept clean. You can listen to what the *imām* is reciting in the mosque, and follow him in prayer. Do what is suitable for each thing. If it causes difficulty to take the children upstairs, then keep them downstairs. You can pray upstairs whenever you do not bring those children with you.

(Bawa Muhaiyaddeen ☺ addresses various people who have duties in the mosque.)

The *imām* or the *mu'adhdhin* should do the call to prayer, when it is time to assemble. When the *imām* cannot do it, the *mu'adhdhin* should recite the first call to prayer. Why? Because now this is a mosque, and not just anyone can do this. Two or three people can do this, we must appoint two or three people who can recite in a beautiful way. There are some people who are able to recite in this way. They must recite correctly.

There are many people who now come to this mosque, and there should be no disgrace, no fault. Different people come here. What we did earlier was different; we had not learned. Now we have learned, we are at the half-way stage of learning, and we cannot do now what we did earlier. Other people are coming here, and they should not say that we are just playing.

The *imām* should do his duty in the right way. God sees our every fault. Do not look at the faults in the prayers of others, look at your own faults. God is watching. Tomorrow He will question you. He will ask why you fed rice to the child who should be drinking milk and gave milk to the child who should be eating rice; why you gave meat to the child who does not have any teeth and gave milk to the child who has teeth; and why you gave meat to the child who does not have any teeth and bananas to the child who has teeth. He will ask about all of this tomorrow. Like this, God will inquire into what you taught them. He will ask, "How did you do that, how did you do this, how did you do that, how did you do this, what did you teach them?" You have to train them in every aspect, until their teeth are able to chew the meat. He will ask about everything.

Each one will have to answer these questions, not just you. Allāh will not miss even one fault. The two angels are present, and they are writing down everything, the good and the bad. They do not miss even one minute. Tomorrow, what the two angels have been writing will be inquired into. These things will be there tomorrow, (on the Day of *Qiyāmah*). The eyes will say what they did, each thing will say what it did. There will be no lawyer or broker there. We will come to the *mīzān tirāsu,* the scale that weighs good and evil. The Rasūl ☺ will be present there as a witness, and the questions will be asked.

We must think about all of this. A wise man must give the medicine for each one's faults. Each person must know his own faults, he must assess the faults that he has within him. It is a huge matter to understand this. What are the faults of his sight, what are the faults of his eyes, what are the faults in his meanings, what are the faults of his ears, what are the faults of his nose, what are the faults of his tongue, what are the faults of his heart, what are the faults of his mind, what are the faults of his *qalb,* and what are the faults of his body? He must see all of these faults, and then a good, wise man can give the medicine. But, if he keeps looking at the faults of other people, his own diseases will devour him.

Each person must ask forgiveness for his own faults. Do not look at the faults of others, do not disparage others, do not get angry with others, and do not attack others. That is not good.

Hmm. Is there anything else? May Allāh protect you and may He protect us. May God, who protects us, protect our brothers and sisters. May Allāhu ta'ālā Nāyan protect everyone, all the brothers and sisters connected to us. May the millions of groups join with us. May Allāh protect us all, from the newborn babies to the children still in the womb, and take us on the good path. May the Rahmatul-'ālamīn, the Grace of all the universes, join us with His group. May He join us with the one group out of the seventy-three groups, God's one group that will not be questioned. May He join us with that seventy-third group. May He join us in that place, and may He forgive the faults that we have committed knowingly and unknowingly. May Allāhu ta'ālā Nāyan help us and join us with Him in His kingdom of grace.

Allāh is the One who is worthy of all praise and praising. May He give us the ability to receive His grace. Āndavanai, please make our *qalbs* worthy! Give us the ability to receive Your *Qudrah* and Your *Rahmah.* Please give us the *qalbs* that can receive Your love and compassion, and strengthen our *īmān* so that we can give You affection, have faith in You, and love You. Please give us that certitude.

Please strengthen our certitude, determination, and *īmān* so that we can pray with the conviction that there is no God other than

You. May You make our *qalbs* resplend, dispel the darkness that covers us, and give us the qualities that are Your *Qudrah*. May You grant us that grace

Yā Allāh, *yā Rabbal-'ālamīn*, O Beautiful One, the Limitless One, the One who abides within everything and protects us, the Bountiful One! You are the One who is our Param Atmā, the Supreme Soul, God. You are our Param Porul, the Supreme Treasure. You are the Param Pidā, the Divine Father. You are the One who is the Sustainer of everything, You are the Solitary One who is spread everywhere, the one God, illAllāh, Allāh — Allāh, the One who stands alone. You are the One who is our Rabbul-'ālamīn. You are the One who is our Rahmān, You are the One who is ar-Rahīm, the One who protects us and sustains us. You are Allāh, the One who is complete, Allāh who is the undiminishing wealth. Please give us a worthy *qalb* and a worthy *īmān*. Please give us the ability to receive Your treasure into our *qalbs*.

Āmīn, āmīn, yā Rabbal-'ālamīn. Āmīn. As-salāmu 'alaikum.

Children, if we get angry, there will be a lot of difficulty. It is very hard to make something grow, but easy to destroy it. To build a house is very difficult, but to break it down is very easy. We need *sabūr*, inner patience. In each country the customs are different.

My love you. Children, do you understand what I told you, and are you all in agreement? Do it like that. Correct yourselves, little by little, improve and improve, and slowly go forward. Children, make your *qalbs* worthy. There is so much you need to learn.

Rābi'atul-'Adawiyyah ⊛ had so many things happen to her. She was a slave, she ran here, she wandered there, she had to beg. But, in spite of that, she finally fulfilled her *hajj*.

She went from one thing to another. She was sold as a slave. After that she danced, she sang, she had a companion, she drank. She did all of that. Then the words of her Shaikh came to her. The words came again and again and again and again, and because of that, at a later time, her *qalb* opened. After following the words of her Shaikh, her *qalb* opened, and finally Rābi'atul-'Adawiyyah ⊛ was given God's crown, the crown of *gnānam*.

Like this, even though we may have committed faults in so many sections, the Shaikh will come and remind us, and show us the truth. From that very place, if you progress and progress and progress and progress, and grow and grow and grow and grow, you can come to that good state. This is the way you can understand and progress.

Sometimes you forget the words of the Shaikh, and you go your own way. Rābi'atul-'Adawiyyah ☺ was a slave. She drank. Even so, she progressed and grew, did she not? Like this, the Shaikh will speak within the *qalb* of each of his children. You must ask forgiveness for the sins that you have committed. The Shaikh will come and teach you. When Rābi'atul-'Adawiyyah ☺ was drinking, singing, and dancing, the words of the Shaikh came and protected her. Then, at the next step he came and advised her. And then, at the next step he came and advised her about her faults. This is the way that the Shaikh taught her.

Children, it is in this way that you must slowly, slowly progress. *Āmīn.* May Allāh help you.

Right, go and eat.

Do the *imāms* understand? *Sabūraligal!* For God's house we are the *sabūraligal,* those who have inner patience. We are the *sabūraligal* when we are going to God's house. The ones with *sabūr* who are going to God's house are called *sabūraligal,* the patient travellers. What are we called when we are travelling and fasting? *Sabūraligal.* We are travelling towards God's house, with *sabūr.*

We are those who have *sabūr,* travelling from the *dunyā* to His house.

Therefore we need *sabūr,* we need to increase our *sabūr.* We are journeying as the *sabūraligal.* That is our fast, the fast for our journey.

Āmīn, āmīn. As-salāmu alaikum.

Shari. Children, please go and eat.

A'ūdhu billāhi minash-shaitānir-rajīm.
I seek refuge in God from the accursed satan.

Bismillāhir-Rahmānir-Rahīm.
In the name of God, the Most Compassionate,
the Most Merciful.

STRIVE TO COME FORWARD TO THE LIGHT

June 24, 1981, Wednesday, 10:00 p.m.

There is a benefit in following an *imām*[1] in the *sharī'ah* prayer, because even if you do not understand anything, when you follow behind him you can join in and say what he says. When you join with him you can repeat again and again what he says. Since you are following behind him in prayer, you will receive certain explanations for that. That is why it is said that there is a benefit in following an *imām* in prayer. Even if you do not understand, if you pray behind an *imām*, if you follow him and (silently) recite whatever *sūrah*, whatever chapter of the Qur'ān, he is reciting, there will be a benefit. You will come to understand those *āyāt*, those verses, or that *sūrah*. That is why the Rasūlullāh ⊕ said that you should join the lines, follow the *imām*, and do what he does.

Furthermore, when people line up behind the *imām*, it will be the ones who have the love who will want to come forward and stand

---

1 *imām* (A) The word *imām* comes from the rich Arabic root *a m m* which has within its derivatives *umm* and *ummi*, mother and motherly. The latter word also means illiterate. *Ummah* means people or nation, and *amāma* means "in front of." The *imām*, as a leader of the prayers, is in front of the other worshippers, but the word also implies one who is an example to the followers, one who embodies the qualities and character of Allāh. Ultimately, the Qur'ān is the foremost *imām*, and the conveyor of the Qur'ān, the Prophet Muhammad ⊕, is the *imām* for all spiritual levels in prayer, as can be heard in a reminder to the dying, the *talqīn*, in a question that will be asked in the grave: "What is your *imām?*" and its answer: "My *imām* is the Qur'ān!"

259

in the front row. Those who have that love will want to come to the front. A lazy person like me will stand a little further back. Those who hurry in noisily at the last minute will be further back from that. Some others who are quietly sitting, might suddenly come, without washing their backside or anything else, and stand even further back. And then there are those who are even more hasty and more lazy. They have been sitting around, and then say, "Oh, they are praying now!" They might come in when the prayer is ending. So, each person will come according to his state.

If a person who is feeling cold goes and stands near a fire, the chill will leave him. The one who stands slightly back from the fire will feel a little cold. The one who stands even further back will be colder than that. And the one who stands furthest away will remain cold.

When you follow an *imām,* Allāh's *rahmah* works in the same way. The state of your *qalb* determines your connection with that *rahmah,* that grace. The further you distance yourself from that *rahmah,* the more your *nafs,* your intentions, and your jealousy will not leave you. Allāh's love will not come, it will be less. So, you should have the love for joining the *jāmi'ah,* the congregation, early, and for going to the front.

This is in keeping with the principles of *sharī'ah.*

To follow a Shaikh is even more exalted. There is a power in the face, in the *zīnah,* and in the words of the Shaikh. That power, Allāh's *Qudrah* and His Light, will fall in front of the Shaikh. When that falls, and if you are in the front row when you are reciting the *dhikr* with that search and that tenderness, then that Light will also fall on you. When it falls on you, some of what is in your *qalb* will be burnt away. Some of your illnesses and diseases will be burnt away. If the Shaikh is a true *Insān Kāmil,* and if you look into his face as you are doing the *dhikr,* then the Light on his face, the *rahmah* that is Allāh's grace, will shower upon you as it falls from him. If it does, then it will cure your illnesses and your diseases, and it will remove your difficulties. Because of that, some of your evils will be removed.

Therefore, when you are with a Shaikh, those of you who have that love must make an effort to come to the front. According to your effort, you will receive the benefit and the gain. The further away you are, the more your illnesses, diseases, and difficulties will not leave you. Why? Because the further back you are, the less gain you will have. The evils and difficulties that come with your state will pull you. They will remain there with you.

So, the first state is *sharī'ah*. The next state is that of the Shaikh, an *Insān Kāmil*. Further, if a person is going to pray alone, there is another meaning: be alone, be hungry, and be awake! If you have merged with the Shaikh in that state, if you have attained that, then you can pray alone. What will that prayer be like? Allāh is the One who is alone. There is none worthy of worship other than Allāhu ta'ālā. So, how will one be who sits alone and prays? Allāh will be the One who is praying. That person will be *maut*, he will have died in that prayer. He will have died and become an *'abd*, a slave to Allāh. He will have surrendered to Him. His *rūh*, his soul, will be united with Allāh, and Allāh will be the One who is doing the *dhikr*. Such a one will have died in that, he will have died in the love of Allāh, he will have died in that prayer. For meditation there is only one, and for this meditation Allāh is praying to Allāh.

If you are not in that state of prayer, then you are not praying alone, and you will not receive any benefit. To whom will you be praying? You will be praying to the *nafs* and the elements. If you pray to the elements, the *nafs*, attachments, illusion, and darkness, then your evils and difficulties will not leave you. However, if you join with an *Insān Kāmil*, if you merge with that love, if you come forward and unite with those who have joined together, then you will have joined the one group, and you will receive the benefit and the earnings from that.

Furthermore, regardless of how much you pray, when you listen to *āhadīth*, words of wisdom, then the blemishes, suspicions, and doubts in your *qalb* will leave, and certitude will be established. The Rasūlullāh ⸙ said that the benefit gained by listening to *āhadīth* is greater than doing fifty *waqts* of prayer without certitude.

It will establish understanding, certitude, and determination in you. Understanding will come. Then, when wisdom comes, determination will dawn. Therefore, if you listen to one *hadīth* in the correct way, it will give you a greater benefit than if you perform fifty *waqts* of prayer. This is what the Rasūlullāh ⊕ said.

He said further, "Go even unto China to learn *'ilm,* divine knowledge. This is the way." The Rasūlullāh ⊕ said this. When words of wisdom are being spoken, no matter how much work you may have, you must try to listen with a lot of love. Then your suspicions, your doubts, and your differences can be cleared from your heart and your *īmān* will be strengthened. This is why the *āhadīth* are very exalted. This is the word of the Rasūlullāh ⊕.

When you pray, you must pray in the proper way. When you follow an *imām,* you should do what he does. You should not think that you have learned more. The Rasūlullāh ⊕ was unlearned, and he received the *daulah,* the wealth of Allāh. Satan was learned, but he received hell. The Rasūlullāh ⊕ was unlettered, and he received the grace called the *rahmatul-'ālamīn.* Therefore, throw away all of your learning, and strengthen your *īmān,* certitude, and determination. With that certitude you must try to receive the love of God. Join with an *imām* or a Shaikh; join and come forward with that love.

It is according to the amount of your love that you will come and join here. And it is according to your own qualities that you will go further and further back. It is according to your lack of effort that you will regress. As you regress, further and further, your life and your prayer will also regress. The further away that you go from the Shaikh, that is how far the benefits will recede.

So, the extent that you come forward towards the Shaikh will be the amount of progress and benefit that you will see. And the extent that you regress will be the amount of regression that you will see.

When you recite *lā ilāha illAllāh,* you must say it correctly. *Lā ilāha illAllāh,* you must bow your head respectfully. When you say *Allāhu Qādirīn,* you should bow your head to the right side of your *qalb* and to the left side of your *qalb.* You must not just sit with your eyes closed. There is no benefit or respect in your *dhikr* if you just sit there with your eyes closed. If you are going to be silent, *ummī*, your surrender must be complete. Only when the *rūh* is working can you do it like that. But I do not see that any of you have reached that state. I do not see that! Therefore, you cannot do it like that.

Now, when you make that sound (of the *dhikr*), the air comes out from four sides of your body, through the skin, the nerves, and the hair. If we would set up a microphone here, how much sound would you hear? But if, along with that large microphone, we would set up speakers in four places, the sound would be greater, the sound would be heard here, and also over there.

Similarly, the *qalb* is a large microphone. The body has so many openings. When you say the *dhikr* out loud, the sound will come out through those openings. From that microphone, the sound will be heard on all four sides. This is how it is.

If we are alone in *maunam*, silence, then the sound is heard in *'ālamul-arwāh*, the world of the souls. That *dhikr* is also heard in *'ālamul-ajsām*, the world of forms. The *dhikr* of *sharī'ah* is heard in the realm of the *dunyā*, and this *dhikr* should be recited respectfully, with bowed head.

Further, you should not just carelessly say *"as-salāmu 'alaikum"* to someone and grasp his hand. When you say *"as-salāmu 'alaikum,"* it means "I am joined with you, I am your brother. I am also Islām, I am also of the Islām that God loves." To look at the other person's face, and then to bow your head and give *salāms,* is respectful. You should not just carelessly say *"as-salāmu alaikum"* as you pass by. That is just playing around. Only if we do this in the proper way will we receive the benefit. Therefore, if you do not establish this state, it will be a little difficult to obtain the benefit from your prayer. The benefit comes according to your state.

Some people want to sit in an easy chair. Because of this they do their *dhikr* at the side, over there. We do not know why they came here to Sri Lanka. If they wanted to study from an easy chair, they could have stayed in America. So, they are going backwards. However far they go in search of an easy chair is the amount they are going backwards. Because of that, what benefit are they going to receive? The one who is thirsty will come to the place where there is water, and try to drink. If there is water in the spring you should try to drink from it. Only at that time can you get the water. The water will not come there, to you.

Like that, some of you who are here are doing your prayers in this state. That is not good. With love, *īmān,* certainty, and faith, you must come and search in the place you need to search. Then you will receive the benefit. So many illnesses will be cured and so many difficulties will be removed. So much will be removed! You will become clear. If you nurture that state and act accordingly…I am not forcing you to do this. It is according to your striving. But if you do this and complete it, if you establish within yourself that certitude of *īmān,* that love, and that effort, then that will be good. That will give the benefit.

May Allāh give this to you and dispel your ignorance. May Allāh give you the certitude of faith, *īmān,* and His love, and may He show you the way to find Him. May Allāh guide you on this path.

Āmīn, āmīn. As-salāmu 'alaikum wa rahmatullāh.

A'ūdhu billāhi minash-shaitānir-rajīm.
I seek refuge in God from the accursed satan.

Bismillāhir-Rahmānir-Rahīm.
In the name of God, the Most Compassionate,
the Most Merciful.

THE MEANING OF *SALAWĀT*

April 18, 1984, Wednesday, 8:20 a.m.

Verily Allāh and His angels
Bless the Prophet.
O you who believe!
Bless him and give him
The greetings of peace.

Holy Qur'ān, *Sūratul-Ahzāb,* 33:56

QUESTION

In so many of the prayers that we do, we invoke God's blessing on Muhammad ☉. And I'm wondering what that means. What are we doing when we ask God to bless Muhammad ☉ and give him peace?

BAWA MUHAIYADDEEN

That is a big question. *Tambi,* little brother, that is a very big question. Allāh has said, "*Yā* Muhammad, if not for you, I would not have created anything. Through you, I have created all of everything."

If there is a sun, its light will cover everything in the world. If there is a darkness, the darkness will cover the world for the time it is there. For a time there will be sun and for a time there will be darkness. In this way, both the darkness of illusion and the resplendent Light that is Muhammad ☉ will exist.

Seeds germinate in darkness. It is in darkness that they sprout.

And it is in the darkness of ignorance and hypnotic torpor that a male and female join together to procreate. From that union which is in darkness, a Light emerges. As soon as that power emerges, the darkness has to recede.

In the same way, Allāh has said, "*Yā* Muhammad, if not for you, I would not have created anything." It was that Light that was impressed on the forehead of Adam ☺. That was the Light. Having created Adam ☺, Allāh impressed that Light on his forehead. He then placed a *rūh,* a soul, within him.

The meaning of this is that everything that is created comes forth from Muhammad ☺. Adam ☺ also came forth from that. According to this meaning, the children of Adam ☺ in faith are of the family of Abraham ☺ and in *īmān* and purity are the *ummah,* the followers of Muhammad ☺. We call that their lineage. Nothing can appear without the *mīm.* Because everything appears from the *mīm,* we say that we are the lineage of Muhammad ☺. You and I and everyone are of the lineage of Muhammad ☺. All of us came forth from this *mīm. Alif* is Allāh. *Lām* is the Nūr, the Light. *Mīm* is the form. The *mīm* has taken a form and contains all three. The *sukūn,* the circle, is Muhammad ☺, *lām* is wisdom, the Nūr, and *alif* is Allāh, the support. Since these three are joined and dwell together, all three resplend from within man: Allāh, wisdom, and Muhammad ☺. Wisdom is the *lām.* It can take a form, it can come as Gabriel ☺. That wisdom can come as Gabriel ☺.

Because this state exists within a human being, the *salāms* which were given by Allāh to Muhammad, the Rasūl ☺, is given by us to Muhammad ☺. When we pay that respect to Muhammad ☺, it is like an echo. When we offer *salāms* to the Rasūlullāh ☺, many tens of millions of *salāms* are returned to us. For each one we give, ten are returned. It is like an echo. When we praise him with those *salāms,* they are returned to us. Allāh praises and gives peace. And the peace that we offer Muhammad ☺ creates peace for us. That is an echo. Those *salāms* are returned to us. The praise of the *salāms* that we offer becomes our wealth. The prayers that we offer are either *bātil,* fruitless, or they become our *daulah,* our wealth.

In this way, since everything we offer returns to us, the praise that we offer Muhammad ☺ returns as praise to his *ummah*, it is returned to us. The meaning is that when we offer *salāms* and then look within, we will find that those *salāms* have returned as the light that is lighting our *qalbs* and our faces. We are praising him, but since he resides within us, the praise of those *salāms* and *salawāt*[1] is reflected back and benefits us. That praise returns to reside within us. This is why we consider the *salāms* to be so very exalted. Understand?

QUESTIONER

I'm afraid I'm still not clear on exactly who Muhammad ☺ is, exactly to whom or to what I am directing my praise.

BAWA MUHAIYADDEEN

Allāh tells the angels, "O angels, I praise My Muhammad with the *salāms* and *salawāt*. All of you must also praise him with that *salawāt*, all of you must praise him with that word. He then returns that same word to all of creation. I praise My Rasūl with the *salawāt* and you must also praise him with that same *salawāt*. If you say it once, I will say it ten times.

"Muhammad resides in every human being. When you see someone you say, '*As-salāmu 'alaikum.*' That person responds with, '*Wa 'alaikumus-salām.*' Similarly, when you give *salāms* to Muhammad ☺, will a reply not be returned to you? A response does come. But because we do not have the ear to hear it, we think that there is no reply. An immediate response to your *salāms* will come. 'O my *ummah*, O my son, O my brother, *as-salāmu 'alaikum,* I also praise you. *Wa sallallāhu 'alaihi wa sallam.*' "

These are the words that were spoken by Allāh. But, this is a very great matter. I cannot describe this great mystery. I cannot place this great wonder in your hands, I cannot convey this to you. Within this exists *sharr* and *khair,* evil and good. In the world of *sharī'ah,* I cannot do this; I cannot describe this wonder.

---

1 *salawāt* (A) Prayers or blessings, asking God to bless the prophets and mankind. Derived from *salla,* to pray.

(Bawa Muhaiyaddeen ☺ gives a *hadīth*.)

The Angel Gabriel ☺ would bring the *wahy;* he would bring the teachings from God to the Rasūl ☺, saying, "Allāh said this." He would give his *salāms* and then convey the message.

One day, when Gabriel ☺ was carrying a message from Allāh, the thought came to him, "I am the one who brings the messages to Muhammad. I am the one who gives him the *āyāt,* the verses of the Qur'ān. It is because of me that all the praises and praisings are coming to Muhammad." This is what Gabriel ☺ was thinking. So, when he arrived there, he said, "*As-salāmu 'alaikum,* O Muhammad. Allāh sends *salāms* to you."

Muhammad ☺ replied, "*Wa 'alaikumus-salām.* I reply with the *salāms* Allāh has given. Who are you?"

"O Muhammad, do you not know who I am? Do you not know me? Do you not recognize me?"

"No, I do not know you."

"Am I not the one who has brought you the *wahy* so many times? Am I not the one who has brought you the *āyāt?* I am Gabriel."

"Ah, is that so? I do not recognize you. It is true that Gabriel brings me the revelations, but you are not he. I do know him. I know him, but I do not know you."

"I am the Angel Gabriel."

"No, no, no! I know him very well, and you are not he."

"I have come so many times bringing you the word of Allāh. Now I am giving you *salāms.*"

"Have you seen Allāh? Have you seen Allāh?"

"No, I have not seen Him."

"If you have not seen Allāh, how can I accept this? I cannot accept this. Therefore, please go. I do not know you. Come again when you have seen Allāh."

Gabriel ☺ returned to Allāh and said, "*Yā* Allāh, Muhammad says he does not know me."

Allāh replied, "*Shari,* that is correct. You did not go as Gabriel, therefore, he did not recognize you."

"He asked me if I had seen Allāh, and when I said no, he told me he could not accept those words."

Allāh said, "*Shari,* that is true. That is true. Look at the guarded tablet that is *al-lauhul-mahfūz.*[2] Look!"

It opened, and when Gabriel ☺ looked, he saw a vast mirror. In that mirror he saw a form that had eyes, a nose, and a mouth, everything. It was a youthful form and it was speaking. He saw Muhammad ☺. It was Muhammad ☺. And all the words that Gabriel ☺ had been carrying were issuing forth from that form. They were the same words that he had been bringing to Muhammad ☺.

That was the form. Allāh has no form. Muhammad ☺ is the form, and it is from within that form that Allāh speaks. Do you understand? Allāh has no form. Muhammad ☺ has a form, and Allāh speaks from within that form. He speaks from within that sign, that manifestation. That is a sign. Muhammad ☺ is a sign, and Allāh resides there and speaks from within that. Muhammad ☺ emerged from within Allāh, and Allāh is revealed through Muhammad ☺. He speaks from within that.

Allāh addressed Gabriel ☺ further, "The same *wahy* that you carried today has come back, and is now issuing forth from this form. O Gabriel, did you see who that was? I am within Muhammad and Muhammad is within Me. The *aham,* the heart, and the *muham,* the face—you have not seen the heart, but now look at the face. I speak from within that. Ahamad-Muhammad. Look! Now do you see? You thought it was because of you that Muhammad was being praised. O Gabriel, I am continually praising Muhammad. I manifested him from within Me and gave him this beauty, and I am praising him from within that form. So, how can it be because of you

---

2 *al-lauhul-mahfūz* (A) The guarded tablet. It is said that when one becomes *hāfiz,* when he has truly assimilated the Holy Qur'ān, his tongue becomes *al-lauhul-mahfūz.*

"Has the story reached thee, of the forces Of Pharaoh and The Thamūd? And yet the Unbelievers (persist) in rejecting (the Truth)! But Allāh doth encompass them from behind! Nay, this is a Glorious Qur'ān, (Inscribed) in a Tablet Preserved!" Holy Qur'ān, *Sūratul-Burūj,* 85:18-22

that he is being praised? I have instructed all the heavenly beings to praise him.

"Since I am formless, I have placed a form for that. The meaning is that I reside within that form. If the words are coming only from this Muhammad, why would I create another form as Muhammad, the *mīm*? If I placed that *mīm* there, it is because I am within that form. Gabriel, you have been created as a witness, in order to give proof to the world. You have been created as a proof, as a witness for this. You are a witness between these words and the people.

"Muhammad is from *ʿālamul-arwāh,* the world of the souls, and I am within that. I am the One who exists there, and I continually praise Muhammad. That exists as a form for Me. That is the place where I reside, and I speak from within that," said Allāh.

"Gabriel, now go and tell this to Muhammad! Go and give your *salāms* and tell him this! Muhammad is there. Muhammad is also here. This is Nūr-Muhammad, Allāh-Muhammad. That is Muhammad, Insān-Muhammad," said Allāh.

Understand? Do you understand?

QUESTIONER

A little better.

BAWA MUHAIYADDEEN

If clarity has not come from all these explanations, then the mind needs to be cleared some more. When you offer the *salāms,* they are returned to you. Once clarity comes, you will get the clear meaning.

This is what Allāh revealed to Gabriel ☺.

Allāh has no form. You yourself are Muhammad ☺. You are worshipping Allāh. His form, that Light, however, is kept within you. Surrender to that within yourself and accept that within your *qalb.* He created that formlessness, that Light, within your own form. This is the meaning.

As-salāmu ʿalaikum wa rahmatullāhi wa barakātahu. This is a very great matter. Every *salām* you give returns to you. When you give one *salām,* thirty *salāms* are returned to you—Allāh's *salāms,* the Rasūl's ☺ *salāms,* and the *salāms* of the *malāʾikah* and the other angels.

For every *salām* you give, you receive thirty *salāms* in return. Every *salām* is multiplied tenfold by the angels, tenfold by the Rasūl ☉, and tenfold by Allāh. What you offer through one mouth is returned through countless mouths.

This is what is said. I have not seen it. For this, we must go beyond. We have not seen it. Well, I *have* seen, but...so many different things...Allāh!

A'ūdhu billāhi minash-shaitānir-rajīm.
I seek refuge in God from the accursed satan.

Bismillāhir-Rahmānir-Rahīm.
In the name of God, the Most Compassionate,
the Most Merciful.

JUM'AH,
THE FRIDAY PRAYER

November 8, 1985, Friday, 1:15 p.m.

O ye who believe!
When the call is proclaimed
To prayer on Friday
(The Day of Assembly),
Hasten earnestly to the Remembrance
Of God, and leave off
Business (and traffic):
That is best for you
If ye but knew!

Holy Qur'ān, *Sūratul-Jum'ah*, 62:9

Out of all the prayers in a week, the Friday *khutbah*[1] is like the head. A body has a head, and the Friday *khutbah* and the *jum'ah*[2] prayer are like the head is to a body. Without a head a body cannot be identified.

This prayer gives proof that you are a *mu'min*, Allāh's *ummah*,

---

1 *khutbah* (A) The sermon given by the *imām* of the mosque before the Friday *jum'ah* prayer.

2 *jum'ah* (A) The special Friday midday prayer performed in congregation.

273

and Allāh's child.[3] The head shows the proof that you are the *ummah* of Muhammad ☺, that you are a child that Allāh has accepted.

For the other parts of the body, all of the other prayers are like the light of the true qualities. They will transform darkness. They will give power to the good qualities. But out of the seven days of prayers, this *jum'ah* prayer is the most important one. This is called the Friday prayer. It would be very good if we attend this prayer.

Both *subh*, the early morning prayer, and *'asr*, the mid-afternoon prayer, fall at times that are a little difficult. The time of *subh* is difficult because satan does not allow one to wake up in time. So, if one does wake up and attend the *subh* prayer, then God will give a *zīnah*, a beauty, to his face. Why? Because that person has escaped from what has hold of him, he has escaped from satan who is trying to capture him. If he escapes from that *ummush-shaitān,* the mother or source of satan, then his face will have that *zīnah.* Once he has completed the prayer, he will be happy wherever he goes, no matter how much poverty he has and no matter how many difficulties he is experiencing. He will show that happiness to children and to all the people that he meets. He will display that happiness, wherever he goes. Regardless of the circumstances he will have a smile, and peace, happiness, and serenity will be radiating from his face.

You can investigate this for yourself and see whether this is correct. You can compare this to the other times of the day. Even if you have an illness, if you pray this early morning prayer, the illness will be made less severe.

The *'asr* prayer is difficult to attend because people are at work.

---

3 Allāh's child: Allāh has revealed in the Holy Qur'ān, *Sūratun-Nisā',* 4:171:
   "Then believe in Allāh and His messengers. Do not say 'Trinity.' Stopping it will be better for you, for Allāh is one God: Glory be to Him, (exalted is He) above having a son. To Him belong all things in the heavens and on earth. And Allāh is sufficient as a Disposer of affairs."
   M. R. Bawa Muhaiyaddeen's ☺ phrase "Allāh's child" therefore adamantly does not refer to the concept of *walad,* a son or child that is the result of procreation. He qualifies the phrase "Allāh's child" and makes clear his meaning saying that "you are a child that Allāh has accepted." This applies to all instances where "child" or "son" is used.

They find it a little difficult to go to the mosque for that *waqt* of prayer. If the mosque is close by, it is good if you would go there. Otherwise, even if you are at work, you should somehow pray that *waqt* of prayer in some quiet place. The *'asr* prayer is considered to be the most exalted of the five prayers. If you can complete the *rak'ahs* of that *'asr* prayer without missing even one *waqt,* then a place will be reserved for you in heaven. And just as you overcame all of the difficulties and performed that prayer, in the same way, your difficulties might be removed from you.

The *waqt* of *zuhr,* the noontime prayer, is when you eat lunch. So, at that time, you can pray. You might come home for dinner at the time of *maghrib* and pray at home, or you might go to the mosque to pray. The times of *'ishā'* and *maghrib* are easier.

If you look into each of these, you will find that some of the prayer times are easier, while others are more difficult.

Some people who have the means go to Mecca and Medina each year on *hajj,* the holy pilgrimage. It is said that they have fulfilled the *hajj* once a year. But for those who do not have the means to go on the *hajj,* this Friday prayer becomes their *hajj*. These fifty-two or fifty-four times in the year become their *hajj*. For the *miskīns,* the poor people who are unable to go to Mecca and Medina, God has given the *rahmah* of this Friday prayer, for fulfilling the obligation for *hajj*. This Friday *khutbah* prayer is equivalent to that. So, it is good if you do not miss this prayer.

No matter what *waqt* it is, you must somehow try to perform each of the five *waqts* of prayers. God has given you a way to do this, even if you are ill. Therefore children, it is good if you establish these prayers, somehow or other.

Before praying we must complete the prayer within ourselves. Precious jeweled lights of my eye, in earlier times, before we could light a lamp we would need to have oil. After the oil was ready, we would pour the oil into the lamp, and then prepare the wick. Having placed the wick, we would then strike a match and light the lamp.

Similarly, before prayer, what do we need? In the same way as the lamp needs oil, before we go to pray, our *qalbs* need Allāh's qualities and actions, His beautiful ideals, faith, certitude, and determination. Before we go to pray we must make these complete. Having made these complete, what else do we need for that prayer? We need to prepare the wick of our intention. Once we have prepared that wick, we then surrender to God. Only then will our prayer catch fire. In this way, we must connect our intention to Him and light the lamp.

So, this has to be done before the prayer begins, even before we go to pray. Prayer is not something that we do when it is convenient. Prayer has to be a natural thing within us. Before praying we must prepare our prayer, just as we prepare a lamp before actually lighting it.

What should happen when you perform *dhikr*? If you take a magnifying glass, put a piece of cotton wool underneath it, and focus the rays of the sun onto it, the cotton wool will catch fire. In the same way, our *qalbs* should be like a magnifying glass. If we change our thoughts, qualities, and actions into Allāh's qualities, then our *qalbs* will become a brilliant mirror. Once the *qalb* changes, it becomes fire. Then, if we place a piece of cotton wool underneath it, if we place the *dhikr,* the remembrance of Allāh, underneath that magnifying glass, that *dhikr* will immediately catch fire. That is the *wilāyah,* that is *gnānam*—Light. Allāh's Light will be attracted to that *qalb.* That power will be focused there, and every word, action, and behavior will become Light, that fire.

This is the true way to do *dhikr,* where we can understand about that *wilāyah,* about that power. If we fail to make those qualities ignite like the cotton wool, then just saying the words will not be enough.

Dhikr is much more subtle than *toluhai. Toluhai* is performed five times a day, but what is known as *dhikr* has 43,242 *sujūd,* prostrations, a day. With each breath, without forgetting, we perform *tasbīh* to Allāh, and ask forgiveness from Him, *taubah.* With each breath, we prostrate at His feet, and give *salāms.* If we surrender to His qualities, His actions, His words, and His compassion, then that *dhikr* will come. Only then will that power, that state come; that Light will come into our *qalbs.*

It is this mirror that Allāhu ta'ālā Nāyan showed to the Rasūl ☺ on *mi'rāj*. Who did the Rasūl ☺ see in that mirror? He saw himself. When he said to Allāh, "I want to see You," this is what he was shown. When the Rasūl ☺ looked in that mirror, he saw a youth of sixteen years, with a fine, soft moustache. He saw himself.

Like that, when your *qalb* becomes that mirror, when you have Allāh's qualities, Allāh's actions, Allāh's three thousand gracious attributes, His ninety-nine *wilāyāt* and His actions and conduct—when you have that state and those qualities—then who will you see in that mirror? You will see yourself. Within that resplendence, you will see that human being, you will see that blessed being, that one who has no death.

We need to understand all of the various meanings of prayer. Just talking and talking is not the way. Each one of us must have an open heart. We must recite God's words with so much awe and devotion. We must conduct ourselves with fear of the words of God. We need to have a great deal of reverence for the state of God. Our every state, word, and action must be filled with awe. Why? Because God is everywhere. He dwells in every place. Even if we do not fear other human beings, we need to fear God who is everywhere. If a man is far away, you can say what you like, because he cannot hear it. If a man turns another way, he cannot hear what you say. If he turns this way or that way, you can find fault with him because he cannot hear you. But Allāh can hear everything, everywhere. So, we should be careful about what we say.

Therefore, He is the One who can hear every word that we say. He is the One who is omnipresent, and we should fear Him with every breath. We should have reverence and awe in our words, in our actions, and in our every speech. We should be aware that Allāh is there. Our *qalbs* should have that awe. We must do His duties with that fear in our hearts.

May Allāh forgive us. May He forgive us for all the faults we have committed knowingly and unknowingly. *Āmīn*. May He forgive our many wrongdoings, the faults we have committed in the time we were without knowledge, without understanding, and without wisdom. May Allāhu ta'ālā Nāyan, the Compassionate One, forgive those faults. May He forgive all of us. May He bless us with His grace and take us to His divine feet. May He join us with the one good group. May God help us.

Āndavanai, please bring us to that group of the *mu'mins,* the true believers, and forgive us our wrongdoings! We are not aware of how many faults we have committed. Please forgive us. *Āmīn.* May You accept me, my brothers and sisters, and my children, those who have faith in You. May You join us with the group of the *mu'mins* who believe that You are our *Pidā,* our Father.

Please take us to Your feet as Your slaves and protect us. Please bless us with wisdom, ability, and good qualities, and give us Your grace. Please take away our illnesses, diseases, and poverty.

Please give us the *rahmah* of Your qualities, truth, knowledge, and *gnānam.* May You give us Your wealth of grace. May You protect and bless us.

Āmīn, āmīn, yā Rabbal-'ālamīn. You are the great One. *Allāhu akbar. Āmīn. As-salamu 'alaikum wa rahmatullāh.*

A'ūdhu billāhi minash-shaitānir-rajīm.
I seek refuge in God from the accursed satan.

Bismillāhir-Rahmānir-Rahīm.
In the name of God, the Most Compassionate,
the Most Merciful.

SŪRATUL-FĀTIHAH AND THE SEVEN SHIRTS

December 27, 1975, Saturday, 8:30 p.m.

You have to study the Qur'ān with substance. You should not merely read it. When you say something, there must be a basis for it; there must be truth. To go on speaking without truth is useless.

When an explanation is given, there must be a foundation for it. That is true learning, is that not so? We should not merely learn something and then start speaking about it. While we are learning, we must cultivate the fundamentals of that learning, with wisdom, ability, and good qualities. That is God's work. This is not easy, it is not a small matter.

Lā ilāha illAllāh, Muhammadur-Rasūlullāh.

(Bawa Muhaiyaddeen ☺ holds up a calligraphic drawing of the *Sūratul-Fātihah*.)[1]

---

1 The calligraphic drawing of the *Sūratul-Fātihah* is reproduced on page 280, and a numbered key which corresponds to the Arabic on the drawing is included on page 281.

279

NOTE: CALLIGRAPHIC DRAWING TO BE INSERTED
HERE. YUSUF WILL NEED TO SUPPLY NEGATIVES (2
TONE)

SŪRATUL-FĀTIHAH
(The Chapter of The Opening)

(1a)   *Ash-hadu al-lā ilāha illAllāhu,*   (1b) *wa ash-hadu*
       anna Muhammadar-Rasūlullāh.
       I testify that none is God except Allāh, and
       I testify that Muhammad is the Messenger of Allāh.

(2)   *Bismillāhir-Rahmānir-Rahīm.*
       In the name of Allāh, the Most Compassionate,
       the Most Merciful.

(3)   *Al-Fātihah*
       The Opening

(4)   *Al-hamdu lillāhi*
       Praise be to Allāh

(5)   *Rabbil-ʿālamīn;*
       The Cherisher and Sustainer of the Worlds;

(6)   *Ar-Rahmānir-Rahīm;*
       The Most Compassionate, the Most Merciful;

(7)   *Māliki yaumid-dīn.*
       Master of the Day of Judgment.

(8a)   *Iyyāka naʿbudu*   (8b) *wa iyyāka nastaʿīn.*
       Thee alone do we worship,
       and only Thine aid do we seek.

(9)   *Ihdinas-sirātal-mustaqīm,*
       Show us the Straight Way,

(10a) *Sirāt*   (10b) *al-ladhīna anʿamta ʿalaihim,*
       The way of those on whom Thou hast
       bestowed Thy Grace,

(11a) *Ghairil-maghdūbi ʿalaihim*   (11b) *wa lad-dāllīn.*
       Those whose (portion) is not wrath,
       and who go not astray.

(12)   *Āmīn.*
       So be it.

BAWA MUHAIYADDEEN
This is the *Sūratul-Fātihah.*

(Bawa Muhaiyaddeen ☺ asks someone to read the Arabic aloud.)

This is the *surah,* the form (of man).

READER
A'ūdhu billāhi minash-shaitānir-rajīm.

BAWA MUHAIYADDEEN
The head, the brain, is Allāh.

READER
(The numbers correspond to the numbers on the drawing.)
(1a) *Ash-hadu al-lā ilāha illAllāhu,*   (1b) *wa ash-hadu anna Muhammadar-Rasūlullāh.*

BAWA MUHAIYADDEEN
With that *kalimah* we accept God. That *surah* accepts God. The brain exists as Allāh, it exists as His *dhāt,* His essence. That is Allāh. That is the crown. The head is *lā ilāha illAllāh, Muhammadur-Rasūlullāh.* That is the head, God's house. That is the sign. Below it is the *Sūratul-Fātihah.*

READER
(2) *Bismillāhir-Rahmānir-Rahīm.*

TRANSLATOR
That is the necklace on the drawing.

BAWA MUHAIYADDEEN
He is the One to whom creation, protection, and sustenance belong.

READER
(3) *Al-Fātihah.*

TRANSLATOR
The heart.

BAWA MUHAIYADDEEN

All praise and praising belong only to Him. He is the only One who can accept all that we give. If we give Him praise, He accepts it. Whatever we give, He accepts.

Al-hamdu lillāh, al-hamdu lillāh. He accepts what we give.

READER

Al-hamdu lillāhi Rabbil-ʿālamīn, ar-Rahmānir-Rahīm, māliki yaumid-dīn, iyyāka naʿbudu wa iyyāka nastaʿīn.

BAWA MUHAIYADDEEN

He is the One who rules. *Al-hamdu lillāhi Rabbil-ʿālamīn.*

(4) *Al-hamdu lillāhi,* all praise and praising is to Him alone.

(5) *Rabbil-ʿālamīn,* for all of everything He is the King. He is the Almighty One, the Ruler.

(6) *Ar-Rahmānir-Rahīm:* He is the One who gives food, the One who protects, the One who sustains. Ar-Rahīm. He exists as the *qalb,* He exists as worship. Ar-Rahīm. He exists as the *duʿāʾ,* as the One who listens, and as the One who gives. He gives what the *sūrah* requests. Ar-Rahīm. He exists as prayer.

READER

(7) *Māliki yaumid-dīn.*

BAWA MUHAIYADDEEN

He is the King to all kings. He is the One who rules alone. He is the One who gives the verdict. *Māliki yaumid-dīn.* He is the One who rules the pure kingdom. He is the King to all other kings. All justice is in His hands. All judgment and fairness is determined by Him. He is the One who gives judgment tomorrow for the good and the bad. He is the One who gives grace. That is how He is, how He exists.

READER

(8a) *Iyyāka naʿbudu*   (8b) *wa iyyāka nastaʿīn.*

BAWA MUHAIYADDEEN

He is the One for the beginning and for the end. He is the One for truth and for the explanation. He is the One who gives love, the One who gives wisdom, the One who gives affection, the One who gives light. He gives His good thoughts, He gives His good qualities, and He gives His good love.

READER

(9) *Ihdinas-sirātal-mustaqīm.*

BAWA MUHAIYADDEEN

Ihdinas-sirātal-mustaqīm. He is the One who created the body and the One who gives the body to hell, the One who gives the portion of earth to the earth, the One who gives the portion of fire to the fire, the One who gives the portion of water to the water, the One who gives the portion of air to the air, and the One who gives the portion of maya to maya. He is the One who separates and apportions these. Allāh takes His share and gives them their share.

READER

(10a) *Sirāt*   (10b) *al-ladhīna an'amta 'alaihim.*

BAWA MUHAIYADDEEN

He is the One who can show us the path that enables us to go beyond and beyond hell and finally reach the shore.

READER

(11) *Ghairil-maghdūbi 'alaihim wa lād-dāllīn.*
(12) *Āmīn.*

BAWA MUHAIYADDEEN

He is the One who gives the explanation of good and evil. He gives His crown to us. He crowns us with His crown in the heavenly kingdom, the divine kingdom. He is the One who gives His grace and helps us. *Nasta'īn*—He is the One who nourishes and sustains us.

This *sūrah,* this chapter of the Qur'ān, and these *āyāt,* these verses, are *insān.* This is what is called man, the *Sūratul-Fātihah.* If man contemplates and realizes this, then only God's story, God's *rahmah,* will be within him. Only God's story will be within him. Man is not, he does not exist. Only Allāh's *takht,* throne, His state, and His responsibility are within him. The "I" does not exist, the "mine" does not exist. There are no relations or blood ties for him. There is no Judgment Day and no Day of *Qiyāmah* for him.

Since man is within God, since the body is God's, and since man has God's state, man has been created in the *sūrah*, the form of the Qur'ān. God has created His story as man. He has created that kingdom as man. He has created all of everything within man, and He is the One who rules over this.

Man is the leader of all of everything. He is the vice-regent. This is the *Sūratul-Fātihah*. This is the *sūrah* of the *kalimah*.

If *insān* can understand this, then — *opposites!* The story of Allāh is *insān* and the story of *insān* is Allāh. That is what is called the *Sūratul-Fātihah*. This is that *sūrah*, the *Sūratul-Fātihah*.

If a person understands this, then that is *ma'rifah*, that is Sufi. That is the *vanakkam* of Sufi. If one has established this state, then that is Sufi. As long as one has not understood this, he is not Sufi.

What is the point in just talking? There is a foundation, a basis for this. Man is not a simple being. When man knows himself, he will see that he is not a simple being.

I have been speaking about the *sūrah* of five letters *(al-hamd)*, the *Sūratul-Fātihah*.[2]

All power, all benevolence, and all *rahmah* belong to the One God. May He protect us. Within our body and outside our body, here, there, and everywhere, may He protect and sustain us with His compassionate qualities. *Āmīn.*

My children who are the gems of my eye, when we say *sūrah*, it means "form." What is known as the *Sūratul-Hamd* refers to the human form. What is known as *Qul Huwallāhu* refers to the *qalb*. That is the *qalb*. *Ahad:* that is His grace, the *dhāt*. That is where His story resides. We need to think about this state.

This did not just come about fourteen hundred years ago through the Arabic language. It does not belong to "my race" or "your race,"

---

2   The *Sūratul-Fātihah* is also known as the *Sūratul-Hamd*, thus the five letters are *alif, lām, hā', mīm,* and *dāl.*

it does not have a connection to a race or a religion. When Adam ☺ was created, when *insān* was created, he was created with these letters. When God collected the earth from the four directions of the world, it was then that He created the *sūrah* called *al-hamd*. The covering for that *sūrah* is its shirt. That shirt is earth, fire, water, air, and ether. God covered His story with these *malā'ikah*, these archangels. With these, He made this shirt to cover this *sūrah* called *al-hamd*—His story, His might, His benediction, and His kingdom, His divine kingdom.

This is the shirt that we are now wearing, the shirt of the elements of earth, fire, water, air, and ether. This is the shirt that we have put on. Within this is God's *sūrah*—*al-hamdu lillāh*. What is called *al-hamd* is God's form. Once we remove this shirt of ours, then His story is what remains. Once His story is there, then the meaning I explained earlier is there. When this meaning is there, then that is His kingdom. That is He. Allāhu alone exists.

We, as *insān*, have to understand this explanation. We have to remove this form, this shirt. God has placed this shirt as a covering over His kingdom and His story. This is a secret. What He has placed on top is a secret. Within it is His kingdom, His *dhāt*.

My children who are the gems of my eye, this cannot be understood through race, religion, or creed. These things that we call race, religion, creed, and scripture are the shirt that we are wearing. This is the shirt of the elements. This is the shirt of the *malā'ikah*. This shirt that we wear, which covers this body as a protection, is made from a portion of the earth, a portion of the fire, a portion of the water, a portion of the air, a portion of the ether, a portion of the *nafs*, and a portion of desire, the portion of the dog. These seven portions are a *jubbah*, a gown.

Having put on this gown and having taken on the qualities of this gown, we have forgotten the inner *sūrah* of *insān* that is *al-hamd*. When God created Adam ☺, He created this beauty and said, "This is My kingdom, this is God's divine kingdom." He said, "This is God's kingdom of purity." He said, "This is the kingdom of God." He said, "This is heaven, this is God's house."

We should remove this form, this shirt, and try to analyze a little. It is possible that this shirt is the religions. Earth is the religion of Hinduism, fire is the religion of Hanal, air is the religion of *al-injīl*, Christianity, and water is *al-furqān*, the religion of Islam. Earth, fire, water, and air. Ether is the darkness of maya. This mind is the *nafs*, the section of satan—the jinns, the fairies, the *nafs*, the ghosts, and the demons. The dog of desire is a section of hell. We have put on these seven different *jubbahs* as a covering. When we put on this gown, we take on the qualities of the gown. We take on the arrogance of the earth, we take on the arrogance of karma, we take on the connection of maya, we take on the qualities of the fire, and we take on the qualities of the air. With these qualities of earth, fire, and water, and with mind, desire, and ether, we fight and say, "This is my country." This form is a different form. It is a shirt. One day we will have to remove this shirt. One day we will have to separate and give back each of these portions. One day this shirt will tear. It has an estimate, a limit. So, this is not something that is permanent.

Therefore, children who are the gems of my eye, this is true for everyone. It may be the religion of Hanal, it may be the religion of *al-injīl* (Christianity), it may be the religion of Hinduism, or it may be the religion of *al-furqān* (Islam), but regardless of what religion it is, this house, this shirt, will have to be removed. This is a shirt that will eventually tear. This is a form that is covering the grace that is His *dhāt*.

Therefore, that body is *insān*. That body of *insān* is the story of God. The beauty of that story is the kingdom of God. The beauty of that kingdom *is* God. This is what we have to understand. As long as we do not understand this, then all of the fighting that we do is fighting that is done by this shirt. All of the worship that we do is worship that is done by this shirt. All of the faults that we commit are done by this shirt. And all of the sins that we commit are done by this shirt.

This is not it, gems of my eye! The *dhāt* of limitless grace, that *sūrah* called *al-hamdu lillāh*, is not this. As soon as you remove these seven *jubbahs*, when you remove this gown and look within, then

God and God's story will be there. God and God's justice will be there. God and God's law will be there. God and God's power will be there. God and God's justice and judgment will be there. God and God's light will be there. God and God's *rahmah* will be there. God and God's wealth will be there. God and God's sweet fragrances will be there. God and God's beauty will be there. God and God's *beauty-form,* His form, that beauty-form will be seen. That is the story.

Therefore, my children who are the gems of my eye, you must reflect on this state a little. If you understand this form, if you realize this beauty, and if you understand this state, then that will be the state of man-God, God-man. If you remove this *jubbah,* God will be there. If this *jubbah* is not there, His story will be there. Ar-Rahīm. That is worship, ar-Rahīm. *Yā* Rahīm. You alone are the One who gives all of everything. This is *vanakkam. Yā* Rahīm. This is meditation. *Yā* Rahīm. He is the One who gives, He is the One who sustains, and He is the One who protects. *Yā* Rahīm.

Therefore, we must try to understand the explanation of *vanakkam,* the subtleties of *vanakkam,* the connection of *vanakkam,* the meanings of *vanakkam,* the inner aspects of *vanakkam,* the deep, deep, deep, deep aspects of *vanakkam,* and the clarity of *vanakkam.* Further, we must try to understand the clarity of *'ibādah,* the unity of *'ibādah,* the unity of *dhikr,* God's unity, the unity of God's kingdom, the unity of the heavenly kingdom of God—the unity between that Light and man, that story and that *dhāt*—the clarity and beauty of that kingdom, that food and that bliss. We must understand that only this love, and nothing else, exists.

Once man understands this, once he removes this shirt, he will not exist. When this form, when these *malā'ikah* are taken away, he does not exist. When he removes the connection to the earth, to Adam ⊕, he does not exist. When he removes the connection to water, to Mīkā'īl ⊕, he does not exist. When he removes the connection to air, to Isrāfīl ⊕, he does not exist. When he removes the connection to fire, to 'Izrā'īl ⊕, he has no death. When he removes the connection to ether, to maya, he does not exist. When he removes the connection to the mind, he has no *nafs;* he has no birth and he has no *nafs.* When he removes the connection to desire, there is no hell. Then he has no hell. So, he is Light.

This is man. He is the *Sūratul-Hamd,* the *Sūratul-Fātihah. Sūrat-ul-partiyā.*[3] Have you looked inside? What you are wearing on the outside is this shirt. Have you removed it and looked inside? Have you seen the connection between Him and you and you and Him? If you have seen it, then this is *al-hamdu,* the *Sūratul-Hamd.*

Upon seeing that you will say, "*Al-hamdu lillāh,* Allāh! Everything is You. The entire body is You. This kingdom is You. All of this is You. I am not. *Al-hamdu lillāh, Sūratul-Fātihah.* You exist as this *surah. Lā ilāha illAllāh, Muhammadur-Rasūlullāh.* This is the beauty of the face and the heart. Your crown is on my head. Your beauty-form exists as *lā ilāha illAllāh, Muhammadur-Rasūlullāh.* That beauty exists there. *Ar-Rahīm.* What is in my hand is Your kingdom, the heavenly kingdom. *Ar-Rahīm* is Your kingdom. Therefore, everything is Yours. I do not exist. I have put on these seven robes, these seven *jubbahs.* They are the *arts-work* that cover Your story. I have wasted all of this time saying, 'I, I,' 'mine, mine.' *Āndavanai, yā* Allāh, how (exalted) is Your *Qudrah!*" This is what you will say.

This is not a religion, this is the truth. This is the truth about *insān.* This is not about race. When Adam ⊛ was created, this *surah* was created, *al-hamd.* When Adam ⊛ was created, this was created. This explanation was created, this beauty was created, this *jubbah* was put on. And one day this *jubbah* that was put on will tear.

Therefore, what is it that we need? We need to search for wisdom, we need the wisdom to understand this. That is not a mantra. We need to search for the qualities that will understand this. That is not magic. We need the wisdom that can penetrate into it. We need to find the deep, original, subtle wisdom that can penetrate it. This is not just "this" or "that." We need the state where we can go within and find the understanding.

---

3 *sūrat-ul-partiyā* (A & T) "Have you looked inside your form?" This is a pun on *Sūratul-Fātihah. Sūrah* (A) means form; *ul* (T) means within; and *partiyā* (T) means "Have you seen?"

Children, jeweled lights of my eye, we have to do this. We need to understand this, we need to realize this. It is not "my share" and "your share." It is not what the mind searches for or what the body searches for. That state is only associated with the *jubbah,* the gown that we put on. That is just a covering, an outside covering. You put on this outside covering and you fight for its sake, saying, "I." You say, "That person is different," or "This person is different." This is *no good!*

If you look at the truth, you will see that only God exists. His kingdom exists. His justice exists. His qualities, His plenitude, His verdict, and His judgment all exist within man. This is what your inner form is. This is your title of man-God, God-man. Once you understand this, you will see only Him: "In that form I exist as God. Once I remove this shirt that I am wearing, God exists in my form and I exist in His form." If this is not removed, then man will exist in the form of the shirt.

We need to understand this. *Īmān* must come, wisdom must come, clarity must come, compassion must come, the love for other lives as our own must come, love must come, tolerance must come, peacefulness must come, justice must come, integrity must come, mercy must come, pity must come, and charity must come. We need to establish justice. Once we establish this state, once we establish faith, then we will realize that man is the vice-regent for God's kingdom. There is only one point, there is only one truth, and there is only one worship. If not for God, if not for Him, not even an atom would move. We must understand this *jubbah* a little.

Children, jeweled lights of my eye, sometimes we blame God. The fire of the five elements, the *nafs* of maya that is the mind, and the dog that is desire...we put our hand into the fire and when it burns, we say, "*Aiyō,* it is burning!" Is that God's fault? It is *not* His fault. If we fall into the ocean of maya and the water carries us away, is that His fault? It is *our* fault. If we fall into the wind of the *nafs* and if it tosses and rolls us around, is that His fault? Are we not the ones who have been caught by this? You go and fall into the *nafs,* so whose fault is that? When the earth tries to make you take many rebirths, is that the fault of the earth? You go and fall into the earth, into that karma. Now, karma is what is creating rebirth. Is that the fault of the earth? Is it the fault of God? Arrogance is the quality of satan. You fall into that and that takes you to hell. You get angry and that takes you to hell. Is that the fault of God? You go and fall into the *nafs* that are the seven hells and they roll you and burn you. Is that the fault of God? It is not His fault. You yourself go there and fall into it. You go there and fall into the air and the fire, you fall into the water, you fall into karma, you fall into anger and arrogance, you fall into lust. We go there, fall into these, and then blame God for it.

Without understanding what your form is, without understanding what that grace is, without understanding what your body is, without understanding what your prayer is, without understanding what God's kingdom is, without understanding that you are the prince of God, without understanding that your form exists in the kingdom of God, without understanding that state, you have put on these seven *jubbahs*. These gowns have to be removed, they have to be cleared. You have put on these gowns in the world and everywhere there is fighting, everywhere there is war, everywhere there is arrogance, everywhere there is hell, everywhere there is karma, everywhere there are differences, and everywhere there is pain being inflicted. This is not the way it should be. Please try to think about this a little.

My children who are the gems of my eye, please try to think about every letter (of your *sūrah*). Try to think about your body. There are two forms, one that is inside and one that is outside. The shirt that you are wearing is a shirt that will tear. It is created, it is not permanent. It will have to be removed. It is something that will have to be shared out. It is something that will have to be distributed, the shares will have to be given back. You are wearing these (*jubbahs*) for the sake of the cold, the sun, and the rain, but they will change.

Look! You put on these things to protect you from the cold and the snow. You put on mind and desire. But as soon as you go out in the sun, you take everything off! This is how it is. It is like this. When you go to Atlantic City, you take off all of your clothes. Look at these *jubbahs*. They are useless. These *jubbahs* change with the seasons. This is simply a shirt. We put on this shirt and we fight.

Man is not this shirt. Man's form is God's beauty, His Light, His effulgence, His compassion, His love, and His pure kingdom, the kingdom of God, paradise. It is a great Light, an effulgence that is spread out shining everywhere.

My precious children, jeweled lights of my eye, please think. You put on these *jubbahs* and fight. You say "my religion" and "your religion" and you wage war. This *jubbah* is a gown that has to be removed. It is something that will have to be returned to the shareholders. It is something that will go back to the earth, it is something that will go back to fire. Do not fight for the sake of this. Do not burn for the sake of wearing this. If you fall into the fire, it will burn you. If you fall into the water, it will kill you. If you fall into the *nafs,* they will roll you around. If you fall into maya, it will scorch you and burn you to ashes. They will do all this.

My children who are the gems of my eye, please think about this; reflect on this. Think with wisdom. Please consider this and understand. Please find out what is right. Please find out what man is. Please find out what the body of man is. If you understand this, if you discover this, that will be very good. *Al-hamdu lillāh.* All praise belongs to Allāh.

This is just a small explanation. If you think about this, it will be good. All praise is to Allāh. Everyone can see this (drawing) once it is printed in a book. *Al-hamdu lillāh, vanakkam. Anbu. Anbu, vanakkam.* Compassion, love. May God protect us.

Is this enough? Ah, it is enough! *Anbu.*

SONG: CLAP YOUR HANDS AND BEAT THE DRUMS WELL

from *Gnāna Oli Mālay,* c.1946

Clap your hands, *adi,*[1] beat the drums well, *adi.*
Clap, so the *kufr*[2] within you rises up on its toes to
run away, *adi.*

Clap your hands blissfully for the Noble Prophet ☮
who pervades everything everywhere.
—Clap your hands, *adi,* beat the drums well, *adi.*

Clap your hands for the Dastagir, the Divine Helper,
who is as valuable as gold, pervading everything everywhere, *adi.*
—Clap your hands, *adi,* beat the drums well, *adi.*

Clap your hands for our Master, the golden Guru-Nabī ☮.
Know his good nature.
—Clap your hands, *adi,* beat the drums well, *adi.*

He will gather the people on all four paths and walk with them.
Clap your hands for our Nabī, our Prophet ☮, *adi.*
—Clap your hands, *adi,* beat the drums well, *adi.*

---

1   *adi* (T) *Adi* shows us that the song is addressed in a familiar manner to a woman. Since Allāh is the only male, this applies to all of us.

2   *kufr* (A) The qualities that have no belief in God.

293

He is the Prophet ☺ who understood the five and
gave them to us.
Clap your hands for our Ādi³ Nabī , our Primal Prophet ☺.
—Clap your hands, *adi,* beat the drums well, *adi.*

Clap your hands with melting bliss
for our Nabī ☺ who knows everything, *adi.*
—Clap your hands, *adi,* beat the drums well, *adi.*

He is the Nabī ☺ who taught us the five *kalimahs,*
He is the one who speaks with God.
—Clap your hands, *adi,* beat the drums well, *adi.*

He is the Nabī ☺ who invites heaven into himself.
He is the Nabī ☺ who makes the good, resplendent *du'ā'.*
—Clap your hands, *adi,* beat the drums well, *adi.*

Why do you not yet understand
the five *furūd* described by the Ādi Nabī ☺, *adi?*
—Clap your hands, *adi,* beat the drums well, *adi.*

Come, find him, *adi!*
Reach the Holy Nabī ☺ himself, *adi.*
—Clap your hands, *adi,* beat the drums well, *adi.*

Catch the bull and control it, *adi.*
Search by knowing the path, *adi.*
—Clap your hands, *adi,* beat the drums well, *adi.*

How many more days will we live, *adi?*
Why do you not know that even now, *adi?*
—Clap your hands, *adi,* beat the drums well, *adi.*

---

3 Ādi (T) Literally, primal, source, causal, original.

Will wealth and worldly pleasure go with you, *adi*?
Aim for heaven instead, *adi*.
—Clap your hands, *adi*, beat the drums well, *adi*.

Do not walk in such a way as to slip off the path, *adi*.
Tomorrow destruction will come in *maut*,[4] *adi*.
—Clap your hands, *adi*, beat the drums well, *adi*.

Do not live without performing the five-times prayer, *adi*.
If you give it up, you will become a *kutti* shaitān,[5] *adi*.
—Clap your hands, *adi*, beat the drums well, *adi*.

Do not go to watch the street theater, *adi*.
If you do, hell will commingle with you, *adi*.
—Clap your hands, *adi*, beat the drums well, *adi*.

If you allow your own husband to drink,
you will ruin your own family, *adi*.
—Clap your hands, *adi*, beat the drums well, *adi*.

Do not die telling lies.
If you do, you will enter hell and burn there, *adi*.
—Clap your hands, *adi*, beat the drums well, *adi*.

Do not lend money on interest, *adi*.
If you do, a fire will burn in your mouth, *adi*.
—Clap your hands, *adi*, beat the drums well, *adi*.

Do not lie, steal, or slander, *adi*.
Take in only the virtue of *īmān*, *adi*.
—Clap your hands, *adi*, beat the drums well, *adi*.

---

4 *maut* (A) Death.
5 *kutti* shaitān (T & A) A small, young devil.

Please search for the five *furūd, adi.*
Merge with our Noble Nabī ☺, *adi.*
—Clap your hands, *adi,* beat the drums well, *adi.*

Do not say that you have recited the *kalimah, adi.*
Endeavor to hold the reins and actually practice it, *adi.*
—Clap your hands, *adi,* beat the drums well, *adi.*

The first of the five *furūd, adi,*
will be the good *kalimah, adi.*
—Clap your hands, *adi,* beat the drums well, *adi.*

The second of the five *furūd, adi,*
will be to pray the beautiful prayer, *adi.*
—Clap your hands, *adi,* beat the drums well, *adi.*

The third of the five *furūd, adi,*
will be the liberation that comes from *khairu khairāt,*[6] *adi.*
—Clap your hands, *adi,* beat the drums well, *adi.*

The fourth of the five *furūd, adi,*
will be exalted fasting, *adi.*
—Clap your hands, *adi,* beat the drums well, *adi.*

The fifth of the five *furūd, adi,*
will be that one *hajj, adi.*
—Clap your hands, *adi,* beat the drums well, *adi.*

Do not ever think,
"I have transcended the five *furūd* and left them behind, *adi.*"
—Clap your hands, *adi,* beat the drums well, *adi.*

---

6 *khairu khairāt* (A) Charity, generosity. Here, *khairu khariāt* refers to the third *fard,* obligatory duty, in Islām, the paying of the annual *zakāt,* charity. Literally, the best of good deeds.

Earnestly climb up step by step, *adi.*
Praise the Most Generous Rahmān, *adi.*
—Clap your hands, *adi,* beat the drums well, *adi.*

Do not place your feet on the final step, *adi,*
saying, "I have attained *īmān* by reciting the *kalimah.*"
—Clap your hands, *adi,* beat the drums well, *adi.*

Do not possess a cunning and thieving heart, *adi.*
Reject your wild criminal state, *adi.*
—Clap your hands, *adi,* beat the drums well, *adi.*

The jealousy-demon, lying, and lust are truly horrible, *adi.*
Terrible consequences will come to join you, *adi.*
—Clap your hands, *adi,* beat the drums well, *adi.*

Do not be uselessly vain.
Overcome it so you do not die in the hot flames, *adi.*
—Clap your hands, *adi,* beat the drums well, *adi.*

Do not step down onto the final step, *adi,* saying,
"It is enough to say the *kalimah.*"
—Clap your hands, *adi,* beat the drums well, *adi.*

Keep the knowledge of the five, *adi.*
And after that, search for the Rahmān, *adi.*
—Clap your hands, *adi,* beat the drums well, *adi.*

Do not die, arrogantly saying,
"I have come to know all that is limitless."
—Clap your hands, *adi,* beat the drums well, *adi.*

Do not move your mouth just to gain fame, *adi*.
Do not live your life by going astray and losing your way.
—Clap your hands, *adi,* beat the drums well, *adi*.

Do not think, "I am great," *adi*.
Destruction will come on that day, *adi*.
—Clap your hands, *adi,* beat the drums well, *adi*.

He who exists as the One who knows everything, *adi*,
is our one and only Rahmān, *adi*.
—Clap your hands, *adi,* beat the drums well, *adi*.

He is the Almighty One not bound by any limits, *adi*.
He is the Ruler of all the universes, *adi*.
—Clap your hands, *adi,* beat the drums well, *adi*.

He is the One who possesses the glory and the greatness.
He is beyond all description, *adi*.
—Clap your hands, *adi,* beat the drums well, *adi*.

Do not depend on the earth, *adi*.
Doing that will not take you to *Ma'shar,*
the Assembly at Judgment Day, tomorrow, *adi*.
—Clap your hands, *adi,* beat the drums well, *adi*.

Do not strike out at the stomachs of the poor, *adi*.
Tomorrow you will burn in a hell of want, *adi*.
—Clap your hands, *adi,* beat the drums well, *adi*.

Do not think, "I alone am a virtuous woman," *adi*.
Your suffering will come tomorrow, *adi*.
—Clap your hands, *adi,* beat the drums well, *adi*.

In heaven the Rahmān will be a Father to all, *adi,*
He is the Haqq that is Ādi Rahmān, *adi.*
—Clap your hands, *adi,* beat the drums well, *adi.*

He is the One who sees knowing the *qalb, adi.*
The sight He will see is the meaning that is He, *adi.*
—Clap your hands, *adi,* beat the drums well, *adi.*

You are not the known meaning,
you are not the unknown meaning.
The meaning that needs to be known is
for you to know yourself, *adi.*
—Clap your hands, *adi,* beat the drums well, *adi.*

Know Ādi Rahmān within love, *adi.*
He is the One who is Āmīn Yā Rabbal-'ālamīn, *adi.*
—Clap your hands, *adi,* beat the drums well, *adi.*

A'ūdhu billāhi minash-shaitānir-rajīm.
I seek refuge in God from the accursed satan.
Bismillāhir-Rahmānir-Rahīm.
In the name of God, the Most Compassionate,
the Most Merciful.

TRUE MAN

July 16, 1981, Thursday, 6:55 a.m.

*B*ismillāhir-Rahmānir-Rahīm. All praise and praising belong to Allāh. There is none worthy of worship other than Allāhu ta'ālā. May our property and Allāh's property be one and the same property. Allāh's property is pure. It is indestructible, undiminishing, and without differences. It is without the "mine" and the "yours." It is common to all lives. It belongs to all, is common to all, is equal to all, and gives peace. It gives peace to the body and to the soul.

God gives His qualities of grace, that treasure of equality, peace, and tranquility to all lives in this world, the world of the souls, and the world of God. This is the way He performs His duty, His actions, and His service. As the One who is the Doer and the One to whom everything is done, He gives His treasure. That is plenitude, that is His wealth. He gives the wealth of peace, tranquility, and serenity to every *qalb.* His treasure of grace, treasure of *'ilm,* and treasure of *gnānam* are the treasures that can end our sorrows and suffering. His treasure is the wealth of His qualities that can give peace to every *qalb.* That is His paradise, it is called *swarkkam,* paradise. That wealth is common to all lives. He dwells in all lives and gives to all. That alone is wealth.

Man should strive to attain that same wealth, that same quality, that same action, and that same behavior. If he attains that wealth, then that will be real wealth. Having that peace will be wealth. To conduct oneself with those actions and to establish that state is prayer. That is *toluhai, vanakkam,* and *'ibādah.* That is called prayer.

If we can establish the state in which we can give the treasures that He gives, the wealth of His qualities, the wealth of grace, the wealth of His property, the wealth of the soul, and the wealth of plenitude, then that is prayer. If we can possess that wealth and establish that state, then we will share that wealth in the same way that God does. To be able to give peace to others is wealth. This is called *vanakkam, toluhai, 'ibādah, tiyānam,* and *tavam,* worship, five-times prayer, service to God, contemplation on God, and meditation. Prayer is referred to in many different ways. Only this wealth can be considered to be real wealth. If we attain this treasure, then God's wealth and man's wealth are one, they are one wealth. God's wealth is man's wealth and man's wealth is God's wealth.

All other wealth, everything else that man considers to be his wealth, whatever he searches for and collects, is *jahannam,* hell. The things that he collects are the hypnotic fascinations of the *dunyā,* the hell of the *dunyā,* torpor, darkness, differences, separations, loathing, selfishness, jealousy, envy, backbiting, hatred of race, hatred of color, hatred of religion, hatred of language, hatred of Āndavan, hatred of Kadavul, hatred of Allāh, hatred of God, hatred of mankind, hatred of lives, hatred of prayer, hatred of *vanakkam,* hatred of *toluhai,* hatred of learning, hatred of sight, and hatred of thought. Property, kinship, and titles are the self-business of the *nafs.* These qualities are the qualities that separate you from Allāh. They must change. Man must change these qualities and receive the wealth of grace, the wealth of the soul. This is the reason that God has sent down the 124,000 prophets. They give proof that there is one family, one group, one race, one God, one truth, and one prayer.

The sun, the moon, the stars, the sky, and the earth are all placed here as examples. The movements in the sky, the thunder, the light, the clouds, the colors, the storms, the lightning, the tremors, the darkness, the greens, blues, reds, and yellows, the gold and the gems, all of these show a connection to the sky. We must realize this.

In the same way as the connections to the sky are shown, the connections to the earth are also shown. Gold, silver, thunder, tremors, and earthquakes are shown. Through the connections of the earth and the sky, hypnotic fascinations are revealed. What is seen in the earth can be seen in the sky and what is seen in the sky can be seen in the earth.

These connections can also be seen in man's body. The sun and the moon, the tremors, vibrations, earthquakes, lightning, thunder, torpor, clouds, sorrow, and happiness exist in this body. In the same way that the sun can be hidden or that a snake can be hidden, man's heart can be hidden by desires, attachments, religions, separations, differences, bad qualities, snake-like evil qualities, poisonous qualities, poisonous actions, selfishness, divisions, egoism, jealousy, envy, vengeance, deceit, treachery, blood ties, maya, arrogance, and karma. These display a connection to the earth and a connection to the sky. They exist within the body.

For man, the head is the most important part of his body. It has seven openings, seven heavens. Further, there is the 'arsh and the kursī, making nine openings. There are seven, plus two. What is called the kursī is in man's forehead, at the bridge of the nose. This is the eye of grace, the gnāna kan. What is called the 'arsh is the takht, the throne of Allāh. It is the brain. It is from here that Allāh explains and rules. These are the nine openings, the nine causes. These nine causes are explained through unarvu, unarchi, putti, madi, nuparivu, pahut arivu, and pērarivu: perception, awareness, intellect, judgment, subtle wisdom, divine analytic wisdom, and divine luminous wisdom, the wisdom of plenitude. It is through gnānam that Allāh's qualities are explained, His plenitude is explained, and His wealth is explained.

The seven causes that are on the head must be understood. When you look at the external body, you will see that there are nine causes: two below, and seven above that are outwardly visible. These are the nine zodiac signs, the nine causes. They are the reason for man's agitation and sin.

What we see on the outside with our eyes mesmerizes us and causes torpor, happiness, sadness, attachment, and craving. The qualities of torpor search for external smells and say, "This smells good.

That smells good." The ears are fascinated by the external sounds they hear. The tongue tastes the external tastes and enjoys them, it speaks the outer speech. One of the openings below enjoys the external *līlai vinōtham,* the sixty-four sexual games, and the *kalai gnā-nam,* the sixty-four arts and sciences. It is fascinated by them. The other opening below is the opening of the fanaticism that is arrogance. The egoism that says "I" arises from the fecal arrogance. That fecal arrogance decreases the good qualities and actions and increases the bad qualities and actions. That fanaticism is arrogance.

There is the torpor of earth, woman, and gold, these three—desire for earth, desire for woman, and desire for gold. From these arise the attachments of the body, the attachments of hell, and the attachments of torpor. Wife, children, babies, calves, cows, house, titles, status, property, kinship, joy, and sorrow, all these are mingled within man. When your mind gets entangled and you are governed and fascinated by these, your actions will separate you from God, and you will receive hell.

This is the state of the nine planets that cause agitation. When you look within these, you will see that there is clearly a connection to the sky above and a connection to the earth below. The two lower openings have a connection to the earth. It is the earth that generates arrogance. What is just below the neck—the heart and the breast—is connected to the sky: the sun, the moon, and the stars. The heart, that world which is below the neck, generates the world of illusion. The heart is the central world. The sun, the moon, and the stars are hidden by lightning, thunder, rain, water, and clouds. All of these cause suffering. Similarly, man's wisdom, truth, light, and plenitude are hidden by darkness, clouds, and storms. This central place is affected in this way by poisons, snakes, and thunderous quakes. Just as the light from the sun, the moon, and the stars can be hidden, so too can man's heart, his *qalb,* be hidden. His qualities, his light, his grace, his *'ilm,* and his learning can all be destroyed by the clouds of his attachments.

The heart is the central place. The sun, the moon, the stars, God, truth, wisdom, and *'ilm* are there in this central place. But this place can be covered by clouds, darkness, storms, tremors, and lightning. The planets seize hold of the sun, the planets seize hold of the moon, and the planets hide the stars. God's qualities, the resplendence of the sun called *'ilm,* and His Star, which is the Light of the *mīm* called the soul, are hidden. The attachments of the world, the qualities of the world, the actions of the world, the religions of the world, the visions of the world, the thoughts of the world, the selfishness of the world, the arrogance, karma, and maya of the world, and sexual craving, hatred, miserliness, greed, fanaticism, envy, intoxicants, lust, theft, murder, falsehood, earth, woman, and gold—qualities like these cover man's heart. Light, the soul, purity, God's qualities, God's grace, God's resplendence, God's *'ilm,* His light-creations, His plenitude, peace, tranquility, and serenity are hidden in his heart in the same way that the sun is hidden by lightning and thunder. This is the central place, this world.

One is the world of creation. One is the world of the *ānmā,* the soul. And one is the kingdom of God, the head. You must understand this.

In the same way that the sky is hidden, in the same way that the light in man's heart is hidden, his birth is destroyed from below by arrogance, karma, and maya. We dance and are mesmerized by the sexual games, by sex, and by the arts and sciences. This is torpor. We must understand this.

If we can triumph over these three worlds, if we can go beyond them, then we will understand the *'arsh* and the *kursī.* We will realize *gnānam,* the *gnāna kan* of *'ilm,* the eye of wisdom that is in the forehead. We will see all of the universes and all lives. This is *gnānam,* this is the sun. God! That eye will see God, it will see God's kingdom. It will see God's qualities and make them complete. It will not accept anything other than Him. It will understand that the clouds, the storms, and everything else have a limit. The eye that can understand all three worlds is that eye of *'ilm.* For man, this has become closed. Yet, it is through this eye that God is explained.

Mīm is the world of the souls. *Lām* is the world of the heart. And *alif* is the world of God. The *alif* comes from the *'arsh* and extends down the bridge of the nose. That is *alif.* That is Allāh. Man must give sound to Allāh. An *alif* itself has no sound. With wisdom and with *'ilm,* man must give that sound. To give that sound and to speak with Him is *gnānam.* If you place a diacritical mark above or below an *alif,* it is immediately given sound, it can speak.

Like that, the sound with which man is able to speak with God is God's qualities. To speak with God, to hear Him, and to worship Him...to hear His sound, man must place his sound on That: God's qualities, those actions, that conduct, behavior, goodness, prayer, and *vanakkam.* Through God, he must give sound to Him. With His qualities he must give sound to Him. With His actions he must give sound to Him. With His speech he must give sound to Him. God's qualities and actions are *al-asmā'ul-husnā. Al-asmā'ul-husnā* are His ninety-nine *wilāyāt.* These ninety-nine speak with Him. His duty, service, actions, *wilāyāt,* and grace speak with Him. Like that, this is the state in which we must speak with Him. We must give sound to Him.

That is a Mystery. The Mystery is Allāh. God is Allāh, ar-Rah-mān is Allāh, ar-Rahīm is Allāh, al-Karīm is Allāh, al-Latīf is Allāh, Subhānallāh is Allāh, Al-hamdu lillāh is Allāh, al-Kabīr is Allāh, ar-Rabb is Allāh, Kadavul is Allāh, Yahweh is Allāh. Whatever the language, whatever word each one uses, that word signifies Allāh.

To pray to Him you must pray from within His qualities. You must establish that state. His speech gives sound to His speech. His tongue gives sound to His tongue. His qualities give sound to His qualities. His thoughts give sound to those thoughts. His prayer gives sound to that prayer. His taste gives sound to the taste of *'ilm.* His peace gives sound to that peace. Like this, the countless compassionate qualities must give sound to those qualities. It is through this sound that we can understand Him.

That is a Mystery, a mysterious Treasure. It is beyond form, shape, figure, relationships, blood ties, attachments, race, religion, scriptures, and philosophies. It has no connection to these. It is beyond colors and hues and beyond languages. It is a beauty beyond all beauty. It is beyond torpor. It is a Treasure that exists in the place where there are no likes and dislikes. It is a Treasure that has no desires or aversions. It is a Treasure that has transcended beginning and end. It is a Treasure that has no appearance or destruction, no joy or sorrow, no hell or heaven, no wife or children, no food or drink, no desire, attachment, or blood ties.

A fragrance is mingled with a flower, is that not so? Like this, many flowers are planted and arranged in a flower garden. Many species, many fruits, many fragrances, many colors, and many tastes are displayed there. When we look at a flower garden or an orchard, we can see this. That is God's kingdom, His equality. The many colors, hues, and fragrances of the flowers are there. All of these are contained in His flower garden.

Like that, your flower garden, which is the kingdom of God... What we are shown on the outside is an example. You would have understood and seen the many different flowers, fruits, fruit trees, and tastes in your garden. You would have understood the many different tastes in the flowers and fruits that you planted in your farm and garden. One by one, you would have understood the many different fragrances that are there.

So, one by one, you would have appreciated the tastes, the fragrances, and the colors that are there, is that not so? This is what is found in a flower garden or an orchard. It is made beautiful by the different things that are there. It is made beautiful by the different languages that are there. It is made beautiful by the different colors that are there. It is made beautiful by the different sounds that are there. It is made beautiful by the different words that are there. It is made beautiful by the different actions that are there. The different fragrances, words, actions, colors, hues, and smells are displayed there.

We can see God's kingdom in our hearts. As you eat each fruit you will find that each one has its own taste and its own fragrance. Yet, they are all found in the same garden, are they not? That is beautiful, is it not?

Like that, God's beauty, His wisdom, His goodness, and His qualities can be seen as one. That is the flower garden of your *qalb*. God has created that flower garden of the heart, the *qalb*, for man.

He has planted the flowers and the seeds in man's heart in this way. He has planted these orchards in this way.

This is the orchard called the world. It is a flower garden, it is a flower garden and an orchard. It is a garden that has taste, it is an orchard that gives joy. God created this with so many colors and flowers. We must realize that we are God's flowers, we are God's fruits in the heart of this body. He created the flowers in the same way that He created man. This is the *qalb,* the *qalb-pu,* the flower of the heart. The *qalb,* the heart: this is the orchard, His garden.

God must protect us, this property. He is the Master of the garden. He is the Rabb, the One who created it. Just as He created the many different flowers in that garden, He created human beings, each with different colors, each with different sounds, each with different hues, and each with different languages. Man has been created in many different ways. The colors and hues are varied, the tastes are varied. Each one is different, yet they are all kept in that flower garden, in that orchard. There, God extracts their essence. The essence of each one belongs to Him. The flowers have form, but their essence is His. As He keeps on squeezing the flowers and extracting that essence, it becomes one point.

Whatever the language, whatever the color, whatever the hue, there is only one God. He is the Guardian. We have not seen our Father, have we? The One who protects us is the Guardian who created us. We have not seen our God, have we? We have not known That. That is a Mystery. It is a Mystery. We have not seen our Allāh, have we? That has no shape and cannot be seen. We have not seen our Rabb, have we? That has no form and cannot be seen. God, Yahweh, Kadavul — That is God. We have not seen That, have we? We have not seen It.

What *are* we able to see? We are able to see His examples: the colors, hues, and languages of man, the colors, fragrances, and hues of the trees, and the fragrances, qualities, and tastes of the fruits. The flowers are examples like that, the fruits are like that, the colors are like that, the constellations are like that, the moon is like that, the rays of the moon are like that, the rays of the sun are like that, the gold color of the moon is like that, the stars are like that, the clouds are like that, the thunder is like that, the lightning is like that, and the rain is like that. Is that not so? All of these are present in the sky, are they not? The sky is like that. What is seen is like that. Earth, gold, silver, mercury, and flowers are also present, is that not so? This is His farm, the flower garden that He created. It is a garden. Yet, we cannot see Him, can we? He is the Guardian. Who is that Guardian?

There are nine kinds of wisdom: feeling, awareness, intellect, judgment, subtle wisdom, divine analytic wisdom, divine luminous wisdom, *meignānam*—the wisdom of the Nūr—and the wisdom of God. God has given us these nine kinds of consciousness and wisdom, and He demonstrates His qualities through them. His qualities and actions are revealed through them.

This is a garden; it is *'ilm*, the *bahrul-'ilm*, the ocean of divine knowledge. Inside! You have to go within and within and vanquish the nine places. You have to go beyond and discover the qualities that can speak with that mysterious Treasure. You must vanquish these nine places and go within. That garden, the kingdom of God, will be there. Thus, having vanquished the nine places, having broken them and cut them away, you must then enter the flower garden.

You must open *unarvu,* feeling, *unarchi,* awareness, and *putti,* intellect, and proceed further. *Madi,* judgment, must open life and proceed, it must open the limit of our life and proceed. *Nuparivu,* subtle wisdom, must with even more subtlety go within that, like lightning. It must go like lightning. *Pahut arivu,* divine analytic wisdom, must separate everything; it must analyze and cut away everything. *Pērarivu,* divine luminous wisdom, must reach Allāh's peace, tranquility, and serenity. *Gnāna arivu,* the wisdom of *'ilm,* is Allāh's speech, the speech between Him and us, the direct speech. That speech is the speech where there is a connection between the Mystery and us. *Full arivu.* With that power we will see Allāh, we will see one point, one Mystery, one God, one family, and one prayer. We will see Him.

He is the Guardian for our life, for subsistence, for *'ilm,* for learning, for everything: for food, for nourishment, for the soul, for the light in the eyes, for sound, fragrance, speech, and taste, and for the heart. He is the Guardian for the body and the soul. We must understand that He is the Guardian. He is the Guardian who watches over our life.

When you come to that correct, mature state He will give you your rightful property. Until then, He is the Guardian. Until you attain that state, until you receive that property, He will be the Guardian who protects you. What is your property? God! He is your property. What is that state? He is your life, your soul, that perfect Treasure. What are you searching for? That is what you are searching for, that Treasure. When you attain that state, then your rightful property will become your paradise. Paradise. You will receive your rightful property: God's kingdom, a kingdom without birth, a kingdom that does not diminish, a wealth that does not diminish, a property that does not perish, a property that is the *ānmā*, a property that is eternal and complete, a life that is complete, a perfected life that belongs to you, a complete perfection and the perfect peace that is without joy or sorrow.

You must attain this property, this state. In this garden you must understand this Guardian, the Gardener who protects you. To be able to understand this and receive your rightful property, is prayer. You must do this prayer. For this there is *nōnbu,* fasting. If you are not attentive to this state, then that will be *no-anbu,* no love. If you have not understood your Guardian, then that will be *no-anbu.* When you have understood this, then it is *nōnbu, anbu,* love. You will have *anbu* for every life, you will have *anbu* for every unity, you will have *anbu* for every brother and sister, you will have *anbu* for every hunger, and you will have an understanding of every sorrow. You must understand this.

My love you my children, sisters and brothers: my life, my eyes, my heart—unity, my life, my eyes, my heart, my life, my brethren. We must realize this. Having realized this, we must understand our Father, the Guardian. First and foremost, if we do not understand the One who is protecting us, how can we understand our *Pidā,* our Father?

'Ilm is the food given for the soul. *Unarchi,* awareness, is for the body. To make this understood, God gives His explanations. That is the food. Sight is for the eyes; light lets you understand what you are seeing. Sound is for the ears; to understand the separations, the joy, and the sorrow is your peace. Taste is for the body; that taste is explained to you. Every section of this body is analyzed and explained, section by section, for you to understand.

What is that food? He gives plenitude in the world of the souls. He gives the food of *'ilm,* He gives the food of His qualities, He gives the food of prayer, He gives the food of fragrance, He gives the food of light, He gives the food of completeness, He gives the food that has no death, He gives the food that has no birth. Similarly, He gives the food that you eat for the body. Fruits, trees, shrubs, leaves, and flowers provide you with food, is that not so? This is for the body.

God keeps on giving food for the inside and for the outside. He is the Guardian who gives food for the section of life, for the section of wisdom, for the section of *'ilm,* and for the section of the qualities. He gives food for the section of the body and for the section of the life of the body, and He protects you. This protection is given for whatever you need in the world. He is the Guardian, the Rabb. He is your Rabb, the Protector. He creates. *Bismillāhir-Rahmānir-Rahīm.* He creates, protects, and sustains. He is the Rabb, the Rahmān, the Rahīm. We need to understand this.

According to this explanation, we can see that He gives you this food in so many different sections, is this not so? He gives food for the body: for the outside body, for the center of the body, for the inside body, and for the light body. He gives food for the body of hell, He gives food for the world of the *nafs* and for the five elements. He gives food to them. He gives food to hypnotic fascinations, to the sun, and to the moon. Whatever the section, He gives food to each one individually so that it can grow, is that not so? He gives to the flowers and the trees. He is the One who gives to each section individually. This is the explanation of how He gives food. He gives food for your search, for your prayer. You must understand this.

When you understand this, you will understand that Rabb, that Mystery known as Allāh. To speak with that Mystery you need His sound. Therefore, we need wisdom and this sound. This is what Allāh, the Guardian, is teaching us. He is showing this to us through *unarvu, unarchi, putti, madi, nuparivu, pahut arivu, pērarivu, gnāna arivu,* which is Nūr *arivu,* and through Allāh *arivu.* With this wisdom He shows and teaches us. It is through this teaching, through these lessons that He gives us food and explains, is that not so? It is through these qualities that He teaches us.

From the time of Adam ☾, then, now, and forever—after and before—that Guardian has been doing this. Whatever you are going towards, whether it is hell or heaven, He gives you the explanation for that. Whatever you need to understand, whether it is hell or heaven, this Guardian shows and teaches you. We need to know this.

From the time of Adam ☾ there has been prayer. From the time of Adam ☾ there has been fasting. From the time of Adam ☾ there has been this search for God. From the time of Adam ☾ there has been heaven and hell. From the time of Adam ☾ there have been eight heavens and seven hells, and the proof of their existence. From the time of Adam ☾ there have been explanations about good and evil. From the time of Adam ☾ there have been explanations about good speech and bad speech. From the time of Adam ☾ there have been explanations about good smells and bad smells. From the time of Adam ☾ there has been a verdict, a justice, a judgment, an inquiry, and a Day of *Qiyāmah* for us. God has explained this to us so that we can understand. From the time of Adam ☾ we have been given the explanation that there is one group, one community, one God, one family, and one prayer.

God alone is the Sustainer for everything, from the time of Adam ☾ to the end of the world. *Bismillāhir-Rahmānir-Rahīm:* He is the Creator, the Protector, and the Sustainer. "You alone are the Sustainer." This is the prayer we must do. We must understand this. My love you, precious jeweled lights of my eye. This is called *'ilm.* You must understand this state.

The other day I spoke to you about the Shaikh, and yesterday I spoke to you about *toluhai,* the five-times prayer. Today I am speaking about the doubts in your minds. Many people in America, as well as here, have these doubts. Your hearts have become covered as a result of your attachments to the different religions, sects, scriptures, and languages. It is like the sky that is hidden by the clouds. Your attachments, your karma, the desire for earth, woman, and gold, and the six evils of lust, hatred, miserliness, greed, fanaticism, and envy are covering your heart.

Lightning, thunder, clouds, poisons, snakes, scorpions, animals, birds, winged creatures, eagles, vultures, pigs, elephants, cats, and rats can be found in your heart. These animals are dwelling there. As long as these qualities are dwelling there, we will not be able to acquire the qualities of God. We will not be able to perform His pure prayer, we will not be able to receive His pure *'ilm,* we will not be able to find that tranquility, we will not be able to find that peace. And because we are unable to find that peace, we will have sorrow.

It is to show us how to dispel these things and to find happiness that God sent down the 124,000 prophets. The Qur'ān speaks of twenty-five prophets. The Bible speaks about them and Judaism also speaks about them. The Tamil (Hindu) religion speaks of many tens of millions of gods. Each religion says many things, but no matter what each one says, no matter how many flowers, or how many trees, or how many fruits there are, the essence is one. God is one. The wisdom that understands that one point explains that God is the Guardian, the One who protects. It demonstrates this every single day. God has given us the wisdom that explains this each day. He has given us *'ilm.* This is how He gives us the explanations.

Az-zabūr, the Hindu religion, speaks of fasting and *gnānam.* This religion speaks of *tānam,* charity, and *dharma,* duty,[1] it speaks of unity, justice, and prayer. Although it has many tens of millions of

---

1   *tānam* (S) Literally, charity; donation, meritorious giving, commonly with a religious motive; generosity.
    dharma (S) Literally, justice; law, charity; prescribed duties.
    tānadharma (S) A combination of the two words, *tānam* and *dharma.* Depending on the context, it is translated as prescribed duties, charity, or justice.

different kinds of prayers, it also speaks of the Paraparam Vastu, the one Supreme Being. It says that once you transcend everything else, the one God will be there. It says that after you transcend all of these other things, the one Treasure is what remains within. That is why the people in this religion do so much charity, prayer, and fasting. Next is Hanal, the Zoroastrian religion. There, they worship the fire. They worship the sun and the moon. This is what they do. Then there is Christianity, 'Īsā ☺.

Like this, all of the prophets, Mūsā, Ibrāhīm, Ismā'īl, Nūh, Ādam, Dāwūd, 'Īsā, Muhammad, Idris, Ishāq, Ayyūb, Ya'qūb, Yūnus, Yūsuf, Sālihu, may the peace of God be upon them all, gave certain explanations. They spoke about one race, one God, one truth, and one prayer. This business is God's business. God! God! His qualities are His business. His resonance is His business. His sound is His business. He needs His qualities, actions, wisdom, unity, equality, and peacefulness. This is what He needs. So, we must give Him the treasure that is His, His actions.

Buddhism separated from Hinduism. From the time of Adam ☺, there have been *gnānis,* or representatives, or spiritual teachers, or *auliyā',* or *nabīs,* or *olis* who have come. Yet, from the time of Hinduism, we have not left off these difficulties, separations, and differences. We have not understood. We are caught in these clouds of darkness. One by one, over and over again, God sent down His representatives, but we still have these separations. We keep on destroying the world and the lives of the people. We say "my scripture, your scripture," "my race, your race," "my religion, your religion," and we destroy the world. We destroy lives. We destroy the world and other lives through colors, hues, and speech. We destroy lives through languages. We have created a sea of blood. We destroy the world and we destroy lives with our thoughts, and for the sake of woman, wealth, gold, silver, houses, and land. We destroy lives through jealousy, selfishness, and self-business.

We murder our own brethren. Through ignorance we murder our brethren, and what follows is that we ourselves are consumed by sorrow and suffering. We cause misery to the soul, which results in our own suffering. Whatever we kill, whatever we cause anguish to, results in the hell that we ourselves receive. We cause suffering to the pure soul. We cause suffering to the pure heart. We hurt good actions with our evil actions. We murder what God has created. We destroy God's good treasure. We forget the Sustainer, the Guardian.

In this state, for the sake of earth, woman, and gold, for the sake of race, religion, and color, for the sake of language, for the sake of blood ties, and for the sake of these differences, we make other lives suffer. We have fashioned these differences within us, we have fashioned this doubt within us, we have fashioned this ignorance within us, we have fashioned this lack of wisdom within us, we have fashioned this selfishness within us, we have fashioned this jealousy within us, we have fashioned this treachery within us, we have fashioned this deceit within us, we have fashioned this black magic within us, we have fashioned this maya within us, we have fashioned this torpor within us, we have fashioned this karma within us, we have fashioned arrogance within us, we have fashioned egoism within us, we have fashioned anger within us, we have fashioned hell within us, and we have fashioned shaitān within us.

We are destroying God's treasure, we are destroying God's love, we are destroying God's qualities, we are destroying God's equality, and we are destroying God's tranquility. We are murdering those born with us. We cause suffering to those born with us, and destroy them. We disrupt their peace and take on their karma and their attachments. As animals, as bears and lions, we drink the blood of others with each thought. As snakes, rats, and eagles, we change into demons that eat corpses. We change into vampires that drink blood.

It is to transform these qualities that God sent down the 124,000 prophets. They were sent for us to realize peace, tranquility, and serenity, and to reach God's kingdom. They were sent so that, through them, we can know our Protector and Guardian and learn the lessons that are necessary for understanding the learning of *'ilm,* the learning of grace, the learning of *gnānam,* and the learning of the soul. They were sent so that we can understand and realize the teachings of this Guardian who is the Protector. These representatives

were sent so that we can understand God. We must realize and reflect upon this. We must understand the prayer of Jesus ⊕, Moses ⊕,
and Abraham ⊕.

What is prayer? What is *toluhai*, the five-times prayer? What is
the *panjasīla*, the five precepts? What is *tānadharma*, the prescribed
duties that you should do? In every religion they say that you should
perform *tānadharma*. In all of the scriptures they say that you should
perform *tānadharma*. They say: have faith in God; pray to Him; show
love to all lives; treat all lives as your own life; feel the sorrow of
other lives as your own sorrow; show compassion and affection
towards all lives; love others as you love yourself; give your own
food to those who are hungry; if someone is angry have *sabūr*, inner
patience; and do not cause suffering to another life. God instructed
the prophets to teach this.

Like this, all of the religions—Hinduism, Hanal, Christianity,
and Islām—say this. Finally, this was made complete. Everything that
each of the prophets taught was collected together and given by God
to the Rasūl ⊕ as the 6,666 *āyāt* of the Qur'ān and as the *ahādīth*.
What each of the prophets brought as proof is revealed there. We
must think about this.

You must consider carefully what each religion says, what
Jesus ⊕ and Moses ⊕ said. But you cannot truly understand what
they said through the world, through religions, through races, or
through languages. If you analyze the scriptures, if you analyze hell
with hell, what will you find there? You will find worms and insects.
The world and the differences are hell. With the exception of God's
qualities, everything else is hell. If you investigate, using the religions,
you will see only destruction.

If we analyze a snake, what will happen? We will find that it has
poison within it. With that poison it might try to kill something else.
An eagle eats corpses. If we analyze that eagle, what will we find? We
will find that it has bad smells within it, it has the smell of corpses.
Like this, if we go to analyze evil qualities, if we analyze what should
be discarded, we will only find the evil things that are there.

Like that, if we go to analyze religions, races, differences, separations, colors, and languages, what will we find inside them? We will find selfishness, differences, and separations. It will be selfishness, differences, separations, jealousy, envy, and vengeance that will be seen. We will see only divisions. If you extract the essence from those divisions, what will happen? You will murder the truth. You will kill the truth and cause harm to others. You will destroy wisdom, truth, the heart, and God.

This is what is revealed there. If you use these divisions to analyze, if you try to find clarity through religions, this is how it will be. If you try to find clarity by using things that have differences, this is how it will be. If you try to find clarity through religions and separations, this is how it will be.

You must transcend all of these things and find clarity in God, in His qualities. To achieve that clarity there is prayer, faith, charity, fasting, and *hajj*. There is prayer to God. These must be done. Christianity, Jesus, Moses, David, Adam, Noah, and Muhammad, may the peace of God be upon them all, have told you this. They have all spoken about charity, justice, compassion, patience, and prayer to God. You must understand this.

If you understand and research into this, if you research into these actions, you will see that all the religions speak about this. The teachings of Jesus ☺, the teachings of Moses ☺, the teachings of Adam ☺, the teachings of Noah ☺, the teachings of Abraham ☺, the teachings of Ishmael ☺, and the teachings of Muhammad ☺ are the same. You must understand this.

Therefore, this teaching has always existed. *Nōnbu, toluhai, vanakkam, tiyānam*—there are many different types of prayer.

No matter what meditation you do you will take on its qualities. If you act like a snake you will take the quality of the snake. If you surrender to a cow you will take the quality of the cow. If you surrender to a serpent you will take the quality of the serpent. If you surrender to a lion you will take the quality of the lion, you will take that form. If you surrender to a horse and if you make the horse into god, you will take the quality of a horse. If you pray to a rat you will take the quality of a rat. If you pray to an eagle you will take the birth, the quality of an eagle. If you pray to a vulture you will take that birth. Whether it is a horse, lion, tiger, goat, cow, donkey, monkey, dog, or fox, you will take the birth of whatever it is you believe in and surrender to. You will take that quality and you will perform that action.

These are the many tens of millions of births. You yourself are the cause of these births. Truth is the instrument that will end these births. You yourself are the instrument to end these births and you yourself are the reason that these births occur. Ignorance takes many births, while wisdom destroys these births and shows you how to not be born again.

There is a Guardian who gives you whatever you desire. He asks, "Is this it, is this what you need? Go there!" and He gives it. "Is this what you desire? Come here!" Whatever you want, He gives. He gives whatever you ask for. You alone experience the sorrow and joy resulting from what you seek. If you desire something that gives sorrow, you will receive that sorrow. If you desire something that gives happiness, you will receive that happiness. That will be your birth. God will give you whatever you ask for. If you ask for evil things and hell, He will say, "Ah *shari,* all right, here it is," and you will receive it. If you want heaven, "Ah *shari,* all right, here it is. Ah *shari.*" The joy or sorrow resulting from what you seek will be understood by you.

We have to analyze this state with the nine different wisdoms, with *'ilm.* God is inside. You must know what is wrong. You must know what your sorrow is and what your happiness is. To know this, there are the five and the six obligatory duties. First, you must understand the five. You must accept God, with certitude. If you want to cut away this birth, you must understand that there is Something that created you and is protecting you. You must understand that there is Something, a Guardian, that is accompanying you. Now you are an orphan. Do you think that it was your mother who gave birth to you? No. You need to know who it was who brought you up before you came into the womb of your mother. Was it your earthly mother who created you? No.

You must realize that God is the One who made water into blood, the One who made blood into a piece of flesh, the One who placed an atom within that piece of flesh, the One who placed a zygote within that atom, the One who created a *mīm* within that zygote, the One who created a light within that *mīm,* the One who created a wisdom within that light, the One who created a soul within that wisdom, the One who created a clarity and a beauty within that soul, the One who placed His plenitude and His qualities within that beauty, the One who resplends within those qualities, the One who placed His paradise within that resplendence, and the One who exists within that paradise, giving explanations and protecting you.

So, He is the One who protects and feeds you in the womb and who is feeding you now. He is your *Pidā,* your Father. He is your Guardian. You must realize that He is the One who created you and who is giving you food. You must accept Him. He is your Father, He is the One who is always protecting your house. He keeps you in a place, a cage, and protects you and makes you grow. This house is a house that has a limit. This is the house where you are kept, and it has a limit. This is the house that your Mother and Father gave you, is it not? This house has a limit, it is where you are kept. A piece of flesh is kept in this house. That house has a limit, it has an end and it will leave. Once your house is destroyed, it is finished! That house is gone, it is a house with a limit. So, does it belong to you? No. That house did not come from you, did it? It was given to you by your Father. You must understand who gave it to you. Once you understand, you will know it is your Father who gave you this.

As long as we do not know that Father, we are orphans. We are orphan-people, we are *miskīns,* paupers. Once we understand our *Pidā,* our Father, then we are wealthy. So, when we understand our Father, when we understand our Allāh, our Father will be there; our Mother and Father will be there. God is the One who gave us milk, so that is the Mother. He is the One who made water into milk, the One who made water into blood, the One who made water into a piece of flesh, the One who made water into *hayāh,* life, the One who made water into a form, a light, and the One who made water into clarity. He is the One who made water into light, into resplendence. If we understand all of this, we will understand that He is both the Mother and the Father.

Only when you understand your Father will you know your family. Then you will discover the One Father that is indestructible, the One Soul that is indestructible, the One Life that is indestructible, and the One Completeness that is indestructible. That will be your wealth.

Everything else is a house that has a limit. God created this house for you. He built it and gave it to you. Earlier, He created this house for you, and then He gave it to you. *Limit!* He first constructed a house, this body, and later He gave it to you. Then, after He created you, He placed another point within you. But, first He created the house, and it has a limit.

None of this belongs to us. Does our body belong to us? No. Do our eyes belong to us? No. Do our ears belong to us? No. Does our nose belong to us? No. Do these teeth belong to us? No. Does this tongue belong to us? No. Do these hands and legs belong to us? No! No! Does all this belong to us? Whose property is it? Who is the One who built it? Who is the One who created it? Who is the One who understands it?

We need to think about whose property this is. Who does this property belong to? How can you say that this property is your property? Is the soul yours? Is the body yours? Is the house that was given to you yours? Is the earth yours? Is the portal yours? Is the silver and gold found in the earth yours? Are the fruits that grow from the earth yours? Are the unripe fruits and flowers yours? Are the fragrances yours? No!

When you extract a beautiful essence, when you extract the fragrance that is joined with a flower and then rub it on your hair, that fragrance has a limit. In a little while it will fade. Similarly, the fragrance from a fruit will fade. If you squeeze a beautiful fruit, extract the juice and drink it, its fragrance and taste will last only for a short time. Will it remain with you after that? No. It will not remain. You may wear a very beautiful dress for a time, but will it stay that way?

These are things that do not stay with you permanently. What is it that will always stay with you? Allāh! Only His qualities and His treasure will remain with you forever.

So, what do you possess that you can give away? What is your treasure? To whom are you going to give it? Your Father is your treasure. You must accept that. To whom does your life belong? It belongs to your Father. Therefore, you must accept that everything is your Father's property.

Your work is to give your Father's property back to Him. The Father's property belongs to all the children of the Father. Who are all of these children that you see? They are your brothers and sisters. There is only one Father and there is only one Mother. Who is that Mother? The One who gives you the milk, God's *Rahmah*. That *Rahmah* is your Mother who gives you milk. Who is the One who made water into blood, who made that blood into milk, and who gave you the nipple to drink from? Can your mother give this to you, can your temporary mother give this? No. It is God who changes the water and gives it. That is the Mother. You embrace that Mother and that Mother gives you the milk. You must understand this. He is the Mother and the Father for this. He does this for all lives.

So, what is your property? It is Allāh's property, Allāh's treasure. It belongs to everyone and gives peace to everyone. If you understand this, you will understand your Father. You will know your Father and you will know your Father's property. From that, you will know where your rightful property is and where your kingdom is. You will understand the Protector. For you to realize this, you need to give charity; you need to know, in your *qalb,* that your Father's property belongs to your brothers and sisters.

A thousand seeds come from one seed. A thousand fruits come from one seed. Do the thousand fruits belong to the tree? No. Who gives those thousand fruits? The Guardian, the Father. He gives them to His children. He gives the thousand flowers to His children, He gives the thousand seeds to His children. We need to understand this. He gives peace to everyone, to all.

If we can live having this state, then we will understand that all

good things are God's property and all evil things are the property of
the demons, the property of hell. We must understand this and act
accordingly. To understand this, each religion says that we should
fast, perform *hajj,* pray, and give charity. What is this *tānam,* charity?
We need to understand it.

It is said that there is a society that separated a little from Hinduism.
That is Buddhism, the Buddha-*dharma.* What is that Buddha-*dharma?*
The *panjasīla.* What is the *panjasīla?* It is *sharī'ah, tānadharma,* the five
duties. This is what is said. First, you must do *tānadharma.*

*Buddham saranam gacchāmi. Dhammam saranam gacchāmi. Sangham
saranam gacchāmi.*

I take refuge in the wisdom of Buddha. I take refuge in the ultimate truth. I take refuge in that which is good.

There is one family. *Dharma:* Have one justice for all. How is this
done? *Dharma:* Do not kill a life, share what you have with everyone.
We need to realize this state.

It is the same in Christianity; Jesus ☺ said this. Moses ☺ also said
this. You should not take as your own the treasure that God created in common. That property is common to all. You need to give
away that common property. You must move away from the other
things and search for your rightful property. You must search for
your property. What is that property? You must understand what
your rightful property is.

In Buddhism they say they have reached *nirvāna.* What is *nirvāna?*
It is to be *niravarati,* one who is blameless. That word means to be
one without sin, one without fault. When one has become *niravarati,*
that is *nirvāna.*

To become *niravarati,* what is needed? If you have the world you
cannot be *niravarati.* If you have arrogance you cannot be *niravarati.*
If you have blood attachments you cannot be *niravarati,* you will not
be able to dispense justice. If you have religion you will not be able
to dispense justice, you will side with your religion. If you have race
you will not be able to dispense justice. If you have language you
will not be able to dispense justice. When a person considers only
his own scripture, his own language, his own wife, his own children,

his own property, and his own possessions, he will not be able to dispense God's judgment. He cannot do it.

So, one who does not have that justice cannot be *niravarati.* He will only see differences. One who holds on to his own property, his own land, his own house, his own possessions, his own kith and kin, his own status, his own religion, and his own titles and honors cannot be *niravarati.*

You must give up all of these things. *Tānadharma.* Having given up all these other things, you must meditate on yourself. You must meditate on your own self, and sacrifice yourself. If you give up everything else, you will be able to do what needs to be done. You will surrender, you will separate away from these differences and go beyond. You will become *niravarati.* That is *nirvāna,* where you have nothing.

Nirvāna, you have nothing. You are one who has no fault. You are *niravarati,* and you have no attachment to anything that has fault, whether it is the earth, fire, land, illusion, selfishness, or religion. You have discarded everything that has sin. Whatever followed you has been sacrificed and thrown away, whatever touched you has been discarded, and whatever caught you has been removed. Therefore, you are *niravarati,* you are faultless. You are faultless to God, faultless to truth, and faultless to justice. You are one who is without fault and without sin. In life, that is called *niravarati.* In the Tamil language it is called *nirvāna.* One is said to be *niravarati.* In Arabic one is said to be an *insān.* He has become a human being, an *insān.*

Beyond this, what is the state that we must attain? Only if we transcend *niravarati* can we see the One who is *Niravarati,* can we see the One who is Faultless. When we become faultless, beyond that we will see the One who is Faultless. After that we will realize our connections. We will understand where we came from, what we are doing now, where we are going, and who exists there.

Thus, when you have transcended *niravarati,* you will understand your earlier place, what you did in the place you came to, what you should do now, where you are going, and who will be there. Then you will understand your Original Father, the Guardian who protected you when you came here, the Father who created you. After this, there will be further lessons that you will need to understand.

My love you. In Buddhism they speak about *nirvāna*. You must discover what is beyond that *nirvāna*. Buddhism also speaks about the *panjasīla*, where you become *niravarati*, where you become a human being. Once you become a human being, there is still more that you must do. Now you must find yourself. You must find your Father. From what place did you appear? Where were you before? What did you come from? What are you doing now? What are you going to do in the future? Where will you see your Father? You have to discover yourself and your Lord. For that, there is a different section.

The *panjasīla* exists in each religion. *Tānadharma:* until you become a human being, there are certain duties that you must perform. After you become a human being, what is the work that your soul must do? After you become *niravarati*, after you attain *nirvāna*, what is it that you have to do? What must you do beyond that? Each religion has explanations for this. God's words are the words that you must follow.

My love you. *Anbu,* children. We have to think of each thing. We need to reflect. We had to speak to you about this. This is the fast of Ramadān. I must speak about *nōnbu, toluhai,* and *vanakkam,* individually. I must tell you about each of these sections.

I will rest for three minutes and then speak further.

A'ūdhu billāhi minash-shaitānir-rajīm.
I seek refuge in God from the accursed satan.

Bismillāhir-Rahmānir-Rahīm.
In the name of God, the Most Compassionate,
the Most Merciful.

HOW TO BECOME ONE
WITH GOD

July 16, 1981, Thursday, 8:30 p.m.

M y love you, jeweled lights of my eye. We will now speak about the 124,000 prophets. We will speak about the twenty-five mentioned in the Bible, in the Torah, and in the Qur'ān. Each of the prophets, up to the end, spoke about how to become a human being, and about the *panjasīla,* the five precepts. Buddha also spoke about the *panjasīla.* The prophets spoke about the *furūd,* the *panjasīla,* and *tānadharma*—the prescribed duties.

You need to understand the Guardian who is protecting you, and realize that the world has a limit. You need to understand what hell contains. You need to understand what the property of hell is, what business is being conducted by each of the religions, and what the prophets have said.

Everyone is making a business of their birthright. We are making a business of God, a business of birth, a business of deities. We are making a business of arrogance, a business of hunger, a business of God, a business of prayer, a business of *vanakkam,* a business of *tiyānam,* a business of *toluhai,* a business of *nōnbu,* and a business of *hajj.* Businesses are being conducted in this way.

A church is a business, a temple is a business. Prayer is a business. We are making the shrines, temples, churches, and mosques into businesses. For the sake of reaching God we are doing business using earth, woman, and gold. In the kingdom of God, we are attempting

325

to do business using religions, creeds, prayer, and charity. We are attempting to do business using *toluhai,* prayer, languages, scriptures, religions, and worship. We are making businesses of earth, property, and woman. We are conducting these businesses with money, cash, gems, gold, and silver. We are making God into a business.

The prophets have told us that these businesses that are being conducted in the churches, the houses of prayer, the temples, and the mosques should be cut away. Businesses should not be conducted in these places. They should be cut away. You should be doing God's Business. This is your common wealth, it is God's wealth. One seed contains many seeds, and this is a common wealth for all.

God's kingdom is a common wealth. This world and the *ākhirah* belong equally to all. This wealth belongs to all lives, it is not your wealth alone. This wealth, which is God's wealth, belongs to God, and He has given that treasure to you. But here (in the world) you have made that wealth into a business. You need to understand that wealth. That is *fard,* an obligatory duty. This *tānadharma,* the prescribed duties, is spoken of in all of the four religions. They all speak of charity and fasting. In the Arabic language they speak of the five *furūd,* the obligatory duties. In the end, all of God's teachings were brought together in *al-furqān,* in the Qur'ān.

You cannot reach God through worldly wealth. God's wealth is a common wealth. This is the world, but for God, the connection to this world has been cut away. His wealth is for all, you cannot give away what belongs to Him. He has discarded the things that belong to the world. These discarded things are not His wealth. His wealth is the treasure of Truth—Light.

You need to understand His wealth. Allāh has made it *fard,* He has revealed it as a duty. In the end, Allāh said, "O Muhammad, *yā* Rasūlallāh, say this. Tell the people that they should perform *tānadharma* and observe the *panjasīla.*" In the Arabic language there is a separate word for this. It is called *furūd.* The *furūd* is known as the five duties. We must understand these five duties.

First, have faith in God. Believe that there is no God other than the one God, that there is one family, one race, one God, and one prayer. God has said this. God is a Mystery, He is your *Pidā.* Understand that Father. He is the Rabb. His *Qudrah,* His Power, exists. He is your Guardian. He is the Guardian who gives you what you need. Therefore, understand this, and take what you need.

He is the Sustainer who has no companion or helper, the One who creates, protects, and nourishes. The One who is said to do this is your Father. He cannot be seen as an example. He is the One who shows every example, and He is the Protector of everything. That Guardian is within you. You need to think about this.

You need to believe in Him with absolute certainty. You need to have that faith within you. Have the determination and *īmān,* the faith that He alone is God. Pray to Him. Accept Him and worship Him. Accepting Him is one point and praying to Him is another point. Prayer is to Him alone. There is none worthy of worship other than Him. Not all created beings in the world will accept that Treasure. The one who does accept God will know that He is the One who gives judgment. If you are one who accepts Him, then you will know that He is the One who is guiding you, and that tomorrow He will raise you up. He is the One who will make the inquiries, the One who will ask you the questions. That Day will be your Judgment Day, that Day will be your Day of *Qiyāmah,* that Day will be the Day that you are given what you have searched for. It will be the Day your deed is written.

Your deed will be given according to what you sought and according to your prayers. You will be questioned about your determination, and then given your earnings. On that Day the proof will be given to you. This deed will be given to you in the presence of all of the *malaks, malā'ikah,* the heavenly beings, the heavenly messengers, the *auliyā',* and the *ambiyā'.*

God has given you a grave for your *ānmā,* your soul. He has given you His ray, the soul. That ray was within Him. You came forth from Him in *'ālamul-arwāh.* After emerging from Him you were sent down within His Light, you were sent down within the Nūr. When you came forth from that Nūr, you came forth as a ray. Then you accepted God and His representatives. You emerged from

Him and accepted Him, His representatives, and the Truth. His representatives are Truth. That Truth came from Him, as Light. The representatives are that Light, the prophets are that Light.

God has said, "It is not the body of the prophets in which you should place your faith. Within them, I have placed the Light that is the *bahrul-'ilm,* have I not? Grace! That Light is My representatives, My words are My representatives, My actions are My representatives, My conduct is My representatives, and My deeds are My representatives. These actions are working within the prophets. Just as I gave you a house, I gave the prophets a house. You should not be looking at the house, but at what is within that house.

"Like that, I have given them a house. Have you seen the *olis* and the *nabīs?* They have a house, just as you have a house. They were given a house in the same way that you were given a house, and it is from within this house that I send out My words and power, so that you will have a way to grow.

"I am their Guardian. I am *their* Guardian and My representatives are *your* guardians. I sent those Lights from Me, to be your guardians. Once they came forth from Me, they became your guardians. The house that I gave them is made of earth and the house that I gave you is made of earth: it is made of earth, fire, water, air, and ether. This is the house that I gave them and the house that I gave you. In the same way that I protect you, I protect all of My treasures that are contained within the prophets—light, form, qualities, actions, *'ilm,* resonance, sound, and speech. I have placed everything within them. I gave them speech and they are speaking with Me. They are My representatives. Truth is My representatives.

"It is that truth that I am now teaching you. They have understood and accepted Me with certitude and you must understand them with certitude, you must understand what is within them, and accept that. They have My speech, My qualities, and My actions. I have placed the explanations within them. They have these explanations, and you must accept them. Their bodies can be seen in the same way that your body can be seen. But, they grow within Me. You should look at what is inside them and accept that word, that action, and that behavior; you should accept the qualities that they have."

Allāh then said to Muhammad ☺, "*Yā* Muhammad, please tell this to your *ummah*. I am giving this to you in the end, in completeness. I am showing you the totality of what was given to the other prophets. The people saw these prophets individually. The prophets came one after the other, but the people looked at their bodies, and slandered them. They ridiculed the prophets, renounced them, hurt them, and destroyed them. They attempted to murder them, and did murder some of them. Tell your followers this.

"I was there, within the blood and flesh of those prophets, as the qualities and the light. Those prophets were filled with light. I filled them with My sound, I filled them with My qualities, I filled them with My actions, I filled them with My sight, light, compassion, and love. Tell the people that they should look there, in *that* place. Tell them to go within that place. Tell them to go within that place, and accept the prophets. Tell them that there, from within *that,* they should speak with them.

"*Yā* Muhammad, earlier I sent down so many representatives. The children of Adam looked at the bodies of those representatives, and accepted only their bodies. They did not look inside, they did not accept what was within them. Some said they accepted them, but they only accepted them with their tongues; they did not accept them with truth or with their hearts. So, they caused harm to those prophets. They did not look at the story that the prophets contained, they only looked at the story of their bodies.

"*Yā* Muhammad, I am sending you as the Rasūl for the *awwal*— for the beginning, for the time of birth, and for the end. Tell them this! According to this meaning, tell them what I have been telling you. Tell them that what I am revealing to you is the final word.

"I have sent many different messages at the different times. I have told the people to practice charity. I have told them to pray to Me alone. But they have created gods that are opposite to Me, they have performed actions that are opposite to Me, and they have discarded My qualities and acquired different qualities. They have discarded My speech, taken a different speech, and are speaking that. They have made that into their songs and discourses. They are using the wisdom that I gave them to do ignorant things. They are using the good that I gave them to do evil. They are mixing evil with the truth that I gave them. They are mixing the 'ilm that I gave them with ignorance, lack of wisdom, and sin, and are using that. They are failing to use the good things that I gave them to do what is good.

"This has been happening from the time of Adam. They have not reached completion, they have not changed into an insān, a human being, they have not chased away the animals that are within them, they have not chased away the poisons that are within them, they have not discarded the evil hell that is within them, they have not discarded the qualities of killing and eating other lives, they have not discarded the qualities of murder or the qualities of animals, and they have not discarded the qualities of drinking blood or the qualities of arrogance, karma, and maya that are connected to that. They have not understood that connection, and they have not discarded these sins. They have not used wisdom to cut this away!

"A bird can fly in the air by beating its wings against the air. I have given the birds the power to fly. And to human beings, I have given the two wings of wisdom and truth so that they can fly. I have given them these wings so that they can beat against evil, but they have not come forward to beat away this evil. As a result, they are experiencing sadness.

"No matter how many storms or gales may come, I have given them two wings, as strength against these winds. I have given them certitude. Like this, no matter how many sorrows may come to the people, I have given them the strength of wisdom and My truth to beat back these sorrows. They are not using that power. I have given them the strength to beat back these sorrows so that they can come forward and meet Me, but they are not using the wings of wisdom and truth to come forward. Instead, they crawl like ants, eating everything that is evil. They are searching for discarded things; they are not searching for what is good.

"Yā Muhammad, tell them this. Tell them to change into human beings. I am giving you the five duties. Earlier we gave many different explanations about tānadharma, the prescribed duties, and about prayer. Here, I am giving you more explanations about prayer and the prescribed duties. Please tell them this.

"What is prayer? What is charity? What is fasting? What is *hajj*? I am giving the proof here of what the prophets have said regarding the *panjasīla* and *tānadharma*. The five *furūd* are duties that each one must do. Tell this to your people, your *ummah*. They should live as the children of Adam, the family of Abraham, and the *ummah* of Muhammad. Tell them to have the faith of Abraham. Tell them to grow in unity in the way David grew in unity.

"O Muhammad, because you came from Me, and because you came from the Nūr, tell your *ummah* that they should become like you. Tell them to change into your Light. Explain to them that I am their *Pidā*, their Father.

"These are easy things that I am telling them to do. Tell them to do these five *furūd*, tell them to do these five obligatory duties. First, tell them to accept Me, to have faith, certitude, determination, and *īmān*. Second, tell them to pray to Me. I am the only One who is worthy of worship, the One who will ask the questions on *Qiyāmah*. I am the One who created the *nabīs*, the One who created the *olis*, the *malaks*, and the *mala'ikah*, and the One who created the earth, fire, water, and air. Tell them to realize that I am the One who has created all of this, and to accept Me. Tell them to accept that I am the One who gives the *rizq*, the food, the One who raises them on the Day of *Qiyāmah*, the One who asks the questions, the One who gives the judgment, and the One who accepts their prayers. Tell them to believe in this with absolute certitude, to accept Me, and to pray to Me. I am the only One worthy of worship.

"*Yā* Muhammad, there are a few who have this state, there are a very rare few who have accepted this. For those who have accepted Me, I am their wealth, I am their treasure, I am their life, I am their soul. I am their wealth of *'ilm*, their wealth of grace, the wealth of their property. I am their food, I am their nourishment, I am their qualities. I am their wealth, qualities, and actions. I am their conduct, their house. That is their paradise. Tell the people to understand this.

"Yā Muhammad, earlier I told you that you emerged from Me. All of the prophets grow within Me. The house that I gave them is the same as the house I gave others, but the prophets grow within Me. They have been given My qualities. Tell the people to accept that the prophets grow within Me. The prophets are not what the people see with their eyes. Tell them that the prophets must be seen with My qualities. Tell them to accept these prophets who grow within Me and who hear My sounds. In the same way that you have accepted Me, tell them to accept Me and to accept that there is no one who is worthy of worship other than Me.

"Further, O Muhammad, tell the people that I sent you down to have *īmān*, absolute faith, in five places. First, the *rūh*, the soul, had *īmān* in Me. There are some who have accepted that you emerged from Me, that I created you. I am their wealth and you are their guardian. For the ones who have understood this, you are their guardian. They do not have the property of the *dunyā* or the section of the *dunyā*, they have only My section. The section that I gave you is what they have as their life. Your qualities are their life. Please tell them this.

"So, there are some who have *īmān* in Me. Those who have this state have that *īmān*. They have *īmān* in you and in Me. Others have accepted Me only with their tongues, they have not accepted Me with their hearts. They are the ones who have not accepted Me with their hearts. Their hearts have accepted four hundred trillion ten thousand different things. Please make their hearts accept Me.

"When I first sent them down I made them accept Me in the womb. I made water into blood, blood into a piece of flesh, and in that piece of flesh I created My ray. In that ray I created a Light, and told them to accept Me. I protected them there, I fed them with milk and honey. I fed the mother, I nourished their bodies. I gave them this food, and through that they were made to grow. They stayed in that place for nine months, nine days, nine hours, nine minutes, and nine seconds, and in that place they said the *kalimah*[1] to Me.

---

1 *kalimah* (A) The First *Kalimah: Lā ilāha illAllāhu Muhammadur-Rasūlullāh.* None is God except Allāh, and Muhammad is the Messenger of God.

"After that, I brought man into the world. Even then, I am the Guardian who is protecting him. Once he emerges from the womb, I show him My examples. When he was with Me I did not show him examples. I was the Protector; when he was in the womb I was the Support. There, I did not show him the examples. Only when he comes into the world is he shown the examples. But then, it is only those examples that he accepts.

"Tell him that there, in the world, he must accept Me and he must accept you! Tell him to have *īmān* there. Tell him to accept you and to accept Me. Tell him to say the *kalimah* there, for the third time. Tell him to accept Me in that place, for the third time. Tell him to say the *kalimah,* tell him to have faith in Me, and tell him to accept Me.

"Fourth, tell him to have *īmān* in My *'ilm*—in My wisdom and *'ilm*. Tell him that in his *qalb,* he should have *īmān*. I am there. Tell him that in his worship he should have *īmān* in Me. I have given him a house here, in his *qalb*. Earlier, I gave him a house within Me. Then I gave him a house within you. After that I gave him a house in the womb. And after that I gave him a house in the *dunyā*.

"So, first I gave him a house within Me, then I gave him a house within you, then I gave him a house in the womb, and after that I gave him a house in the *qalb*. That house of the *qalb* is a *qabr,* a grave. The house of the womb is also a grave. He has three graves: the *qalb* is one grave, the womb is one grave, and the place where he is finally buried is another grave. He has three graves. These are the three houses where he is buried. Tell him that I am the One who is the Protector of the three houses where he is buried. He is buried in three places. I will raise him up. I will raise him from his *qalb*. I will raise him from the room of the womb; I created him from Me and kept him there. And I will raise him up from the *qabr,* the grave in which he is buried, and will ask him the questions.

After that, in *hayāh,* on the Day of *Qiyāmah* I will again raise him up, and I will question him. He will speak with Me. In *hayāh,* I will raise him up and question him, and then he will be given his earnings.

"O Muhammad, first, he said the *kalimah,* the affirmation of faith, accepting you and Me. Second, he said the *kalimah* to Me when he was in the womb. Third, he said the *kalimah* in the *dunyā.* Fourth, tell him to say the *kalimah* in his *qalb,* and to accept Me with *'ilm* and with truth. Fifth, tell him that he must recite the *kalimah* to Me with his *hayāh.* His soul must say the *kalimah* to Me. Just as the soul said the *kalimah* in the beginning, the soul must say the *kalimah* to Me at the end. These are the five times that he must recite the *kalimah.*

Thus, I have buried him in three places, in three graves. The fourth time I will raise him up in the unchanging place, and question him there. He must triumph over the three graves. He must rise up from these three graves. The house of the *qalb* is a grave, the house of the mother is a grave, and the house where his body is buried is a grave. Tell him that I am the One who will raise up the *hayāh* in these three places. Since I will raise the *hayāh* in these three places, tell him to search for the path that has life, that is eternal. He must become one who has no birth or death, one who has *hayāh.* He must accept Me. He should understand this.

"I am ruling through My *malaks, malā'ikah,* and *nabīs.* I am explaining My qualities. *Yā* Muhammad, tell man to understand this. Tell him to accept Me with absolute certitude," said Allāh.

"To make the people understand this, I am revealing here the five *furūd,* the obligatory duties. Tell those who have accepted the bodies of the *nabīs* to accept that those prophets are kept within Me. Tell them to accept that the prophets grow within Me and that I speak with the prophets. Just as the people are buried in a grave, I have buried the prophets within Me. I have placed them in My *Qudrah,* My Power. Tell this to the people, tell them to accept this. Each prophet was created in this state. Tell them this.

"Further *yā* Rasūl, O Muhammad, tell them that I created you first, for the beginning and for the end. You came forth as the Nūr, the Light. I created you from Me. You appeared here as Muhammad, you came forth as Ahamad. Tell them that I created you as the beauty for the heart and for the face. That beauty is created through Me, within *'ilm.* To make that Light complete, there is *'ilm.* The *'ilm* that they have should be My *'ilm,* their qualities should be My qualities, their actions should be My actions, and their conduct should be My conduct.

"The ninety-nine *wilāyāt* and the three thousand gracious qualities are My qualities. My actions are My *asmā'ul-husnā.* I have created the body with *al-asmā'ul-husnā,* with the twenty-eight letters. From within these twenty-eight letters I taught you the 6,666 *āyāt* of the Qur'ān so that you can teach them. I have created and placed everything within it. I have revealed this to you so that you can reveal it to them. Tell them this.

"Through My *rahmah,* I make everything that is dead come alive. I created you as a representative so that they can have *hayāh,* life. They have died through darkness, they have died through maya, they have died through their *nafs,* they have died through desires, blood ties, blood attachments, and injustice. They have made their *hayāh* die. They keep dying, again and again, and they keep being reborn as animals, again and again. Tell them to discard these animal births and to change into *insān.* This is the reason I am sending you.

"First, tell them to accept Me. Second, tell them to pray to Me. Third, My wealth is the Support. I am the Support. The *dunyā* is the example. Whatever you look at and search for is the *dunyā,* all of the praise and blame is the *dunyā.* Everything people desire, eat, and enjoy is an example. I am the One who is the Support. I am the Cause, the Creator. *Yā* Muhammad, I have placed you as the guardian, the Nūr, the Light. Go, and protect them! I made you the Light, and with your Light, I am making you their guardian. As the guardian, you must protect them.

"There is one lineage, one race, one prayer, one God, and one family. Tell them to realize this and to acquire My qualities. All wealth is a common wealth, it belongs to everyone. Tell them not to take it as their own. Tell them to love all lives as their own life, to consider all sorrow as their own sorrow, all brethren as their own brethren, all hunger as their own hunger, all illness as their own illness, all suffering as their own suffering, all eyes as their own eyes, all *qalbs* as their own *qalb,* all ears as their own ears, all noses as their own nose, all mouths as their own mouth, all tongues as their own tongue, and the limbs of others as their own limbs. I created their skin with many different colors. I have placed many colors in that flower garden, and it is beautiful.

"Like that, I have placed each of the languages and each of the colors and hues in the cultivation of My *dunyā.* I look at the beauty of all this, and enjoy it. I have created the people with this beauty. Through this beauty I take the essence that is in their *qalbs.* I take that truth and smell it. That is My fragrance, their *qalbs* are My fragrance. If there is a good fragrance, I take it and smell it. If there is a bad smell, I discard it. Their *qalbs* are My flower garden, while the flower garden of their *nafs* is the hell of the *dunyā.*

"Tell them that I am their flower garden. Tell them that My fragrance is the happiness of their flower garden. Tell them that their *qalbs* are fragrant to Me. My flower garden is their *qalb* and their flower garden is My *Qalb.* Also tell them that the joy they experience from their bodies is the stench of hell. Tell them that all of the smells from the body and the *nafs* are hell.

"When they love what I love, that will be paradise, it will be fragrance. In that state, when that *'ilm,* that wisdom, that prayer, that certitude, and that determination come, that will be the fragrance of their *hayāh,* their life. O Muhammad, please tell them this!

"In order to correct them I sent down the four *vēdas* and the prophets. *Sariyai, kiriyai, yōgam, gnānam — sharī'ah, tarīqah, haqīqah, ma'rifah — az-zabūr, al-jabbūrat, al-injīl, al-furqān* are the four religions. Tell them that I created the four religions for them.

"*Az-zabūr* is creation, I placed this below the waist. That is the *zabūr vēda,* Hinduism.

"Hanal is the fire that I placed within the stomach, the fire of hunger, the fire of arrogance, and the fire of anger. They should understand this.

"Christianity: I placed it as the heart. There are so many *āvis,* spirits, there. They should understand that there is only one perfectly pure *āvi,* the soul. That is man.

"Then, there is the head. I am *Gnānam*, *'Ilm*, Resplendence, and the Nūr. This is *al-furqān*, (Islām).

"These are the four. The four religions show the proof of the one Qur'ān, one man, one God, and one family. The four religions are the four steps of *sharī'ah*, *tarīqah*, *haqīqah*, and *ma'rifah*. These four steps must be understood. The people must understand these explanations.

"They must understand creation. That is the Hindu religion; it is below the waist. Next they must understand the fire of hell, Hanal. Tell them to understand and take the Truth from it. I am That, I am Truth. Then there is the heart, the *qalb*. It contains so many *āvis*. There are four hundred trillion ten thousand spiritual *āvis*. Each thought takes a form, each intention takes a form. Tell them that in that heart We are the only pure ones: I and you, My Light. That Light and I exist as the purity within the prophets. The people should understand this. Other than that, everything else is hell. Tell them that all thoughts are hell, that they are the *āvis* of hell. They should realize this. *Sharī'ah*, *tarīqah*, *haqīqah*. Tell them to realize that oneness in the *qalb*, to have unity with Me. That is Christianity. And then there is *al-furqān*, the fourth step. I have made the head essential for *insān*. If he does not have a head, then he cannot read My *purāna*, My history. This *purāna* is the Qur'ān. The Qur'ān is the head for these four steps. Understand these four steps. The Qur'ān is the head.

"I have made seven causes for this head. Tell them to understand Me from within these seven causes. There is the cause and there is the effect. I am the Doer. I am the Doer within the effect. Tell them that I am the Creator, the Great One. I am the Lord of the cause and the effect. I am the One who conducts everything. Tell them to understand that I alone am the cause for all of this. This is the state of *gnānam*, *ma'rifah*, and *sūfiyyah*. This is the state where one is speaking with Me and living his life with Me. His qualities are My qualities.

"These steps must be understood. These are the four religions, the four paths of *sariyai*, *kiriyai*, *yōgam*, and *gnānam*. They are *sharī'ah*, *tarīqah, haqīqah,* and *ma'rifah.* Tell them to understand these four. When this is understood, there will be one *sūrah,* one man, and one Qur'ān. Man is a world. Man is the leader of the kingdom of hell and the kingdom of heaven. And man is the cause of destruction and non-destruction. The one family, one God, one man, and one prayer will be seen as proof. Tell them to make these four steps into one—one race, one family, one truth, one prayer, and one God.

"These are the four steps. The *zabūr vēda* says to accept that there is one race. Hanal says to accept with certitude that there is one truth. *Al-injīl* says to accept that there is one prayer to God and that there is one point for that. And *al-furqān* says that there is one God, that there is only one God.

"These are the four. Man is the Qur'ān, he is the world, he is heaven, he is hell, he is the *dunyā.* Tell him to understand these four steps. Then he will receive *'ilm,* then he will have My qualities. Sound will arise from Me. My sound will come, then My speech will come, and then My sight will come. Then My speech, voice, sound, language, melody, tone, and resonance will be complete. Then he will be My *mahan,* My son. 'My God.' 'My son.' I am his Father and he is My son. It is so that this can be understood that I am giving so many explanations."

Let us stop for two minutes.

(Bawa Muhaiyaddeen ☺ continues.)

This is what Allāh has said. "In each of the religions I have given different meanings. *Yā* Muhammad, of these, there is *sharī'ah.* We will now speak about the five *furūd,* obligatory duties. The five *furūd* are:

"First, accept that prayer is to Me alone.

"Second, pray to Me, the One alone.

"Third, give a share of My wealth to everyone. From one seed I give a thousand seeds. Others must be given their portion. Each person must take his *rizq,* the food that belongs to him, and give the others their *rizq.* There are some who have accepted this and understood it. Only a few have accepted this. Many have not.

"Because of this I created the fourth obligation—*nōnbu*, fasting. I am always fasting. I was fasting before and I am fasting now. I gave charity before and I am giving charity now. Tell them this. They should accept that there is no treasure other than Allāh, the One alone. They should give away everything else, and become a *mu'min*, a true believer. That person will be an *insān*. But for the one who does not give in this way, there is this duty, this *fard*. Tell them that it is easy to do this.

"If he has a hundred shares, tell him to give ten shares to the poor, to the mendicant, the widow, the orphan, the blind, and the deaf. Tell him to search for these people, and give to them. Find them! Find out who is hungry and who is old, and give to them. Help them in their death and in their life. Help them when they are hungry and in their old age. Give to them.

"Only a very few have accepted this, many people have not accepted this. So, I have ordained *nōnbu*. I have made fasting obligatory in this month of Ramadān. Tell your *ummah* to do this. This is not like the fasting that was done earlier. In this fast you should not swallow your saliva.

"In the same way that I have kept a flower on a tree, in the same way that I give air, water, and earth to that flower to protect it from wilting, in the same way that I give happiness, joy, and fragrance to that flower and protect it—in the same way that I protect that flower that is on the tree, their fasting should take Allāh's fragrance of love and place it in their *qalbs*. Tell them to have those qualities, tell them to have those actions, tell them that their prayer should have My breath, tell them to have My speech, and tell them to have My intention. Tell them that when they are fasting they should have My actions, My intention, and My compassion. They should be in this state. Tell them to give fragrance to the *qalbs* of others. Tell them to give fragrance to Me and to others. They should fill the hearts of others with that fragrance.

"They should not swallow their saliva, they should not sleep, they should not have any desire. They should protect their *qalbs* in the same way as a flower is protected. Their breath and speech should do *tasbīh* to Me, their words and actions should do *tasbīh* within My qualities. No matter how many other explanations of fasting there are, they should fast in the way that I have described.

"O Muhammad, if an insect falls into a flower, it instantly causes pain to that flower. When the wind blows hard, the flower fades. When the sun is too hot, the flower fades. When the rain falls hard, the flower fades. Like this, countless numbers of things can damage the flower and make it lose its color.

"Similarly, during this time of fasting, countless things can come and attack the *qalbs* (of your *ummah*). If *nafs*, attachments, blood ties, ties to religion, separations, colors, differences, anger, hastiness, selfishness, jealousy, deceit, backbiting, showing conceit, causing divisions, thinking bad thoughts, performing bad actions, crying, and laughing—if even one of these four hundred trillion ten thousand different thoughts come and attack their *qalbs*, it will be the same as a flower that is attacked. Their *qalbs* and their fasting will fade. If these four hundred trillion ten thousand gales and storms—the winds of hell, the winds of blood, the winds of attachments, the winds of separations, and the winds of differences—injure their *qalbs*, their *qalbs* will fade. These things will not give strength to their fast. They will not give beauty to it, is that not so?

"I have shown the flower as an example. Through this example, they should realize that when they are fasting, the flower of the heart can be affected by these winds, in the same way that a flower is affected.

"Like this, tell them to do *tasbīh* with Me and I will do *tasbīh* with them. Tell them that they should stand with Me and do *tasbīh*. I have never forgotten them. Tell them that they should stand with Me and never forget Me. Their breath and their speech should be one with Me. I am the One of peace, the One of tranquility, the One of patience, the One of *sabūr*, the One of *shukūr*, and the One of *tawakkul* and *al-hamdu lillāh*. When they praise Me, I praise them. I am the One who has this state. Tell them to establish this state so that their hearts will not fade.

"This is fasting. They should do this. If they have this state they will understand every *qalb* that I have created and they will understand every sorrow and joy that I have created. They will give away everything other than Me, and give peace to others. They will take on My qualities, and treat everyone with good qualities and love. They will consider everyone's happiness as their own happiness and they will consider everyone's sorrow as their own sorrow. In the same way as a flower suffers and fades when it is struck, their own hearts will fade when they see others struck by sorrow. When these storms of sorrow, suffering, and difficulty strike someone else, it will be as if these storms are striking their own hearts. They will feel that. If they become aware of that, and give peace to others, then that is fasting.

"We have ordained this fasting so that man can realize the sorrows and joys of others within himself. To understand this through one's own self, is *'ilm*. What is called *hadīyah, sadaqah,* and *nōnbu* were created for them as a way to learn and attain *'ilm*. It is for this reason that we have decreed fasting and charity. If they understand these two, they will become *mu'mins,* true believers. When they become *mu'mins,* I alone will be their wealth.

"I have created a guardian that can protect this. I have placed this guardian in their *qalbs* to protect the wealth of the *dunyā* and the wealth of the *ākhirah.* For that guardian, I am the Supreme Being. I am the One who conducts everything. That guardian must give the explanations, and show love. Tell them to understand that I am the Creator of that guardian.

"It is because they did not understand charity that I revealed fasting, and because they did not understand fasting that I sent down the fifth *fard* of *hajj,* the holy pilgrimage. Tell them that they must fulfill this *hajj* in their *hayāh,* they must complete a *hajj* in their lifetime. If they understand fasting, it will be easy to do the *hajj* with Me. If they understand *toluhai,* they will join with Me in *hajj.* Those who have faith in Me and have certitude in you will not be separate from Me. One who truly prays to Me, having understood that there is no one else worthy of worship, will always reside in My house. He will not be separate from Me.

"He will do *tasbīh* to Me and I will do *tasbīh* to him. He will breathe within Me and I will breathe within him. He will speak within Me and I will speak within him. He will live within Me and I will live within him. He will be an embryo within My *Qalb* and I will be an embryo within his *qalb*. He will be a light within My *Qalb* and I will be a light within his *qalb*. He will receive My house and I will receive his house. He will sleep within Me and I will sleep within him. He will receive My kingdom and I will receive his kingdom. He will understand My life and I will understand his life. He will perform My actions and I will perform his actions. He will have My qualities and I will have his qualities. He will realize My *hayāh* and I will realize his *hayāh*. He and I will be joined. We will be merged as one, without any separation.

"When this is his prayer, when I am his *hayāh* and his treasure, and when he has received the wealth of My *rahmah,* only then will he not need any other wealth. He will not desire the wealth of the *dunyā.* That will not be his wealth.

"But for one who does not have that faith and that prayer, I have given these *furūd,* obligatory duties. It is because his certitude is weak that I have revealed this charity, this fasting, and this *hajj.* I have revealed this so that he can reach a more exalted state, so that his heart can understand.

"If he does not understand this fasting, he will not understand himself. There are very few people who understand themselves. That is why, *yā* Muhammad, I have given you so many *ahādīth* for them. I have sent down so many *ahādīth* for them. I have sent the 6,666 *āyāt,* verses of the Qur'ān, so that you can teach them and give explanations to them. But they have not understood. They have made the *dunyā* their own, and discarded Me and you. They have discarded the truth, and made hell their property. They have discarded the *ākhirah,* and accepted satan. They have discarded the light of truth and *hayāh,* and kept their *nafs* as *hayāh.* They have built a house of earth, fire, water, and air. They have built this as their house of hell and as their house of the *ākhirah.* They have made all the treasures of hell their own. They have made, as their own, a house that will be destroyed, and have allowed the indestructible house, the house that We gave them, to decay. They have given over that house to satan and demons. They have given it over to animals, dogs, and foxes.

"*Yā* Muhammad, tell them to give My house back to Me, to give My wealth back to Me, and to have My qualities. Prayer is the state where My three thousand gracious qualities are established. My *wilāyāt* are My prayer. They must understand that prayer. Once they understand that prayer, they will understand everything.

"Tell the people that in their lifetime they must perform a *hajj* with Me. I sent down this *fard* of *hajj*. They should give to others all of the sins, the karma, and the property of the *dunyā* that they have accumulated. They should distribute this among their relatives, children, neighbors, family, and brothers and sisters, and then come to Mecca and Medina and perform the *hajj*.

"I built the Ka'bah and gave it to Abraham. *Yā* Muhammad, I made that a seal for your *ummah*. Tell them to come to that Ka'bah and complete their *hajj*. When they come, tell them to wear the shroud of death; they should wear the shroud that they will wear when they die. The *dunyā* within them should die, and they should come alive within the house of the *ākhirah,* and grow within Me. They should make the *dunyā* die, and make the house of the *ākhirah hayāh.* Their *hajj* should be completed in a state where their *rūh* can live in My house. *Yā* Muhammad, tell them this," said Allāh. "This *hajj* is one of the five *furūd.*

"These are the five *furūd:* to know Allāh and accept Him; to pray to Him; to take His wealth and give it to the people; from that, to understand oneself through fasting; and from that, to make oneself die when performing the *hajj*—to come to Allāh's house on *hajj* and accept Allāh's wealth. Tell them to realize this. Tell them to understand this," said Allāh.

"We have to realize this. Every child should understand these *furūd,* they should be told about them. These have been established as five *waqts* of prayer. It is because the people did not understand these *furūd* that I revealed the five *waqts* of prayer, *toluhai.* We must first think about these five times of prayer.

"At *awwal fajr*, the time of the *qunūt* prayer, iblīs, the one who has received hell, is eating away at man. Iblīs' mother's name is jadda, his father's name is badda, and his name is jāhil, the one who has gone astray. Satan, the one has gone astray, is mingled within man's body of earth. Tell man to destroy that quality of satan that is within him. He must annihilate that quality. For that, he needs the *awwal fajr* prayer.

"The first house that Allāh built is the house of man's *sūrah,* his form. That first prayer is the prayer to the mosque. Tell him that he should perform two *rak'ahs* of prayer for the sake of Allāh, the One who built this house. He should pray two *rak'ahs* to Allāh who built his house, this mosque of the *qalb.* When he goes to a mosque, he should first pray these two *rak'ahs.*"

("O Muhammad, tell man:)

"Allāh built that house and gave you His *rizq,* and He is the One who is protecting you. That is the prayer to the mosque, the two *rak'ahs* that you must pray to Allāh. This mosque is the *ka'bah.* You must pray two *rak'ahs* for the sake of this *ka'bah.*

"Further, at the *awwal fajr* prayer, the time of the *qunūt* prayer, the qualities of satan are eating away at you. Satan is licking, licking, licking you, he is licking, licking your *qalb,* he is licking, licking, licking that rock mountain. His qualities are trying to come out from your *qalb.* Allāh has bound satan with seventy thousand iron chains, he has been tied down in every *qalb.* In the *alif*—in Allāh's Sound — there are seventy thousand *nuqat* and seventy thousand *sukūns.* Within you Allāh has bound satan with these seventy thousand *nuqat,* with these seventy thousand iron chains. It is with these chains, with the seventy thousand *nuqat,* the angels, that the *qalb* is being protected. But those chains can be broken, and satan's qualities can escape.

"You have four hundred trillion ten thousand spiritual thoughts, the thoughts that are within you, within the *nafs ammārah,* is that not so? You have qualities such as jealousy, envy, hypocrisy, and deceit. These are the qualities of the one who has gone astray. Therefore, you need to perform the two *rak'ahs* of the *qunūt* prayer to tie down these qualities so that they are not able to escape. You must do this prayer so that every *nuqtah* of the chain is secure. With each *sukūn,* the angels are protecting you. These angels are protecting the 4,448 nerves. If satan's thoughts arise in the blood, skin, and flesh, each *nuqtah* of that chain should tie down those thoughts. When those qualities try to enter through the blood and the hair follicles, they should be chained up. Like this, every day, in your every gaze, thought, intention, and focus, satan must be chained so that he cannot arise.

"This is the meaning. The first prayer is to the mosque, it is the prayer to the *ka'bah,* the *qalb.* The body is our first house, the mosque. The meaning of this is that you must clear that house. An outer mosque is shown as an example, and when you understand from that place, you will then see your own house, the *qalb,* which is Allāh's house. You must have the intention to stand in prayer and clear this *ka'bah,* the *'arshul-mu'min,* the throne of the true believer. You must understand this.

"O Muhammad, I am telling you about the five *waqts* of *toluhai.* These five times of prayer consist of the *nafl, witr, sunnah,* and *fard* prayers.

"I have instructed man to perform sixteen kinds of *wudū',* ablutions. You must do the *wudū'* of purity. It is not just for the body, you must do *wudū'* on the *qalb.* You must clear the *qalb* for prayer. It is not enough to just wash your eyes, face, and ears. It is not enough to just do *wudū'* on your feet and hands. You must do *wudū'* on your heart. In your heart there are four hundred trillion ten thousand impurities. There are sixty-four demons in your heart, there are sixty-four kinds of magnets and currents in your heart, and there are sixty-four different attachments in your heart. There are illnesses and demons in your body that are eating you. Every thought is a demon that is eating and destroying you, every intention is like that. You need to understand this.

"Tell the people to understand this. When they understand this, they must cut away these things. They must understand and do this. *Yā* Muhammad, tell them this.

"I have created a secret house inside man. His body is a *sirr,* a secret. His *qalb* is a *sirr.* I am a *sirr* within his *qalb,* and his *hayāh* and *'ilm* are a *sirr* within Me. He should understand the house of that *sirr*. *Yā* Muhammad, this is why I have sent down the 6,666 *āyāt* to you, and have directly told you countless *ahādīth*. I have sent down all the angels as witnesses for your people, your *ummah,* so that they will accept you. I have sent down so many prophets and I have sent down so many angels so that the people will accept you.

"I have created the seven *malā'ikah,* archangels: Jibrīl, Mīkā'il, Isrāfil, 'Izrā'īl, Rūqā'īl, Munkar, and Nakīr. (Also, there are two angels on your shoulders, Raqīb and 'Atīd, who record everything,) and I have created the two angels Ridwān and Malik, (who guard heaven and hell).

"The seven *malā'ikah* protect this house of the body. Everything in your every breath and speech is written down (by the recording angels). They know everything, and tomorrow, on *Qiyāmah,* they will show the proof. Tomorrow, on *Qiyāmah,* the record, the picture, and the breath will be revealed. This will all be revealed on that Day, through your speech, sound, words, hearing, and pictures— through everything. When you come to Me, you will not have a lawyer or a broker. Your breath and your speech will bring proof of what you have done. In that place you will bring that record. That record will come, your breath, speech, pictures, gaze, and thoughts will come. This is the record for *Qiyāmah.* This speech, this sound, these words, and these pictures will be gathered together, and come to Me. O Muhammad, I have placed these angels within the people, as a protection. Please explain this secret to them.

"I sent *'ilm* to the *ummah* so that they can understand Me. This is an ocean of great *daulah,* a *bahrul-'ilm. Yā* Muhammad, you are the *mīm* that swims in My *bahrul-'ilm,* My ocean of divine knowledge. Because you swim in this ocean, you understand and know Me. And because you swim in this ocean, you understand the ocean called the *qalb.* I have made you know My beauty, the *zīnah* of Muhammad, and the Light that is Muhammad. From that Light of Muhammad I have made you know the resplendence that is My Nūr, the Light of the ninety-nine *wilāyāt* of *al-asmā'ul-husnā.* From this ocean I have made you understand Me and you.

"Therefore, you and I are swimming in My *bahrul-'ilm*. Because you are swimming in this *'ilm*, because you have understanding, tell them that I have made that *'ilm* into an ocean and that with that *'ilm* they can understand the *dunyā* and the *ākhirah*. I have kept wisdom within them and that wisdom is explained in that place. Therefore, *yā* Muhammad, tell them to learn this *'ilm*," said Allāh.

This is why the Rasūlullāh ⊕ said, "Go even unto China to learn *'ilm*. Go to those of wisdom to learn that *'ilm*. Go to those of truth and learn that *'ilm*."

(Allāh continues:)

"Tell them that only if they learn this *'ilm* will they be able to learn My explanation and your explanation. Only if they swim in this *'ilm* will they understand Me and you. They will understand My *malaks*, *malā'ikah*, *nabīs*, representatives, messengers, My *olis*, and *qutbs*. They will understand hell and heaven, they will understand good and bad, they will understand *halāl* and *harām*, they will understand the *sharr* and *khair* in My creations. They will understand that *sharr* and *khair*, good and evil, are in My *tawakkul*, My responsibility. They will understand that I am the One who is the Cause of all this. O Muhammad, please tell them this.

"There are five *waqts* of prayer. They should do these prayers. These prayers are *fard*. They should realize and perform these obligatory prayers. They should discover that light, they should realize that *'ilm*. They should realize that I am the only One worthy of worship.

"For *subh* there are two *sunnah* and two *fard*. For *luhr* there are four *sunnah*, four *fard*, two *sunnah*, and two *nafl*. Like this, for *'asr* there are four *sunnah* and four *fard*; tell them to pray these eight *rak'ahs* of *sharī'ah*—four *sunnah* and four *fard*. For *maghrib* there are three *fard*, two *sunnah*, and two *nafl*. For *'ishā'*, there are twenty-three prayers (four *sunnah*, four *fard*, two *sunnah*, two *nafl*, two *shaf'ī*, one *witr*, and eight *tahajjud*). Tell them to do these twenty-three prayers," said Allāh.

Yesterday I spoke about the meaning of these *fard* prayers. Yesterday I explained this, so that you would be able to understand. You could understand it. Today I am speaking about this in a concise way. Yesterday I gave a detailed explanation, I showed the meanings so that you would be able to understand and do that prayer. But people are ignoring this. Some are just performing the two *fard* *rak'ahs* at *subh*, the four *rak'ahs* at *luhr*, the four *rak'ahs* at *'asr*, the three *rak'ahs* at *maghrib,* and the four *rak'ahs* at *'ishā'*.

For ablution, there are sixteen (actions), yet they are only doing four. How can they become clean when they only do four? They need to realize this. They need to understand *'ilm* so that they can understand this. They must first wash their *qalbs*, they must clean their hearts. They must have the *niyyah*, the intention to perform ablution in the proper way, and wash away anything that is obstructing the connection between them and God. That connection must be made clear. *Wudū'* is to clear the connection between Allāh and *insān*. This ablution must be done prior to prayer.

Toluhai, the five-times prayer, is when there is a connection of love between Allāh and man. The prayer where Allāh's speech and his speech become one speech, is prayer. That is prayer. They must understand this. Prayer is purity. There is none worthy of worship other than Allāhu ta'ālā. This is what God says.

Children, we have to understand these steps of prayer, one by one. This is *sharī'ah*. This *toluhai* is called *sharī'ah*. If this *sharī'ah* is understood, then when you go beyond this prayer and attain *'ilm*, it will show the proof of what we explained yesterday. You will realize this. Yesterday I gave an explanation about *toluhai, vanakkam,* and *'ibādah*.

First you must understand the meaning of *toluhai. Toluhai* is to have Allāh's qualities, to be filled with Allāh's qualities. It is to be filled with Allāh's three thousand gracious qualities, to be filled with the *daulah* of Allāh, to be filled with Allāh's ninety-nine *wilāyāt*, His actions, behavior, conduct, and goodness, to be filled with Allāh's *sabūr, shukūr, tawakkul,* and *al-hamdu lillāh*. To accept these actions and be filled with them is *toluhai*. To be filled with Allāh's words, *ahādīth,* speech, and *'ilm* is *toluhai*.

After understanding *toluhai,* there is *vanakkam.* Just as a tree, a flower, or a fruit bends low, we bow down in *vanakkam* to Allāh. Every breath bows down, every action bows down, every intention bows down, every word and gaze bows down in *vanakkam* to Him. We must perform that prayer. That is *vanakkam.* The qualities of *toluhai* join together and prostrate to Allāh. Man's life, death, actions, and words prostrate to Allāh. One who prostrates to Allāh and does this duty is an *'abd,* His slave. That is *vanakkam.*

'Ibādah. You take Allāh's property and distribute it. You distribute Allāh's qualities, *'ilm,* and what you have earned, to everyone. You give tranquility to everyone. You give peace and equanimity to everyone, you give comfort to all lives, you give peacefulness and solace to everyone. There is one God and one family. No one is worthy of worship other than Allāhu ta'ālā. *'Ibādah* is to give His property to everyone, to give fragrance to everyone, to give love to everyone, to show compassion to everyone, and to give peace to all lives. You consider all lives as your own life. You take the property of the Rahmatul-'ālamīn, and give a share of that *rahmah* to everyone. You give goodness and peace to all.

Sūfiyyah is to die in Allāh. It is to die in Allāh, to take Allāh's words, His breath, and His speech. It is to take His speech, His words, His actions, His conduct, His behavior, and His good qualities. The "I" is not present. Allāh is the Speaker, He is the Doer, He is the One who does everything. This is *sūfiyyah.*

We must understand this. These are the prayers of *toluhai, vanakkam, 'ibādah,* and *sūfiyyah.* We must think about this. The prayer of *sūfiyyah* is where you perform 43,242 *sajdahs* a day. The breath, the nerves, the flesh, the membranes, the muscles, the hair follicles, the skin, the bones, and the marrow, all of these resplend within Allāh's resonance. Every limb does *tasbīh* to Allāh, every hair follicle does *tasbīh* to Allāh, every breath and speech does *tasbīh* to Allāh. This is the state, the prayer of *sūfiyyah,* where you perform 43,242 *sajdahs* and *rak'ahs* to Him. Every day you do 43,242 prostrations to Him. That is *sūfiyyah.*

Precious jeweled lights of my eye, you, the American children, must understand this. What is the first thing we told you? I gave you certain explanations so that you could learn. It is good wisdom. You must search for it. I thought that I could take you rapidly on the good path and that I could make my children attain *hayāh*, life that is eternal. I first described the prayers of *ma'rifah* and *sūfiyyah* to you. I showed this to some who are here, and to many who are there. I gave you the explanations about *dhikr*—about how to do *tasbīh* to Allāhu ta'ālā with the *dhikr* and about the 43,242 *sajdahs*. We explained about how you could strengthen your *īmān*.

Some of you grew in that *īmān*, but many of you were not able to do that *dhikr*. Some of you were not in that state, you were in a state of tiredness and fatigue. You could not complete the *dhikr* in the correct way. You were unable to understand the explanations about the connection to Allāh. Because of that tiredness some of you had various intentions and thoughts. Some of you had the thoughts of religion, some of race, some of scriptures, some of "my religion and your religion," some of "my *vēda* and your *vēda*." Some of you had envy. Because of that, because you did not understand all of the steps of the religions and scriptures, when I showed you only the last stage, the explanations did not set correctly. You were unable to do it. You could not complete it, you could not do that *rukū'*. You could not understand that one prayer. You could not understand yourselves.

I saw this in you. When I saw this in you and realized that you could not complete this, the thought came to me that if you do not start from the beginning, you will not be able to understand the end. You will not be able to understand it.

I need to teach you this in person, I need to show you the four explanations. So, in this way, here in Ceylon, I am now explaining and teaching this to you. I need to explain about death and life, about where you should die, where you should say the *kalimah*, where you need determination, where you should do *rukū'*, where you should reach peace, where you should show tranquility, where you should reach eternal life, what the connection is between Allāh and you, and what the protection of the Creator, the Great One, is.

I am now giving you this explanation. You were unable to do what I said earlier, you were unable to complete it. Some of you have doubts. Some have differences of religion. Some are thinking, "This is Islām." Some are thinking, "This is wrong." Some say, "It is this way," and some say, "It is not this way." Some say, "He said something earlier and later said something else."

But what I explained yesterday supports what I am saying today. Today I am giving certain explanations. Yesterday I spoke about certain things. And before that I spoke about the Shaikh, I spoke about what the relationship should be like between the children and the Shaikh. Yet, certitude has not developed in some of you.

For a Shaikh, when a current is taken from the sun with a magnifying glass, no other talk is necessary. If cotton wool is placed under the magnifying glass, the cotton wool will catch fire. Now look, according to science they are using the current from the sun to generate light without a motor, are they not? You can see this. Like that, in the past, to create fire the rays of the sun were directed onto a magnifying glass, and if cotton wool was placed under the magnifying glass, the cotton wool would catch fire.

Just as you extract current from the sun, if you want to take the qualities of the Shaikh—that truth, that resplendence, that wisdom, and that light—you must be like the cotton wool. If you are like the cotton wool underneath the magnifying glass of wisdom and if Allāh is the Light, then you will catch fire. But you do not have this state. You are trying to be Allāh. Or you are trying to be the magnifying glass. Or you are trying to make the Guru, the Shaikh, into the cotton wool. What is the use of trying to make *him* into cotton wool and trying to make *him* catch fire? You have not understood the explanation.

Some of you have *qalbs* that are like this. Some of you have not become a flower, yet you are trying to become a fruit. Some of you think you are already a fruit. So, since your hearts are in these various states, I must start at the beginning. I have to start at the beginning with the four religions, and finally show you *sūfiyyah*. If you have reached that state of *sūfiyyah,* it will be very easy to do the *dhikr.*

If you can do the 43,242 *sajdahs* called *ma'rifah*, then it is not necessary for you to do this beginning prayer. But, if you are not doing that *ma'rifah* prayer in this way, then come forward and I will tell you what to do. I will show you the path. If you say that you cannot do that *ma'rifah* prayer, then you can do this, and slowly progress. You can go on understanding each step, and move forward.

If you do not understand something, please tell me. If you are able to do the 43,242 *sajdahs* that I spoke about earlier, well, *shari*, that is fine. If, however, you cannot do that, if instead of wisdom you have ignorance, then you need to come here. If you do come, that would be good. If you like, do it this way, or if you have matured, then do it that other way. But as long as you have doubt, suspicion, and religious bigotry in you, you will not understand justice. As long as you have divisiveness, separations, and color differences, you will not understand. As long as you have anger, hastiness, and the quality of keeping one thing on the inside and another on the outside, you cannot go along this path. You need to think about this.

Some of you are thinking, "What is this Ramadān fast?" Some of you are thinking this. Some of you are saying this and some of you are keeping these thoughts to yourselves. This has been eating away at you, it has been gnawing at the insides of some of you. Some have been saying this aloud, and beating others with it. These diseases that are eating away at some of you should not continue to grow within you. If they are growing within you, if they are continuously gnawing at you, they will consume you. It is not good for your body to let these poisons grow.

Therefore, end this. Speak with me. Do what I tell you, whatever it is! If you are unable to do this *ma'rifah* prayer, you can do the *haqīqah* prayer. I will teach you and you can try to do it. If you are unable to do that, if you do not have certitude, I can teach you about *īmān*. Ask about *tarīqah* and I will tell about that. If you cannot do that, then ask about *sharī'ah*. If you are in that place, if you are in the place that belongs to birth, I will tell you about that. There are these four steps. No matter what place you are in, I will teach you about that particular place. If you do not understand the first place, how can you understand what is beyond that? Even if you have understood one place, there is still more to tell you.

If you do not understand *ma'rifah,* we will speak about *haqīqah,* the unity of God. If you do not understand that, I will speak about the unity of *īmān.* If you do not understand that, then I will tell you about the unity of creation. I can tell you about all of this.

My love you. It is good if you can clear yourself. Perform *wudū'* on your *qalb* and make it clear. All this time I have been talking about prayer. This is needed in America and it is also needed here. Here we have been speaking about *toluhai, vanakkam, 'ibādah,* the grave, and burial, and each one of you needs to understand these explanations.

Today is Thursday. I started at seven o'clock in the morning. We are going to finish at eleven o'clock at night. Now we are going to conclude. I have been speaking now for four hours….Ah! Three hours have passed by. What time did I start? Ah! How much time has gone by? Three hours have passed.

I am not well. But you are even more unwell than I am. My illness is in the body, while your illness is in the *qalb.* Your illness is worse than mine. There are so many of you who have an illness in the heart. I am a single person with a body that is not well, but I see that your illness is causing you so many difficulties. So, I had to speak. I must first cure *your* illness.

Therefore, precious jeweled lights of my eye, some of you have a very great illness in your *qalbs.* I have only the illness of the body, so I must bear up that illness and help you get rid of your illness. Some of you are quite ill. That is why I had to speak; there were four or five points I had to speak about. If I find the time, I might speak further. Having said this…

My love you children, precious jeweled lights of my eye, please type this and I will have it sent to America. Elam Pun, Pudia Pun, Dick Tambi, Mitch Tambi, Myrna Pillai, Sonia Pillai, please make this into a book there. Edit it and print it and give this book to everyone. This is urgently needed. Quickly, make this into a book.

These diseases should not come into your hearts. They will cause great difficulty. It is better for an illness to stay in the body. When it comes to the *qalb,* the heart, it is very difficult.

An illness has entered the hearts of some of the very young children. The hearts of the baby children have an illness. There are some children who have a sickness in their hearts. God must take care of that.

Some children who have wisdom do not have an illness in their *qalbs,* while some children who have less wisdom have an illness in both their hearts and their bodies.

These illnesses should not be there, in the *qalb.* Therefore, the children who have wisdom should give the medicine for these illnesses of the *qalb.* You children who have wisdom must give the medicine for the illnesses of the *qalb.* Also, please give me the medicine for *my* illness!

We must find a way to cure our illnesses. *Āmīn. As-salāmu ʿalaikum wa rahmatullāhi wa barakātuhu,* may the peace, the beneficence, and the blessings of God be upon you. We need Allāh's help.

My love and my *salāms.* May Allāh give you His beneficence and His *rahmah.* May He grace you. *Āmīn, āmīn, āmīn.*

As-salāmu ʿalaikum wa rahmatullāhi wa barakātuhu.

A'ūdhu billāhi minash-shaitānir-rajīm.
I seek refuge in God from the accursed satan.

Bismillāhir-Rahmānir-Rahīm.
In the name of God, the Most Compassionate,
the Most Merciful.

SONG: THE ONLY MEDITATION THAT COMPLETELY FILLS MY HEART

June 25, 1979, Wednesday, 11:30 a.m.

A QUESTION IS TRANSLATED TO BAWA MUHAIYADDEEN
For a little while she has been doing something that is like a meditation. That is what she is asking about. Without using a particular method, her meditation is just to sit. For some time, it seems as if something has been waking her at four o'clock in the morning. At times, it seems as if it is like a long-distance telephone call, but when she picks up the phone, no one says anything. It is as if someone is waking her, she doesn't know anything else. The other thing she said is: "When I meditate, I see something like a light. Sometimes it seems as if something like a face appears, but then it disappears and I don't know what kind of face it is. I just see it as a light."

BAWA MUHAIYADDEEN TO QUESTIONER
What *tiyānam,* meditation, are you doing?

TRANSLATOR
That is what she is asking Bawangal, she is asking what meditation to do and will Bawangal teach her. She is not doing any meditation.

BAWA MUHAIYADDEEN
This is not the way. There must be a meditation.

355

(Bawa Muhaiyaddeen ☺ begins to sing.)

The only meditation that completely fills my heart,
the only meditation that completely fills my heart
is the only meditation awakened by divine grace.
The only meditation that completely fills my heart
is the only meditation awakened by divine grace.

The only meditation that completely fills my heart
stops thought and simply is.
To melt and dissolve the innermost heart
until the rising flood of compassion overflows its banks,
to melt and dissolve the innermost heart
until the rising flood of compassion overflows its banks—
that is the only meditation that completely fills my heart.

To understand the self and to experience
gnāna-tavam, the ultimate austerity of divine wisdom,
to understand the self and to experience gnāna-tavam,
to live life forgetting the earth, and to experience
arul-maunam, the ultimate silence of grace,
to live life forgetting the earth, and to experience
gnāna-maunam, the ultimate silence of divine wisdom—
that is the only meditation that completely fills my heart.
That is the only meditation that completely fills my heart.

To destroy the multitudes of thoughts and
to turn to the good path,
to destroy the multitudes of thoughts and
to turn to the good path—
that is the only meditation that completely fills my heart.
To melt and dissolve the innermost heart
until the rising flood of compassion overflows its banks—
that is the only meditation that completely fills my heart.

Intending the One Being devoid of the six evils,
devoid of any one else,
intending the One Being devoid of the six evils,
devoid of any one else,
to melt and dissolve in love,
to melt and dissolve in the love of
the Bestower of Immeasurable Grace,
the One who is Incomparable Love—
that is the only meditation that completely fills my heart.

Rejecting and driving out the five,
cultivating wisdom until it grows tall,
rejecting and driving out the five,
cultivating wisdom until it grows tall,
reaching the state of *īmān,*
filling the heart with resplendent grace,
filling the heart with resplendent grace—
that is the only meditation that completely fills my heart.

Understanding both sin and virtue and
bringing light to the fully developed heart,
understanding both sin and virtue and
living life so as to enable the opening blossom of the heart
to reach its fully developed state—
that is the only meditation,
the only meditation that completely fills my heart,
the only meditation.

To melt and dissolve the innermost heart
until the rising flood of compassion overflows its banks,
to melt and dissolve the innermost heart
until the rising flood of compassion overflows its banks—
that is the only meditation that completely fills my heart.

Having cut away and discarded the evil qualities,
having cut away and discarded the evil qualities,
having destroyed all the evil,
having cut away and discarded the evil qualities,
having destroyed all the evil,
having closed these eyes and opened the eye of *gnānam,*
having closed these physical eyes and opened the eye of *gnānam,*
having opened the door of the *qalb,*
having opened the door of the *qalb,*
having closed these eyes and
having been there in *maunam,* in absolute silence,
having placed into the house of my heart,
Allāhu, the One Being who is
the Bestower of Boundless Compassion,
Allāhu, the One Being who is
the Bestower of Boundless Compassion,
having placed Him into the house of my heart,
having placed Him into the house of my heart forever—
forever, then and now,
forever, then and now,
having existed within that enduring remembrance,
that enduring remembrance,
without forgetting Him for even a moment—
that is my only meditation,
the only meditation that completely fills my heart,
the only meditation.

To melt and dissolve the innermost heart
until the rising flood of compassion overflows its banks—
that is the only meditation that completely fills my heart.

To destroy the fraudulence of the mantras,
to dispel those evil tricks,

to destroy the fraudulence of the mantras,
to dispel those evil tricks, and
to give them to someone who wishes
to obtain celebrity, praise, and fame,
to give them to someone who wishes
to obtain celebrity, praise, and fame,
so I can know the One, the Master, who created me,
so I can know the One, the Master, who created me.

Being alone, being alone at His side and embracing Him,
being alone, being alone at His side and embracing Him,
that is the only meditation that completely fills my heart.
Being alone, being alone at His side and embracing Him,
that is the only meditation that completely fills my heart.

To melt and dissolve the innermost heart
until the rising flood of compassion overflows its banks—
that is the only meditation that completely fills my heart.

To sit in prayer embracing
the Bestower of Immeasurable Grace,
the One who is Incomparable Love,
the Bestower of Immeasurable Grace,
the One who is Incomparable Love,
embracing Him as Love within love and
uniting with Him within wisdom,
incorporating Him into wisdom as Love within love
and uniting with Him within wisdom,
incorporating Him into wisdom until the two exist as One,
and then sitting in prayer—that prayer,
that is my only meditation,
the only meditation that completely fills my heart,
the only meditation that completely fills my heart.

To melt and dissolve the innermost heart
until the rising flood of compassion overflows its banks—
that is the only meditation.

To simply stand by the path,
the one path that reaches peace,
to simply stand by the path,
the one path that reaches peace,
if I can simply stand by that path—
that Word which is without birth, without death,
without birth, without death—
having known it before and knowing it after,
having known it before and knowing it after,
merging with it on the day the self is lost and
the austerity is complete,
merging with it on the day the self is lost and
the austerity is complete,
and then to pray—
that is the only meditation that completely fills my heart,
the only meditation that completely fills my heart.

To melt and dissolve the innermost heart
until the rising flood of compassion overflows its banks—
that is the only meditation that completely fills my heart.

When I leave behind the maya-mantras and the magic,
when we leave behind the maya-mantras and the magic,
when I transcend the hypnotic delusions, the lust, the hatred,
when we transcend the hypnotic delusions, the lust, the hatred,
when we leave the hypnotic delusions of religion and separation,
with the one Word *Allāhu* that rules this world,
that rules all these worlds,
with the one Word *Allāhu* that rules this world,

that rules all the worlds and that is our support,
with the one Word *Allāhu* that rules this world,
that rules all the worlds and that is our support,
when I slip into the Word within that Word,
the day I slip into the Word within that Word,
going beyond the outermost limit and sitting in prayer,
going beyond the outermost limit and sitting in prayer—
that prayer, that prayer is the only meditation
that completely fills my heart,
the only meditation.

To melt and dissolve the innermost heart
until the rising flood of compassion overflows its banks—
that is the only meditation that completely fills my heart.

To open the *qalb* and to look into the mirror there
at the divine grace of the Creator resonating, resonating there,
to open the *qalb* and to look into the mirror there
at the divine grace of the Creator resonating there,
so that after having journeyed past the outermost limit,
the One seated there will see Himself,
so that after having journeyed past the outermost limit,
the One seated there will see Himself.
It is then that my heart will resonate,
my heart will resonate and worship only that One.
To always live without any separation from Him,
that is the only meditation that completely fills my heart,
the only meditation that completely fills my heart.

To melt and dissolve the innermost heart
until the rising flood of compassion overflows its banks—
that is the only meditation.

To understand peace and tranquility within myself
so the grace-awakened wisdom of the quality of virtue
comes to resonate within me,
so the grace-awakened wisdom of the quality of virtue
comes to resonate within me,
so that all the *ambiyā'*, all the prophets, shine resplendently there,
so that all the *ambiyā'* shine resplendently there,
so that my heart blooms with flower blossoms of absolute purity,
so that my heart blooms with flower blossoms of absolute purity,
so that the fragrance of *zam-zam* becomes a resonance,
so that Allāh, the One who permeates everything,
will dwell there and be pleased,
will dwell there and be pleased,
that is the only meditation that completely fills my heart,
the only meditation that completely fills my heart.

To melt and dissolve the innermost heart
until the rising flood of compassion overflows its banks—
that is the only meditation that completely fills my heart.

So that the heart resonates with *illAllāhu,*
the One who knows everything,
so that my words and actions unite with Him
as I walk following Him,
so that my words and actions unite with Him
as I walk following Him,
to embrace in my heart the One who exists
beyond the outermost limits,
to embrace the One who dwells there
as the grace and the meaning,
to give Him milk there,
to embrace Him in my heart and to give Him milk,
to dispel all my cares,
to cling to and to embrace my only Companion,

to cling to and to embrace only that One,
until my heart resonates, saying, "This is the only happiness,"
until my heart resonates, saying, "This is the only happiness,"
until the two merge and become One,
until the two merge and become One —
that is the only meditation,
my own meditation,
the only meditation that completely fills my heart.

To melt and dissolve the innermost heart
until the rising flood of compassion overflows its banks —
that is the only meditation that completely fills my heart.

To understand within wisdom the five and the six obligations,
to understand within wisdom the five and the six obligations,
to see Ādi Rahmān there,
to stand resonating as effulgent Light within effulgent Light,
to stand resonating as effulgent Light within effulgent Light,
to follow that pure and true meaning and to embrace it,
that is the only meditation,
the only meditation that completely fills my heart.

To melt and dissolve the innermost heart
until the rising flood of compassion overflows its banks —
that is the only meditation that completely fills my heart.

To peacefully exist in the only place known as peace,
to reach peace through the true meaning of peace,
to destroy the mouth's opinions,
to dispel idle talk,
to discover this myself before the days of my life are gone,
to discover this myself before the days of my life are gone,
to live merged within love as One and to reach the grace,
to live merged within love as One and to reach the grace,

that is the only meditation that completely fills my heart,
the only meditation.

To melt and dissolve the innermost heart
until the rising flood of compassion overflows its banks—
that is the only meditation that completely fills my heart.

Having cut out the very roots of my own faults and
thrown them away,
so that peaceful qualities can enter into me,
having cut out the very roots of my own faults and
thrown them away,
so that peaceful qualities can enter into me,
having merged with the Great Light of Ādi,
having merged with the Great Light of Ādi,
then and now, so that the two can live as One—
that is the only meditation that completely fills my heart,
that is the only meditation that completely fills my heart.

To melt and dissolve the innermost heart
until the rising flood of compassion overflows its banks—
that is the only meditation that completely fills my heart.

To say the Word *lā ilāha* and to experience bliss,
to say the Word *illAllāhu* and to have it fill
and overflow from your heart,
to say the Word *lā ilāha* and to push the world away,
to say the Word *illAllāhu* and to bring it down into your heart,
to experience bliss,
to say it without saying it,
to raise and lower it breath after breath,
to say it without saying it,
to raise and lower it breath after breath,
until the liberation in the Word *illAllāhu* resonates alone,

until the liberation in the Word *illAllāhu* resonates alone,
until it shines as Itself within Itself,
until it shines as Itself within Itself,
expanding, resplending,
expanding, resplending,
merging with that One Being who is illAllāhu,
merging with that One Being who is illAllāhu —
that is the only meditation that completely fills my heart,
that is the only meditation that completely fills my heart.

To melt and dissolve the innermost heart
until the rising flood of compassion overflows its banks —
that is the only meditation that completely fills my heart.

To understand *īmān,* to see the shore, and to hold on to it,
to understand within myself
the many explanations in my heart,
the many qualities in my heart,
to live without losing my dignity, and to know,
to take shelter in God who dwells without anything else —
that is the only meditation that completely fills my heart,
the only meditation.

To melt and dissolve the innermost heart
until the rising flood of compassion overflows its banks —
that is the only meditation that completely fills my heart.

To understand without seeing anything parallel or equal,
without seeing anything parallel or equal,
to see that One Being,
to serve God who resides in all living beings,
to be One with them as Life within life and to understand them,
to be One with them as Life within life, and to understand them,
then I too can dwell with that God,

then I too can dwell with that God—
is the only meditation.
That is the only meditation that completely fills my heart.
That is the only meditation.

To melt and dissolve the innermost heart
until the rising flood of compassion overflows its banks—
that is the only meditation that completely fills my heart.

To efface the sights that I see,
to observe and to push aside all my dreams and ideas,
to observe and to push aside all my dreams and ideas,
to annihilate the attachment to the relatives
who have been trying to seize me, then and now,
to see in my heart the immutable God
who cherishes and serves me,
to see in my heart the immutable God
who cherishes and serves us,
to see the precepts of righteousness and to understand them,
to see the precepts of righteousness and to understand them,
to see the One Eternal Being who exists alone
without deviating from truth,
to see Allāhu who shines alone as the One Being
and to embrace Him in my love—
that is the only meditation that completely fills my heart,
that is the only meditation that completely fills my heart.

To melt and dissolve the innermost heart
until the rising flood of compassion overflows its banks—
that is the only meditation that completely fills my heart.

Āmīn.

   This is meditation that is good; this is what is good. This is a
good song.

A'ūdhu billāhi minash-shaitānir-rajīm.
I seek refuge in God from the accursed satan.

Bismillāhir-Rahmānir-Rahīm.
In the name of God, the Most Compassionate,
the Most Merciful.

THE TRUE QUR'ĀN

November 29, 1981, Sunday, 6:10 a.m.

(Bawa Muhaiyaddeen ☺ recites the Third *Kalimah*.)

Subhānallāhi
wal-hamdu lillāhi
wa lā ilāha illAllāhu
wallāhu akbar,
wa lā haula
wa lā quwwata
illā billāhi
wa huwal-'alīyul-'azīm.

All glory is to Allāh
and all praise be to Allāh
and none is God except Allāh,
and Allāh is greater,
and there is no majesty and power
except with Allāh,
and He is exalted, supreme in glory!

Bismillāhir-Rahmānir-Rahīm. In the name of Allāh, the Most Compassionate, the Most Merciful. Allāh is the One of limitless grace and incomparable love. All praise and praising are to Him alone. *Āmīn.*

My precious brothers and sisters, may you, may everyone, may all of us live as those who love Allāh alone. May we all live as one group, as one assembly, and as one family. May we join together and praise the One who is the Rahmatul-'ālamīn. May we pray to Him, may we worship Him alone, and may we praise Him alone. May we glorify Him, pay obeisance to Him, and perform *sajdah* to Him. May we prostrate at His feet and worship the Lord, the only One who is worthy of worship. *Āmīn.*

My precious brothers and sisters, many meanings are revealed in the Qur'ān and the *ahādīth.* In *'ālamul-arwāh,* the world of the souls, Allāhu ta'ālā Nāyan created man as the Qur'ān. Allāh made His qualities, His actions, His conduct, and His *rahmah* into the Qur'ān. His actions are the Qur'ān, His conduct is the Qur'ān, His love is the Qur'ān, His justice is the Qur'ān, His unity is the Qur'ān, and His peacefulness is the Qur'ān.

Like this, Allāh made His countless qualities complete, and made them into the Qur'ān. He made that Qur'ān as the *amānah,* the entrusted treasure, as Light. He made that Qur'ān into a *mīm,* into the Nūr, into plenitude, and He is there, as Himself. He is One who has no (visible) form. The Qur'ān is Allah's form. All the actions and conduct of that Qur'ān are His form. That Light is Allāh's form.

In *anādi* before *ādi,* in the beginningless beginning before creation, when Allāh was in darkness, He dispelled the darkness from Himself. He found clarity within Himself, and then made that Light of plenitude complete. It is that Light of plenitude that He kept within Himself. He eliminated everything else. He discarded darkness, torpor, comparisons, helpers, attachments, selfishness, jealousy, pride, and the "I" and "you." Having discarded these, He looked at Himself with that Light and created everything. Whatever appeared from Him was kept as His *sirr.* Whatever appeared from Him is *sirr;* it is called *sirr,* it is a secret. There is the *sirr,* the secret, and there is the *sifāt,* the creation. This is what they are called. There is *dhāt, khair,* and *sharr.* Whatever manifested outwardly from within Him is shown as *sharr,* evil. And that which remained as Himself is shown as *khair,* goodness. That is how creation was made. All that was *khair* remained as His state, while the *sharr* was made outwardly manifest and was kept as an explanation. This is the *sharr* and the *khair*. His qualities are the *dhāt*. What separated from Him is what is *harām*, impermissible. He kept Himself as what is *halāl*, permissible, as the food for the *rūh*, the soul. And what was *harām* for the *rūh*, He kept as an example. This is the clarity that Allāh found in *'ālamul-arwāh* itself.

Precious jeweled lights of my eye, we must think about this. With one dot He created Adam ☺. He took earth from the four directions and instructed the *malā'ikah*, the archangels, to deposit this earth in the place called Karbalā'. He gave this order to the archangels. That is a dot, it is a *nuqtah*. With this *nuqtah* and with Allāh as the support, that *nuqtah* became the *mīm*. He fashioned this within Himself. The Light that emanated from Him became His rays, and those rays became the Light of the *rūh*. Having brought forth that Light of the *rūh*, He fashioned the earth, and within that earth He placed His qualities. He fashioned the earth using His *malā'ikah* of earth, fire, water, air, and ether. Within this He placed His form: His perfect actions, His conduct, His qualities, and His beauty. He formed that beauty within Himself as the Qur'ān. That is Light. It is the beauty of Allāh that is called the Qur'ān.

It is said that *insān*, Adam ☺, was created with Allāh's beauty. What is Allāh's beauty? It is the Light of the Qur'ān, His actions. What remained after Allāh discarded everything else was the Light of perfection, the Light of plenitude, the Light of the cause and the Light of the effect. That Light is the Qur'ān. That is He. He created *insān* with that beauty. Within that, with the *rahmah*, the beauty called His *dhāt*, He created the *mīm*. He created Adam ☺, and within Adam ☺ He remained as Himself. He remained as all of His qualities, actions, and behavior—that beauty, that Light, and that wisdom. That is what is meant when it is said that He created man with His own beauty, in His own image. The *rūh* that is within man and the qualities that are within him are Allāh's beauty, and that is the Qur'ān.

Allāh created all creations with the *mīm*. He created them from that *nuqtah*. He extends as the support, the *alif*, for all of these creations.

He extends from this *nuqtah*. That support, the *alif,* and that *nuqtah* became the *mīm*. From that, Allāh created the prophets, the representatives, and Muhammad ⊕—both before and after. He created this with three *mīms*, with three *sukūns*—one in the *awwal,* one in the *dunyā,* and one in the *ākhirah*. In the *dunyā* it was as an embryo, and in *'ālamul-arwāh* it was as a *nuqtah*. He is the support for that. In the *dunyā* it was as the embryo, as the *mīm,* as Muhammad ⊕. Allāh is the support for that. In the *ākhirah* it was as the *sukūn*. He is within all of everything. That is the support for the Nūr-Muhammad ⊕. It is to that beauty that the name Muhammad ⊕ is given. It is to that beauty, Muhammad ⊕, that the causal names were given.

Anādi-Muhammad ⊕ is the *sukūn*. The Anādi-Muhammad ⊕, before *ādi,* is that s*ukūn,* the beauty that was created from Him. That *sukūn* is that beauty.

Ādi-Muhammad ⊕ is the Light that was born from Him. It is the Light that was born from His qualities.

Awwal-Muhammad ⊕ is what appeared from Him. Allāh is the support for that. He fashioned the name Muhammad ⊕ for the Light that He created. When this was created as the causal manifestation, when this appeared, He created it with the five. He created it with the *malā'ikah:* Jibrīl ⊕, Mīkā'il ⊕, Isrāfīl ⊕, 'Izrā'īl ⊕, and (Rūqā'īl ⊕), ether. Allāh manifested this form and placed His beauty within it. That is the Qur'ān; those qualities are the Qur'ān. It is through these qualities that Allāh sees His own beauty. That Qur'ān was made beautiful within Allāh's own beauty and is said to be His form. That form exists within *insān* as Himself. After that Allāh created Adam ⊕. He impressed His qualities as the Light, which is the *amānah,* on Adam's ⊕ forehead. Allāh's beauty, His Light, was impressed on the forehead of Adam ⊕.

There are these causal names:

Anādi-Muhammad ⊕ came from Him.

Ādi-Muhammad ⊕ appeared from Him and the qualities came.

Awwal-Muhammad ⊕ manifested from Him and is shown as the basis of His *sharī'ah*.

From Hayāt-Muhammad ⊕ He sent forth the *rūh*.

From Annam-Muhammad ☉ He gave the *rizq*, the nourishment. From that Muhammad ☉, from that *sukūn* He brought forth the *rizq*, the support.

Ahamad ☉. He made the resplendence come forth from His *qalb*. He made His qualities and actions come forth, and He is the support for that.

Muhammad ☉. From Him the *zīnah*, the beauty and Light of the face, and the cause were revealed and gave explanations. The Light and the *zīnah* imparted wisdom.

Nūr-Muhammad ☉. All darkness was dispelled, and the plenitude of His qualities, the beauty, and the perfection were revealed as Himself.

Allāh-Muhammad ☉. That treasure that manifested from Him returned to Him, and remains with Him as His beauty. When this beauty merged with Him, it became Allāh Himself—Allāh-Muhammad ☉. It is complete. This plenitude is His beauty, and with His beauty He created Adam ☉. This is the meaning.

Man is not this outer *sūrah*, this outer form. Within *insān* is the *sūrah* of Allāh's qualities. That is what is meant when it is said that Allāh created Adam ☉ in His own image. The *sūrah* of *insān* is an earth-form, but within *insān*, Allāh fashioned His beauty as a Light-form. He fashioned that within a *nuqtah*. Within the *qalb*, known as the *'arshul-mu'min*, Allāh created a *nuqtah*. Within that He made the *mīm*, within that He made Muhammad ☉ as a *sukūn*, and within this *sukūn*, Allāh extends as the support. That was placed as the *mīm*, that is the *mīm*. That *mīm* comes from His qualities, and could not have come without this *sukūn*. This was given as an *amānah*, an entrusted treasure, to our body that is made of earth, fire, water, air, and ether. It is said that this is an *amānah* within these five. Allāh said, "This entrusted treasure must be returned to Me at a later time."

What was discarded from Allāh is satan. What is called satan is darkness, that which has faults. All the qualities that were discarded from Allāh are called satan, and everything that remained resplendent within Allāh is said to be Himself. What remained as Himself is that beauty, and the resplendence of that beauty is Truth.

We must realize this state. This is Muhammad ☻. This is what is called Muhammad ☻ in the *awwal*, in the *dunyā*, and in the *ākhirah*. It is that Light that is called by that name. It is not the form of Āminah's ☻ son that is Muhammad ☻, nor is it the form of the son of 'Abdullāh ☻.

If we want to understand this we must understand what Allāh has said: "*Yā* Muhammad, if not for you, I would not have created anything." What is known as Muhammad ☻ refers to Allāh's "form," His Light, the cause, the effect, and the plenitude. Not an embryo would have manifested without having a connection to that. Allāh is the support, the *alif*, for this *nuqtah*, this *sukūn*, this *mīm*. Nothing would have been created without this. This *nuqtah* must be within every created being. Nothing could be created without this *nuqtah*, without this connection, whether it is a seed, a tree, a kernel, a fish, an egg, an embryo, or any other form. No matter what the creation, whether it is grass or a weed, no matter what has appeared, it cannot exist without this connection. Insects, viruses, and cells cannot exist without this. The angels and archangels cannot exist without this. The jinns and fairies cannot manifest without this *mīm*. No creation can come forth from Him without this *nuqtah*.

There are five kinds of *rūh*. There is the *nuqtah* and the *sukūn*. The form is the *sukūn*. It manifested as the *nuqtah* and came as the *sukūn*, the *mīm*. Without the *Qudrah*, the Power of Allāh, nothing would have appeared. That is the meaning.

It is to realize this state that Allāhu ta'ālā created Adam ☻, man, and impressed His Light on man's forehead. It was impressed on the forehead of man. That is the Qutbiyyah, Allāh's Light, the causal Light, the *gnāna kan*, the *kursī*. That is the *gnāna kan*, the eye of wisdom. His plenitude becomes the *'arsh*, the throne of God. The eye with which he sees becomes the *gnāna kan*. That becomes the Nūr, the Light, and that becomes the Light of the *zīnah*. Then, the beauty of the heart, the *aham*, the beauty of Ahamad ☻, can be seen on the face, the *muham*.

These nine Muhammads ☻ are shown as the cause. Allāh explains these as the nine causal Muhammads ☻. Even though there are countless meanings, they are explained by these nine. He placed the seal of the Qur'ān within the *sūrah* which is the house, and within the seal that is the Qur'ān, He reveals His qualities, His actions, His prayers, His *'ibādah,* and the wisdom that realizes what is *khair* and *sharr.*

There are the causal wisdoms of *unarvu, unarchi, putti, madi, nuparivu, pahut arivu,* which is the Qutbiyyah *arivu,* and *gnāna arivu*—the Nūr *arivu,* which is the wisdom of Allāh's *rahmah.* These seven causes are there as seven basic principles, and from these seven, we must understand and gain clarity.

With these seven, Allāh fashioned the sound for the Qur'ān. He made this sound into the Light for the *qalb,* and from this sound He opened out the state that makes it possible for man to understand himself and to understand the cause and the effect. He fashioned all these and placed them within the *qalb* as a drop of His secret. Within that He placed His house and all of His qualities, His actions, His conduct, and His behavior. Within that He placed His Qur'ān, Himself, the Light of His *mīm,* Muhammad ⊕, the Nūr, and His *malaks, malā'ikah, olis,* and *nabīs.* He placed them as a *sirr,* within that house of the *sirr.* They reveal the meaning. That is the beauty of His Qur'ān. This Qur'ān, His actions, His conduct, and the cause and effect become the Light of the *sūrah* within the *sūrah* that is Muhammad ⊕. They exist as the inner Qur'ān. It is these qualities that Allāh sent down to Muhammad ⊕ as the Qur'ān. That is the Qur'ān.

The *sūrah* of *insān* was created with the four *malā'ikah:* Jibrīl ☺, Mīkā'īl ☺, Isrāfīl ☺, 'Izrā'īl ☺, and the fifth, Rūqā'īl ☺. Within it is the Qur'ān—Allāh. It is this Qur'ān that we must understand. If this Muhammad ⊕, this *mīm,* and this *nuqtah,* along with the seven principles were not there, if that explanation was not there, we could not understand Him and ourselves, *khair* and *sharr, sirr* and *sifāt,* good and bad, hell and heaven, Allāh and *insān,* creation and created beings, wisdom and ignorance. We could not understand darkness and light. Allāh formed and placed His house within the *qalb* in a subtle way, so that this could be known. That is the house of the *sirr,* the *dhāt.* That *dhāt,* the *sirr* within that *sirr,* exists as His qualities. That is His Qur'ān.

It is this Qur'ān that was revealed to Muhammad ⊕. This was revealed in *'ālamul-arwāh*. Allāh said, "*Yā* Muhammad, I will reveal this to you in the end, in completeness. I will make complete what I gave to the other prophets, and will give it to you at the end, in its entirety." This is the meaning.

This is what is known as the Qur'ān. It is His qualities. This is the meaning. If this Qur'ān is to be understood, it cannot be understood through the actions that we perform. It exists within that Light and form that is the Light-Muhammad ⊕ — those qualities. It is through this that we must understand. Those qualities are the sound of the Qur'ān. They are the sounds, the actions, the conduct, and the explanations of the Qur'ān. This is what He placed within Adam ⊕. This is Allāh's form. Allāh is the One who is without form. Therefore, we must reflect upon how He created Adam ⊕. Allāh's "form" is complete resplendence. He fashioned this *sūrah* of Adam ⊕ within that resplendence; He fashioned that form within that. We must understand that this is the Qur'ān. It is to understand this that Allāh created the Rasūl ⊕ and made the Qur'ān complete. The Rasūl ⊕ said, "Go even unto China to learn *'ilm*." He gave the Qur'ān into the people's hands and said, "To understand this go even unto China to learn *'ilm*, to learn wisdom. The treasure is in your hands, but seek wisdom to understand it. If you seek that essential principle, you will understand." This is the meaning. This gem has been given into the hands of a baby. It has been given to the baby to play with. But to understand the value of this gem, one has to go to someone who knows its value. This is what was said, this is the meaning. To know the value of this gem, your own value, the value of your house, the value of your Rabb, the value of His *Rahmah,* the value of your *ākhirah,* the value of your *qalb,* the value of the *dhāt,* and the value of the *sirr,* you must, in that state, go and learn. You must go even unto China to learn *'ilm*. These are the words that the Rasūl ⊕ spoke.

You who were without form have been placed within a form, and within you is Allāh. He has no form. The Qur'ān has no form. His sound has no form. And His qualities have no form. That resplendence is a complete resplendence. You need to understand that. This is a house, and within it He exists as the essential principle. This is a *sukūn,* and within it He exists as the support, the *alif.* This is a *mīm,* and He is the Light within it. Within this is a *qalb* and within this is Light, resplendence, and wisdom. We must understand this. Please understand this, precious jeweled lights of my eye.

What is the Qur'ān? What is the *sūrah?* What is Allāh? What is Muhammad ⊕? You must understand these essential principles. As long as you do not understand these, you will only have understood the five archangels of earth, fire, water, air, and the ether, which is Rūqā'īl ⊕. You will only have understood the earth, the fire, the water, the air, and the ether.

Your *sūrah* is an example. If you only understand that map-body, you will not understand the inner state. You will not understand Allāh's form or your form. Your form is the *rūh* and Allāh's form is resplendence. Your form is the *rūh* and Allāh's form is Light. That house is the state of the complete resplendence of the *ākhirah,* Allāh's kingdom.

You must think of this, each child must reflect on this. It is to establish this state that, in the end, Allāh revealed the Qur'ān in completeness to the Rasūl ⊕. He said, "*Yā* Muhammad, I have given everything to you in completeness. There will be no other prophet after you. I have completed this. I have finished this and given it into your hands."

It is this perfected Qur'ān that we have today. This Qur'ān is Allāh's qualities, Allāh's actions, Allāh's equality, Allāh's justice, and Allāh's beauty. That perfection—the three thousand gracious qualities and the ninety-nine *wilāyāt*—is the Qur'ān. It exists with the beauty of those qualities. That is within us, that is Muhammad ⊕. In the world of the souls, it was given to Muhammad ⊕; Allāh's actions were given as the Qur'ān.

The Qur'ān that we see today is in the form of a language, the Arabic language. It has the *sūrah* of language. But the *sūrah* that is formless, the *wahy* that came from Allāh without form, as Light, is *that* Qur'ān. It came from His qualities. That is the Qur'ān. You must look within that Qur'ān. To see that you must go even unto China, you must go even unto China to learn 'ilm.

The thirty juz', divisions of the Qur'ān, can be read very easily. Within two years, a child can memorize them. But to read that inner Qur'ān, to attain that beauty, those qualities, and that perfection takes a very long time. Qiyāmah after qiyāmah will pass. Many qiyāmahs will be needed to finish this.

Even if all the water in the oceans were made into ink, and all the trees in the world were made into pens, you can never finish writing the entire meaning of that Qur'ān. Allāh's qualities, actions, and behavior are that Qur'ān. Who can find an end to this complete perfection? Who can discover how great it is? Even if you keep on cutting and cutting, there is no end. Even if you keep on looking and looking, there is no end. Even if you keep on learning and learning, it will be beyond and beyond this. And even if you keep on understanding and understanding, there will still be more to understand. Therefore, you cannot find the end to Truth. Is that not so? How can you ever find an end to His beauty? Therefore, that is 'ilm. That is something that has no end. That is the meaning. You cannot find an end to it, whether it is in this ocean of illusion or in life. No matter what you have learned you will find no end, whether it is in the purānas, the scriptures, the religions, or the philosophies. Through these, you will never complete your studies. Through languages or the many other paths, you will not find clarity or completion.

This ocean is the ocean of 'ilm. It is the ocean of Allāh's rahmah. That is a secret. You cannot find an end to that secret form, His beauty. You can only disappear into That. You cannot know Its end. You will have to disappear into that Power. But even if you go into That, you cannot say, "It is only this much and no more." You will not be able to reach Its end. Allāh said to the Rasūlullāh ☉, "You must understand this."

What is called the Qur'ān is a very great matter. What is called the Qur'ān is Allāh: His Light, His plenitude, His completeness. What is called the dunyā is what Allāh discarded from Himself. The dunyā, the darkness, the hypnotic fascinations, and all that we make use of, were discarded from Him. Everything we desire was discarded from Him. What Allāh loves is wisdom within wisdom. He accepts that plenitude and those qualities. All of the qualities that were discarded from Him are known as satan and hell. These are not who He is. You have to understand this.

The Qur'ān is called *tauhīd, gnānam,* and *maʿrifah.* The Qur'ān is *maʿrifah,* and it is from this place of *maʿrifah* that Allāh speaks. The Qur'ān is within. It is sent down to the *ummīs,* those who are unlettered. When this *dunyā* does not speak within you, then you are *ummī.* When attachments do not speak within you, when relatives and blood ties do not speak, when the divisions of religions and the divisions of races do not speak, when the "I" and the "you" do not speak, when arrogance and karma do not speak, when falsehood and jealousy do not speak, when intoxicants, lust, theft, murder, and falsehood do not speak, when the six evils of lechery, anger, miserliness, fanaticism, bigotry, and envy do not speak, when earth, woman, and gold do not speak, when self-business and your desire and monkey mind do not speak, when *tārahan, singhan,* and *sūran* do not speak, at the time that none of these sections speak—when the four hundred trillion ten thousand different things do not speak— then you are *ummī.* When none of these speak with you, then you are *ummī.* And when you are *ummī,* this Qur'ān will speak with you. Then you are *ummī.* You will have learned that learning. As soon as all these other things stop speaking to you, then you will hear the sound of that Qur'ān. When you stop listening to these books, these *purānas,* and these scriptures, these scenes, when you stop listening to them and they no longer speak within you, then the Qur'ān will become *wahy* to you. Then you will understand the sound, you will understand the quality with which Allāh speaks with you, you will understand the words that were sent down, and you will understand correct behavior. You will understand those qualities, that compassion. That is the Qur'ān.

That is the Qur'ān, and then you are *ummī.* The Rasūl ☺ was *Ummī* when it was sent down to him, and once you are *ummī* it will be sent down to you. That is *ʿilm,* that is wisdom. After that you will know what worship really is, that there is none worthy of worship other than Allāhu ta'ālā. You will say the *kalimah*. When you become *ummī*, you will recite the *kalimah*, having realized Him. Then you are a *mu'min*, a true believer. You have become Islām. When you become Islām, that is *ma'rifah*. Islām is *ma'rifah*. After you have discarded from yourself what Allāh has discarded from Himself, you can say the *kalimah*. Only then can you accept the Rasūl ☺ and Allāh. Then you can accept the truth of *īmān* and clarity. You will have become *ummī*.

When you become *ummī*, your speech will be the speech that comes from Him, your actions will be the actions that come from Him, your behavior will be the behavior that comes from Him, your love will be the love that comes from Him, and your compassion will be the compassion that comes from Him. You will understand His peace, His justice, and His equality. You will understand this, and it is at that time that Allāh will recite your prayers.

So, recite the *kalimah* and accept it. There is none worthy of worship other than Allāhu ta'ālā. You must firmly establish this *īmān* with certitude. Then, He will speak with you. The words will come, the conduct will come, the actions will come, the gaze will come, and the thoughts will come, in the same way as they came to Muhammad ☺.

When you become the *mīm* and reach the state where none of these other things speak to you, then Allāh will speak to you. His *wilāyāt* and His *dhāt* will come within you. Then you will understand. In that state, you will speak and understand with absolute certitude. You will have *īmān* and you will pray to Him. You will know and understand Him. You will speak only to Him. You will no longer speak to these other things. You will know Him. You will know yourself and you will know your Lord, Allāh. You will hear His sound in your *qalb*.

As soon as you hear that sound, you will perform His *tasbīh*. You will take in His breath and you will adopt His actions. At that time you will accept with firm certitude that there is no Lord other than Him. Your soul, your actions, your conduct, your love, your com-

passion, your justice, your ways of integrity, your peace, your tranquility, and your unity, all of these will be His. In that state, you will
not see anything other than Him. None of your property here will
mean anything to you. Property will no longer speak to you. Once
these things do not speak to you, He will be your property, He will
be your house, and you will see only His beauty. That will be your
heaven, that will be your life, that will be your existence, that will
be your speech, that will be your taste, and that will be your food.
You will realize this.

But if you fail to attain that place, you will go on speaking with
the things that are speaking with you. You will go on speaking with
the things that He discarded from Himself. That will trouble you, it
will cause you difficulty. When these things speak, they will bring
you sorrow. When they speak in this way, you will become sad.
When you listen to all the things you hear, you will become sad.
When you accept all that they say, you will become sad. Because you
accept what they say, you will suffer. When you speak with them in
this way, when you accept what He has discarded from Himself, that
will be your suffering in the *dunyā,* in the *ākhirah,* and in the *awwal.*

When we become *ummī,* having understood this and having firm
īmān without any doubt, we will be able to hear His sound in our
hearts. We will do His *tasbīh* and pray to Him. That is known as
vanakkam. That is worship, knowing that there is none worthy of
worship other than Allāhu ta'ālā. That is called Islām.

Those who accept this state and speak with Him alone are
mu'mins. They are the one group. That one group of *mu'mins* is the
group that accepts Allāh, that accepts Allāh's qualities, His sound,
and His speech. The *mu'mins* are the ones who read His Qur'ān.
That is the group that exhibits His beauty, the group that praises His
glory, the group that enjoys His speech, and the group that accepts
His thoughts and then acts upon them. That is the group that exhibits His actions, His behavior, and His qualities. That is the group of
the *mu'min.* It is this group called *mu'min* that sees Him directly, pays
obeisance to Him, honors Him, praises Him, and worships Him.
That is the prayer that they do. They do only that.

Yet the number of those who have forsaken this state is increasing more and more. So, for those who accept the *dunyā* and the discarded things of the *dunyā,* for those who are increasing in this way, three obligations were sent down. Previous to this, there were two obligations: first, you must accept God without any doubt, and second, you must do *tasbīh* and pray to Him alone. These two obligations were for the group that prayed to God, the only One worthy of worship. But for those who had forsaken these, He gave three more obligations. Those three things...You have given up His treasures and have accepted the discarded things of the *dunyā*. You have accepted that sound and that speech. So, for these other seventy-two groups, Allāh ordained something further: Give *sadaqah,* charity. Give away what you have taken for yourself. If you refuse to do that, at least give away one-tenth of it. If you refuse to give even that, it means that you have not firmly established your *īmān*.

Next, *nōnbu,* fasting was ordained to correct this. Understand this. Do this to correct yourself. Consider all lives as your own life. All of Allāh's creations are in your heart. You yourself are the world. The world is within you. Hell is within you. Hell, evil, sorrow, and joy are within you. Hunger, disease, old age, and death are there. Torpor and darkness are there. Attachments and differences are within you. Realize this. Understand this through fasting. Do this for thirty or forty days. When you have done this, you will understand these meanings. Certain things will be revealed to you. During that fast you should give to others what you have kept for yourself. Make those who are speaking with you retreat. Drive away from you those inner beings who are full of desire. Attain peace and tranquility, dispense justice. Have God's qualities, perform God's actions, and act with and exhibit God's good conduct and behavior. See God's compassion, see His three thousand gracious qualities. Everything you see is connected to you. Adam ☺ and the children of Adam ☺ are connected to you. Truth and deceptive things are mingled within you. You should understand this.

Fasting was the fourth *fard* that was ordained, but for those who did not accept this, a fifth *fard* was revealed. God said, "*Yā*

Muhammad, you must tell them this." This was explained and re-vealed to that Light that is Muhammad ☉. It was shown to that wisdom, to that *rahmah,* to that plenitude.

Allāh said, "Tell them to perform the *hajj,* the holy pilgrimage. The children of Adam live in the four directions of east, west, north, and south. I exist as one point. I am one point. All four directions belong to Me. I am that point. My qualities are the Qur'ān. I am the *rahmah* that you cannot comprehend. I am the plenitude that is that *rahmah.* Tell them that they should unite the four directions, make them one, and look at Me in the center, in the *qalb,* the *ka'bah.* That is the *ka'bah.*

"Man's *qalb* is his *ka'bah.* Tell them to complete the *hajj* of the *ka'bah* and to understand that *ka'bah.* I am a dot within it, and Muhammad ☉ is a *sukūn* within that. I and My *malā'ikah* recite *sala-wāt* to Muhammad. I have told My *malaks, malā'ikah,* and *nabīs* to recite *salawāt* to his name. That dot is truth. That truth was placed in that *ka'bah.* That (truth) is the *kalimah.* What is called *īmān* is that dot, it is that stone.[1] That stone that was placed in this *ka'bah* is the stone that was placed in the *qalb.* That is the stone called *īmān.* The light called the *kalimah* is there, in the center. That is the stone in their *qalbs;* that is that stone. I have placed that stone of truth in the *ka'bah.* That stone called *īmān* and that light called the *kalimah* are placed there. Tell them to know Me through that. Tell them to go there, and perform the *hajj.*"

The explanation is this...Muhammad ☉ was born in Mecca. He went to Medina, is that not so? That place was shown as an example to the *qalb.* It was revealed as an example, as an essential princi-ple. That stone of the *ka'bah* is *īmān.* The *ka'bah* was built with the *kalimah.* It was built with the *kalimah,* and the stone of *īmān* was placed there. Within that is Light—Allāh. The Light and the quali-ties that are Allāh are within that. They were told to look at That. That is that *hajj.*

---

1 stone: Outwardly, the stone refers to the Black Stone that is in the Ka'bah in Mecca.

Allāh said, "Tell them to wear the shroud of death. That is the *hāl* of *maut,* the state of death. *Yā* Muhammad, tell them to wear the shroud of death and complete the *hajj.* Tell them to burn away everything in the *dunyā,* to burn away all the things in the world that speak to them, all of the people who are calling out to them. That is the *hāl* of *maut.* Tell them to perform this *hajj,* which is the fifth *fard,* by making the *dunyā* die."

This is the *hajj* that Allāh ordained. This is the *hajj* to the *ka'bah* that is built with the *kalimah,* where the stone of *īmān* is kept. That is the place of worship. Prayer is performed there. That is the *ka'bah;* it is the house of the *'arshul-mu'min.* The *ka'bah* has been constructed there, and Allāh is the *sirr* within this. All of His explanations are within this. You must think about this. This *fard* was ordained by Allāh. It is said that people from all four directions should come to that place, to that house that was built with the *kalimah.*

That stone of *īmān* was brought and placed within the Rasūl ☺. Allāh is the Light and meaning within this stone of *īmān.* "Tell them to come here to complete their *hajj.*" One is Mecca, the cause, and the other is the *qalb,* the *ka'bah,* the effect. Allāh's angels, archangels, prophets, and saints are praying there. They send out a resonance and a light. They are speaking with Him, standing in rows upon rows, praying. We must realize this. This must be understood. We must understand this *'ilm.* We must truly understand this ocean of *'ilm.*

It is in this state that Allāh, Allāh's Rasūl ☺, Allāh's prophets, angels, and archangels exist. The *īmān* of Muhammad ☺ exists there. In *'ālamul-arwāh* itself Allāh is the support for the *īmān* that is Muhammad ☺—that *sukūn,* that *nuqtah.* Allāh praises that. That is the group of the *insān kāmil* and the *mu'min.* They are one group. Allāh sent His prophets, His representatives, and His vice-regents as witnesses to guide people on the straight path, to dispel all the others who are speaking to them, and to give them peace. These representatives are witnesses. They tell the people to understand this and to do this. We who have *īmān* must understand this explanation.

This is *tauhīd.* *Ma'rifah* is Islām. Only after one understands this does he become Islām. If you can establish this state, then you will be the one group. To say that this one group is Islām means that all of everything is one group, that all are the children of Adam ☺. That is Islām. All of everything is one group. When the Qur'ān speaks within you, then that is the one group. But if the Qur'ān does not speak within you, and if instead what was discarded from Allāh speaks within you, then that is the seventy-two groups; it is not the seventy-third group, (the one group). When you accept Allāh with firm certitude, you are the one group. Then you will see no differences. But when what was discarded from Allāh speaks within you, then you have separated into the seventy-two groups. You have separated into the groups that undergo suffering, *'adhāb*.

When you understand your *īmān*, wisdom, and love of Allāh, when you understand the Qur'ān, when you understand Allāh's actions, and when you understand that perfection, then you are the one group, you are Adam's ☺ children. You will be seen as one assembly. You will pray to Allāh alone. You will see clearly that there is one group, that the Rabb is one, and that prayer is one. But if you have not established this state, you will have divided into the seventy-two groups. You will have joined with the groups that speak to all of these other things. That is not the group of the *mu'mins*. That is not the assembly of prayer. You will be the group that undergoes difficulty, the group that speaks to the many people.

For this reason, Allāh sent down the *nabīs*, the *olis*, the *qutbs*, the *auliyā'*, the *malaks*, and the *malā'ikah*. He created them with His Qudrah and sent them down. He and all of His vice-regents recite the *salawāt* to that truth. That (truth) is Muhammad ☺. It is that *sukūn*, that *mīm* that is called Muhammad ☺. That is mingled within everything. What came from Allāh is called Muhammad ☺. So, it is to this that the *salawāt* and *salāms* are recited. Allāh Himself recites the *salawāt* and praises Muhammad ☺. The Qur'ān reveals this.[2] That Qur'ān is you. It is within you. When you become *ummī*, you will understand this. When you become *ummī* like Muhammad ☺, you

---

2 "Verily Allāh and His angels bless the Prophet. O ye who believe! Bless him and give him the greetings of peace." Holy Qur'ān, *Sūratul-Ahzāb*, 33:56.

will understand the Qur'ān. Only then will you know this. All the time that you are not *ummī*, you will not be able to understand this.

It is for this reason that Allāh has revealed the Qur'ān. It is a witness. The *nabīs*, the *olis*, the *qutbs*, the *malaks*, and the *malā'ikah* are witnesses. We have to realize this. In the *dunyā*, the prophets were shown as examples, Allāh's prophets and saints were placed here as examples, and it is through them that we must understand and know *'ilm*.

Islām is *ma'rifah*. The first learning in *ma'rifah* is to have *īmān*. From that you will learn about His beauty. To merge with Him is that learning. When you reach this state where you can disappear within Him, then you will become His Light. There is still more to learn beyond this. When you accept Him and worship Him, when you learn that prayer, you will become one with Him, you will disappear in Him. You will become an *'abd*, a slave, within Him. The name for that is 'Abdullāh, a slave of God. Only after you become a slave of God will you be called 'Abdullāh. 'Abduh, 'Abdullāh. Before that, we are not 'Abdullāh, we are the children of many other things. We are the children of satan, of earth, fire, water, and air, of the *nafs ammārah*, of desire, maya, darkness, and envy. Among the children of Allāh, we are the children who have separated off. There are many people like this. We need to understand this.

This is the reason that Allāh has placed the *olis*, the illumined beings, in certain places, as examples. Allāh has placed them there to protect us. When they are there, they are a protection. And even after they disappear, their light remains. Even though you and we may forget them, they have not really disappeared. They are here. They are the *mu'mins* who have nothing other than Allāh. They are *ummīs*. They speak to Him alone. They are the support for the earth.

When the earth said "I" and started shaking, the mountains were created. When the earth moved and shook, the mountains were created to stop this shaking. Very large mountains were created in different places.

When the earth became proud with the "I" Allāh created the mountains to control it. When the wind became proud He created the mountains and the trees to control it. When water became proud He controlled it with the air. When fire became proud He controlled it with the water. When ether became proud He controlled it with the sun, the moon, and the stars. When satan became proud He controlled him with *īmān* and the *kalimah*. When man became proud Allāh controlled him with His own qualities. When man said "I" He controlled him with *jahannam,* hell. When wisdom became proud He controlled it with His qualities and with His Light. When the "I" became proud He controlled it with His justice. In this way, whenever something acquired pride He created something else to control it. Whenever any creation became proud He put something else there to control it. That is Allāh's duty, Allāh's work. These are His actions. Every child must think about this.

There are some people who say that the *salawāt* should not be recited to Muhammad ☙ or to any of the other prophets. But the Qur'ān and Allāh say that the prophets are *mu'mins* and that these *mu'mins* have eternal light. Others will not be able to speak to Allāh. Instead, they will speak with their *nafs,* with desires, with monkeys, and with donkeys. They will not understand. They (the *mu'mins*) speak with Allāh. The others speak with the *nafs.* They do not understand. They do not understand the Qur'ān. They do not understand *īmān,* yet they say we should not praise that *mu'min,* they say that it is *shirk*[3] to do this. He himself is the one who is a *mushrik.* He is the *nafs.* His thoughts are the thoughts of satan. His speech is treacherous. All of his looks are the looks of *zinā,* adultery. All of his thoughts are the thoughts of the *nafs* and hunger. His entire nature is that of the joy of maya and darkness. His happiness is like the happiness of the jinns and the fairies. In this way, he has four hundred trillion ten thousand different qualities. The qualities of satan, monkeys, donkeys, dogs, foxes, cats, rats, pigs, scorpions, four-legged animals, snakes, frogs, and fish, of magic and the qualities of hypocrisy, envy, and vengeance are found within him.

---

3   *shirk* (A) To worship something else along with Allāh; idolatry. It comes from the root denoting partnership, making a partner to or associating something with Allāh. A *mushrik* is one who practices *shirk.*

When these qualities are speaking with him, how can he know that resplendence? How can he know that which speaks with Allāh? These other things exist within him as *shirk*, as *sirr*, and as comparisons to God. He has so much *shirk*, so many secrets, so many qualities that are *harām*, and so many animals within him. So how can he know about the one who has cut these away and speaks with Allāh alone? He is a *mushrik* to himself, he is satan to himself, he is a *hayawān*, an animal, to himself, and he is a snake to himself. All of these exist within him, as comparisons. These are parallels that are within him. Only when he dispels these will he exist in the state of equality, peacefulness, and tranquility. Only when he is in the station of *ummī* will he understand. But, as long as he remains as the four hundred trillion ten thousand *hayawāns*, poisonous qualities, satans, darknesses, and torpors, how can he understand this? It is the one who does not understand this who speaks in this way.

If one is to understand the Rasūl ☻, he must understand what the *mīm* is like, how it is supported by the *alif*, what the *sukūn* is like, what the *nuqtah* is like, when it was created, what kind of Light has come to it, what kind of beauty Allāh has, and what that *rahmah* is like. Only when he stops speaking to these other things will he understand. When he becomes *ummī*, he will understand. As long as the entire world and all of the seven hells are speaking with him, how can he understand? It is the one who does not understand who continually speaks in this way.

The *mu'mins* are those who understand. They are those who have *īmān*, those who have read the Qur'ān after becoming *ummī*, and those who have realized that *'ilm*. They can always speak to the Rasūl ☻, that Light. One who has wisdom must realize this.

With the use of scientific instruments, we who are here in Sri Lanka can hear the voice of someone who is speaking in the north, in America. Does the sound just disappear? No. When someone telephones from America, you can hold the phone to your ear and hear him speak, even though he is such a long distance away. This is happening in this age, in this century. The voice, the tone, and the sound can all be heard. You can make out the speech of someone who is speaking from there. You can hear it from thirteen thousand miles away, you can hear it even from beyond twenty thousand miles away. Scientists have discovered how to do this. They have invented something that you can hold up to your ear to hear what is being said elsewhere. Man can watch television, listen to the radio, and speak on the telephone. He can do all of this. In this age, it is possible for man to do this.

But those who have received the *rahmah* of Allāh...That is *meignānam*, true wisdom, while the other is *vingnānam*, scientific wisdom. That is *meignānam*; that *'ilm* is true wisdom. So, are those who have *meignānam* not able to speak from Mecca? Are they not able to speak from the *ākhirah?* And are they not able to speak with Allāh, with His representatives, and with His prophets from *'ālamul-arwāh?* It is justice that speaks, it is true wisdom. Are not Allāh's *gnānam*, qualities, actions, and behavior able to speak in this way? If you can speak from so many miles away, why are they not able to speak?

There is *poignānam*, false wisdom, *agnānam*, ignorance, *vingnānam*, scientific wisdom, and *meignānam*, true wisdom. How does *meignānam* speak? How can anyone say that true wisdom has disappeared? Allāh has not disappeared and truth has not disappeared. We pray and we worship. Is Allāh not there? Does He not see? How does He hear that sound? Does He not hear?

The *mu'adhdhin* calls, "Come to the mosque." You cannot see Allāh, so how does Allāh hear that? How does He hear what that man is saying? Is not the One who hears this able to hear what His representatives are saying? And are not the ones who came here as His representatives able to hear Allāh's sound from there? Can they not speak with Him? Are they dead or are they alive? How can we understand this?

They do speak. Those who speak will always go on speaking. Why? They are not two. If the *dunyā* is no longer speaking and if those representatives are speaking with God, then they will have disappeared in Him. They will have merged with and disappeared in Him. They are beyond all of the demons. But for those who are speaking with the *dunyā*, truth is cast away from them.

For the one who speaks with the *dunyā, īmān* is cast away from him, the *kalimah* and *īmān* are cast away from him. One who is like that will not be able to speak with Allāh. Only when he becomes *ummī* will he speak with Allāh. As long as he is not *ummī*, the demons will speak with him and the *dunyā* will speak with him. So, when he cannot hear that sound of Allāh, he will say, "That is *shirk*, this is *shirk*." He is the one who is a *mushrik!* Regardless of what sound he hears, everything within him is *shirk*, everything within him is hell, and all of the speech within him is filled with deceit, with satan's qualities. That is what he understands.

Therefore, one who has discarded this *dunyā* is *ummī*. He speaks with Allāh, and he understands. If one has that *'ilm*, that wisdom, and those qualities, that is *īmān*-Islām. That is what is understood. The one who does not understand will speak in this other way, while the one who understands the Qur'ān...

What is the Qur'ān? What is the meaning of the Qur'ān? What is an *ummī* like? Only when one becomes *ummī* will he understand the Qur'ān that is within him. That is resplendence, Light, the three thousand gracious qualities, equality, peace, tranquility, unity, the ninety-nine *wilāyāt*, and Allāh's qualities, actions, and conduct. That is the Qur'ān that is within him. That is Light. When one realizes and accepts that state, when he speaks with Allāh and hears His sound, he will see only the One. Until then, the one who is a *mushrik* will see only what is *shirk*; everything will be *shirk*. He is a *mushrik*. You must understand this.

Allāh's Rasūl ☉ said in a *hadīth*: "*'Ilm* is a very great matter."[4] Some may say, "That is *shirk*, this is *shirk*," but great men, those with wisdom, say that those in the seventy-third group, those who have

---

4   *'ilm* (A) Divine knowledge, including knowledge of the Qur'ān.

In *Sahīh Muslim*, Abū Mūsā reported Allāh's Apostle ☉ saying: "The similitude of that guidance and knowledge with which Allāh, the Exalted and Glorious, has sent me is that of rain falling upon the earth. There is a good piece of land which receives the rainfall and as a result of it there is grown in it herbage and grass abundantly. Then there is a land hard and barren which retains water and the people derive benefit from it and they drink it and make the animals drink. Then there is another land which is barren. Neither is wa-

hayāh, the *olis* who have made this *dunyā* die, those who are *ummī,* whether they live in the *dunyā,* in the *ākhirah,* in the *awwal,* in hell, or in heaven, they will be in heaven. When one no longer speaks with the world, when he hears only the sounds of Allāh and speaks only Allāh's speech in the world, whether he lives in the *dunyā* or the *ākhirah,* he will be in heaven. He will be living in heaven here.

When one has not become *ummī,* when he is speaking with the *nafs,* with desire, with satan, with the earth, with blood ties, with languages, and with his thoughts, when he is speaking with these kinds of things, when what is called *jahannam,* hell, is speaking, then he will hear only those sounds, he will not hear Allāh's sounds. He will only hear the sounds of *shirk.* He will listen to the sounds of *shirk* that are within him, he will listen to what is deceitful and *shirk.* He will not hear Allāh's sounds, he will not hear the Qur'ān. His ears will not hear the Qur'ān, he will not hear Allāh's qualities, he will not hear His actions, he will not hear His voice, and he will not hear His speech. To the one who is a *mushrik,* those sounds are *haram,* they are parallels to God. But, for an *ummī,* it is not like that. Those who are *mushriks* keep comparisons. They have discarded the truth. Truth will never come to them.

When a *mu'min* goes to a *qabr,* a grave…there are so many graves, and in those many graves there is so much suffering. There is the questioning, there is the Day of Judgment, and there is the punishment. In those graves there are those who are suffering, those who keep these parallels, and those with *nafs.* The many who are there are undergoing so much suffering from the questioning and the punishment in their graves. Those of wisdom, the *auliyā',* and those of truth can hear the sounds that come from that place. When the

---

ter retained in it, nor is the grass grown in it.

"And that is the similitude of the first one who develops the complete knowledge and understanding of the religion of Allāh with which Allāh sent me and it becomes a source of benefit to him. (The second type is) one who learns knowledge and imparts it to others. (Then the third type is) one who does not pay attention and thus does not accept Allāh's guidance with which I have been sent."

prophets heard these sounds from the graves, when they heard this, they said, "The *malaks* and the *malā'ikah* are questioning and giving punishment according to the command of Allāh." They said further, "When you see a grave, do not worship in that place. That is not a place to pray. Do not worship at a graveside. Because of the punishment that is going on there, you should, in Allāh's name, recite a *Fātihah*, a *Yā Sīn* from the Qur'ān, and a *salawāt*."

So, when a *mu'min* sees a grave, he recites these and says, "Allāh, please help them." Then for that amount of time that he is doing *tasbīh* to Allāh, the angels who are giving the punishment will raise their hands in praise, and that punishment will stop. When the angels hear a *Yā Sīn* being recited, the suffering and punishment in the grave will be lessened for that amount of time. When a *Fātihah* is recited, the punishment will stop for five minutes. As long as the angels hear the sound of this *tasbīh* being recited to Allāh, they will raise their hands and that punishment will be lessened.

When someone offers praise to Allāh upon seeing a grave, it is to reduce the suffering in that grave. That is what the great ones, the wise ones have said. The prophets have told us this. Therefore, when those who have wisdom in the world see a grave they recite a *Yā Sīn* and a *Fātihah* to lessen the suffering, not because the dead are gods, but to give them relief. The *mu'mins* are not worshipping in that place. Rather, they are doing a duty that needs to be done.

When someone is crying, it is our duty to comfort that person. This is what a *mu'min* will do. When a wise man sees a grave and hears the suffering and crying that is going on there, he will give comfort upon hearing that sound. Those of wisdom will do that. For one who does not hear those sounds, that (recitation) will be a comparison. He will not understand, nor will he know what to say to give comfort. He will not know what to say during this time. He cannot hear the suffering that is going on in that grave because he himself is suffering. He has no understanding, he has no wisdom. So, he does not hear those sounds.

One who does hear that torment, one who does hear the suffering that is going on there, will recite a *Yā Sīn,* do *tasbīh* to God, and recite a *Fātihah* for that person. And for as long as he does this, the punishment will be reduced. That is one meaning. Only the *ummī* who has learned *'ilm* will understand this.

However, when someone (other than an *ummī*) recites a *Khatm*,[5] and a *Fātihah,* he recites for his own sake, not for the dead. He is offering praise to Allāh and giving food to feed ten poor people from what he has gathered, but he is not doing this for the sake of the dead. He is not reciting for the sake of the *mayyit,* the corpse. He himself is a corpse, he is a living corpse. He keeps the *dunyā* within him and is a corpse within this *dunyā*. He is a corpse to the *nafs,* he is a corpse to desire, he is a corpse to money, he is a corpse to children, he is a corpse to race, he is a corpse to color, he is a corpse to his house — he is a corpse to everything. He is a walking corpse. This walking corpse is heavy, it is a heavy weight. So, because he is a corpse, if he feeds ten people he will feel a little peace because he has given to others some of what he has gathered for himself. At least his own suffering will be lessened. Whatever he does when he is alive is done for his own sake. This will help him in his own grave.

Therefore, the reason he does this is not to help someone else. He feeds the ten people for his own sake, he recites a *Yā Sīn* for his own sake, he recites a *Khatm* for his own sake, and he glorifies and praises the prophets, recites, and beseeches God for his own sake. Is this done for the corpse? No.

For one who has wisdom, this is the correct duty to do, but for the one who has no wisdom, it is *shirk*. He keeps comparisons; he associates something with Allāh. The one who has placed his *nafs* as a comparison to Allāh will not understand. Only one who understands *'ilm* will understand this. One who has earth, fire, water, air, ether, *nafs ammārah,* arrogance, karma, deceit, falsehood, and jealousy within him will not understand this. Those who have these qualities have separated away from Allāh.

When Allāh's *rahmah* came, it was sent down to the Rasūl ☉ who was *Ummī,* unlettered. He was not learned. It came at that time to

---

5 *Khatm* (A) Recitation of the entire Qur'ān. Literally, seal.

those in the *dunyā*. The Qur'ān was sent down, it was completed and sent down in the end. The 6,666 *āyāt* contain the histories and explanations that were given to the earlier prophets. This was given in the Arabic language. It was sent to a land where Arabic was spoken. Through this, Allāh has explained the earlier prophets. Allāh revealed and gave all these explanations to that *Ummī*.

Like this, only after one has become *ummī* can he read the Qur'ān that is within him. That is what is *khair*. *Yā* Haqq! *Yā* Haqq is Truth. *Yā* Haqq is that Truth. Only then can he understand his Haqq that is within him. What is his Haqq? It is Allāh. He will understand Allāh's sound and speech. If he has not understood *yā* Haqq, he will not know "My Truth." What is "My Truth?" That Truth is Allāh. He has to understand this. That is His Qur'ān. He has to understand this. Allāh explains these meanings through the *nabīs*, the *olis*, and the *malaks,* and He reveals it through His creations. This Haqq—*yā* Haqq is the Truth that they need to understand.

In this state, there are the four *vēdas* and religions. From the time of Adam ⊕ the four *vēdas* and religions separated from this Truth. So many of these sections, so many languages, and so many, many *vēdas* have separated from this *dīn*. There are so many languages, so many divisions, so many *vēdas,* so many *vēdāntas,* so many prayers, and so many comparisons. There are so many of these things. There is *az-zabūr, al-jabbūrat, al-injīl,* and *al-furqān,* the four *vēdas.* Although there are all of these, there is only one thing that has been spoken about. There is one thing.

In Hinduism the wise men are called *gnānis*. In Christianity they are called saints. In Islām they are called *auliyā', ambiyā', qutbs,* and *olis.* Like this, in the four religions there are wise men. In one religion they are called *gnānis* and *sannyāsis,* in another they are called saints, and in still another they are called *auliyā'* and *ambiyā'.* It is through all of these wise men that these various states were revealed.

From the time of Adam ⊕, for generation after generation, these states that Allāh showed Adam ⊕ in *'ālamul-arwāh* were explained through these wise men. Allāh keeps revealing explanations in this way. This has been happening for the past two hundred million years. The Qur'ān speaks about this. The Qur'ān speaks about these *ambiyā', auliyā', qutbs, olis,* and *nabīs;* it speaks about the representatives of Allāh, and about the *malaks* and *malā'ikah.* Depending on the language, whether it is Tamil, Latin, Hebrew, or Arabic, those of wisdom are referred to as saints, messiahs, *auliyā', ambiyā', olis,* or *nabīs.* This has been going on for two hundred million years.

One who is a *mushrik* says that the words of Allāh are *shirk,* but it is his own body, he himself, his actions, and his thoughts that are *shirk.* For generation after generation, for two hundred million years these (words) have been coming, they have been coming for four yugas. Yet now, in Islām, in this century, some people who are *mushriks* are trying to destroy the words of Allāh by denying the words of the *auliyā'* and *ambiyā'.* They say they should not be mentioned or spoken about. They say there are no *auliyā', ambiyā',* or *olis.* They do not accept what the Qur'ān says. It may be that they themselves are *mushriks.*

We must accept what the Qur'ān says. This is something that one who is a *mushrik* does not understand. Why? Because what speaks with him is one thing, while what speaks with Allāh is a different thing, it is *īmān.* As soon as the call to prayer is recited, the name of the Rasūl ⊕ comes. Allāh sent down the Qur'ān, and that word was mentioned even before the call to prayer originated. Without that, without that word, and without that point, what work has the Qur'ān here, what function does it have? That which has form has no work here. Allāh's qualities and actions exist formlessly, and that is necessary for one who has wisdom, it is necessary for that state. But for the one who does not have wisdom, the *sūrah,* the form, is necessary. To understand that form he must be in the form of *shirk* itself. He will be a *mushrik,* he will have the *shirk* of earth, fire, water, air, ether, and the *nafs ammārah.* So, how can one who is a *mushrik* know Allāh's *rahmah* and qualities? How can he know the *auliyā'* and *ambiyā'?* How can he know Allah's prophets? He cannot know! He cannot know! How can he know how to speak with them? He cannot know! He cannot know!

Allāh praises His prophets. He sent them down as His representatives and lights. But those who are *mushriks* do not understand this. They say that it is these representatives who are the *mushriks*.

One needs to understand himself. The one who does not know about eating rice says that rice is *harām*, so he drinks milk. He says that rice is *harām*, but when he is hungry he will eat the very thing that he says is *harām*. On the outside he will say something is *harām*, but when he is hungry he will eat that very same thing. That is his impurity, his *shirk*. If his actions do not follow his words, then that is his *shirk*. The one who is a *mushrik* sees Allāh's words as *shirk*, sees Allāh's speech as *shirk*, and sees Allāh's representatives, messengers, and saints as *shirk*. This was going on in the four religions in earlier times, and it is still going on now. In this century, in Islām, these precepts and words come from people who are *mushriks*. Those who are *mushriks* express these ideas.

Those with wisdom will understand the Qur'ān, but others may be ignorant. They will not understand what the Qur'ān is. To understand the Qur'ān one must become Muhammad ☮, one who is *ummī*. An *ummī* is one who can understand the Qur'ān. The Qur'ān speaks only with the one who understands.

There is light in a stone. A stone itself is *shirk*, but light is not *shirk*. If you see the light that is within it, then you will know the value of the stone. If you think it is just a stone, then it is *shirk*, but if you see the light that it contains, then it will not be *shirk*. It will be valuable, it will not be *shirk*. Blood too is *shirk*, but when blood changes to milk, it is not *shirk* anymore, it becomes food. You do not drink blood, but when it turns into milk you can drink it, it will become *halāl* for you; it will become *halāl*. If you slaughter something and eat it, then that is *harām*, but if you slaughter it in the proper way, then it might become *halāl*.

Like that, your thoughts are *harām* to you, your thoughts are *shirk*. The animals within you are *harām*. Your qualities are *harām*, your actions are *harām*, they are *shirk*. However, if you go on cutting them away, then later they will become *halāl* for you. If you take Allāh's food, then that will be *halāl*. Blood is *harām*, it is *shirk*, but milk is *halāl*. A stone is *shirk,* but the light, the truth that is within it, is *halāl*.

Like this, if one can extract the taste, if he can extract that treasure of *yā* Haqq, which is the Truth, from his learning, from the explanations of wisdom, and from his qualities, then that is Truth. That is *halāl,* it has no comparison. Like this, if he can extract the Truth called al-Haqq from *'ilm,* from his learning, from his actions, and from his qualities, then that is *halāl*. That is Light, it is Resplendence. It is nourishment, milk.

The nectar that the bee extracts is *harām*. The bee removes it with its mouth, but when it gathers the nectar and stores it somewhere and when it becomes sweet, then that becomes *halāl*. It is *halāl*. What the bee first extracted was *harām,* but when it was gathered and stored in the proper way it became *halāl*.

All food is *harām,* all of it is *harām*. It comes from the earth and contains so many shaktis. For that food to have the right taste and become *halāl,* it has to be changed. One must work hard. He must earn with the sweat of his brow and give to others. He must give food to others. If he himself eats only after he has given food to those who are hungry, then the food that was *harām* will be transformed and become *halāl*. That is truth.

Like that, when one understands each thing and discards what is *shirk* and *harām,* then that will be *halāl*. If he discards what is *shirk* on the inside and the outside, from his body, his breath, his qualities, and his actions, then that is correct, that is true. If one does not discard those qualities and actions, they will remain as *shirk* within him. The one who has not understood this, the one who is a *mushrik,* will look at the truth, will look at that milk and say it is *shirk*. He will look at food and say it is *shirk*. He will say that what is right is *shirk*. He will say Allāh is *shirk,* he will say prayer is *shirk,* he will say wisdom is *shirk,* and he will say the light of the Qur'ān is *shirk*. The one who is a *mushrik* will say so many things like this. When you speak with one who is a *mushrik,* the one who has these comparisons within him, he will say that what is true is *shirk*. But those who have wisdom...We must accept Allāh's Truth and act accordingly.

When a dog barks, we should not bark back at the dog. When a dog bites, we should not bite it back. It will bark and bite and die on its own. Feces will taste sweet to the dog. It will lick itself; the dog will lick its own wounds. Its own phlegm and saliva will taste sweet to it, *lalalalnnng*. Like this, just because a dog barks, we should not bark back.

We need to know, understand, and do what we must do, in accordance with the words of the Rasūl ﷺ. He said that unity, love, tranquility, peace, and the qualities of Allāh are Islām. That is the Qur'ān. Those qualities are the *rūh*. That is Islām. That state is Allāh, Allāh's *rahmah*. He made those qualities, His actions, His conduct, His essence, and His perfection into His form. When one speaks with Allāh, that person is said to be a *mu'min*. We must understand this.

The one who does not understand this, the one who is a *mushrik,* the one who has *sirr,* the one who is *harām,* the one who has faults, the one who goes on speaking on the path of *shirk*—all of the sounds that that person hears are from the *shirk* of the demons and ghosts. There are some people who are *mushriks* who speak of these many things. But we must not accept these; we must accept Allāh's words. We must learn His teachings, we must teach His teachings, and understand the explanations that were sent to the Ummī Muhammad ﷺ. According to that, we must discard everything that is speaking with us. We must discard all the things of the *dunyā* that were discarded by Allāh, and understand Allāh's qualities and actions, His grace, His wealth, His completeness, and His truth. It is only after we become *ummī* that His sound and speech will come. Only then will we understand the Qur'ān that is within us.

We must change in the same way that the blood was changed into milk. The milk of grace, the honey, the milk called the *rahmah* of Allāh must come forth. We must strive to take it and taste it. In the same way that light comes from a stone, we must change the stone that is called the *sūrah,* the *qalb*. We must break it apart, and polish and facet what is within it. We must clear it and take the resplendent Light that is Allāh, the valuable Treasure that is within it.

Then we must give our *qalb* to that One of value. We can then realize that value and that beauty. We must change our blood-drinking
quality and transform our *qalb* into milk. We must melt it and give
everyone a share of that quality, that grace, and that wealth. This is
the duty we must do.

Even so, those who are *shirk*, those who have *sirr*, have emerged
in this century to make the world *shirk*, to make prayer *shirk*, to
make our intentions and *īmān shirk*. They keep parallels to God
within themselves. Satan, *nafs*, demons, pride, arrogance, and bad
qualities are speaking with them and they are speaking with these
things. They are not *ummī*. They do not speak with Allāh.

Therefore, we must give up these sounds and listen to Allāh's
sound, the sound of the *rasūls*, and the sound of the *olis*. If we can
learn to do this, all of these other sounds will not be heard. Only the
sounds of the *nabīs* and those of truth will be heard. We must comfort those who are suffering, give goodness, and then proceed. This
is the right path.

There is more to be said about this, but it is now early morning.
It is nearly eight-thirty a.m. Therefore, we must stop now and speak
at another time. If God gives His grace and allows us to speak again
about this, if He comes and speaks, we will speak.

(Bawa Muhaiyaddeen ⊕ recites the Third *Kalimah* and everyone joins in.)

*Subhānallāhi wal-hamdu lillāhi wa lā ilāha illAllāhu wallāhu akbar, wa
lā haula wa lā quwwata illā billāhi, wa huwal- 'alīyul- 'azīm.* All glory is to
Allāh and all praise be to Allāh, and none is God except Allāh, and
Allāh is greater, and there is no majesty and power except with Allāh
and He is exalted, supreme in glory!

Allāhu akbar, Allāhu akbar, Allāhu akbar, Allāhu akbar! Allāh is
greater, Allāh is greater, Allāh is greater, Allāh is greater!

Lā ilāha illAllāhu, Muhammadur-Rasūlullāh. None is God except
Allāh, and Muhammad is the Messenger of God.

As-salāmu 'alaikum wa rahmatullāh. May the peace and beneficence of God be upon you.

A'ūdhu billāhi minash-shaitānir-rajīm.
I seek refuge in God from the accursed satan.

Bismillāhir-Rahmānir-Rahīm.
In the name of God, the Most Compassionate,
the Most Merciful.

Epilogue
Song: Eternal Prayer

September 1, 1974, Sunday

G od who knows everything in the *qalb,*
God who knows everything in the *qalb,*
is the Almighty One who bestows heavenly bliss.
God who knows everything
is the Almighty One who bestows heavenly bliss.
The Good One who is God,
the God who knows everything,
is the Almighty One who bestows heavenly bliss.
The Good One who is God
is the Protector who gives us grace,
the Creator who knows and understands the *qalb,*
the One who does everything with compassion.

He is the Great One who understands and
prays with a clear heart.
God, the Great One who loves,
is Ādi, the Beginning,
who makes our wisdom clear,
and Anādi, the Beginningless,
who shows us the path of love.
He knows our thoughts before we think them.
He is God.

We must have determined faith in Him with absolute certitude.
He is the Great One who sees and understands before we see.
He is our God, the Pādishāh, the King of kings.

When the state of *īmān* and certitude arises
and overflows from within us,
when we truly focus on His grace,
we will see the Divine Luminous Bliss that has no pride,
the resplendence of the Most Great One,
God who is our birthright.

We must know Him and realize Him within ourselves.
We must place all our intentions within His intention
and we must know that all goodness belongs to Him.
When that state arises from within us
and overflows from the *qalb,*
we need to firmly establish that state and pray to God.

The Absolute, the Rahmān, the Most Compassionate, is One.
The One who exists in this state is God.
He is intermingled as the *Aham* within our *aham,*
as the Heart within our heart.
He is the One who dwells within Ahamad ☺.
He is absolutely intermingled with everything everywhere.
We must know that One who is free of all affliction.
There is the Light known as Ahamad ☺, and
there is His beauty known as Muhammad ☺.

Look in the mosque of *īmān,*
see how the Light of the Nūr shines and fills it.
The happiness there is God.
There is nothing other than Him.

When you realize with all your certitude
that there is no God other than illAllāhu,

knowing that He is the Pure One
who knows your words before you speak them,
that He is God without beginning or end,
that He is the One who stands before you
as the Thought within thought,
you must establish Him within your compassionate *īmān*.
You must live with justice and fairness.
You must absolutely have His qualities within you.
You must act with His qualities.

All of you who have *īmān* need to know what Islām is.
The light of the *dīn,* the path of purity, is on one side.
The reverberation of the *dhikr* is on the other side.
The *aham,* the heart, is the resplendence,
Muhammad ☽ is the *zīnah,* the beauty of the face.
The Completion that is the Nūr is the reverberation.
Within it is the explanation that wondrously understands.

When you see the nature of the Completion,
then that is the *asmā'ul-husnā,*
the ninety-nine beautiful attributes and actions of God.
For that Completion, Allāh is the only One.
The *sūrah,* the form, that appears when you stand
is Nūr-Muhammad ☽.
When the meaning is clearly known, it is *dīn.*
When the karma is absent, it is Islām.
When that is understood, it is *dīnul*-Islām.
When that is understood and known,
when that is understood and known,
it is *īmān*-Islām.
When you freely know this,
it is Sūratul-Insān-Muhammad ☽.
When this is known,
it is illAllāhu.

Then Adam ☺ is the Light there
and within him is Nūr-Muhammad ☺.
Nūr-Muhammad ☺ in *awwal,* the beginning,
will be the explanation that comes from
within the center of the forehead.
If you know this clearly, it is *gnānam,*
the Light of the eye that knows the three worlds.

That is the explanation of *gnānam.*
If you do not know, it is the *sūrah* of a *hayawān,*
the form of an animal.
If you understand, it is the state of *īmān,*
and that is the art with which to know
the commandments and the *furūd.*

The grace of God does everything with a melting heart.
May we know this fully
and understand the actions of that Most Wondrous God.
He knows our thoughts before we think them.
He realizes what we see before we see it.
He gives the truth before we know what is to be known.
He comes to us when we are in danger,
when we play and when we are in karma,
and He protects us.

Believe in that compassionate God.
Place your intention, your *īmān,* and your certitude
in the Treasure that is your birthright.
O *insān,* stay in that stable state.
Do not believe what is written on water.
The five *malā'ikah* are contained
within the form that is within the form.
If you open that form, there will be five letters.
If you know the explanation, they will become the messengers:
Ādam ☺, Jibrīl ☺, Mīkā'īl ☺, Isrāfīl ☺, and 'Izrā'īl ☺.

When you look at them closely in order to know them,
they are *malā 'ikah.*
When you look at them as the *qudrah,*
they will be His heavenly messengers.
If you know them truly,
then Munkar ⊙ and Nakīr ⊙ will be there.

If you know the meaning and pray in your *qalb,*
you will see the good and evil there
and understand them.
Your own *qalb* will become your *qabr,* your grave,
and you will know the questions contained in that *qabr.*
If you die before death,
the seven *nafs* will move seven feet away.
Once they walk seven feet away from your grave,
that will be your Day of Questioning, Reckoning, and *Qiyāmah.*
The seven feet will become seven *nafs.*
If you dissolve them,
that Day will be a Day without questions, without reckoning.

This heart is the *qabr,* the grave that is the *maut,*
the death in which you will be contained.
If you know this and open your heart,
and if you drive the seven *nafs* seven feet away,
then the state of *īmān* will speak.
It will tell you to accept the heaven of the *sūrah* of Muhammad ⊕,
to open the *qalb* that is Ahamad ⊕,
and to accept Muhammad ⊕
who is the beauty of the qualities of Allāh.
The reverberance of the Nūr will reverberate.
The grace of Nūr-Muhammad ⊕ will be minutely understood
and shine clearly there.
That expanding Light will be clearly evident there.
Our shining Rahmān will be resplendent there.
That is the fundamental *Qiyāmah.*

If you know and understand this in the grave that is your *qalb,*
then on the Day of Reckoning
you will see your Day of *Qiyāmah* there.
Then Munkar ☻ and Nakīr ☻ will be there, fully open to you.
There will be no other day for you in which to understand.

Your own *qalb* is the pit that is the grave of all graves.
You can see it as heaven if you understand.
The eight heavens are there.
The state of *īmān* arises and overflows there.
Perception, awareness, intellect, judgment, wisdom,
divine analytic wisdom, divine luminous wisdom, and *īmān*
are the eight heavens that shine there.
The Nūr shines and reverberates there.
Our Original One, Allāh, resplends there.
These eight heavens shine in the *qalb,*
once they are known within.

The *aham,* the heart, is Ahamad ☻.
The *muham,* the face, is the beauty of Allāh.
That is Muhammad ☻.
The resplendent *wahy,* revelations, of Allāh
will illumine the *qalb* as the Messenger ☻.
All of the revelations of Allāh are there.
They will be brought by the Angel Jibrīl ☻
and will resplend there.
The Ahamad ☻ and the Muhammad ☻ of the *qalb*
and all the secrets of *'ālamul-arwāh*
will come to shine there.

The reverberation of Allāh in the *ākhirah*—
all the *wahy* will gather there,
they will gather there.
They will be clearly evident and reverberate from there.

The explanations will be
the *sūrah* of Allāh,
the *wahy* of Allāh,
the reverberation of Allāh,
the explanation of Allāh,
the Qur'ān of Allāh,
the *hadīth* of Allāh,
the *dhikr* of Allāh,
the *vanakkam* of Allāh,
the *toluhai* of Allāh,
the reverberation of Allāh,
the explanation of Allāh,
the intention of Allāh,
the patience of Allāh,
the tolerance of Allāh,
the peacefulness of Allāh,
the *tawakkul* of Allāh,
the *shukūr* of Allāh,
the *sabūr* of Allāh,
the intention of Allāh,
the focus of Allāh,
the reverberation of Allāh.

All of them will be clearly evident there.
It is there that they will be radiant.

Jibrīl ☺ will bring the *wahy*.
He will be radiant there.
Everything in the heavens, the worlds, the underworlds,
all of the creations of the Almighty One
will be opened out before you,
their explanations will shine before you.
Everything in the *'ālam* and *'ālamul-arwāh* will exist
as an atom within an atom
and be contained there.

All the *sirr* and the *sifāt*,
the resplendent *dunyā*, the *ākhirah*,
and the eighteen thousand universes
will be contained within the *qalb*,
condensed within Ahamad ☉.
The beauty of that *sūrah*, that form,
will shine clearly within Muhammad ☉.
The explanation of *īmān*-Islām will shine within the Nūr.

He who knows this state,
he who stands and understands this
will be *Ummī*, the Unlettered One.
The *Ummī* that is the *īmān*,
the certitude that is the Qur'ān,
the Muhammad ☉ that is the *sūrah*,
the beauty of Muhammad ☉,
that mysteriously subtle Nūr
is the Light of the explanation.

Knowing this with the meaning
and being clear about it,
will become the state of merging
with the Lord who is beyond all imagination.
Your words and your breath will become Him.
When you open your eyes,
everything you see will become His beauty.
Your entire life, your *'ibādah*, and your *vanakkam*
will become His straight path.
All of the methods designated for that special purpose
will become the state in which you can meet Allāh.
That will become a life without Questioning, heaven.
It will be a life without Judgment
in His state of *hayāh*, completion.

The *dīn* that knows this,
the *dīn* that knows this,
the *dīn* that comes into the *dīn,*
the Dīn-Muhammad ﷺ that comes in the Light
is the *dīn* that exists as Light.
The *qalb* that dawns from Ahamad ﷺ,
the beautiful Muhammad ﷺ that dawns from within that,
and the explanation of the Light that
is the Nūr that dawns from that,
is the radiance of the *Rahmah* that reverberates as Allāh alone.
He who sees this state is Islām.
He who does not know it
is a *hayawān,* an animal.

This is the *fard,* the obligatory duty, in your *toluhai,*
your five daily prayers.
There are six *furūd* that shine inside and
five outer *furūd* that resplend as the five *malā'ikah:*
Ādam (عم), Jibrīl (عم), Mīkā'īl (عم), Isrāfīl (عم), and 'Izrā'il (عم).
They reverberate as outer worship.
They reverberate as the outer explanation.
This is the radiance that comes from the outer *furūd.*
This is the explanation of *sūratul-insān.*

Know the six subtle and mysterious *furūd.*
If you know and understand the resplendent meaning there,
then that is Islām,
īmān-Islām,
īmān-Islām.

Resplending in the Breath within breath,
shining as the Intention within intention,
reverberating as the *Qalb* within the *qalb,*
is the One who is the Wealth of Wisdom within *īmān,*
radiant in our hearts

as the blossoming flower that is Muhammad ☺.
The fragrance in that flower is the Nūr.
The Light within the Nūr is Allāh.
He alone is the Good One.
That is what exists as the Lord.
When we believe in this and know it,
it is *īmān*-Islām.

To make a connection with the method of worship
that is known as *toluhai,*
you must accept that method of worship with purity.
We must know the first *shart,* the first condition:
We need to have certitude in God
who has always resplended in the past
and will always resplend in the future.
Day and night you have to know that He is God.
You need to understand the *sirr* and the *sifāt*
that He created one after the other.
You need to establish Muhammad ☺ in your *qalb,*
as your birthright,
taking him deep into your *qalb,*
and transforming that into Ahamad ☺.
You must make that *aham,* that heart, your *qalb.*
You have to transform that into Ahamad ☺,
transform Ahamad ☺ into your *qalb,*
transform your *qalb* into *īmān,*
and make your *īmān* complete.
You need to make that Completion beautiful,
transforming it into Muhammad ☺,
transforming Muhammad ☺ into truth,
transforming truth into the Nūr,
and transforming the Completion of the Nūr into Allāh.

You need to believe in that state with firm determination.
All the *sirr* and the *sifāt* will be there.

You need to transform all the blessings
of the completely open Rahmān
into faith, determination, and certitude.
You need to know that illAllāhu,
the Almighty One who is the Pādishāh of prayer,
has no equal.
He has no support.
He has no equal.
He has no support.
He is pure.
This must be in your *qalb.*
This must be radiant in your *qalb.*
You need to place the Pure One there.
Focus your intention: there is no God other than Him.

He has no equal, no wife, no birth, no end, no destruction.
Establish the reverberation that exists as the bliss that is Allāhu.
Establish the meaning within it.
Establish the determination to know
that the state of this *shart* is *īmān*-Islām.
Focus on God:
have the faith and determination
that He exists without equal, without support,
that He is the Great One without wife, without child.
Have determined faith:
He has no form, no image,
He is not contained by anything,
He is the Fire in the Gem that has no equal,
He is everywhere,
He is God, the Ultimate Unique One,
He is Allāhu.

He is Allāhu, the Pādishāh of both worlds.
Engrave this for all eternity in your heart:
He is the Lord of *Qudrah,* the Lord of Power,

the Creator, the Protector, the One who feeds us,
the One who lives in the truth,
God—without beginning, without end,
the Pure One, the Perfect One,
the One who gives the Judgment,
the One who asks the questions on the Day of *Qiyāmah,*
the One who destroys, the One who creates.
He is Allāhu.

Establish this state of determined *īmān* with love.
Make your *īmān* determined
with the Determination within determination.
Make your *īmān* sure that there is no one other than Allāh.
When you establish this state with love, with determination,
when you establish *īmān*
with the Determination within determination,
when you worship Allāh like this without equal,
then that will be the prayer that worships the Pure One
with knowledge of the *shart* of *toluhai.*

On the correct path, place Him on His *takht,* His throne.
Establish faith and determination in your *qalb* to make it His *takht.*
He is the Creator, the Protector,
the One who feeds all of creation,
the Pādishāh of everything in the *'ālam* and *'ālamul-arwāh.*
There is no God other than Him.
He is the Pure One without any support.
He is the Watcher,
the One who knows the *qalb,*
the One who knows the meaning,
the One who knows the eyes.
He is the One who shines and understands everything
in the microcosm and the macrocosm.
He is Ādi Nāyan, the Lord of the Beginning.
In order to make your *īmān* strong,

you must understand the *shart* of how to worship Him,
with certitude and determination.

Awake at *awwal fajr*.
Awake with *adab*, with good conduct.
Focus your intention and place it with His intention,
giving all your intentions and aspirations to Him.
In sleep, in wakefulness,
in happiness, in sadness,
have *tawakkul*, trust in Him.
Keep His qualities and His intention in your heart,
in the *qalb* itself.
No matter the problem, the sadness, the happiness,
the illness, the poverty, or the difficulty,
place your *tawakkul* in Allāh and
awake at *awwal fajr*.

Perform the *wudū'*, the ablution.
As you walk towards the mosque,
say *lā ilāha illAllāhu* with the reverberation of His intention.
With the explanation of the *salawāt*,
walk believing in the One God.
Go to the mosque.
Go to perform the *fard* of *wudū'*.
Perform the twelve *furūd* of *wudū'*.
Do it properly with *tartīb*, in order,
placing your unwavering intention upon Him.
When you make your intention to
perform the *wudū'*,
stand in the form of your Lord.
When you perform the *furūd* of the *wudū'*,
transform yourself truly into Muhammad ⊕
and dedicate your intention to Allāh,
with the *'ibādah* of the Divine Messenger of our Lord.

When you stand and pray behind Muhammad ☻,
the *'ibādah* belonging to that prayer
becomes the Shaikh, the Ustādh, our Imām al-Mustafā.
The leader of your religion,
the king of your religion,
the explanation and the Light of your religion
is the *sūrah* of Nūr-Muhammad ☻.
As the Light, as *īmān*-Islām,
place Muhammadur-Rasūlullāh ☻ in front of you,
so your eyes can see him,
so your *qalb* can see him,
so your eyes can see him,
so your *īmān* can see him,
so your heart can see him.
Place Muhammadur-Rasūl ☻ in front of you for *'ibādah*.
Place Muhammad ☻ in front of you for the meaning.
This is the *fard* of *wudū'*.
Do this correctly.
Establish your intention, focus your attention,
and stand behind the good Nabī ☻.

Pray two *rak'ahs* in the mosque perfectly.
After that, do the two *rak'ahs* of the *qunūt* prayer perfectly,
with certitude, determination, and faith in Khudā.
This is the exalted obligation.
Do the *fajr* prayer perfectly in an exalted way.
Then recite the *dhikr* and the *salawāt*.
With God's qualities, do *dhikr* to Allāh and stay with that intention.
Place your intention and focus upon the *'ibādah*,
upon the Pādishāh to whom worship belongs,
the Almighty One, illAllāhu, God.
Place your focus and your intention and pray a good *toluhai*.
Stand at the *waqt* of *subh*.
Stand as *wudū'* with the *wudū'*,
stand up and pray the two *rak'ahs* that are *sunnah*.

As the meaning with the meaning,
pray the two *rak'ahs* that are *fard*.
Before you see the sun rise
keep reverberating with the *salawāt* and the *dhikr*.
Finish your *toluhai* with understanding.
In the most correct way
keep your intention and focus there.

In our eyes and our *qalb*,
in our *īmān*,
in our eyesight,
Muhammad ⊕ has to stand before us as our Imām.
To understand and see this in your eyes and in your *qalb*,
you must see the Rasūl ⊕ of Allāh.
You must pray seeing him.
You have to pray with that objective
to the Pādishāh to whom all prayer belongs, illAllāhu, Allāh.
When you see Muhammad ⊕ and pray,
you will see Allāh who is the Rahmatul-'ālamīn in front of you.
If you see Muhammad ⊕, you will see Allāh.
You will know the beauty of Allāh.
You will know His Light.
This state of tenderness becomes prayer.
This becomes the connection to *toluhai* and *'ibādah*.
This state becomes the *'ibādah* and *vanakkam* of the Pure One,
the intention.
Those who pray with purity like this
belong to the purity of *īmān*-Islām.
O you who have been born with me,
know this and stand in prayer.
This is the state of true prayer.

To know the *shart* and the *fard* of the Pure One,
you must establish this prayer,
and remain there

until that *waqt* is over.
Stay there at that specific time and place until eight o'clock.
Stay there until eight o'clock,
and then again perform the *wudū'* with the *wudū'*,
according to the *fard*.

After performing the *wudū'*,
according to the *shart* with the *shart*,
after the sun has risen higher,
you must again pray another radiant prayer.
Stay there, praying until ten o'clock with the meaning.
Do the *salawāt* and the *dhikr*
with that intention and reverberation.
After you pray clearly and with understanding,
perform the part that is
the *salawāt*, the reverberation, and the *dhikr*.
Perform thirty-three *dhikrs* and the *salawāt*,
performing *sajdah* to Allāh each time.
Place Muhammad ☮ in front of you
when you do *sajdah*.
Do one hundred and one *sajdahs*.

Do *wudū'* at twelve in a way that is *tartīb*
when the *waqt* of *zuhr* arrives.
After that, pray the *waqt* of *zuhr*.
Pray the four *sunnah*, the four *fard*, and the four *sunnah*.
Pray with clear understanding.
Pray correctly according to the *fard*.
Recite with excellent qualities,
the part that is the *dhikr* and the *salawāt*
keeping Muhammad ☮ in front of you.
See Muhammad ☮ in each *sajdah*.

When you establish the correct state for
your *qalb*, your thoughts, your *īmān*, your eyes, and your eyesight,

Muhammad ☧ must stand before you as Light.
When you stand in this state,
Allāh and the Rahmatul-'ālamīn will stand before you.
In the prayer that is your *toluhai, vanakkam,* and *'ibādah,*
you will see Allāh, you will see Muhammad ☧.
The prayer that you pray in this way is the key to your *qalb.*
This is the key to *īmān.*
This is the explanation of *īmān*-Islam.
The prayer in which you see the Rasūl ☧ of Allāh
is *toluhai* and *'ibādah.*
When that *toluhai* is completed in the correct way,
you will remain in this state of *Toluhai* with *toluhai.*
When you finish that prayer,
after the reverberation of
the *salāms* and the *salawāt,* the *dhikr,* and the *sajdah,*
after you do a *sajdah* for each of the thirty-three,
and a *sajdah* for the hundredth,
after you do the one hundred and one *sajdahs,*
the *waqt* of *zuhr* will be over,
and it will be time for the *waqt* of *'asr.*

Then you must perform the *fard* for *'asr*
in a way that is *tartīb.*
You must correctly perform the twelve *furūd* for the *wudū'*
in a way that is *tartīb.*
When you do that you need to fill your heart
with the Light of Allāh and Muhammad ☧.
Establish your *qalb* there,
focus upon Him,
have firm faith in Him
and continue to pray.

While you stand there with understanding,
place the Jeweled Light of Our Eyes,
the Nabī ☧ who is the Messenger of God,

before you as your Imām.
Look at him and exist as Light.
Do the four *sunnah*, the four *fard*, and the four *sunnah*—
the twelve *rak'ahs*.
Stand behind Muhammad ☙.
Pray, worship God,
perform your *'ibādah* there in this way.
Do the twelve *rak'ahs* of the *waqt* of *'asr*.
Pray this *waqt* and after that recite the *dhikr* and the *salawāt*.
Recite them, stay there, recite them
and then perform the *waqt* of *maghrib*.
Two *sunnah*, two *nafl*, and three *fard*.
Pray the seven *rak'ahs*.
After that do the *salawāt* and the *dhikr*.
Place your intention on Allāh,
establish that state.
Stand behind Muhammad ☙,
and then do the seventeen *rak'ahs* of *'ishā'*.
Complete them in that *waqt*.

Only if you act in this way,
only if you follow the Rasūl ☙ and
perform the *toluhai* and the *'ibādah* behind him,
will that be a prayer and a *toluhai*
in which you will see Allāh.

In the *fard* of *wudū'*
you must forget everything other than Allāh.
You must forget yourself,
you must forget the *dunyā*,
and see Muhammad ☙ and his beauty.
That is *wudū'*.
Place your *qalb*, your eyes,
your aspirations, your focus, and your intention
all in the *tawakkul* of Allāh.

Stand behind the Rasūl ☺ of Allāh.
Performing that *toluhai* is *Toluhai*.
That will be worship of the Pure One.
Then Allāh will be the Pādishāh for that prayer
and that prayer will be loved by Allāh.

If you follow the Mighty Nabī,
that will be worship that is not wasted.
That will grant you the blessing of the Rahmān
who is the King of Ma'shar, the Assembly at Judgment Day.
The kingdom of His grace will belong to you,
and the intention, the focus, and the Completion
of the Almighty One who knows everything will belong to you.
You can obtain the blessing of your Lord.

If you do not know that state,
if you do not realize that state now,
if you do not know this *fard,*
and if you pray,
then all of your intentions,
all of your intentions,
all of your aspirations
will be known to Allāh who is One,
and you will be subject to the questioning tomorrow.
You will be subject to questioning
on the Day of Judgment, the Day of *Qiyāmah.*
You will know that this decision was made on that Day
and then you will receive the profit and the loss
on that Day of Judgment.
Where will you be?
You will be in hell.
You will have looked for hell.
You will receive there everything you have gathered here.

But if you are in heaven here,
if you see the Rasūl ﷺ of Allāh here,
if you see him and perform your *'ibādah*—
hell will be far away from those who
have seen the Rasūl ﷺ of Allāh.
If you pray standing behind the Rasūl ﷺ of Allāh
in every *sajdah,* in every prayer,
hell will be far away from you
and it will be heaven wherever you are.

If you know the truth of the Pure One,
if you know the reverberation of radiant Islām,
if you know the *furūd* of *īmān*-Islām,
if you know the *toluhai,* the *'ibādah,* and the *vanakkam,*
if you pray knowing how to pray to the Pure One,
then that is *dīnul*-Islām,
that is *īmān*-Islām.

If you realize the meaning of *īmān*-Islām,
if you know and then perform your *'ibādah,*
what hell will you have,
what Day of Judgment,
what Day of Questioning?
On the day that you see
the One who is the Kingdom of Grace,
you will have heaven,
the grace and the beauty of the Pure One,
His *zīnah* and His form.
That will become the Completion.

If you know this *dīn* and act accordingly,
performing *'ibādah* only to Allāh,
it will be good.

Āmīn. Āmīn. Yā Rabbal-'ālamīn.

GLOSSARY

The following traditional supplications in Arabic are used throughout the text:

- ﷺ *sallallāhu 'alaihi wa sallam,* may the blessings and peace of Allāh be upon him, is used following the Prophet Muhammad, the Rasūlullāh, the Messenger of Allāh.

- ﷽ *'alaihis-salām,* peace be upon him, is used following the name of a prophet, wives of the prophets, or an angel.

- ﷺ *radiyallāhu 'anhu* or *'anhā,* may Allāh be pleased with him or her, is used following the name of a companion of the Prophet Muhammad ﷺ, Qutbs, and exalted saints.

(A) Indicates an Arabic word
(T) Indicates a Tamil word
(S) Indicates a Sanskrit word
(P) Indicates a Persian word
(H) Indicates a Hebrew word

Note: Tamil and Arabic words that have become common usage in the English language are not italicized. Also, proper names have not been italicized. For simplicity's sake, we have most often used the English "s" for the plural form of foreign words.

The Footnotes and Glossary have been assembled by the editors. Wherever possible explanations and definitions have come directly from Bawa Muhaiyaddeen ﷺ.

419

PRONUNCIATION KEY

The non-Arabic and non-Tamil reader of this book will encounter unfamiliar words and names. We have tried to make them as simple as possible to pronounce.

While there are standard ways of transliterating Arabic letters into Roman script, there is no standard system of transliterating Tamil. Thus, we have not adopted any system in its entirety, but are indebted to many.

We have simplified the consonants — for the typical English speaking person, it would not be particularly helpful to distinguish between the two types of s or h or t in Arabic or the two types of t, the three types of n or l in Tamil.

- gn is pronounced like the n in the Spanish word *mañana*.
- k has been variously transliterated as k or j or g, depending on whether it has a hard, medium, or soft sound.
- th (a confusing and inconsistently applied legacy transliteration that has come down from the German) has been simplified throughout as t or d, depending on sound.

We have adopted the phonetic spelling of words, such as *mee-cham* and *shari,* that we have incorporated into common usage in Philadelphia.

Both Arabic and Tamil have long and short vowels: the long vowels have been indicated by long marks in most cases. Thus, in Arabic and Tamil,

- a is pronounced as in agree,
- ā is pronounced as a long ā in father;[1]
- i is pronounced as in pin,
- ī is pronounced as a long ī as in pique;
- u as in pull,
- ū as a long ū in rule;
- o is pronounced as in opaque,

---

1 In Arabic the long ā is generally pronounced with a flatter vowel sound, more like man than father, except after "r" and six emphatic consonants.

 ō is pronounced as a long ō in ore;

 e is pronounced as in end,

 ē is as a long ē in they;

 ai is pronounced as in aisle except at the end of a word, where it is generally pronounced as in day.[2]

Any good transliteration system needs to be logically consistent. However, the idiosyncrasies of both languages must be considered; a few well-placed exceptions serve to clarify a sound that would otherwise be mangled. For instance, *nāi* (dog—pronounced as in high) could not be spelled *nāy* without causing confusion, even though that is what the Tamil spelling would seem to indicate.

A

'abd (A) Slave, servant; slave of God.

adab (A) Good manners, decency, humaneness, culture.

ādavan (T) Sun.

aday (T) An exclamation; "hey!"

'adhāb (A) Punishment; suffering, the torment of hell.

adhān (A) The call to prayer for the five-times prayer in Islām.

adi (T) A term used in addressing women in a familiar manner.

ādi (T) Primal beginning, the source, the origin. The period after *anādi,* the time when the Qutb ☺ and the Nūr manifested within Allāh; the time of the dawning of the Light; the world of grace where the unmanifested begins to manifest in the form of resonance. In contrast to the *awwal,* when the creations became manifest in form, *ādi* is the time when the first sound or vibration emerged.

Ādi (T) God, the Primal One.

---

2 However, in Arabic the *ai* is pronounced as the *ay* in day, except after "r" and six emphatic consonants when it is pronounced like the *ai* in aisle.

Ādi-Muhammad ⊕ (A) The Manifested; one of the nine names of Muhammad ⊕.

Ādi Nāyan (T) The Lord of the Beginning.

Ādi Param Porul (T) God, the Supreme Being.

Ādi Pidā (T) God, the Original Father.

Ādi Rahmān (T & A) God, the Most Compassionate.

agnānam (T) Ignorance.

ahad (A) One, absolute oneness, unity.

āhadīth (singular, *hadīth*) (A) The reported sayings and actions of the Rasūlullāh ⊕; words of wisdom.

aham (T) Heart.

ahamad (A & T) The beauty of the heart brings about the beauty of the countenance (*muham,* T) of Muhammad ⊕. That beauty is the beauty of Allāh's qualities. This is a name that comes from within the *bahrul-'ilm,* the ocean of divine knowledge. Allāh is the One who is worthy of the praise of the heart. Spelled in Arabic *ahmad;* literally, more praised.

Ahamad ⊕ (A & T) The *qalb,* the heart; one of the nine names of Muhammad ⊕.

aiyō (T) Oh; oh no.

al-ākhirah (A) The kingdom of God. Literally, that which exists after an appointed time, the hereafter, the last day.

'ālam (A) World, universe.

'ālamul-ajsām (A) The world of forms.

'ālamul-arwāh (A) The world of souls.

al-hamd, al-hamdu (A) The praise, praise to God.

al-hamdu lillāh (A) All praise is to Allāh. Allāh is the glory and greatness that deserves all praise.

alif (A) The first letter of the Arabic alphabet, equivalent to the English letter "a" and to the Arabic numeral "1," which stands, within the realm of wisdom, for Allāh, the One who stands alone.

al-'Alīm (A) God, the Omniscient, the All-Knowing.

'ālim (A) A person learned in religion.

Allāh, Allāhu (A) God.

Allāh-Muhammad ⊕ (A) Allāh is within Muhammad ⊕ and Muhammad ⊕ is within Allāh. The Light known as Muhammad ⊕ is within Allāh and the Light known as Allāh is within Muhammad ⊕. One of the nine names of Muhammad ⊕.

Allāhu akbar (A) God is greater.

Allāhu Qādirīn (A) God who is the Power.

Allāhu ta'ālā, Allāhu ta'ālā Nāyan (A & T) God, the Exalted, is the Ruler. Allāhu: the beautiful, undiminishing One; ta'ālā: the One who exists in all lives in a state of humility and exaltedness; Nāyan: the Ruler who protects and sustains.

al-lauhul-mahfūz (A) The preserved tablet upon which everything has been written. It is said that when one becomes *hāfiz,* when he has truly assimilated the Holy Qur'ān, his tongue becomes *al-lauhul-mahfūz.* Literally, the guarded tablet.

amānah (A) Trust property; a trust; the treasure given in trust by God to man which must be returned to God in full.

amāvāsi (T) Darkness, torpor; the twenty-eighth letter of the house of the body; the new moon.

ambiyā' (singular, *nabī*) (A) Prophets of God.

āmīn (A) May it be so.

anādi (T) The beginningless beginning; the state of darkness before creation; the state in which God meditated upon Himself alone; the period of pre-creation when Allāh was alone and unmanifest, unaware of Himself even though everything was within Him; the state before *ādi;* the state of unmanifestation.

Anādi-Muhammad ⊕ (A) The Unmanifested; one of the nine names of Muhammad ⊕.

'anāsir (A) Elements; as used here, the five elements or states of matter.

aṅbu (T) Love.

Āndava, Āndavan (T) God; God who is One.

Āndavanai (T) O God!

āṇmā (T) Soul, life.

Annam-Muhammad ☉ (A) The food for the *rūh* and for all creations; one of the nine names of Muhammad ☉.

arivu (T) Wisdom, subtle wisdom; the fifth of the seven levels of wisdom.

'arsh (A) The throne of God.

'arshul-mu'min (A) The throne of the true believer.

arul-maunam (T) The ultimate silence of grace.

ash-hadu al-lā ilāha illAllāhu, wa ash-hadu anna Muhammadar-Rasūlullāh. I testify that none is God except Allāh, and I testify that Muhammad is the Messenger of Allāh.

'asr (A) The late afternoon prayer; the third of the five-times prayer of Islām.

as-salāmu 'alaikum (A) May the peace of God be upon you.

as-salāmu 'alaikum wa rahmatullāhi wa barakātuhu (A) May the peace, the beneficence, and the blessings of God be upon you.

astaghfirullāhal-'aliyyal-'azīm (A) I beg forgiveness of Allāh, the Exalted, the Supreme.

athe shari (T) That is okay, that is right, very well.

at-tahiyyāt (A) "*At-tahiyyātu lillāhi was-salawātu wat-tayyibāt:* the divine greetings, the blessings, and the pure things belong to Allāh." This is a short phrase that is said while in the sitting position during *salāh*.

a'ūdhu billāhi minash-shaitānir-rajīm (A) I seek refuge in God from the accursed satan.

auliyā' (A) Saints, those beloved of God, those who are near God, guides.

āvi (T) Breath, exhalation; vapor; spirit.

al-awwal (A) The beginning; the stage in which forms begin to manifest. Literally, the first.

awwal fajr (A) The early morning prayer prayed before *subh* which is the first of the five-times prayer. Usually used to refer to *ash-shafʿī wal-witr* prayer.

Awwal-Muhammad ☺ (A) The beginning; the emergence of creation; one of the nine names of Muhammad ☺.

āyāt (*āyah,* singular) (A) Verses of the Qurʾān; signs or miracles.

B

bāʾ (A) The second letter in the Arabic alphabet corresponding to the English consonant "b."

badda (A) Father of dajjāl, the antichrist.

bahr (A) Ocean.

bahrul-ʿilm (A) The ocean of divine knowledge.

bakti (T) Devotion.

Banū Isrāʾīl (A) The children of Israel. Prophet Jacob ☺ was called Israel ☺ after he wrestled with the Angel of Death. Prophet Jacob's ☺ descendants are known as the children of Israel, the Jews.

barakāt (A) Blessings; the wealth of Allāh's grace.

bātil (A) Useless; wasted, ineffective, fruitless, nullified; worship not carried out in accordance with its conditions.

Bismillāhir-Rahmānir-Rahīm (A) In the name of Allāh, the Most Compassionate, the Most Merciful.

Buddha-*dharma* (S) The teaching of the Buddha.

Budddham saranam gacchāmi. Dharman saranam gacchāmi. Sangham saranam gacchāmi (S) A Buddhist chant: I take refuge in the wisdom of Buddha. I take refuge in the ultimate truth. I take refuge in that which is good.

D

dajjāl (A) The antichrist, satan, jahīl.

Dastagir (P) Divine Helper. The title Dastagir often refers to Muhyid-dīn 'Abdul-Qādir al-Jīlānī ☺. Depending on the context, it may also be a title for Allāh or Prophet Muhammad ☺. Literally, helping hand.

daulah (A) Wealth, the wealth of the grace of Allāh. The wealth of Allāh is the wealth of *'ilm,* divine knowledge, and the wealth of perfect *īmān.* Literally, good fortune, or change of fortune from bad to good; also power, state, empire.

Dēva (T) God.

dēva (T) A heavenly being.

dharma (S) Literally, justice, law, charity, prescribed duties.

dhāt (A) The essence of Allāh, His treasury, His wealth of purity, His grace.

dhikr (A) The remembrance of God. Of the many *dhikrs,* the most exalted *dhikr* is "*Lā ilāha illAllāhu:* There is nothing other than You, O God. Only You are Allāh." All *dhikrs* relate to His *wilāyāt* or His actions, but this *dhikr* points to Him and to Him alone.

dīn (A) The path of absolute purity; Islām. Literally, religion, faith, path.

Dīn-Muhammad ☺ (A) Muhammad's ☺ path of perfect purity.

dīnul-Islām (A) The path of perfect purity; the resplendence of absolute certitude of *īmān.* This explanation is supported by what Allāh said in *Sūratur-Rūm,* a. 30, 31: "So set your true countenance towards the *dīn* inclining away [from all else], the *dīn* being the nature of Allāh upon which He has shaped mankind. There is no change to the nature of Allāh! That is the pure, straight *dīn,* but most of mankind does not know. And be of those who are repenting to Him. And guard your morality before Him and establish the daily prayers *(salāh)* and do not be of those who worship other than Him." Literally, the religious path of complete submission to the will of Allāh.

du'ā' (A) A prayer of supplication to God.

dunyā (A) The world; the earth-world in which we live; the world of physical existence; the darkness which separated from Allāh at the time when the Light of the Nūr-Muhammad ☺ manifested from within Allāh.

E

elam pun (T) Young wife.

F

fard (A) Prescribed duty; obligatory prayers.

Fātihah (A) The *Sūratul-Fātihah,* the first *sūrah* of the Holy Qur'ān. Literally, to open out.

fikr (A) Constant contemplation and immersion in Allāh.

firdaus (A) Paradise.

al-furqān (A) Islām. This is the fourth step of spiritual ascendance, the teachings revealed to Moses ☺ and Muhammad ☺. When asked, Bawa Muhaiyaddeen ☺ included Judaism in this step, explaining that these two religions are like two brothers descending from one father, Abraham ☺.

In the body of man, *al-furqān* corresponds to the head. Literally, *al-furqān* is the criterion which distinguishes between good and evil, right and wrong, lawful and unlawful, truth and illusion.

furūd (singular, *fard*) (A) Obligatory duties. The five *furūd* refer to the five pillars of Islām: declaring absolute faith in God with the *shahādah, salāh, zakāh,* or the annual charity, fasting the month of Ramadān, and *hajj.*

G

ganja (*ganjā,* S) A selected preparation of marijuana.

gnāna arivu (T) The wisdom of *'ilm.*

gnāna kan (T) The eye of wisdom.

gnānam (T) Divine wisdom, divine luminous wisdom, grace-awakened wisdom.

gnāna-maunam (T) The ultimate silence of divine wisdom.

gnāna-tavam (T) The ultimate austerity of divine wisdom.

gnāni (T) A wise man, a man of divine wisdom; one who has *gnānam,* or divine wisdom; one who has received the qualities and wisdom of God by surrendering to God, and having received these, lives in a state of peace where he sees all lives as equal; one who has attained the state of peace.

Guru (T) The true Shaikh; the Teacher who awakens the truth within the disciple; the Guide who takes the disciples to the shore of the heart.

guru (T) Teacher.

H

hadīth (plural, *ahādīth*) (A) Reported words and deeds of the Prophet Muhammad ⊜; words of wisdom; a discourse of wisdom; a story.

hādiyah (A) Gift, present.

hajj (A) The holy pilgrimage to Mecca, the fifth prescribed duty in Islām.

hāl (A) State; a transient state or condition.

halāl (A) Permissible; those things that are permissible or lawful according to the commands of God and which conform to the word of God.

Hanal (T) The religion of Zoroastrianism or Fire Worship; *al-jabbūrat.*

haqīqah (A) The third step of spiritual ascendance. Literally, truth, reality.

al-Haqq (A) God, the Truth, the Reality.

haqq (A) Truth, ultimate reality, justice; the wealth within each heart; man's possession, God.

harām (A) Impermissible; forbidden; that which does not conform to the commands of God or to the word of God.

hayāh (A) Life; the plenitude of life that is eternal.

Hayāt-Muhammad ☉ (A) The emergence of the soul; one of the nine names of Muhammad ☉.

hayawān (A) Animal.

himmah (A) Resolve, determination, will; high aspirations for the sake of Allāh.

houris (*hūr,* A) Celestial maidens who dwell in paradise. The beautiful divine qualities that a person displays during his worldly life become the eternal youths that serve him or her in paradise.

I

'ibādah (A) Worship, service to God.

iblīs (A) Satan; the one with degenerate qualities.

illAllāh (A) You are Allāh. Literally, if not, or except Allāh.

'ilm (A) Divine knowledge.

imām (A) Leader of prayer; the leader of the congregation; one who conducts the *salāh,* the five-times daily prayers of Islām.

īmān (A) Absolute and unshakable faith that God alone exists; the complete acceptance by the heart that God is One; faith, certitude, and determination.

īmān-Islām (A) Perfect certitude and purity of faith in Allāh; the state of the spotlessly pure heart which contains Allāh's Holy Qur'ān, His divine radiance, His divine wisdom, His truth, His prophets, His angels, and His laws. When the resplendence of Allāh is seen as the Completeness within this pure heart of man, that is *īmān*-Islām. When the complete, unshakable faith of this pure heart is directed towards the One who is Completeness and is made to merge with that One, when that heart trusts only in Him and worships only Him, accepting Him as the only perfection and the only One worthy of worship—that is *īmān*-Islām.

al-injīl (A) Christianity, the third step of spiritual ascendance. In the body of man, this relates to the region of the heart.

insān (A) Man, a human being.

Insān Kāmil (A) A perfected human being; one who has realized Allāh as his only wealth, cutting away the wealth of the world and the wealth sought by the mind; one who has acquired God's qualities, performs his own actions accordingly, and immerses himself within those qualities; one in whom everything other than Allāh has been extinguished.

Insān-Muhammad ☺ (A) Prophet Muhammad ☺.

'ishā' (A) The evening prayer, which is offered after darkness has fallen; the fifth of the five-times prayer of Islām.

Islām (A) Purity; unity; the state of total and unconditional surrender to the will of God; the state of absolute purity; to accept the commands of God and His qualities and actions and to establish that state of purity within oneself, worshipping Him alone.

J

al-jabbūrat (P) The religion of Fire Worship or Zoroastrianism, the second step of spiritual ascendance. In the body of man, this relates to hunger, disease, and old age, corresponding to the area of the stomach, the element fire, and the Angel Israel ☺. Literally, power.

jaddah (A) Mother of dajjāl, the antichrist.

jahannam (A) Hell.

jāhil (A) Satan, the one who has gone astray; evil qualities. Literally, ignorant, unrestrained.

jāmi'ah (A) Congregation.

jib, jib (A) To stand in straight, parallel rows.

jinn (A) A being created of fire.

jubbah (A) A robe or gown. For women, this is usually called an *abaya*.

jum'ah (A) The special Friday midday prayer performed in congregation.

juz'ul-Qur'ān (A) A portion equal to 1/30th of the Qur'ān.

K

Ka'bah, *ka'bah* (A) The place in the grand Mosque of Mecca where the earlier prophets and the Final Prophet, Muhammad ☺, gathered together in prayer. On the path of *sharī'ah,* one of the five obligations is the *hajj,* the holy pilgrimage, to the Ka'bah.

The *ka'bah* is the place where *insān,* the human being, meets Allāh face to face. Whoever brings his heart to that state of perfection and prays to God from that heart will be praying inside the *ka'bah.*

al-Kabīr (A) God, the Great, the Vast.

Kadavul (T) God.

kalai, kalai gnānam (T) The sixty-four arts and sciences.

kalimah (A) *Kalimah* is used by M. R. Bawa Muhaiyaddeen ☺ to refer to several different phrases. In most contexts it either is the statement, *lā ilāha illAllāh, Muhammadur-Rasūlullāh,* or the *dhikr, lā ilāha illAllāh.* If twenty-four letters are mentioned, it is the former. However, it may also refer to the *dhikr* used by specific prophets, or to a series of statements Bawa Muhaiyaddeen ☺ referred to as the five *kalimahs,* which include the *shahādah.* Literally, a word, phrase, or short sentence.

Kamil Shaikh (A) The perfect spiritual guide; the true teacher; the one who, knowing himself and God, guides others on the straight path to Allāh.

al-Karīm (A) God, the Most Generous; the Noble; the Kind.

karma (T) The inherited qualities formed at the time of conception; the qualities of the essences of the five elements; the qualities of mind and desire.

khair (A) That which is right or good; that which is acceptable to wisdom and to Allāh, as opposed to *sharr,* that which is evil or bad.

khair khairāt (A) Charity, generosity. Literally, the best of good deeds.

khalas (T) Finished.

Khatm (A) Recitation of the entire Qur'ān. Literally, seal.

Khudā (P) God.

khutbah (A) The sermon given by the *imām* of the mosque before the Friday *jum'ah* prayer in Islām.

kufi (A) Cap worn by Muslims.

kufr (A) The qualities that have no belief in God; ingratitude; rejection of belief in God.

kunjam (T) A little, a small quantity, a bit.

kursī (A) Allāh's chair or throne. In Sufism, Allāh's seat in the forehead between the eyes; the eye of wisdom between the physical eyes in the center of the forehead.

kutti shaitān (T & A) A small, young devil.

L

lahannam: The accursed hell. This may be a combination of the Arabic words, *jahannam,* hell, and *la'nah,* accursed.

lā ilāha (A) Other than God nothing exists; in Tamil: *unnay tavira vēr illay:* There is nothing other than You.

lā ilāha illAllāh, Muhammadur-Rasūlullāh (A) None is God except Allāh, and Muhammad is the Messenger of Allāh.

lā ilāha illAllāhu (A) There is nothing other than You, O God. Only You are God. There are two aspects. *Lā ilāha* is the manifestation of the *sifāt,* creation. *IllAllāhu* is the *dhāt,* essence. All that has appeared, all creation, belongs to *lā ilāha.* The One who created all that, His name is *illAllāhu.* To accept this with certitude, to strengthen one's *īmān* or absolute faith, and to affirm this *kalimah* is the state of Islām. Literally, none is God except Allāh.

Lailatul-Qadr (A) The Night of Power or Destiny. *Lailatul-Qadr* is the night the entire Qur'ān was revealed to Prophet Muhammad ☉.

lām (A) A letter in the Arabic alphabet, corresponding to the English consonant "l," which stands, within the realm of wisdom for the Nūr, the Light, the Light of wisdom.

al-Latīf (A) God, the Most Subtle and the Most Gracious; the Kind; the Gentle.

lebbe (T) One who recites the call to prayer in a mosque and performs various other duties there.

līlai, līlai vinotham (T) The sixty-four sexual games.

M

mādargal (T) Females.

madi (T) Judgment, assessment, estimate; the fourth of the seven levels of wisdom.

maghrib (A) The prayer soon after sunset; the fourth *waqt* of the five-times prayer in Islām.

mahan (T) Son.

malā'ikah (A) Archangels. Literally, angels.

malak (A) Angel.

Mankumbān: The site of the Mosque built in Sri Lanka by M. R. Bawa Muhaiyaddeen ☉, completed in February 1975.

mantra (*manttiram,* S) An incantation of a magic word or a set of words; sounds imbued with the energy of the five elements.

ma'rifah (A) *Al-furqān,* Islām; the fourth step of spiritual ascendance. Literally, gnosis; knowledge of God.

ma'shar (A) Assembly; the Assembly at Judgment Day.

mas-hun (A) Wiping the entire head during ablution.

maunam (T) Silence.

maut (A) Death.

maya (*māyā,* S) Illusion; the unreality of the manifest world of form; the glitters seen in the darkness of illusion; the 105 million rebirths. Maya is an energy, a shakti that assumes various forms and shapes, causes man to forfeit his wisdom, and confuses and hypnotizes him into a state of delusion. It can take many, many millions of hypnotic forms, and although he "sees" those forms, he will never catch them. Whenever man tries to grasp one of these forms with his intellect, it will elude him by taking yet another form.

maya shaktis (T) Forces of illusion.

mayyit (A) Corpse.

meecham nallam (T) Very good.

meignānam (T) True wisdom; wisdom of God; wisdom of the Nūr.

mīm (A) A letter in the Arabic alphabet, corresponding to the English consonant "m," which represents Muhammad ﷺ, and the fact that nothing could have been created without him.

minnal (T) Lightning.

mi'rāj (A) The ascension through the heavens during the night journey of Prophet Muhammad ﷺ when he went to meet with Allāh. The name of the night journey is the *Isra',* and *Al-Isra'* is the name of the seventeenth chapter of the Qur'ān that begins with its description. Literally, an ascent.

miskīn (A) Poor person, pauper, needy, impoverished.

mīzān tirāsu (A & T) Balance scale; justice; the scale that weighs good and evil.

mu'adhdhin (A) One who recites the call to prayer in a mosque, and performs various other duties there.

mubārakāt (T & A) The supreme, imperishable treasure for all three worlds, *al-awwal, ad-dunyā,* and *al-ākhirah.* Allāh's wealth is the wealth of the soul, of wisdom, and of His grace, which is the resplendent wisdom of the Nūr. *Mu* is a Tamil prefix meaning three; *barakāt* (A) means blessings.

mūdēvi (T) The Hindu goddess of misfortune and suffering. She resides in all places that are unclean and represents falsehood, darkness, and what is wrong.

Muhaiyaddeen ☺ (A) A name given to the Qutb ☺, the being who brings the divine explanation; the one who gives the clear light of wisdom and the clarity of *īmān* to the heart of man. Literally, the giver of life to the true belief.

muham (T) Face, countenance.

Muhammad ☺ (A) Muhammad ☺, the Messenger of God, the last of the line of prophets; the beauty of the Light of Allāh's essence present in the heart and reflected in the face.

Muhammad Mustāfār-Rasūl ☺ (A) Prophet Muhammad, the Chosen Messenger of God ☺.

mu'min (A) True believer.

murīd (A) Disciple.

Murugan (T) A Hindu god.

mushrik (A) An idolater; one who practices *shirk,* worship of something along with Allāh.

al-Mustafā (A) The Chosen One. The Prophet Muhammad ☺ is often referred to by this title of honor.

N

nabī (plural, *ambiyā'*) (A) Prophet.

Nabī Peruman Mustāfār-Rasūl ☺ (A) The Noble Prophet ☺, the Chosen Messenger of God.

nafl (A) Optional supererogatory prayers in Islām.

nafs, nafs ammārah (A) The seven kinds of desires; that is, desires meant to satisfy one's own pleasure and need for comfort. Literally, person, spirit, personality; inclination or desire which goads or incites one towards evil.

nafsāniyyat (A) Delusion arising from the darkness of maya; the desires and aspirations of the lower self that cause evil actions.

nānam, madam, atcham, and *payirppu* (T) The four virtuous qualities of modesty, reserve, shyness, and fear of wrongdoing.

nasīb (A) Fate, destiny.

nastaʿīn (A) We seek Allāh's help alone.

niravarati (S) One who is blameless; one without sin; one without fault.

nirvāna (S) To be in a blameless state; to have no attachment to anything that has fault. In Buddhist and Hindu teaching, *nirvāna* is the highest state that one can attain, a state of enlightenment.

niyyah (A) Intention.

no-anbu (T) No love.

nōnbu (T) Fasting.

nūn (A) A letter of the Arabic alphabet, corresponding to the letter "n."

nuparivu (T) Subtle wisdom; the fourth of the seven levels of wisdom.

nuqtah (plural, *nuqat*) (A) A dot; a dot placed over or under certain Arabic letters to differentiate one from another.

Nūr (A) Light; the resplendence of Allāh; the plenitude of the Light of Allāh that has the resplendence of a hundred million suns; the completeness of Allāh's qualities. When the plenitude of all these becomes One and resplends as One, that is His Light, His Nūr. That is Allāh.

Nūr-Muhammad ⊕ (A) The Light, the completion that is Muhammad ⊕; the Light has attained the completion in Allāh, appearing as that completion; one of the nine names of Muhammad ⊕.

Nūrus-samāwāti (A) The Light of the heavens, i.e., Allāh.

O

oli (T) Light-being, light of God.

P

Pādishāh (P) Emperor, Ruler, great King.

pahut arivu (T) Divine analytic wisdom; the sixth of the seven levels of wisdom; Muhaiyaddeen ☺, the wisdom of Allāh that explains His mysteries to the soul.

palakkam (T) A training exercise, habit, practice, custom.

panjasīla (S) The five basic precepts in Buddhist teaching; prescribed duties.

papum (T) We will see.

Paramasivan (T) A name for Adam ☺ in Hinduism.

Param Atmā (T) The Supreme Soul.

Param Pidā (T) The Divine Father.

Param Porul (T) The Supreme Being; the Supreme Treasure.

Paraparam Vastu (T) The one Supreme Being; God, the Supreme Being.

Pārvati (T) The goddess of earth; a name for Eve ☺ in Hinduism.

pērarivu (T) Divine luminous wisdom; the seventh of the seven levels of wisdom.

pidā (T) Father.

pillai (T) Child.

Pillaiyār (T) The elephant-headed Hindu god, Gānēsa.

po (T) Go.

poignānam (T) False wisdom.

poitch (T) Finished.

pudia pun (T) New wife.

pūjā (T) A form of Hindu worship; to perform ritual ceremonies.

purāna (T) Hindu scripture. In the teachings of Bawa Muhaiyaddeen ☺, the seventeen *purānas* are the seventeen worlds of arrogance, karma, maya, *tārahan, singan,* and *sūran,* sexual desire, anger, miserliness, attachment, fanaticism, envy, intoxicants, lust, theft, murder, and falsehood.

putti (T) Intellect; the third of the seven levels of wisdom.

Q

qabr (A) The grave.

Qadr (A) Power or divine decree; the Night of Power or Destiny. *Lailatul-Qadr* is the night the entire Qur'ān was revealed to Prophet Muhammad ☺.

qalam (A) The pen with which Allāh is said to have pre-recorded the actions of men.

qalb (A) Heart, the heart within the heart of man, the innermost heart.

qalb-pu (A & T) The flower of the heart.

Qāsim (A) The Prophet Muhammad's ☺ *kunya* or honorific name was Abul-Qāsim, meaning "Father of Qāsim." Qāsim was his son, who died in childhood.

qiblah (A) The direction one faces in prayer. For Muslims, the *qiblah* is the Ka'bah in Mecca. Within man, the *qiblah* is the *qalb,* the innermost heart.

Qiyāmah (A) The standing forth; the Day of Reckoning.

al-Quddūs (A) The Most Holy; the Purest.

Qudrah (A) Power; the Power of God's grace and the qualities which control all other forces.

qunūt (A) *Du'ā's* or supplications recited at *witr* and *subh* prayers. Literally, obedience to God, humility before God, devoutness, piety.

The following is the *qunūt* prayer recited at *subh:*

Allāhummahdinā fiman hadait. O dearest Allāh guide us among those You have guided. *Wa 'āfinā fiman 'āfait.* And wipe away our sins among those whose sins are erased. *Wa tawallanā fiman tawallait.* And take charge of us among those you have cared for. *Wa bārik lanā minal-khairi fimā a'tait.* And bless us with what is good in whatever You have granted. *Wa qinā sharra mā qadait.* And guard us from the evil which you have ordained. *Fā'innaka taqdī wa lā yuqdā 'alaik.* For indeed Your decree prevails and none can overrule You. *Wa innahu lā yadhillu maw-wālait.* And indeed he will not be humiliated whom You have befriended. *Wa lā ya'izzu man 'ādait.* And he will not be honored whom You have opposed. *Tabārakta Rabbanā wa ta'ālait.* Blessed are You our Lord and most exalted. *Falakal-hamdu 'alā mā qadait.* Then to You belongs all the praise for what you have decreed. *Nastaghfiruka wa natūbu ilaik.* We beg Your forgiveness and turn in repentance towards You. *Wa sallallāhu 'alā sayyidinā Muhammadinin-nabīyil-ummīyi wa 'alā ālihi wa sahbihi wa sallam.* And shower Your blessings O Allāh on our Master Muhammad, the Unlettered, and on his followers and his companions and grant them all eternal safety and peace. *Āmīn. Yā Rabbal-'ālamīn.* Amen. O Lord of the universes.

Qur'ān (A) The words of Allāh that were revealed to His Messenger, Prophet Muhammad ☻; those words that came from Allāh's Power are called the Qur'ān; Allāh's inner book of the heart; the Light of Allāh's grace which comes as a resonance from Allāh.

qurbān (A) The ritual sacrifice of animals to make them *halāl.* Inwardly, one purifies one's *qalb,* heart, by sacrificing and cutting away the animal qualities that exist within the self, thus making one's life *halāl,* acceptable to God. The *Subhānallāhi Kalimah* is recited for the purpose of destroying these animal qualities within the *qalb.*

Qutb ☻ (A) One who has attained the power of the Light of grace-awakened *pahut arivu,* divine analytic wisdom, that dawned from the throne of God and that investigates, understands, and analyzes everything in the eighteen thousand universes and beyond.

Through this inner analysis, the darkness of evil is dispelled and the beauty of goodness is made clear and radiant. The Qutb ☺ is sent by Allāh, through His grace and mercy, to reawaken mankind's faith in God and to establish certitude in our hearts. He is the wondrous embodiment and illustration of *īmān,* absolute faith in God, in all three worlds.

Qutbiyyah (A) The state of *pahut arivu,* divine analytic wisdom, which is the sixth level of wisdom; the state that explains the truth of God to the wisdom of the human soul.

R

ar-Rabb (A) God, the Lord, the Creator and Cherisher of all lives.

Rabbul-'ālamīn (A) The Lord of the universes.

ar-Rahīm (A) God, the Most Merciful; the Most Compassionate; the Kind.

rahmah (A) God's grace; His benevolence, compassion, mercy.

ar-Rahmān (A) God, the Most Compassionate; the Most Merciful; the Most Gracious; the Kind; the Cherisher.

Rahmānai (A & T) O God, Most Compassionate!

Rahmatul-'ālamīn (A) The Grace of all the universes.

Rahmatullāh (A) God, the Merciful.

rak'ah (A) A complete set of words and movements during the five-times prayer of Islām, including standing, bowing, prostrating, and sitting. Literally, a bowing.

Ramadān (A) The ninth month of the Muslim year during which fasting is observed from sunrise to sunset.

rāsis (T) The signs of the zodiac.

Rasūl ☺, Rasūlullāh ☺ (A) Muhammad ☺, the Messenger of Allāh. Literally, messenger, apostle.

rizq (A) Sustenance, food; nourishment given by Allāh.

rounding: This is a colloquial expression used by Bawa Muhaiyaddeen ☺ describing the circular nature of going out and then coming back to where you started.

rūh (A) The soul, the Light-Ray of God, the Light of God's wisdom. Bawa Muhaiyaddeen ☺ explains that the *rūh* is life, *hayāh*. Out of the six kinds of lives the soul is the light life. It is a ray of the Nūr, the Light of Allāh, a ray that does not die or disappear.

rūhānī (A) The spirit of the elements. There are six kinds of lives within man. One is human life which is the light life. That is the soul *(rūh)*. Associated with this are the lives of earth, fire, water, air, and ether. These constitute the *rūhānī*.

When all the four hundred trillion ten thousand intentions and thoughts take form they are called *rūhānīs*. All the things to which the mind roams in its thoughts are called *rūhānīs*. Even after a person dies, his desires bring him back. It is those desires, those *rūhānīs*, that bring him back to be born again.

rukū' (A) The bow in the five-times prayer of Islām; to bow down in worship to God.

S

sabūr (A) Patience; inner patience; to go within patience, to accept it, to think and reflect within it. *Sabūr* is that patience deep within patience which comforts, soothes, and alleviates the suffering caused by the mind. Literally, *sabūr* is the intensive form of *sabr*, patience.

sabūraligal (A & T) Those who have inner patience.

sadaqah (A) Charity.

sajdah (plural, *sujūd*) (A) The prostration in prayer.

salāh (A) The five-times prayer of Islām.

salām(s) (A) "May the peace of God be upon you." Literally, peace, the peace of God, greetings of peace.

salawāt (A) The recitation of peace and blessings upon the Rasūl ﷺ; prayers or blessings; usually used to refer to the supplications asking God to bless the prophets and mankind. Derived from *salla,* to pray.

sallallāhu 'alaihi wa sallam (A) "May the blessing and peace of Allāh be upon him." A supplication traditionally spoken after mentioning the name of Prophet Muhammad ﷺ. Most often abbreviated with a calligraphic circle: ﷺ.

samad (A) Equality; eternal, everlasting, absolute. As-Samad, God, the Eternal-Absolute.

sarihay, kiriyay, yōgam, and *gnānam* (T) The four parts of the body, corresponding to the elements earth, fire, air, and ether; the four steps of spiritual ascension: Hinduism, Zoroastrianism, Christianity, and Islām.

sattiya vēdam (T) The religion of truth.

Serendib (S) An ancient name for the island of Sri Lanka.

ash-shaf'ī (A) A prayer in Islām which consists of two *rak'ahs* usually performed after the *'ishā'* prayer in the last third of the night.

Shaikh (A) The teacher who takes the disciples to the shore of the heart; the spiritual teacher.

shaitān (A) Satan.

shakti (T) The energy or force of creation arising from the five elements. Shakti also refers to the consort of Shiva.

shānti (T) Peace, tranquility, serenity, stillness.

shari (T) All right, correct, good, very well.

sharī'ah (A) The first step of spiritual ascendance; the revealed law of al-Islām.

sharr (A) That which is evil or bad.

shart (A) Condition.

shī-nai (S & T) *Shī* is an interjection of contempt and disgust. *Nai* means dog. "Get away, dog!"

shirk (A) To worship something else along with Allāh; idolatry; from the root denoting partnership, making a partner to or associating something with Allāh. A *mushrik* is one who practices *shirk*.

Shiva and Shakti (T) Adam ☺ and Eve ☺; the section of earth, creation.

shukūr (A) Gratitude; contentment with whatever may happen, realizing that everything comes from Allāh; contentment arising from gratitude.

sifāt (A) (singular, *sifah*) Form, creation, manifestation.

sirātul-mustaqīm (A) The straight path.

sirr (A) Secret; the secret of Allāh.

sittar (T) An ascetic who has attained supernatural powers; one who controls the shaktis of the elements and maya and performs *sittis*.

sitti (T) Miracle, supernatural feat, occult power.

subh (A) The early morning obligatory prayer; the first of the five-times prayer in Islām offered between the break of dawn and sunrise.

Subhānallāh (A) All glory and exaltedness is to Allāh.

Subhānallāhi Kalimah, Subhāna Kalimah (A) The Third *Kalimah*:
   Subhānallāhi wal-hamdu lillāhi wa lā ilāha illAllāhu wallāhu akbar, wa lā haula wa lā quwwata illā billāhi wa huwal-'alīyul-'azīm.
   All glory is to Allāh and all praise be to Allāh and none is God except Allāh, and Allāh is greater, and there is no majesty and power except with Allāh, and He is exalted, supreme in glory!

Sufi (*Sūfī*, A) A genuine Sufi is in a state of *maunam*, silence, within God. He prays with God as God. He performs 43,242 prostrations in prayer each day. His every breath goes out to unite with God. His every intention goes to Him and unites with Him. His every idea goes to Him and unites with Him. His every thought goes to Him and unites with Him. A Sufi establishes the state of the ninety-nine meanings of the ninety-nine beautiful Names of God, the *asmā'ul-husnā,* in his *qalb.* Literally, from the Arabic word *tasawwuf,* derived from *sūf,* which means wool.

sūfiyyah (A) The fifth step of spiritual ascendance; the state where one has transcended the four religions and merged with God.

sujūd (singular, *sajdah*) (A) Prostrations.

sukūn (A) A diacritical mark in Arabic in the form of a tiny circle placed over a consonant, indicating that it has no vowel and is therefore without movement. Literally, silent, quiet.

sunnah (A) Additional prayers that the Prophet Muhammad ⊕ usually performed.

supi (T) A pacifier that a baby sucks.

sūrah (A) A chapter of the Qur'ān (initial letter *sīn*). Literally, row, series.

sūrah (A) Form (initial letter *sād*).

Sūratul-Fātihah (A) The Chapter of the Opening; the first chapter of the Holy Qur'ān.

Sūratul-Hamd (A) The Chapter of Praise; another name for the *Sūratul-Fātihah.*

Sūratul-Ikhlās (A) The Chapter of Sincerity (Purity); the 112th chapter of the Holy Qur'ān.

sūratul-insān (A) The form of man.

sūrat-ul-partiyā (A & T) Have you looked inside your form?

sūriyan (T) Sun.

swarkkam (T) Paradise, heaven.

swarnapati (T) Heavenly kingdom.

T

tahajjud (A) A *sunnah* prayer in Islām, offered individually between midnight and dawn; the night prayer.

takbīr (A) To raise the hands and say "*Allāhu akbar,* God is greater," in *salāh* and then to tie the hands placing the right hand over the left.

takht (P) Throne of God.

tambi (T) Little brother.

tānadharma (S) A combination of *tānam* and *dharma*. Depending on the context, it is translated as prescribed duties, charity, or justice.

tānam (S) Literally, charity, donation, meritorious giving, commonly with a religious motive; generosity.

tānam, nidānam, avadānam, and *gnānam* (T) Surrender, perfect balance, absolute focus, and divine wisdom.

tantra (*tantiram,* T) Trick, stratagem, scheme.

tārahan, singan, and *sūran* (T) The three sons of maya, related to aspects of the sexual act.

tarāsu (T) Scale.

tarīqah (A) The second step of spiritual ascendance. Literally, path.

tartīb (A) Step by step, in order.

tasbīh (A) A *dhikr* containing the words *"Subhānallāh*—all glory and exaltedness is to God;" prayer beads.

tattwa (T) The strength or power inherent in the qualities of creations, manifested through the actions of those qualities.

taubah (A) To repent, to do penance.

tauhīd (A) The affirmation of the unity of Allāh; the state of oneness without any trace of duality; the indivisible and absolute Oneness of God.

tavam (T) Austerity; meditation.

tawakkul, tawakkul-ʿalAllāh (A) Trust in God, surrender to God, putting all into God's responsibility.

tiyānam (T) Meditation; contemplation on God.

tollai (T) Difficulty, trouble.

toluhai (T) Prayer, worship; the formal five-times prayer in Islām.

turshshanam mountain *(malai)* (T) The mountain of the evil qualities of the mind; evil, wickedness, lewdness.

U

ummah (A) Followers; people, community, nation, family.

ummī (A) Unlettered; mute; silent; a title that refers to Prophet Muhammad ☺.

ummush-shaitān (A) The mother or source of satan.

'umrah (A) The pilgrimage to Mecca which may be performed at any time during the year.

unarchi (T) Awareness, feeling, consciousness; the second of the seven levels of wisdom.

unarvu (T) Feeling, perception, awareness; the first of the seven levels of wisdom.

ustādh (A) Master, teacher, professor.

V

vanakkam (T) Prayer, worship; also a greeting.

vēda (T) Scripture; religion.

vēdānta (T) Philosophy.

veena *(vīnā,* S) An Indian stringed instrument; a lute.

vingnānam (T) Science; scientific wisdom.

W

wa 'alaikumus-salām (A) And may the peace of God be upon you also.

wahy (A) Revelation.

waqt (A) Time; time of prayer.

wilāyah, (plural, *wilāyāt*) (A) Power; that which manifests through God's actions; the ninety-nine beautiful names and actions of God; the miraculous duties and actions of God.

witr (A) According to Abu Hanīfah ☺, a necessary *(wājib),* single bow or cycle of prayer, performed after *'ishā'* and before *fajr,* immediately following a pair of bows or cycles of prayer known as *ash-shaf'i.*

wudū' (A) Ablution, purity, cleanliness.

Y

yā (A) The vocative O! Perhaps, originally, an exclamation of praise, a title of greatness or praise.

Yahweh (H) God, Jehovah.

yā Rabbal-'ālamīn (A) O Lord of all the universes; the Creator who nourishes and protects all of His creations forever.

Yā Sīn (A) The thirty-sixth *sūrah* of the Qur'ān.

Z

az-zabūr (A) Hinduism, the first step of spiritual ascendance. In the body of man, Hinduism corresponds to creation, to the area below the waist, to the element earth, to form, and to Adam ☺.

az-zabūr, al-jabbūrat, al-injīl, and *al-furqān* (A & P) The four steps of spiritual ascendance, the four religions, the four scriptures: Hinduism, Fire Worship, Christianity, and Islām.

zam-zam (A) The spring which God caused to flow for Hagar ☺ and her son, Ishmael ☺, when they were alone in the desert, frantically searching for water.

zinā (A) Adultery, fornication.

zīnah (A) Beauty.

zuhr (A) The noon prayer; the second *waqt* of the five-times prayer of Islām, which is offered after the sun begins to decline at midday.

INDEX

Passim denotes that the references are not to be found on all of the listed pages; e.g., 24-29 *passim* would be used where the reference is on pages 24, 25, 27, and 29.

A'ūdhu billāhi minash-shaitānir-rajīm.
I seek refuge in God from the accursed satan.

Bismillāhir-Rahmānir-Rahīm.
In the name of God, the Most Compassionate,
the Most Merciful.

M. R. Bawa Muhaiyaddeen ﵦ

The words of Muhammad Raheem Bawa Muhaiyaddeen ﵦ reveal the mystical Sufi path of esoteric Islām: that the human being is uniquely created with the faculty of wisdom, enabling him to trace himself back to his Origin—Allāh, the Creator and Cherisher of all the Universes who exists in Oneness with all lives—and to surrender to that Source, leaving the One God, the Truth, as the only reality in his life. This is the original intention of the purity that is Islām.

Bawa Muhaiyaddeen ﵦ spoke endlessly of this Truth through parables, discourses, songs, and stories, all pointing the way to return to God. Over fifteen thousand hours of this ocean of knowledge were recorded.

People of all ages, religions, classes, backgrounds, and races flocked to hear and be near him; he interacted compassionately and lovingly with all of them, opening his heart to them equally, regardless of who they were. Presidents of countries and fakirs from the streets, the proud and the humble, the high-ranking and the low-ranking, the ordinary and the extraordinary, the extremely poor and the extremely rich all sat side by side in his presence.

An extraordinary being, Bawa Muhaiyaddeen ﵦ taught from experience, having traversed the path and returned, divinely aware—sent back to exhort all who yearn for the experience of God to discover the inner wisdom that is the path of surrender to that One.

Bawa Muhaiyaddeen ☺ did not tell us much about his life, although there were rare moments when he spoke to those gathered around him of certain memories.

What we know is that he was first sighted by spiritual seekers—a man we know only as Periari and a few others from the town of Kokuvil—at the edge of the jungle near the pilgrimage town of Kataragama in what was then known as the island country of Ceylon.

The tiny island that is shaped like a teardrop falling from the tip of southern India is a place known for its legendary as well as its sacred geography. Adam's Peak in the center of the island is said to have retained the imprint created by the impact of Adam's foot from when he first touched the earth after being cast out of the Garden of Eden.

Referred to in the ancient text of the Ramayana as Lanka, it was the site of Princess Sita's captivity by her abductor, Ravana, the evil demon-king of Lanka. The Ramayana contains details of the battlefields where the armies of her husband Prince Rama fought the armies of the demon-king, and describes the groves of exotic herbs dropped by Hanuman, the monkey-king who helped Prince Rama rescue his wife.

When the island was called the Isle of Serendib, the voyage of Sinbad was described in the Thousand and One Nights. Medieval Arabs and Persians made regular pilgrimages to Adam's Peak. The fourteenth century Arab traveler and scholar Ibn Batutah made that pilgrimage. Legends record the visit of the Qutb ☺, who after visiting Adam's Peak, meditated for twelve years in what came to be known as the hermitage shrine of Daftar Jailani that lies at the edge of a pre-cipitous granite cliff in the south central portion of the island, a site that has become a place of saintly visitation and mystical meditation.

Living in that land of legends, those seekers from Kokuvil rec-ognized Bawa Muhaiyaddeen ☺ as a uniquely mystical being when they began to interact with him, begging him to teach them. Bawa Muhaiyaddeen ☺ has told us his voice was like a bird's then. He had lived peacefully alone in the jungle for so long that he had almost forgotten human speech. Gradually, he began to speak with those seekers, although his voice retained its high bird-like pitch for many years.

Telling those seekers that God was the only Teacher, he consented only to study side by side with them. Working long hours in the rice fields as a farmer by day, he spoke and sang to them of his experiences of God in the evenings. Eventually, he and that small group of seekers from Kokuvil built an ashram in Jaffna.

Travel was difficult in that small country, yet the refuge of his presence was irresistible. As more and more people came to know about him and to hear him sing and speak of God, many of them began to invite him to stay in their homes. Among those people were Dr. Ajwad Macan-Markar and his wife Ameen Macan-Markar who lived in the city of Colombo. Bawa Muhaiyaddeen ☺ told them it would not be easy: that he was like a tree upon which many birds needed to take shelter. If he was to agree to stay at their home, they would also have to accommodate these birds. He warned them that there could be many at times. Dr. Ajwad and his wife did not hesitate to agree to open their home to all who wished to accompany him. After that, Bawa Muhaiyaddeen ☺ always stayed at their home when he was in Colombo.

For forty years Bawa Muhaiyaddeen ☺ spent his time with those seekers until 1971, when he accepted an invitation from Carolyn Andrews and a small group of people in Philadelphia in the United States who had heard about him. After that, he went back and forth between Philadelphia and what by then had been renamed Sri Lanka until 1982, when he stayed in the United States until December 1986.

In these distressing times, his words are increasingly recognized as representing the original intention of Islām which is the purity of the relationship between man and God as explained by all the prophets of God, from Adam, Noah, Abraham, Ishmael, Moses, David, Jesus, and Muhammad, may the peace of God be upon them, who were all sent to tell and retell mankind that there is one and only One God, and that this One is their Source—attainable, and waiting for the return of each individual soul.

WE INVITE YOU TO VISIT:

THE FELLOWSHIP in Philadelphia, Pennsylvania, where Bawa Muhaiyaddeen ☺ stayed when he visited the United States, continues to serve as a meeting house and a reservoir of materials for everyone wishing access to his teachings.

THE MOSQUE of Shaikh M. R. Bawa Muhaiyaddeen ☺ is located on the same property as the Fellowship. The five daily prayers and Friday congregational prayers are observed.

THE MAZĀR the resting place of Bawa Muhaiyaddeen ☺ is an hour west of the Fellowship and open daily between sunrise and sunset.

For further information about visiting, Fellowship events, branch locations, and
meetings:
The Bawa Muhaiyaddeen Fellowship
5820 Overbrook Avenue
Philadelphia, Pennsylvania 19131
Phone: (215) 879-6300
Fax: (215) 879-6307
E-mail: **info@bmf.org**
Website: **www.bmf.org**
Free catalog or book information: **(888) 786-1786**
To order CDs and DVDs: **www.bmfstore.com**

BOOKS BY M. R. BAWA MUHAIYADDEEN ⌣

Prayer

Al-Asmā'ul-Husnā: The Duties and Qualities of Allāh
website: asmaulhusna.org

The Choice

Bawa Asks Bawa Muhaiyaddeen ⌣ (Volumes One, Two & Three)

Life Is a Dream: A Book of Sufi Verse

A Timeless Treasury of Sufi Quotations

The Four Virtues and Their Relationship to
Good Behavior and Bad Conduct

Sūratur-Rahmah: The form of Compassion

God's Psychology: A Sufi Explanation

The Point Where God and Man Meet

The Map of the Journey to God: Lessons from the School of Grace

The Golden Words of a Sufi Sheikh, Revised Edition

Islam and World Peace: Explanations of a Sufi, Second Edition

A Book of God's Love

The Resonance of Allah: Resplendent Explanations Arising from
the *Nūr, Allāh's* Wisdom of Grace

The Tree That Fell to the West: Autobiography of a Sufi

Questions of Life — Answers of Wisdom (Volumes One & Two)

The Fast of Ramadan: The Inner Heart Blossoms

Hajj: The Inner Pilgrimage

The Triple Flame: The Inner Secrets of Sufism

A Song of Muhammad ⌣

To Die Before Death: The Sufi Way of Life

A Mystical Journey

Sheikh and Disciple

Why Can't I See the Angels: Children's Questions to a Sufi Saint

Treasures of the Heart: Sufi Stories for Young Children

Come to the Secret Garden: Sufi Tales of Wisdom

continued on next page

BOOKS *(continued)*

My Love You My Children: 101 Stories for Children of All Ages

Maya Veeram or The Forces of Illusion

God, His Prophets and His Children

Four Steps to Pure *Īmān*

The Wisdom of Man

Truth & Light: Brief Explanations

Songs of God's Grace

The Guidebook to the True Secret of the Heart (Volumes One & Two)

The Divine Luminous Wisdom That Dispels the Darkness

Wisdom of the Divine (Volumes One to Six)

The Tasty, Economical Cookbook, Second Edition

BOOKLETS

Can We Ever Regain Our Innocence?

Come to Prayer: The Wake-up Song

Du'ā' Kanzul-'arsh (The Invocation of the Treasure of the Throne)

An Explanation of the Benefits of Reciting the *Salawāt*

The Foot of the Qutb ☺

King Solomon ☺ and the Fish & Explanations About Jinns and Fairies

The Opening of the Mosque of Shaikh M. R. Bawa Muhaiyaddeen ☺

Sindanay & I Will Tell You of the Way

Sufism

Why We Recite the Maulids

A CONTEMPORARY SUFI SPEAKS SERIES:

On the Meaning of Fellowship

Mind, Desire, and the Billboards of the World

On Peace of Mind

On the Signs of Destruction

Teenagers and Parents

On the True Meaning of Sufism

On Unity: The Legacy of the Prophets

GEMS OF WISDOM SERIES:
Vol. 1: The Value of Good Qualities
Vol. 2: Beyond Mind and Desire
Vol. 3: The Innermost Heart
Vol. 4: Come to Prayer

THE INSTRUCTIONS:
The Fox and the Crocodile and Do Not Carry Tales
God Is Very Light
Prayer: Starting Over
Unity

PAMPHLETS
Advice to Prisoners
Faith
The Golden Words of a Sufi Sheikh: Preface to the Book
Grieving for the Dead
Keep the Pond Clean
Letter to the World Family
Love Is the Remedy, God Is the Healer
Marriage
A Prayer for Father's Day
A Prayer for My Children
A Prayer from My Heart
Strive for a Good Life
Sufi: A Brief Explanation
A Sufi Perspective on Business
25 Duties — The True Meaning of Fellowship
Who Is God?
With Every Breath, Say *Lā Ilāha Ill-Allāhu*
Why Man Has No Peace (from My Love You, My Children)
The Wisdom and Grace of the Sufis

continued on next page

PAMPHLETS *(continued)*

FROM ISLAM AND WORLD PEACE:

Islam & World Peace: Explanations of a Sufi—
Jihād, The Holy War Within

Islam & World Peace: Explanations of a Sufi—
The True Meaning of Islam and Epilogue

Islam & World Peace: Explanations of a Sufi—
Two Discourses

FOREIGN LANGUAGE PUBLICATIONS:

Ein Zeitgenössischer Sufi Spricht über Inneren Frieden
(A Contemporary Sufi Speaks on Peace of Mind—
German Translation)

*Deux Discours tirés du Livre L'Islam et la Paix Mondiale:
Explications d'un Soufi* (Two Discourses from the Book,
Islam and World Peace: Explanations of a Sufi—
French Translation)

La Paix (Two Discourses—French Translation)

¿Quién es Dios? Una Explicatión por el Sheikh Sufi
(Who is God? An Explanation by the Sufi Sheikh—
Spanish Translation)

OTHER PUBLICATIONS

Bawa Muhaiyaddeen Fellowship Calendar

Morning *Dhikr* at the Mosque of
Shaikh M. R. Bawa Muhaiyaddeen ☺

Songs of Divine Wisdom (a notated version of Sufi songs)

The *Subhāna Maulid*

Al-hamdu lillāh!
All praise is due to God!

Made in the USA
Middletown, DE
29 July 2023

35915928R00275